Religion and the Family in East Asia

RELIGION AND THE FAMILY
IN EAST ASIA

Edited by

George A. DE VOS
and
Takao SOFUE

UNIVERSITY OF CALIFORNIA PRESS
Berkeley   Los Angeles   London

BL
625
.6
.R45
1986

University of California Press
Berkeley and Los Angeles, California

University of California Press, Ltd.
London, England

This reprint originally published as Senri Ethnological Studies No. 11: *General editor*, Tadao Umesao; *Associate editors*, Kyuzo Kato, Mikiharu Itoh, Keijii Iwata, Komei Sasaki, Takao Sofue; *Editorial adviser*, Kenneth Ruddle; *Editorial manager*, Minoru Tarumi.

First California Paperback Printing 1986

Library of Congress Cataloging-in-Publication Data

Religion and the family in East Asia.

    "Originally published as Senri ethnological studies no. 11:—t.p. verso.
    Includes index.
    1. Family—East Asia—Religious Life. 2. East Asia—Religious life and customs.
I. De Vos, George A. II. Sofue, Takao, 1926–
BL625.6.R45 1987   291.1′783585′095   86–6925
ISBN 0–520–05762–7 (alk. paper)

Printed in the United States of America

1 2 3 4 5 6 7 8 9

In memory of
Youngsook Kim Harvey

Contents

Acknowledgments

This volume results from the 5th Annual Taniguchi Symposium for the Promotion of Ethnology, held at the National Museum of Ethnology, Senri, Osaka, between September 1–7, 1981. We would like to express our sincere gratitude to the Taniguchi Foundation, and to its Executive Director, for the financial support which made the symposium possible.

The idea for this symposium originally grew out of informal talks a few years back between Drs. George De Vos and Hesung C. Koh who approached me about the possibility of holding a conference to compare cross-culturally the relationship between religion and the family in East Asia. This plan gradually crystallized with the encouragement of our museum. We formed a Planning Committee consisting of De Vos, Koh and myself (later aided by Lewis Lancaster). The Museum Organizing Committee was constituted of Dr. Tadao Umesao, Director-General of the National Museum of Ethnology, Professors Takao Sofue, Komei Sasaki, Mikiharu Itoh, Kyuzo Kato and Mr. Makoto Kimura, Chief Administrative Officer of the Museum. The Executive Committee comprised Professor Shuzo Koyama and Research Fellows Yasuhiro Omori, Yasuhiko Nagano, Kazuyoshi Nakayama and Mayumi Shigematsu of the National Museum of Ethnology, Mr. Isao Kuboniwa and Mr. Shozo Saito, both Administrative Officers of the Museum, and from the Senri Office of the Japan Ethnological Foundation, Director Eiko Yuasa, Chief of the Operations Division Hidejiro Uji, and Secretary Takeshi Mihara.

I am grateful for the continuing helpfulness given by all the members of the above mentioned committees, to all the multidisciplinary participants and to many others who, in unseen but important ways, contributed to the notable professional and social success of the symposium. I also would like to express my gratitude to Mrs. Miriam Warner for her editorial assistance to George De Vos in turning individual papers into related chapters.

This symposium was a splendid occasion to promote and continue friendly interaction among the varied participants. Further fruitful communication will no doubt result. We of the Museum are indeed grateful to them and to the encompassing group spirit which made of our symposium an unprecedented success.

Editors' Note: In some instances in writing on Chinese subjects, modern Japanese character contractions have been used at the discretion of the authors.

Part I

Introduction:

**The Social Functions of Religious Belief,
Manifest and Latent**

Chapter 1

Religion and Family: Structural and Motivational Relationships

GEORGE DE VOS

THE PURPOSE OF AN INTERDISCIPLINARY APPROACH

In this volume we are juxtaposing two concepts widely studied in social science—that of religion and the family. Our objective is to explore their relationship to one another in the religious traditions of East Asia. It would be presumptuous to consider that we are attempting any exhaustive discussion of either. We have sought to bring together scholars who have been considering religion or the family separately in a diversity of disciplines, directly in religious studies, or indirectly in history, sociology, anthropology or psychology. What we hope to do in the following chapters is to sample some of the concerns of recognized Asian and American scholars who are specialists in these various disciplines. By bringing together the following chapters, we may be able to suggest some interesting perspectives that need further systematic exploration, perspectives that might not result simply from individuals pursuing work in their own given field.

Although we are looking at some historical considerations of religion in East Asia, we are by no means attempting any chronology or study of the development of religious ideas. Although we are examining some specific tenets of folk religions and the major doctrines of Confucianism and Buddhism, we are attempting no integrated interpretation of belief systems. Although we are looking at the institution of the family in East Asia, we are attempting no systematic discussion of family institutions, past or present. However, by juxtaposing the topics of family and religion, which, as Melford Spiro points out, have been intertwined from the dawn of human existence, we are seeking out some possible present relationships of these social institutions in three highly evolved Asian cultures, China, Japan and Korea. In two introductory chapters by Melford Spiro and myself, we will attempt some overview from the standpoint of structural anthropology as well as from psycho-cultural or psychodynamic perspectives. Then in the following chapters we shall turn to a number of more specific approaches to both indigenous cults and the so-called great traditions of East Asia.

RELIGIOUS TRADITIONS IN EAST ASIA—SOME FUNCTIONAL CONSIDERATIONS

East Asia today manifests both the living continuity of folk traditions and religious beliefs that originated before written history, as well as very powerful continuing influences of universal creeds and ideologies that developed with literacy and civilization. One finds mingled in the minds of many Asians both the continuity of shamanistic beliefs and the more universalistic traditions embodied in Buddhism and Confucianism.

Unfortunately, within our present scope, we cannot consider the role of Christianity in East Asia or the more recent influence of Marxism. Both creeds have acted to instigate revolutionary social movements during the modern period. We are also not considering the very important phenomena related to so-called new religions which have made their appearance in contemporary Asian societies; they are deserving of separate treatment in another work.

Religion as Orientation of Self in Time and Space

There have been numerous functional studies in anthropology concerned with religious beliefs as they serve to integrate the individual in his social group. These are usually synchronic studies of a particular culture. However, when we approach religious beliefs historically through time we observe that different religions may also be a disintegrative source of conflict until a new equilibrium is established with the new ascendancy of a given creed within a changing social tradition. Both integrative and disintegrative influences can be observed in Asian religious history, although integrative considerations are usually emphasized when a culture is examined retrospectively.

Emile Durkheim in his study, *The Elementary Forms of the Religious Life* [DURKHEIM 1947], described how religious beliefs and practices embody the collective representations of the group; that is, to say, religious beliefs exist prior to the individual and in infancy through childhood become embodied in the thought processes and forms of language which serve as communication within the society. From early childhood, the individual learns to conceptualize in both religious and secular patterns that afford intercommunication within his social group. Religious beliefs and practices, in effect, orient the individual within social "time" and social "space" as conceptualized within his culture. In this Durkheimian framework, one can analyze how religious beliefs and practices relate to the relative social cohesion of the group. Sharing of religious beliefs strengthens collective bonds, whereas loss of religious communality is related to a general attenuation of social norms which may ultimately result in a condition of anomie or normlessness and a loss of moral tone within the social group.

The functional approach of Malinowski [1948, 1974] and some others considered religious beliefs and practices as expressions of basic human motivations, both social and personal. In *Magic, Science and Religion* [1948] Malinowski attempted to demonstrate how beliefs in the supernatural could be "instrumental" in magical practices or "expressive" of dependent needs. In either case, these beliefs assuage deep insecurities and anxieties in both primitive and modern man. Clyde Kluckhohn in *Navaho Witchcraft* [1944] delineated both latent and manifest functions of particular religious beliefs. Some he saw as socially integrative, some not; some as personally adjustive, some not. By his thorough study of witchcraft beliefs and practices, he indicated how particular beliefs can reflect both social and psychological functions.

Sigmund Freud in *The Future of an Illusion* [1928] discussed the relation of religious beliefs to underlying psychological processes. In this tradition, Melford Spiro in the following chapter examines some of the latent functions of religious beliefs as related to personality variables involving primary family relationships.

In what follows in this introductory chapter, I shall briefly refer to the functions of religious beliefs in reference to the collectivity, families as well as individuals, in East Asian societies.

Religion as Group and Individual Continuity

Viewed temporally, religious beliefs are representations of a collective sense of purpose and continuity. The group in which the individual finds himself is *self-consciously related* as its members share a sense of its past and future. Past generations are part of the social self as it is developed within any social group. One's antecedents are traced back in time to origins represented in some form of sacred mythology defining the origin of the group. Such a mythology foreshadows the increasingly more secular forms of history and legend that become recorded with the inception of writing. Nevertheless, it is well to note that no matter how historians seek for what is termed "objectivity" in recording the past, there remains implicit in their writings a sacred dimension. The tracing of history continues to represent collective values related to group belonging. Collective memory of the past, oral or written, embodies present and future purposes and ideals. Religious representations continue to give temporal direction to human purpose.

Human beings from their earliest period created what are now seen as graphic or plastic works of arts or built astronomical architecture to help predict and control the future. Divination as well as the supplication of divine guidance has been common in all religious systems. Magical practices precede or substitute for "scientific" practices in relation to the future, whether humans are concerned with unpredictable natural events or the vagaries of the stock market acting in complex modern systems of economic distribution. Modern economists do not use the scapula of deer or the entrails of chickens, but they are called upon as diviners to predict future trends.

Ritual and ceremony generally commemorate mythological occurrences. They dramatize the collective concepts of origin or later periods of tribulation and reaffirmation that mark the collective memory of the group and, in some ceremonies, future goals. The group's integrity is continually reaffirmed by recalling specific past events which are reflected in future hope and purpose. Particular historical invasions, cleavages, dissensions, and changes of power relationships are deformed so as to conform to the present sense of continuity and group belonging.

Religions conceptualize time quite differently as related to both individual and group continuity. For example, there are notable differences in cosmology between the linear concepts of time found in Western religions, whether Judaism, Christianity, or Islam, and the cyclical concepts of Buddhism. The Western conception is basically "millinarian" in seeing an eventual end to the present world, with a final judgment of humanity in which individual continuity is affirmed. In Buddhism, in contrast, there are cyclical reincarnations of being, rather than the eternal continuity of the same conscious self.

Religion as a Definition of Social Space and Social Organization

Religious beliefs seen as representations of the spatial dimensions of society help define interpersonal relationships as well as relationships with the environment. Within the group, myths designate why systems of social differentiation have come about and why they remain. Religious beliefs affirm the system of differentiation and stratification according to age, sex, family, clan, classificatory lineage, caste, and class. Social roles are sanctified by rituals of transition that move the individual from one designated role to the next throughout the life trajectory, as well as by rituals that reintegrate the deviant into the group [VAN GENNEP 1960].

Another specially integrative aspect of any religious belief system is the articulation of the earthly member of the group to the supernatural. Ancestors remain integrated geographically as well as socially within the living community. The dead may take on a variety of disparate social roles, benevolent or malevolent. Religious beliefs represent the interaction of the living and the dead, be they demonic or saintly.

Additionally, as Durkheim well contended, religious representations provide more or less personalized embodiments of causality and power operative within the natural environment. Such culturally continued beliefs both delineate the realm of magic and affect one's attitudes toward more scientifically controlled observations of the laws of nature. Religious and magical concepts of power precede physics, and religious geography and geology precede more secular knowledge of the dimensions of space as well as time.

Lloyd Warner in his study of Australian aborigines [1958] provided us a classic example of a structural-functional approach to the understanding of religion. He analyzed the dreams, rituals, and myths of Australian aborigines in both their temporal and spatial conceptualizations. He showed how ritual dramatically integrates aboriginal concepts of the past, called "dream time." It provides representations of the ecological area in which the community lives and indicates how the flora and fauna of the surrounding world are categorized and related to human organization by so-called totemic concepts. Ritual also dramatizes the kinship organization of the community including its relationship with the dead, traced back ancestrally into the dream time of mythological beings. All elements of aboriginal life are integrated in the collective religious representations of the group. These are artistically transmitted by cosmetic alteration of the body, carvings on wood and stone, rock paintings, dance, songs, and mythic tales.

In this volume, we gain brief glimpses of such interrelated systems of thought. The various chapters touch upon Asian folk beliefs and practices and demonstrate how the universalist concepts of Confucianism and Buddhism came to be transmuted into specific meanings within Chinese, Korean, and Japanese cultural traditions.

Political or economic practices are sanctified by religious representations which help bind and formalize agreements, especially when they involve changes in status or role. The dynastic successions in China, Japan, and Korea were legitimated by sacred means. Ascension to political power is universally marked by ceremonies of transition in which an individual is symbolically ordained and made worthy of new office. This sanctification is supposed to qualify the individual as well as to symbolize the consensus of the group.

Some religious practices are "therapeutic" for the group as well as for the individual. There are shamanic ceremonies, as indicated in the chapters by Kendall and Sasaki (Chapters 3 and 4), through which a religious practitioner returns the ill person or the deviant to proper and expected role functions. The shaman will often also resolve the interpersonal difficulties that are diagnosed as a source of physical malaise. Such therapeutic practices have strong representations in folk religions universally. In Asia, shamanistic traditions are operative and well utilized even today as medical practice. Such therapeutic functions were sometimes also found historically in Buddhist practice, but generally speaking its representations were and are today more directed toward moral malaise than are the methods or concerns of practicing shamans. Whether the malaise is diagnosed as physical, moral, or both, therapeutic practices of a medico-religious nature function at the same time to re-integrate the individual and resolve tensions existing within his social group.

There are other ceremonial practices of a religious-legal nature that ostracize. Religio-juridical ceremony can exclude given individuals who are considered toxic to proper functioning of the group. Every society devises some system of punishment or exclusion as a means of social rectification. Very often, this system will evoke religious sanctions as part of its procedures.

Newly introduced religious beliefs, especially of a universalist variety, can be revolutionary for a society. They can become a visible source of conflict by introducing new concepts which seek to reorder the system of life and its meaning. However, when these effects of religious change occur gradually, they are considered reformist rather than revolutionary. For example, Confucianism in Korea progressively lowered the status of women from the beginning of the Yi Dynasty, a trend occurring so gradually that there was little conscious attention paid to how conflicts over inheritance were progressively being resolved in the direction of male inheritance patterns.

Social scientists have usually dealt with religious traditions only after they have become well established; therefore, they usually consider them as functionally integrative for the society in which they are found. However, if one looks at longitudinally at a society from the inception of any new religion, one gains more perspective on how religions can change family functions or bring about tensions that did not exist before their introduction. In some of the following papers, we touch tangentially upon such topics, especially in discussing the relationships of Confucianism to Buddhism as these religions influenced family interaction patterns. Lancaster (Chapter 9) suggests how Buddhism has had periods of conflict with concepts of family integration. Ozaki (Chapter 6) documents how Taoist practitioners moved toward greater separation from ordinary family life in pursuit of their religious goals. Both Buddhism and Taoism have constrained individuals to leave the family and to retreat from the social world in seeking for personal salvation, a search no longer defined as the exercise of a family role.

This social structural approach to religion and the family as it interacts with family definitions and roles is well exemplified by Suenari (Chapter 11) in discussing a pattern found in a contemporary Taiwanese village where there is a continuity of traditional ancestor worship. Suenari provides for us a description of how ancestor worship operates as part of a complex social pattern. The economic functions of the Chinese family are well described as part of this pattern, in which the worship of the dead can also be viewed as a distribution of goods.

Religious functions within the domestic unit demonstrate folk conceptions as well as Confucianist principles. The god of the hearth or fireplace is worshipped as part of the preparation for the eating of food. Other deities are conceptualized as observers of domestic functions who may negatively sanction behavior that strays from the socially expected. Numerous cooperative religious activities take place within the domestic compound.

Suenari traces all these patterns of reciprocity and distribution that revolve around ancestral worship. Participation in ancestral worship helps internalize a sense of obligation in respect to property obtained through inheritance. Succeeding the deceased ancestor entails a reciprocal obligation to continue property into the next generation within the family. In these Chinese practices the relationship between gods and worshippers is contractual. The somewhat instrumental offerings are tokens of a bargain with the deity by which the worshipper's wishes are to be fulfilled. Suenari cites Margery Wolf's analysis [1974] of this bargaining: if the divination practices seem at first to indicate negative omens, the individual will "up the ante" until there is some indication that the god has finally agreed to fulfill what is sought for in the future.

Religious practices are also forms of instrumental cooperation for a common purpose in the lineage unit. There is economic sharing; the shares within any cooperative enterprise are carefully calculated. In effect, in Taiwan there is little difference in how one conceptualizes a business and a religious venture.

Suenari attempts a comparison between the Chinese family observances and those of Japan and Korea. He finds obvious differences in the forms taken by ancestor worship in the three societies. The Japanese corporate *ie* household assumes most of the functions, which may be handled disparately in Taiwan. The ie is a religious unit of worship and also the unit of life crisis rituals. The so-called *dōzoku*, which appears in parts of Japan as main and branch family relationships, is quite different from the compound fraternal units of the Chinese family in Taiwan. In northeastern Japan, for example, it is only the main household that is responsible for ancestral ritual. The descendants of branch households send a representative to attend the ritual at the main household rather than conducting any ritual directly pertaining to their own branch household. Suenari perceptively notes that relationships with the ancestors in Japan are based more on a continuity of emotional feelings than on instrumental contracts. Ancestors are worshipped even though secular gain is not implicitly promised, as it is in Taiwan. The Japanese, observing primogeniture, do not emphasize sharing in ancestral worship. The Chinese do, since inheritance is equally distributed among children.

Suenari notes that the Korean situation, at first glance, seems to resemble the Japanese. However, in the Korean instance, there is much more direct emphasis on Confucian formalism than is found in the typical Japanese household, which uses Buddhist services. When Koreans gather at the household of the eldest son for rituals of commemoration celebrating the anniversary of dead ancestors, the responsibility for the ceremony is assigned to the eldest. This is also true for the Japanese, but there is sharp difference to be noted in the consciousness of participants. In Korea, the ancestor is seen as an ancestor of all those assembled rather than only as ancestor of the main household.

Comparing the three Confucian cultures, Suenari sees the Korean as adhering most closely to the prescribed Confucian manners to be observed by the living toward the dead. The Koreans, in other instances, are intermediate between the Japanese and the Taiwanese in observed practices. As for the Japanese, the emotional incentives for participation seem more important than the instrumental purposes which characterize the Chinese household. The Chinese and Japanese are further apart in formal religious terms. The Chinese family is a symbolic summation of relationships at various levels, including those beyond the immediate domestic one, whereas the Japanese do not formalize as religious units beyond the immediate household or ie.

What Suenari does not analyze is how some quasi-religious functions, related to a psychological sense of security or life dedication in the Japanese case, are found to extend to occupational units that are not related to the family, whereas such religious feelings never seem to be extended by the Chinese into the business or occupational worlds. This emotionalized loyalty and dedication to fictive kinship or mentorship patterns, so often found expressed in the Japanese business world in a quasi-religious way, is lacking in both the Koreans and Chinese.

Laurel Kendall (Chapter 3) uses a social structural approach to explain the differences in the shamanistic activities of Korean women as *mansin* or *mudang* in Korea versus the male and female *tang-ki* of Taiwan. In the Korean instance, shamans, who are overwhelmingly women, perform rituals that involve high gods and ancestors, whereas in Taiwan it is the men and male shamans who deal with the powerful high gods while the female shamans minister to women's particularistic concerns such as childbirth and the prevention of illness in growing children. In effect, the Korean women's ritual dominion manifests a greater range of authority and responsibility in family life than do the more specifically mothering concerns of the Chinese female shamans.

Seen in historical perspective, Kendall's comparative contentions are related to the fact that one can find in the Korean family system the progressive Confucianization that occurred between the fifteenth and seventeenth centuries, which lowered the status of women in the family [DEUCHLER 1977, 1980]. Prior to the Yi Dynasty, women tended to live in their parental home with their husbands during the first several years of marriage. They then joined their husbands' kin as "mothers," matrons in charge of their own household area. They inherited a share of their own parents' ancestral tablets. Not having a son was therefore not a liability nor the birth of a daughter a reason for lamentation as it was in the more strictly patrilineal Chinese families. It was the neo-Confucian reformers in the Yi Dynasty who slowly constrained women to lose their rights of inheritance, and this Confucianist control also set more rigorous standards of feminine modesty and chastity. In the area of ritual practice, however, the Korean woman maintained more status and, unlike the Chinese woman, was less defined as polluting and unworthy of religious communication with the high deities. As Lee points out (Chapter 12), the separate domain of the wife is manifested symbolically in the two-part structuring of the Korean house.

Sasaki's chapter on spirit possession (Chapter 4) in Japan does not directly relate the functioning of shamans in Japan or Okinawa to these issues of family function or women's status. However, he cites Lebra [1974], who sees the relatively higher status of Okinawan women as related to their spiritual specialization both as shamans and priestesses. Sasaki also documents how Japanese women as shamans inferentially are closer in function to Korean women than to Chinese in their relating to higher deities and in their range of spiritual competence. Chinese female specialists have longer reflected their more limited sphere of ritual authority. The Chinese women were circumscribed to strictly uterine concerns and could not deal with representations of the family beyond these functions in relation to the supernatural.

The more broadly efficacious *kut,* or Korean shamanic ritual, was therapeutic and integrative insofar as it was used to ameliorate natural loss, speed recovery from illness, and resolve domestic quarrels. It could also be used more broadly to revitalize the household symbolically as a unit. There were religious representations of purification of a dwelling and its inhabitants, exorcism of the sick, and the removal of pollution and malevolence. The functions of celebrating a cult god's birthday or purifying the household or defending the community against possible malevolent ghostly incursions have in Taiwan been the prerogative of male shamans. This split in function was interpreted perceptively by Ahern [1973, 1975, 1978], who suggested that pollution beliefs limiting the ritual role of women provide a symbolic rationale for the subordinate social status of Chinese women. Women could deal only with the lowly and unclean in the supernatural hierarchy. The ritual concerns of birth, death, and menstruation all had polluting aspects, which were due to the fact that they represented ruptures of social integrity as well as the integrity of the body. In the Chinese system there is a strong conceptualization of women as incoming brides breaking the boundaries of the family as potentially disruptive strangers. This perception was directly related to anxieties over inheritance patterns. In contrast, the underlying bilaterality still to be perceived in both the Korean and Japanese affiliative concerns with the relatives of the wife as well as the relatives of the husband seem to be less emotionally alarming. For the Korean woman, pollution is only a temporary condition during the menstrual cycle, not inherently sullying. When not in an immediate polluted state, Korean women can worship the gods and can be possessed by high gods as well as by the more lowly ones dealing with specific female functions.

Wolf [1972] also suggests why Chinese women are seen as potentially more destructive to family functions and integration . She reasons that as wives of husbands who potentially inherit equally, women are more readily perceived as sources of domestic strife, since they may be seeking to forward the special interests of their own husband over the other brothers. In the Korean and Japanese households, where unequal inheritance is aimed more toward primogeniture, the senior heir inherits the house and a major share of the household lands. Other sons are expected to establish independent households. The underlying tensions of women competing with one another cannot be as disruptive as among the Chinese.

In sum, the Chinese unilinear family pattern, with equal inheritance of sons, extends much further back historically than does the Korean or the Japanese. A Confucianist insistence on the more lowly status of women was a sentiment that took root progressively in Japan and Korea only in more recent centuries. Women lost status and prerogatives with their loss of inheritance and the more insistent shift to patrilocal residence. In effect, the Confucianization of family life as influencing family ritual in Korea is less complete than in Japan or China. The ritual acts of women manifest a greater range of authority and responsibility in household and family life than they do within the Chinese family system. In Japan, the mother-in-law exercises actual power and status, but not through religious ritual (see Tanaka, Chapter 15).

RELIGION AS EXPRESSIVE OF HUMAN MOTIVATION

The same religious beliefs and practices (or "representations" in Durkheim's terminology) that can be analyzed in a social structural framework concerned with cohesion or role affirmation can also be observed as expressions either of human emotional needs or of motives of an instrumental nature. A motivational analysis of religious expression in psychological terms is complementary, not contradictory, to a social structural analysis of the meaning of religious beliefs and practices. In a psychocultural approach, one attempts to discern how personality features normative for a given culture are reflected in the particular nuances found in specific religious traditions. In this sense, religious beliefs and practices are expressive of culturally prevalent psychological features as well as reflective of universals of human psychology found everywhere. Not only are these religious representations expressive for adults but they are formative throughout childhood in the patterning of social adaptation and psychological adjustment characteristic of a specific culture.

A psychocultural approach looks at religion as related to human motivation in both expressive and instrumental ways. Let us briefly delineate these functions. In the "expressive" or emotional dimension, religious beliefs and practices represent dependency and a need for nurturance and protection, the seeking of affiliation, the assuagement of isolation, a need for harmony versus discord and violence, a need for self-acceptance versus debasement, and a basic need to give meaning to suffering and to seek forms of release from human afflictions. On an instrumental level, religion is related to questions of power and dominance, to a need for achievement, the attainment of adequacy, a need for self-regulation, and a means of cooperation among fellow beings toward a common purpose.

A psychocultural approach interrelates a so-called "emic" analysis of consciously experienced concerns with an "etic" analysis of unconscious or latent religious functioning underlying the human experience from birth to death within society [KLUCKHOHN 1944]. The psychocultural approach also examines patterns of thought in various cultures, including particular patterns of religious symbolism, mythology, or magical practices, to see not only how they reflect the concerns of daily experience related to family structure, but also how these beliefs and practices still embody the experiences of childhood, including psychosexual development crises occurring within a given culture. The "logic" of particular beliefs and practices continues to give evidence of the precausal, affectively directed thought patterns characteristic of earlier periods of childhood cognitive development. Such "magical thought" embodies precausal patterns well described by Piaget [1930, 1932]; that is, contiguity in time or similarity of appearance or function are conceptually fused. Metaphorical similarities become causal identities. In early folk ritual in Japan, for example, urination was thought to bring on rain, and sexual congress in the rice fields was thought to induce agricultural fertility. In Chinese practice today, the burning of symbolic paper money is a down payment to a deity toward obtaining one's wish. The degree of focus on precausal linkages of events is proportionately different for different religious systems. Ideally, in Confucianism, for example, little heed is given to what is considered "magic" or mystic concerns; attention is directed instead to moral sensitivity and role responsibility. Ecstatic experiences are considered disruptive. Taoism, in contrast, allows for the irrational and seeks for "meaning" in forms of thought considered undisciplined to the Confucianist (see Tu, Chapter 7).

Seen developmentally in human psychology, the various motives and interpersonal concerns reflected in religious expression start with the panhuman sense of helplessness which is part of the initial experience of separateness arising with the dawn of consciousness. The progressively more self-conscious human never overcomes a need for some form of *dependence* on outside power for nurturance. This sense of deep *need for nurturance* is also reflected negatively in an existential *fear of nonexistence*, that is, the basic sense of death—a threat to the continuous existence of the self—which is an early conscious experience. There is also a deepening awareness of how one's own helplessness is juxtaposed to the presence of external power, be it conceptualized naturalistically or in supernatural terms. Some of the early childhood representations of fearful power, whether thunder or fire or the aggressive behavior of giant adults, remain embedded in religious representations throughout life (Spiro, Chapter 2). From childhood, the human consciousness begins to locate power as an attribute of awesome outside objects or beings. This sense of awe starts early, and the human never completely overcomes a need to relate to such external powers as a means of assuring personal security.

The conceptualization of power never becomes completely secularized in most explanatory systems. A belief in divine benevolence affords deep emotional security and comfort for most human beings. Conversely, the potential of evil force in the supernatural causes one to seek divine protection. Early animistic representations of power are found in various folk beliefs. In the Japanese case, *kami* is vaguely conceptualized as representations of power in sacred mountains, impressive trees, or other unusual manifestations of nature. Deity can be represented in vague concepts of fertility, generativity, sometimes personalized and sometimes not. Power also becomes represented in particularly awesome individuals who become deified objects of worship. Such was the case of the courtier Sugawara, whose death coincided with what were interpreted as malevolent occurrences in the capital during the Heian period. He was propitiated by building a shrine to this now awesome kami.

Some forms of security are gained in the process of cognitive growth by a developing sense of instrumental control through knowledge. The seeking out of explanations for the workings of nature are means of assuaging anxiety. However, the cognitive system of causal knowledge provided within a culture remains inseparable from religious thought except when secularization processes provide alternative modes of thought. A religious system blending magic and science gives the individual some sense of regularity in experiencing the outside world, and affords some hope for control over the awesome powers of nature. Knowledge becomes progressively instrumentalized and related to systems of prediction as well as to immediate control. A religious system very often develops in which knowledge of astronomy allows for the prediction of future events. The need for control through knowledge is related to man's manifestly inadequate control of nature, which despite all efforts remains unpredictable and threatening. Specialists in prediction develop, who through various means of control, such as astrological signs, practice various forms of prediction of the future. Here religious belief becomes thoroughly mingled with magical practices. This intermingling is especially apparent in curative practices for illness, when the individual seeks medical assuagement to guarantee or restore health.

Religious concepts often suggest instrumental means of maintaining relationships with awesome powers, whether these are conceptualized as impersonal or personal. When personalized, religious practices are, in effect, acts of submission and entreaty to sway divine will or purpose. Humiliation of the self or ascetic practices are means toward having one's humble wishes granted. As Suenari (Chapter 11) points out, in Taiwan, religious practice is envisioned as a contractual type of relationship with a deity. It is evident how similar the methods for gaining benevolent care from the supernatural are to those attempted in regard to the powerful beings who live within one's own social world.

When we look at various societies, we note that the type of control and security obtained through development of knowledge of the world can become heavily secularized. Explanations are progressively developed in naturalistic terms and lose their religious representations as modes of explanation. In some systems, such as that developed under Confucianism, the immediate influence of the supernatural becomes of secondary concern to human control and regulation. Confucianism maintains its providence in the realm of moral and ethical problems, that is to say, in regard to the type of causality that exists in human interaction. The consequences of behavior in a social system continue to be conceptualized in moral terms. In effect, as Tu discusses in Chapter 7, there is the development of a sense of social belonging as related to various consequences of behavior in the social system. The proper exercise of one's family role is made central to moral behavior. In Buddhism and Taoism, conversely, the individual may seek for religious resolution, leaving the family and its obligations in order to realize personal religious salvation.

The seeking out of knowledge acts as a means of security when one is dealing with the most awesome experiences of human life, namely, birth, sexuality, and death. These very emotional experiences, as well as illness and threats to subsistence, when witnessed must be given some kind of representation which aims at regulating them. Experiences of this nature are never free from a sense of individual incapacity and anxiety. Folk cults, such as Shinto, particularly concern themselves with representations of generativity and fertility, whether they be agricultural or familial. There is anxiety about crop failure and the need for continuity through successful childbirth and surviving the illnesses of childhood. It is in the realm of these awesome forces of birth, sexuality, and death that concepts of purity and pollution remain most firmly embedded in religious practice. Humans witness bleeding or the physical decay and pollution of death as frightening occurrences that are both emotionally and socially disruptive. The activity expended in religious behavior focuses one's affective and intellectual control and assures the return of regularity over chaos, of continuity over annihilation.

The human needs and motivations which Buddhism seeks to fulfill in these respects contrasts directly with those involved in shamanistic folk religions. Buddhism provides a more universalist cosmology and sense of order while suggesting withdrawal from expressive needs as a means of salvation. In folk cults, relation to power is sometimes envisioned animistically as in the Japanese concept of kami. In Buddhism one turns from such instrumental or expressive concerns with external power to a more internal sense of guilt related to the need for self-control over inner impulses as well to the giving up of one's dependent needs on others.

Human desire in any form is seen as the cause of suffering in others. Human unhappiness is seen to be caused by lack of self-control in social relationships. Such a sense of moral causality is properly related to internalized guilt, since the individual consciousness is held responsible for improper actions. In Shinto the improprieties can be mechanically incurred without volition. In Buddhism there is a profound recognition of the karmic effects of self-interest, both instrumentally and expressively conceived. In Shinto there is less concern with guilt, and attitudes about behavior are resolved by attention to greater education so that the learner will avoid negative consequences. In Confucianism the ethical directives discussed by Tu are put in terms of self-development and avoidance of selfishness. There is less said about the negatives of sin or pollution and more emphasis on affirmative action rather than assuagement of inadequacy or impurity.

All forms of religions reconcile the individual to his particular circumstances and perceived destiny. On an individual expressive level, they are used to *reconcile problems of internal conflict.* It has only been in the more revolutionary religions of Christianity and Marxism in recent Asian history that religion has been used with great force to *rebel against the status quo.* However, there are many examples in Asian history in which Buddhism or neo-Confucianism was used as a critique of the existing society and in which individuals who followed the dictates of these religious philosophies sought to reform corrupt practices in society. The seeking for reform can of course come in conflict with the state. Although never becoming the impetus of a successful social movement, both Buddhism and Confucianism in Asia were periodically used by social critics to point up the inadequacies of contemporary social systems.

Turning to other, more instrumental considerations of religious belief, we see how religious representation becomes related to *internalized forms of responsibility* and life purpose. As the individual internalizes the normative system of his society, he or she is given a personal sense of purpose which can be related instrumentally to achievement goals in the life course (Koh, Chapter 16). These goals may be defined both individually and collectively. The individual internalizes a sense of responsibility and a need for self-control. One's behavior is not simply determined by the presence of a dominating external power, but a sense of control ideally is moved inward as an internalized code. This code of regulation applies to one's self without the continual intervention of outside constraints.

Religion functions to bolster a *sense of personal adequacy* as well as assuaging *fear of failure*, in the achievement of life goals. The individual often senses himself to be inadequate, and in his own sense of imperfection seeks out *means of assistance* from the supernatural in reaching toward what he conceives to be the ideal level of competence. Moreover, individuals, to varying degrees within any religious system, feel themselves incapable of becoming fully responsible socially. In the Confucian system there is a great deal of emphasis upon attaining a satisfactory level of self-control and responsibility. Buddhist beliefs vary in this regard from sects such as Zen in Japan which emphasize acquisition of self-regulation and a capacity of finding internal strength, to those such as Shinshu which consider human beings inadequate and needing some form of assistance from the outside. These differences are termed *jiriki*, or self-reliance for strength, and *tariki*, or reliance on outside strength, by Japanese Buddhists.

In the domain of emotional needs religious representations in some contexts take on a deeply *affiliative meaning*. They represent a search for deepening *intimacy and understanding* and act as an assurance for the individual against isolation and neglect. Individuals may find represented in their religious practices bonds of closeness as they share in the mutual worship of the supernatural. One finds oneself bonded with others who are adherents of a shared belief. There is a common sense of social belonging that unites the religious community expressively as well as instrumentally as they seek out joint purpose. A need for belonging and group identity is assured by common religious practice. In East Asia such ceremonies take place within the family; in the West under Christianity they are more individualistically conceived. Whereas relationships to the supernatural are somewhat nonreciprocal because of vast inequalities of power, relationships among fellow adherents to a religious sect stress horizontal bonding as well as a vertical relationship with the supernatural. In ancestor worship, such as that which is continued in Confucianism, the affiliative bond remains within the family. In Christianity the so-called Christian brotherhood of the church is religiously more important than individual family units. Monasticism is a type of affective withdrawal that comes in conflict with and therefore must be reconciled with the family as an institution (Koh, Chapter 16).

In Western individualistically oriented traditions, the problems of human isolation are given very direct representation. It is expected that religious conversion can assuage a deep sense of alienation and problems of loss of meaning usually associated with loss of intimate forms of human attachment. The relation of the Christian to his God is manifestly separate from his relationships to others within his family. The resolution of a sense of alienation or isolation is more often resolved in Asian traditions by a symbolic reincorporation of the individual within the family [DE VOS 1980].

Religions have an evaluative dimension by which one judges oneself emotionally in reference to one's own standards of self-acceptance as well as to standards of social acceptability. There are a variety of conceptualizations that define acceptability. The most pervasive are the aforementioned concepts of purity and pollution. In respect to these concepts, behavior is evaluated as bringing one closer to a possible communication with the deity or making one unworthy of contact and constraining others to reject one as being in a state of pollution. In Confucianism, the individual who fails to fulfill social obligations is seen as reprehensible and, if all efforts at reform fail, worthy of social ostracism. In Buddhism, the concern becomes more internalized and similar to the Christian tradition in which there are concepts of sin which remove the person from the potential of salvation. Karma is passed on from past incarnations. Sometimes the afterlife is represented as a place for purging the taints of bad behavior.

In folk religions such as Shinto, conditions of transgression or pollution tend to be mechanically defined, not necessarily related to intentionality, whereas in religious representations of guilt there are questions of moral intention that must be judged. The religious community to a certain degree judges its members by their adherence to social regulations held sacred by the group. Since there are inevitable lapses, most religions have practices that are restitutive, whereby the individual is restored to his or her proper functioning.

In Shinto ritual, there are forms of exorcism of pollution whereby the individual is cleansed and returned to a state of relative purity. In certain instances, however, and under certain conditions, these impurities are considered to be inherent to the individual and not removable. Such representations reinforced the development of a caste system in Japan whereby those born of a polluted family were inherently ritually impure and comprised the Eta caste. In other instances, individuals' behavior could cause them to be outcast into the pariah group known as Hinin. Members of this group, however, under proper conditions could be restored through a ceremony of *ashiarai*.

Considerations of purity and pollution were used, as indicated above, to lower the status of women. Menstruation caused women to be in a state of impurity; sexual practices also led to impurity, as did the process of birth. Death in most societies is ritually polluting as well as materially contaminating, through decay, to those who come in contact with the dead.

All *religions regulate aggression*; they regulate how or under what conditions there can be proper expression of hostility and destructiveness. Conversely, they promise the eventual attainment of forms of *harmony and peace* that are considered an expressive need in all societies. One sees represented in religious beliefs concepts of ideal harmony as well as representations of the sources of discord and unhappiness among individuals. Every religious system embodies concepts of taboos of killing or intra-group destructiveness, whereas they may condone destructiveness directed outside the group under religiously nonpolluting circumstances. The religious system gives moral justification to certain forms of aggression while proscribing others. In this sense, all religious systems regulate harmony and discord on an expressive as well as on an instrumental level, setting up regulations for cooperation and competition within and between societies.

Religions set *boundaries on sexual expression*, defining degrees of relatedness in the family. Religious beliefs enforce incest taboos and define the times and occasions and age of maturity at which sexual practices are condoned.

Religious beliefs offer *explanations for suffering* and may even provide a sense of purpose for the enduring of affliction. In brief, both bodily pleasure and malaise are religiously defined. Religions impose regulations on the individual, but also provide periodic *release from regulation*. One notes in the chapters in this volume a variety of discussions showing differential emphasis in Asian religions in the tolerance of emotional expression through religious conceptualization. Whereas Confucianism aims in its concepts of self-regulation toward the establishment of harmony within society, Buddhism is more concerned with internal experiences which cause suffering for the individual or the collectivity. Buddhist concepts in this sense are more concerned with emotional expression and self-regulation, whereas Confucianist concepts are more related to the instrumental aspects of social responsibility.

THE ADAPTABILITY OF FOLK BELIEFS TO THE GREAT TRADITIONS

Chapters 3, 4 and 11 examine continuities of folk belief in contemporary Korea, Japan and Taiwan. These beliefs and practices preceded the introduction of the so-called "great traditions" of Confucianism and Buddhism in East Asia, causing two-tiered systems of elite and folk beliefs—a topic examined in some detail by Lancaster in Chapter 5.

Chapter 4 by Sasaki deals only with present-day shamanic practices. Some historical notes are perhaps necessary here to acquaint the general reader with what is known historically about Japanese folk beliefs, now generally termed "Shinto." In matter of fact, it is somewhat erroneous to use the word "Shinto" to describe all folk religion in Japan. The word Shinto itself was borrowed and only appeared at the time when literacy allowed for the writing down of native mythology in Chinese script. Modern readers are introduced to Japanese folk religion in ancient times through two basic works: the Kojiki and Nihon Shoki or Nihongi. At the time they were recorded, many of the shamanistic traditions had already been somewhat altered or modified by centralized religious practices. There is less direct evidence of the shamanistic origins of some beliefs than was true for the contemporaneous Korean states. So one must not judge as Japanese folk belief the usages of the state cults of "Shinto" operative at the time they were first represented in writing.

One cannot say that the Kojiki and the Nihongi are sacred books resembling the Bible in all its attributes. Nevertheless, just as the Bible is, in effect, a genealogy that justifies and validates the lineage of certain families, so too do the writings in the Kojiki and Nihongi reaffirm the mythical origins of the imperial lineage and, by extension, the sacred lineages of the major families politically dominant at the time the works were written. The Kojiki and Nihon Shoki chronicle the age of the gods, which was a prelude to the latter legends accounting for the foundation of the imperial system. Some indirect glimpses can be gained from these writings as demonstrated by Sofue in Chapter 14, which allows us to understand better the life and society of early Japan.

Basically Shinto, as it came to be called, was a form of nature worship built on beliefs which are called "animistic" by anthropologists. Divine power was diffusely conceptualized. There was no personalized specificity to the word "kami," which is usually translated as "god(s)" or "spirit(s)". What was "kami" was superior quality or power as held true for Polynesian concepts such as "mana" or even the concept "numen" found in Roman belief. Nor was Japanese homage to the beautiful personalized as it was in Greek or Roman myths. The spirit of kami in early shrines received no personification or concrete representation, but early on we find, just as described by Suenari in Chapter 11, a propitiation of the kami of the hearth and kami governing other domestic functions. Central to Japanese beliefs were ritual purity and ceremonies that had much to do with insuring cleanliness through the removal of taint. Abstention was a means of obtaining ritual purity, and in early Japan there was even a family of specialized hereditary abstainers called "imibe." Beliefs were not uniform throughout Japan, but with the coming of political centralization there was some attempt at a more organized presentation of ritual. The original cults were concerned specifically with the domestic household; separate villages or clans often held in common an ancestral concept of the "ujigami," or clan god, perhaps conceptualized as a founder or forefather from whom all traced their lineage. The main concern was with fertility of the natural environment as well as family continuity. The "uji" of the Japanese had similarity to the Roman concept of the "gens." The leader of such a clan-like unit was respected as the "ujino kami" or the head of the clan who was the chief worshiper of the ujigami.

One question which arises is how much did the early cult behavior resemble the later ancestral worship discussed in the chapters of Part IV?

One question which arises is how much did the early cult behavior resemble the later developed ancestral worship discussed in the chapters of Part IV.

Looking at the first chronicles, there is no question that they were compiled as validations of the contemporary social structure. They had specific political intentions as well as serving the religious function of establishing origins for the group. Sansome [1958: 28], suggests that the earlier observances in Japan were extremely simple and certainly not as elaborate as those practiced by the Chinese of that period. The purifying ritual consisted of sprinkling water and waving branches or wands as purifiers. There appear to have been no sacred edifices of any permanent nature; most likely a small plot of ground was purified for the occasion. There may have been worship in front of an ancestral tomb, tree or stone thought to have a special quality of holiness.

Sansome [1958:31], lists the pollutants chiefly as dirtiness of person, of clothing, menstruation, intercourse, childbirth, disease, wounds, and death. The drawing of blood was polluting. The original Japanese word *kega*, which means wound, refers to defilement, and in modern language the word *kegare* refers to being stained. It is interesting to note how in the mythology Susanowo, in fighting with his sister, pollutes her rice fields by tossing in them the skin of a piebald horse flayed backwards. This had no specific meaning to the Japanese who diligently wrote down the myth. They did not know why this act would be particularly polluting. However, if now we refer to the shamanistic traditions of northeast Asia we do find that shamans there used a pure white horse that was flayed front to rear. The skin was put on an armature of twigs to allow the shaman to ride to the sky in his communication with the supernatural. In effect, Susanowo, by using a horse's skin with black spots removed by backward flaying performed a symbolically reprehensible reversal of ritual in order to cause greater pollution aimed at his sister. No shamanistic continuity of thought was available to the Japanese recording the myth. To discover meaning one must examine practices of shamanism cross-culturally to reestablish what had disappeared in Japanese practice. There is much in the folklore of Japan which Sansome [1958:33] considers demonstrably of Korean origin.

What is interesting historically is that Shinto, as it became termed after the introduction of literacy, learned to live in accommodation with the newer great traditions introduced by contact with Korea and China. Sansome [1958:77] considers how Buddhism and Confucianism actually served to restimulate, in some way, the ancient cult activities and helped systematize them as they sought accommodation. One reason for their persistence, I would contend, is that indigenous shrines served to validate in a religious sense family positions in the political structure of the society. Such validation of old lineages could not be as readily derived from the recently introduced beliefs from the continent. Rather, the newly introduced priesthood could not chance offending the ruling families too greatly by any active suppression of the ancient cults, which were in effect forms of ancestor worship. For this reason "shinto" retained its hold on ancestral religious practices.

In the written documents, it's obvious that many of the rituals performed at the behest of the nobility remained native rather than Chinese in form and function. In the first written account of the prayer for harvest, one notes that it was done in a thoroughly Japanese manner of ceremony under the supervision of officers of state whose titles and functions, however, were borrowed from Chinese practice. Foreign influence had not succeeded in diminishing the position of the sovereign as the direct intermediary between the nation and the gods, or in weakening the religious beliefs of the ordinary people. The great rituals of the harvest were performed not only in the capital but in the provinces as acts of government as well as acts of worship, and Sansome notes that over three thousand shrines throughout the country received offerings on this occasion. This finding attests to the fact that the indigenous cult was by no means in eclipse at this time. Again, there is recording of a great purification liturgy through surviving texts in the 9th century which reflects the myths of the Kojiki concerning concepts of purity.

Although there were brief periods of hostility when Buddhism was first introduced to Japan, before long the native divinities began to be recognized as avatars or manifestations of Buddhism. The cosmic Vairocana was identified with the sun goddess, and Shinto shrines were often put under the charge of Buddhist monks. Many Buddhist emblems became representations at Shinto sacred places.

Shinto remained adaptive; it offered no positive resistance to Buddhism but passively incorporated what would allow it to survive. We must also look to the Japanese mentality in this regard in that Japanese were not concerned, and never have been, with precise points of logic or exclusiveness in thought. Shinto also survived because many of the large shrines were places of family devotion. This was so not only for the Great Shrine of the Imperial Family at Ise but for other shrines of the Fujiwara regents and for the families that were later to become part of the Bakufu. These places maintained a splendor of ceremony and a wealth which supported a Shinto priesthood as celebrators marking the greatness of the families of the politically dominant. Buddhist priests would be asked to go to these Shinto shrines to recite passages from Buddhist scriptures. To refuse probably would have meant a symbolic refusal to acknowledge the worldly power of the family of the supplicant.

The very simplicity of Shinto in belief and observance kept it from being a direct rival to Buddhist thought. Informally, the Buddhist adherents if not the monks could also continue native beliefs. This topic is discussed further by Lancaster in Chapter 5.

In the context of the content of native cults, one must note that the tradition of possession experiences referred to by Sasaki in Chapter 4 is probably continuous from the prehistoric past. It still appears as a very telling part of newly established religious cults.   One can note, in some of the very large so-called new religions, such as Tenrikyo, Tensho-kotai-Jingukyo or Rissho-Koseikai, which have appeared over the past 150 years in Japan, that the shamanistic "possession" suffered by the foundress or founder substantiated the religious beliefs of following generations of adherents.

THE GREAT TRADITIONS AND THE FAMILY IN EAST ASIA

In the religious teachings of the great traditions which developed in China and spread to Korea and Japan, what is the relationship of the individual to the family? What is the conceptualization of the self as related to the family, and how is this relationship viewed as part of religious meaning within the individual? What is the relationship of family membership to religious practice and dogma to psychological security and other functions provided by religious adherence and belief? Looking at the relation of family structure to religion, what is the interaction between given forms of religious belief and the family as an institution? Do religions in East Asia support the family as an institution, or in seeking for religious answers and purposes is the individual brought into conflict with the family? Chapters by Tu, Bito, Lancaster, and Fujii touch upon these questions.

Confucian answers and the use of Confucian ideas in China and Japan reflect basic differences between these two cultures. Chapter 8 by Bito is a description of neo-Confucianist ideals prevalent in Tokugawa during the 17th century. Bito rather succinctly summarizes some incisive thoughts relating the family as a social institution to the forms and ideas of neo-Confucianism as they were accepted, rejected, or modified in Japanese usage.   His main point is that scholars of Confucianism in Japan almost invariably deny a basic proposition of the Chu Hsi school.   Whereas Chu Hsi emphasizes the absorption of basic principles *into the self* in order to discover one's basic nature, the Japanese philosophical commentators see that the *outer behavior* "residing in reverence" accomplishes all of one's moral training.   The so-called penetrating principle of going into the self is not considered because it is enough to unconditionally devote oneself *behaviorally* to the given social norm and the role to which one dedicates oneself in the feudal service of one's lord. This espousal of proper behavior as the ultimate expression of virtue is still found today reflected in Morita therapy [REYNOLDS 1976], a specific form of psychotherapy developed out of Zen Buddhist principles. It is not considered important therapeutically to resolve the inner experience of malaise; rather, what is resolved is an incapacity to act properly in accordance with one's role expectations. The measure of proper virtue is behavior, not thought. Thought can interfere. One learns as well as possible to be "selfless" in one's expected behavioral role.

Bito sees that the Japanese concept of the family has not changed since the eighth century. He too, affirms that the ie system is basically different from the conception of family espoused in the Chinese lineage system. The ie as a unit of social organization and social morality in Japan is not based on concepts of strict kinship but displays many of the characteristics of an artificially contrived social organization formed to preserve the household occupation rather to continue it directly through blood lineage. Bito points out how it is possible for a non-kin member to succeed in the continuity of the ie so that, in given circumstances, the first son as head of the household is circumvented when his succession would be to the detriment of family business or property. The corporate concept of the Japanese family has as its requisite the appointment of an appropriate heir who will maximize the functioning of the ie, not the automatic succession of someone strictly on the basis of birth. Kinship is a principle of family continuity that can be modified in given circumstances. One does not acquire, according to Bito, the qualifications of a member merely by being born into a family. One becomes a full member only after some form of achievement and actualization. Looked at anthropologically, the family, strictly speaking in Japanese conceptions, is characterized not only by status acquired by birth but by a combination of acquired and achieved status. In China, in contrast, one is born into a family and thereby given rights and obligations which become the basis of all social activity. The realization of self is not specifically in the continuity of a given occupation; rather, the individual has some choice as to how to actualize himself, an actualization that may take a different form from that previously taken by other family members. What is required is obedience to the father to ensure the lineage rather than the continuity of a corporate household defined occupationally. It is relationships that are respected rather than one's ability or qualifications. Bito, interestingly, points out how in Japanese the very concept of filial piety itself has to be expressed by a Chinese-derived loan word. There is no "Yamato" word for it. Bito paraphrases Tsuda, a prominent scholar of history and thought, who argued that the reason the Chinese regard filial piety as the basis of morals is because they view all morality as based on the dyadic relationship between individuals. He contrasts this with the Japanese view in which it is the individual's relationship to the group that is the prime consideration. The basis of morality in respect to the ie lies in the performance of one's designated role within the group.

Bito describes how the samurai developed the concept of a pattern of loyalty. It must be noted that the samurai differed basically as administrators from the gentry of China. Japanese feudalism developed in a way different from the continuity of power in China. Bito speculates that the shift from Buddhism to Confucianism in the Tokugawa period was due to the fact that the attempted centralization that occurred under the Tokugawa regime led to some functional similarities to the bureaucratic system extant in China. Under the Tokugawa shogunate samurai retainers were organized into a bureaucratic network that ruled the nation. Like the gentry, the samurai were not a true nobility, but there was no examination system as a qualifier to office. Rather, they were a set of hereditary warriors who by the end of the 14th century had preempted the power of the former court and the nobility with its large landholdings. The samurai continued to draw their power from local communities and maintained a hierarchical system of loyalty in which individuals were assigned roles as they demonstrated ability to perform during the course of the Tokugawa period. However, as the samurai were gradually assembled into castle towns where the *daimyo*—"big names" among the feudal samurai—were headquartered, Confucianist writings on bureaucratic government became more germane to the centralized system that was developing. Nevertheless, the relationship between the shogun and the various daimyo, and then between each daimyo and his retainers, preserved the feudal characteristics of inherited loyalty. The retainers who served the daimyo were regarded as followers of the daimyo's clan. The samurai ie or corporate household included others beside those of the hereditary lineage, which was kept intact by adoption when necessary. Merchants and craftsmen as well as farmers also became organized into corporate ie and widely used adoption and direct mentorship as modes of continuity. This system of group loyalties was a precedent for today's set of specific loyalties toward a "company president" and his retainers which flavors the structure of modern corporations and business in Japan. The pattern of occupational morality based on loyalty is extended beyond direct kinship.

During the early part of the Tokugawa period it was not necessary for samurai to devote themselves to any Confucianist study. However, those who had some special interest in learning or wanted to be scholars themselves had access to Confucianist scholars. These Confucianist scholars as well as Zen priests with their aesthetic and ascetic practices were the teachers and mentors of members of the samurai class. Studying Confucianism became useful for acquiring a position but was not essential for an administrative post, as was true in China with its examination system. Learning for the samurai was somewhat irrelevant to actual politics but helped validate status in the Weberian sense [WEBER 1954]. Confucian ethics could be used also as validation of an ethical code which gave some expression to the religious sensibilities of an individual. Such a code gave him a sense of purpose and regularity in the performance of duty, permitting actualization of the self through the exercise of social duties and roles, in a manner Tu describes in Chapter 7.

In reference to Chinese religious sensibility Tu distinguishes cogently between the state of being religious and religion as an institution with objectifiable dogmas. The sense of being religious involves a sense of self-identification and of self-purpose in relationships and interaction with others. Characteristically, the Chinese sense of self is located, not in a structure or a normative concept of the individual, but more in a sense of process in which the self is continually transformed and developed in social interaction. The "self-transformation," therefore, is transactional rather than located in some kind of "individual" entity that takes on new structural characteristics. In both China and Japan self relates to social role. Bito in discussing the ie as a basic group sees the Japanese concept of self in relation to the total group, whereas Tu emphasizes that the self in China is conceptualized in specific dyadic relationships rather than as an aspect of group membership. For example, the Chinese father-son relationship is an interaction through which the self is developed, whereas for the Japanese it is the role of son, perhaps a first son, or the role of head of family that is actualized in relation to the group or ie as an entity. For the Chinese (Hsu in MARSELLA, DE VOS and HSU 1985), the self is perceived not as structure but as process widening into progressively larger circles of relationships. It is not located in an enclosed world of private thoughts and feelings. Another point made by Tu in discussing the nature of the self is that there is no dichotomy in the Chinese self-concept between the sacred and secular. For a Confucianist, the self is not actualized in a religious separation or departure from society but in a continual return to one's social interaction, with higher and deepening awareness of the meaning of relationships.

There is a profound difference in the Taoist dichotomy related to being within the society and being outside of it (Ozaki, Chapter 6) as well as the Buddhist sense of departure from society (Lancaster, Chapter 9). In Chinese thought as a whole, therefore, one notes a split between those who are more oriented religiously in their self-concept toward a Confucianist type of self-awareness and those who take on a sense of leaving the family, a historical practice in certain Taoist sects as well as in those following the Buddhist tradition, which came into China from its Indian source.

Ozaki, using historical sources, tries to answer the question whether or not Taoism always implied some retreat from the social world and the family or whether this practice, noted as the regular state of affairs for Taoists during the Tang period, had developed historically. Ozaki comes to the conclusion that certain social pressures as well as the influence of Buddhism changed Taoist practice from one in which Taoist religious practitioners or priests could live in a family context to an attitude in the 7th-century Tang period in which Taoists took on some of the characteristics of traditional Buddhism in respect to separating oneself from the immediate social world. Ozaki suggests that the intervention of state policies in religious practice may have caused Taoist priests to take on these special practices. However, considering on balance the other influences bearing on this trend, Ozaki concludes it was the influence of Buddhism itself on certain of the Taoist sects that was most instrumental, since these influences predated government intervention. Hermits and monks were emulated by Taoist priests. The calligraphy for "house" as used by the Taoists was given two further meanings, one being "love of the family" and the other, interestingly enough, being "all existence." Therefore, the characters for "ch'u-chia" meant leaving the love of parents, wives, and children in order to strive to study, but it also meant giving up all existence as the ultimate removal of self from society. Such concepts, clearly of Buddhist influence, grew in certain of the Taoist sects but not in others. Ozaki has also selected certain other symbolic characteristics to show that the Taoists, nevertheless, continued to have respect for the meaning of filial piety in that they did not shave their heads. The shaving of the head was one of the central issues that Confucianists held against the Buddhists because it violated the classic concept that one's body in its totality, including skin and hair, were given by the parents and that it was the obligation of the individual not to damage this gift in any way. However, Ozaki rejects this explanation as the sole reason why Taoists did not shave their heads. He favors rather as the prime motive for not cutting one's hair the Taoist belief that the spirit resides in every part of one's body including the hair. Ozaki also points out that Taoists kept their family names in many instances, whereas Buddhists symbolized their sense of continuity with their teacher rather than their family by using the character for "shaka" (or the living Gotama) as their surname.

Fujii (Chapter 10) attempts to show how aspects of ie thinking in Japanese culture had great influence in the appearance of what might be termed certain "indigenous" developments in Japanese Buddhism from the latter part of the 14th century during the Kamakura period. Chinese Buddhism, according to Fujii, took on some other cultural characteristics as it moved from China and Korea into Japan. The Japanese tended to confound local religious features with Buddhist practice, a tendency especially apparent when popular Buddhism became diffused through the various reformist sects of the Kamakura period. A peculiar form of continuity taken by Japanese Buddhism was what Fujii terms its "founder worship," in which reforming monks themselves became the objects of worship and were venerated as sacred alongside the Buddha. In certain Kamakura sects not only did an image of the Buddha and Buddhist names of ancestors occupy the center of the family altar, but these were joined by images of the sect founder.

Fujii indirectly discusses how continuity of inheritance in Japanese Buddhist sects showed ie corporate characteristics: that is, the Buddhist establishment as an ie continued by adopting an individual who became the "family" head, although blood lineage was seemingly also used. The fact that this succession was possible in the reform sects suggests that Buddhism as practiced in Japan was not, in effect, in any way antithetical to the family, but conversely, that it accommodated itself to a great extent to the ie family structure of Japanese society even if the monkhood offered a means for individuals to escape from the ordinary expectations of society. What none of our authors discuss is how Buddhism offered some children of the poor the only means to practice a form of social mobility by acquiring education. Becoming a monk was also a means of avoiding military conscription and other duties imposed by the government.   It was characteristic of the period of Buddhist reform that many individuals who became monks were from the poorer classes of society, whereas previously Buddhist faith and practice had been more the province of the elite.   Nichiren, one of the most influential of the reformers, in his own auto-biographical writings attests to the fact that he saw himself as someone who had come from what he termed the "sudra" level of Japanese society to take on religious leadership.   Studies of how the spread of Buddhism in Japan was related to shifts in Japanese social structure bear further work by historians.

Finally, again from the standpoint of emotional expression, one must note that religious systems in some form or other are related to patterns of psychological release which can be attained periodically through ritual activity.   Some expressions of a need for power as well as some forms of sexual release by those who are in a usually powerless status position can be found in trance cults in most societies.   Organized religious systems try to contain trance or ecstatic experiences so that they do not become socially disintegrating.   It is to be noted that both the Buddhist and Confucianist higher traditions frown upon such types of religious activities.   They continue to appear, however, in the folk cults and are certainly represented in shamanistic practices.   Trance or possession experience allows for altered states of consciousness wherein the individual "gets out of his own mind" and can either consciously or unconsciously participate in types of experience not condoned for his usual status or sense of self.   We notice two types of trance experience in Japan.   One type is that used by a medium through whom a deity expresses a communication.   Mediumship differs from shamanistic practices, of the second type, since the shaman is not merely a medium but has some form of power to help heal and cure which goes beyond simple states of being passively possessed.

Ecstasy, properly considered, is to be distinguished from trance, in that the ecstatic state is very often a sense of experiencing within the self external forms of power or external experiences which the self is enlarged to encompass, in a psychedelic sense.   In true trance, however, the individual does not remain present while being possessed.   His body and mind are taken over so that he himself does not directly experience the power that is being exercised.   In trance, those aspects of the self that cannot ordinarily be released are not consciously experienced.   In ecstasy, more is experienced than is usually tolerated within the boundaries of consciousness [MARSELLA, DEVOS and HSU 1985].

ANCESTOR WORSHIP IN EAST ASIA

As touched upon in Parts III and IV of this volume, ancestor worship remains a principal feature of religious sensibilities in East Asia.   It is found embedded in indigenous cults, but with the coming of literacy ancestor worship is preempted by the so-called "great traditions."   Confucianism as discussed by Tu (Chapter 7) and Bito (Chapter 8) becomes a very direct social morality in which ancestor worship as religious practice is more concerned with social performance of the living than it is a means of ensuring a benevolent relationship with the powerful dead.   In indigenous religion, there was a great concern about possible malevolent consequences should ancestor worship be neglected.   Under Confucianism, ancestor worship becomes a moral imperative maintaining the social forms and symbolizing inheritance practices within lineage structures.   Whereas ancestor worship in China and Korea became and remained Confucianized, in Japan concern with ancestral tablets became attached to Buddhist memorial practices offering respect to the dead.   In effect, Buddhism plays the same functional role in Japan as the more direct, self-consciously organized Confucianism does in Korea and China.

In Part IV, Fujii (Chapter 10) discusses how Japanese family structure has historically altered the forms taken by Japanese Buddhism.   Succession within religious sects comes to resemble the succession practiced in the Japanese corporate ie. In this sense, it is looser forms of Japanese ancestor worship that give a particular cultural stamp to Buddhism in Japan. Suenari (Chapter 11) and Lee (Chapter 12) as well as Morioka (Chapter 13) point up the social and cultural functions of ancestor worship and show how these functions have continued in some instances into the modern age but in other instances have been radically altered with contemporary modernization of family life within industrial societies.

Suenari is obviously an exponent of functionalism in analyzing a contemporary form of ancestor worship in Taiwan, where the Chinese lineal system is still in force and is not being altered by modern experiences. The inheritance pattern has not changed in contemporary Taiwanese society in as obvious a manner as in postwar Japan, where primogenture has been abandoned. What Suenari further delineates in his chapter is how various household functions are conceptualized as governed by deities ranging from the god of the hearth, the fireplace, through more elevated deities related to other family functions. As indicated, these functions parallel the description of such personalization of household functions found within the Korean household.

What Suenari stresses throughout is that one cannot separate the economic functions of the household from their ritualization in religious practice.   Ceremony governs forms of reciprocity and distribution; it sanctions obligations and role responsibilities in respect to property and ensures proper exercise of inheritance from one generation to the next.   He also notes that in comparison with Korean and Japanese motivational characteristics, the Chinese are more concerned with the instrumental, economic functions of ancestor worship, while expressive, emotional concerns with the dead mark Korean and, especially, Japanese practices.

Morioka, in similar fashion to Suenari, takes a manifest functionalist approach to religion by suggesting that ancestor worship in contemporary Japan is changing with a progressive shift from a unilateral lineage system to a more bilateral orientation among urban nuclear families. He specifically singles out as a continuing dynamic function of ancestor worship a legitimization of succession related to the maintenance of political as well as religious authority in the household.   Second, he stresses the stabilization of intergenerational relationships, in effect making a psychoanalytic interpretation of how ancestor worship resolves ambivalent feelings of an individual toward a living parent (see also Spiro, Chapter 2). Morioka stresses, however, that in the Japanese inheritance system inheritance can take place while the previous head is still alive, so that the resolution of ambivalence toward a dead ancestor is less important. Nevertheless, this relationship of ancestor worship to the emotional stabilization of intergenerational relations remains a potent force. Morioka indicates how some ancestor worship still has the function of family unification or the strengthening of cohesion in times of stress, although the nature of affinity may have shifted in a more bilateral direction.

Morioka suggests another psychodynamic function in ancestor worship for people in the poorer strata of society; for them the worship of ancestors may relieve tension concerning their present low status and ensure against future disaster or misfortune. According to karmic principles one has to rationalize one's present impoverished position as due to bad karma in the past. The rationalization that occurs very often is that a previous generation did not worship properly; hence, in order to ensure the family's prosperity in the future, one has to maintain a more proper form of ancestral worship.

What Morioka points out very graphically in his functionalist analysis is how the Japanese concept of ancestor worship is stretched very readily to include individuals who, properly speaking, are not true members of one's lineage. In effect, this flexibility in regard to ancestor worship is a direct reflection of flexibility in adoption, which maintains "family" occupational continuity through the generations. Morioka also points up that some memorialization of the dead remains the single important inducement for many contemporary Japanese to maintain a Buddhist affiliation. The Japanese may have almost no concern for Buddhist dogma or Buddhist beliefs; nevertheless, the necessity to memorialize the dead causes one to retain allegiance to one's Buddhist sect for ceremonial purposes. Finally, Morioka points up that the weakened influence of established religions has led numbers of contemporary Japanese to accept some new religious form. Curiously enough, some of these "new" religions have reintroduced ancestral memorialization as a means of satisfying this continuing need among their constituents. But as definite as the major change in memorialization is the obvious bilaterality that has come to the fore in contemporary Japanese families.

In Lee (Chapter 12) the points made elsewhere (Chapter 3), about the relative maintenance of status within the household by Korean women despite the pressures of the Confucianist patriarchical orientation, are reflected in the physical independence accorded Korean women in the allocation of space within the Korean house. The inheritance system remains a form of modified primogeniture, with unequal distribution among the male inheritors. The first son receives the superior share, since he is allocated the responsibility of care for the parents within the stem family system still extant in Korea. The Korean housewife is sufficiently "pure" to perform rituals to the household deities, unlike the lower-status Chinese women described in Kendall's comparative analysis in Chapter 3. Nevertheless, the Confucianist principle that ancestor worship is a male function is evident in the division of ritual acts in the Korean family. The male family head is exclusively responsible for ancestral worship.

Lee documents how the more restricted space of city living has influenced the division of roles among family members, especially in the working class but also in the middle class as well. Whereas some forms of labor for the Korean housewife have diminished, her psychological responsibility as wife and mother has been increased.

Household deities are disappearing in the urban apartment. A number of educated women have converted to Christianity, Buddhism, or some form of new religion. Household religious practices have been dropped. Nevertheless, shamanistic rituals are maintained by specialists moving into the urban scene.

The forms of ancestor worship practiced have become much simplified or changed from their traditional modes. Younger men have lost knowledge of how to write ancestral tablets, and they must resort to the use of photographs. The elaborately conceived ceremonial table with its many dishes is now not well prepared. Nevertheless, Lee points out that ancestor worship has maintained some popularity among urban people and is used as a means of bringing together rural and urban dwellers in order to mark the continuity of family integrity. Ceremonies are excuses to bring families together; they are occasions for social interchange among relatives now widely separated geographically.

Lee makes a final comment that the practice of Korean religion, especially that centered around ancestor worship, is really a supplication for family prosperity rather than a means of character formation for individuals. This is true for Korean practices of shamanism, Buddhism, Confucianism, or even Christianity. In this sense, despite the so-called modernization of the Korean family, religion remains in an emotional sense very deeply expressive of traditional cultural patterns.

THE SENSE OF SELF AND SOCIAL ROLE IN RELIGIOUS EXPRESSION

In the final part of this volume, "Women's Role and Status in the Family," we have three chapters that, in effect, turn more directly toward an examination of motivational patterns of a psychocultural nature rather than a functional analysis of social structure. Sofue (Chapter 14) relates the known anthropological material, which strongly suggests that the fundamental family group in Japan during the eighth century was one of bilateral kindred in which both patrilineal and matrilineal principles could be seen as operative. Inferentially, the lower the individual's social status, the more prevalent the bilaterality, whereas patrilineality was increasingly stronger the higher the class. There is good evidence for both dual virilocality and uxorivirilocality as prevailing patterns at the dawn of literacy in Japan. From the 9th century on, women's status became gradually lowered, and by the time of the takeover by the samurai class in the fourteenth century the position of women became very similar to that existing in China at this period. The feudalistic period in Japan accentuated the lower position of women among the dominant samurai, the class that made specific use of Confucianist ideology. Therefore, we find in Japanese history some parallels to what we have stated was extant among Koreans with the ascendency of Confucianism through the Yi Dynasty.

Sofue skillfully considers the expressive relationships of family members depicted in Japanese mythology and literature and suggests that the major preoccupation to be noted in the early mythology was about sibling relationships. This suggests that intergenerational concerns were much less evident than jealousies and sexual tensions among sibs and half-sibs of the same generation. Sofue contrasts this preoccupation with that of the modern period, in which the fantasy life expressed in literature and the mass media focuses very heavily on the mother-son dyad. The close psychological focus on a lack of resolution of dependency and nurturance needs between mother and son suggests certain specific continuing tensions within the Japanese family, marked by the continuing disciplinary as well as nurturant influence of the mother into adulthood. This focus differs from an Oedipal relationship, in which tensions are directed toward the dominant paternal figure. What we see is that the lineage system as practiced in Japan may be formally patrilineal but the focus is upon the powerful and emotionally expressive role of the mother which is also transmuted into the instrumental performance of males, as I have pointed out elsewhere (DEVOS 1973: Chapter 5]. Japanese society with its "socialization for achievement" depends heavily upon the internalization of standards and role expectations through the self-sacrificial definition of the woman's role. Thus in many Japanese families a quasi-religious sense of security and purpose remains located in the performance of role expectations rather than being expressed in a concern with formal religious doctrines.

Chapter 15 by Tanaka reinforces these contentions directly by a detailed consideration of maternal authority in the Japanese family. Tanaka stresses the strong sense of dependency and need for nurturance which continues in the male role as these needs are transferred from the mother to the wife. Through satisfying such needs, the woman gains a very strong moral authority within the Japanese household. The woman's domain includes nurturant care of family members on a daily basis, as well as some care for the ancestors in the domestic setting. The man's domain is almost exclusively outside the house. The woman within the household maintains the moral integrity of the family. More than that, the woman's role is highly internalized, with a "Confucianist" dedication to the role which goes beyond that found either in China or Korea. There is the practice of the Confucianist ethic without the continuity of self-conscious Confucian ideology.

In the last chapter (16) by Hesung Chung Koh, we find a detailed examination of personal motivations in the assumption of a specialized religious role by contemporary women. Koh examines the various expressive emotional motives, especially related to the sense of affiliative loss which stimulates individuals to take on the role of a Buddhist nun. She further compares and contrasts the social status and social background of women in Korea who become Buddhist nuns with women who become shamans as reported by Youngsook Kim Harvey [1979]. Koh makes a very cogent comparison of social structural characteristics and family background which differentiates the individuals becoming Buddhist nuns from those becoming shamans. The nuns were all of upper middle-class status, whereas the shamans were drawn from lower middle-class families. Common to all those becoming Buddhist nuns is a deep sense of role dedication. There is an emphasis on role performance even though there are extenuating circumstances that make these women feel they cannot perform the normal role of woman through entering the married state. It is interesting to see in the autobiographic essays how each woman combined different elements of Christian, Buddhist, and Confucianist considerations in her choice of vocation, without seeing them as contradictory or exclusive of one another.

Looking at these considerations from the standpoint of expressive motivations discussed in this chapter, we see how much affiliative loss enters in as an ordeal to be overcome in these womens' lives. Interpersonal love is transposed into a love for Buddha or love for Christ. The concept of affiliation is transmuted in totally religious terms. Koh states also these women's need for self-acceptance and self-respect as an expressive emotional concern. She says of one nun, "Through her synthesis of beliefs she found courage to meet life's challenges and maintain her *self-respect* as well as justify her life-style."

What is also apparent in all five cases cited by Koh is that becoming a nun meant overcoming strong family opposition. Considering the deep attachment to family, it is impressive how they were able to persevere in the choice of a religious vocation. Again to be noted in this small sample is that all the nuns were eldest daughters, a sibling position of particular responsibility in the Asian household. When Koh compared the mudang with the nuns, again it was apparent that the role of eldest daughter was represented in five of the six cases cited by Harvey [1979]. In each instance these women were intelligent, strong-willed, and self-reliant. Again comparatively, the women cited by Harvey experienced severe internal conflict, but it is to be noted that the conflict occurred at a different stage of the life cycle for those becoming shamans. The nuns had their period of ordeal in their mid-twenties, while the shamans faced a crisis in their lives and resolved it by becoming mudang during their mid-thirties. The symptoms of illness in the mudang tended to be more in the direction of what are usually termed psychopathological problems; there appeared psychosomatic symptoms or symptoms of mental illness such as hallucination or seizures.

What is overwhelmingly apparent in both sets of individuals is the unusual amount of tragedy and highly charged emotional experience, the most excruciating being the death of close family members or lovers. Another feature which may have been typical for postwar Koreans generally but was especially noteworthy among the families of those becoming shamans was the frequent moves in which the individual sought for some more stable financial situation. In their case histories one notes a great deal of physical displacement and insecurity about economic survival.

Koh summarizes the same focus on cultural values found in both the nuns and in the women becoming shamans, although the emphasis was somewhat different between them. The three principal values found as important in all the cases were, first, a deep sense of filial piety. There was in these women a strong sense of dutifulness and the acceptance of responsibility for the support and care of others. Concerning the value of chastity in premarital experience, there was a striking difference between the nuns and the shamans. The nuns placed a high value on chastity; those becoming shamans had been more expressive sexually and had developed liaisons which sometimes brought them into social disrepute. Nevertheless, both nuns and shamans expressed the value of role dedication. All the women were seriously concerned with the role of women and took seriously the expectation that a woman is to be a wife and mother, even though in their personal vocational choice there may have been a rejection of their own ability to fulfill this role. In the case of the shamans, the women assumed the role of economic provider in instances where their spouses were incapable of fulfilling it. What we find in all these cases is no manifest rejection of the status accorded women in society; rather they attempted to take on unusual roles as religious specialists, the better to fulfill a sense of responsibility, despite an inner feeling of incapacity to play the woman's role as it is usually expected. Throughout the lives of these individuals, there was an implicit adherence to Confucian ethics which attests to the depth of Confucian values in contemporary Korean culture. In approaching such cases on a biographical level, we note the necessity to take into account more than simple social structural characteristics in understanding religious behavior. The fact that religious motivation is expressive as well as instrumental is well documented in Koh's biographies.

In sum, in the following chapters we can observe in Asian traditions some universal functions of religion as related both to social structure and to motivations of an expressive or instrumental nature, which are part of human personality, whether in Asia or anywhere else.

BIBLIOGRAPHY

AHERN, Emily
  1973 *The Cult of the Dead in a Chinese Village.* Stanford, Calif.: Stanford University Press.
  1975 The Power and Pollution of Chinese Women. In M. Wolf and Witke (eds.), *Women in Chinese Society*, Stanford, Calif.: Stanford University Press, pp. 193–214.
  1978 Sacred and Secular Medicine in a Taiwan Village: A Study of Cosmological Disorders. In A. Kleinman *et al.* (eds.), *Culture and Healing in Asian Societies*, Cambridge, Mass.: Schenkman Publishing Company, pp. 17–39.
DEUCHLER, Martina
  1977 The Tradition: Women During the Yi Dynasty. In S. Mattielli (ed.), *Virtues in Conflict: Tradition and the Korean Woman Today*, Seoul: Royal Asiatic Society, pp. 1–48.
  1980 Neo-Confucianism: The Impulse for Social Action in Early Yi Korea. *Journal of Korean Studies* 2: 71–112.

DeVos, George A.
1973   *Socialization for Achievement*: *Essays on the Cultural Psychology of the Japanese.* Berkeley and Los Angeles: University of California Press.
1980   Afterword. In David Reynolds (ed.), *The Quiet Therapies*, Honolulu: University of Hawaii Press, pp. 111–135.

Durkheim, Emile
1947   *The Elementary Forms of the Religious Life.* Glencoe, Ill.: Free Press.

Freud, Sigmund
1928   *The Future of an Illusion.* London: Hogarth Press.

Harvey, Youngsook Kim
1979   *Six Korean Women*: *The Socialization of Shamans.* St. Paul, Minn.: West Publishing.

Kluckhohn, Clyde
1944   *Navaho Witchcraft.* Boston: Beacon Press.

Lebra, William
1974   *Okinawan Religion*: *Belief, Ritual, and Social Structure.* Berkeley and Los Angeles: University of California Press.

Malinowski, Bronislaw
1948   *Magic, Science, and Religion.* Boston: Beacon Press.
1974   *The Foundations of Faith and Morals.* London: Oxford University Press.

Marsella, Anthony, George DeVos, and Francis Hsu
1985   *Culture and Self.* London: Methuen.

Piaget, Jean
1930   *The Child's Conception of Physical Causality.* London: Routledge and Kegan Paul.
1932   *The Moral Judgment of Children.* London: Kegan Paul, Trench, Trubner.

Reynolds, David
1976   *Morita Psychotherapy.* Berkeley and Los Angeles: University of California Press.

Sansome, George
1958   *The History of Japan to 1334.* Stanford: Stanford University Press.

Van Gennep, Arnold
1960   *The Rites of Passage.* Chicago: University of Chicago Press.

Warner, W. Lloyd
1958   *A Black Civilization*: *A Study of an Australian Tribe.* New York: Harper and Row.

Weber, Max
1954   Class, Status, Power. In C. Wright Mills and W. W. Gerth (eds.), *From Max Weber*: *Essays in Sociology*, Chicago: University of Chicago Press, pp. 154–165.

Wolf, Margery
1972   *Women and the Family in Rural Taiwan.* Stanford, Calif.: Stanford University Press.
1974   Chinese Women: Old Skills in a New Context. In M. Z. Rosaldo and L. Lamphere (eds.), *Women, Culture, and Society*, Stanford, Calif.: Stanford University, pp. 157–172.

Chapter 2

Some Reflections on Family and Religion in East Asia

MELFORD E. SPIRO

INTRODUCTION

The theme of this volume is especially congenial to an anthropologist because the family and religion were among the core interests of anthropological inquiry from its very inception, and they have remained among its most perduring subjects of investigation. There are, I believe, at least two reasons why this should have been so.

In the first place, although like the family and religion, other sociocultural systems are also universal, none is as easily recognizable across all the etic types which are employed by anthropologists to classify the wide array of sociocultural systems as are family and religious systems. In the case of economic and political systems, for example, those which fall at the polar extremes of any of the recognized typologies by which they are classified are often identifiable as members of the same series only because of their similarities to the intermediate types. We need only remind ourselves of the differences between nomadic-gathering economies and industrial-bureaucratic economies, or between small, acephalous band organizations and large-scale centralized empires in order to grasp this rather simple point. For both comparisons it is difficult to identify an invariant sociocultural core that cuts across all their types or that persists from their earliest to their most recent manifestations.

The contrary, however, is the case in regard to the family or religion, or so it would seem, if I am correct in claiming that the nuclear family is the invariant core of every family system, and that the worship of superhuman beings comprises the invariant core of every religious system. Indeed, the founders of nineteenth century evolutionary thought in Europe were as perplexed by the similarities between their own (Victorian) family and religious systems and those of the non-European societies that they studied as they were intrigued by (and sometimes contemptuous of) the differences.

The second reason, I believe, for the perduring anthropological interest in the family and religion is that these two systems are related to one another in a systematic relationship which holds for no two other sociocultural systems. At first blush, this statement seems paradoxical because while the human family marks man's affinity with the rest of the animal kingdom—especially the class of mammals—religion marks his uniqueness. That is, the family (whether uniparental or biparental) is a generic mammalian institution, and since man evolved from a mammalian (more particularly a primate) species, it is hard to escape the assumption that the human family is phylogenetically rooted in the family system of our pre-hominid ancestors.

Since religion, however, is found (as far as we can tell) in our species alone, if religious systems are also universal it is because (as Robertson Smith and Freud pointed out a long time ago) they are rooted in, and may be viewed as metaphorical expressions of family (including kinship) relations. If that is so, then religion and the family (in contrast, say, to religion and economics or religion and politics) sustain a special relationship with each other, the existence of religion being in large part a function of the existence of the family.

To say that religious systems may be viewed as a metaphorical expression of family relations is to say that while the existence of the family may be explicable in terms of biological characteristics and needs which we share with other mammals, religion is explicable only in terms of the uniquely human capacity for symbolization, for it is in the symbolic process that the privately-constituted world of fantasy, the well-spring of religious belief, is transformed into the culturally-constituted world of religion. That is so because the symbol creates Being (spirits and gods) out of non-Being, and it invests words and gestures with the instrumental power that is imputed to religious ritual. In short, religious symbols often represent the transformation and elaboration, at the *cultural* level, of fantasies and cognitions that are found at the *psychological* level, which in turn are produced by family relations at the *social* level.

Although there is nothing new in this, its implications for the universal dimensions of the family and religion have not always been spelled out by anthropologists who, in their special concern with variation, have more often concentrated on the cross-cultural differences in family and religious systems than in their regularities. Although there can be no denying the importance of these differences, their regularities are equally important, and it is the recognition of the cross-cultural regularities in the family, viewed as a system of social relationships, that enables us to understand its connection with religion, viewed as a system of symbolic relationships.

CROSS-CULTURAL REGULARITIES IN HUMAN FAMILY SYSTEMS

The pan-human roots of the regularities in human family systems are not hard to discover, for however much these systems must adapt to and are conditioned by variations in ecology, economy, demography, the polity, and the like, every family (and kinship) system is a response to certain irreducible biological characteristics of human existence, among which I would stress the following.

(1) Human reproduction is bisexual, and conception is effected by means of sexual intercourse.

(2) Human beings are born helpless, and they remain dependent, both physically and emotionally, for a prolonged period on their caretakers.

(3) Human beings are also born instinctless, so that their caretakers attend not

only to their dependency needs but also to their need to acquire the cultural traditions of the group into which they are born.

(4)   Since relatively permanent pair-bonding, brought about both by the absence of estrus and the need for economic cooperation, has been a human characteristic since at least the origin of hunting, the core caretakers are parents, together with whom children comprise a domestic group.

(5)   Dependency being the child's prepotent need, he develops feelings of affectionate attachment toward his caretaking parents who, to a greater or lesser degree, gratify that need.

(6)   Gratification, however, is always relative to frustration, and caretakers not only gratify, but they also frustrate children's needs.

Caretakers are frustrators, willy-nilly, in a number of ways.   First, since they are agents of socialization and enculturation, they impose restrictions, constraints, and prescriptions on their offspring which are almost always frustrating if not downright painful.   Second, since there is no incompatibility between lactation and sex in human beings, as there is in infra-human mammals (in which the female does not enter estrus until her infant is weaned), caretakers are simultaneously both parent and spouse.   Hence, since the mother, for example, is simultaneously mother and wife, the child must share her attention and love with the husband-father. Third, since humans are dependent for a prolonged period, their dependency does not cease with the birth of a sibling—as it does in infra-human mammals, who either leave or are driven from the domestic group by the time the new infant arrives—which means that the attention and love of the mother must be shared with siblings as well as father. The sharing of love and attention is frustrating enough for adults, as the ubiquity of jealousy and envy indicates; for children, however, the frustration is even stronger.

Given, then, that caretakers both gratify and frustrate children's dependency needs, parents are not only the first and most important objects of their children's affection, but they are also, together with siblings, the first and most important objects of their hostility.

In sum, so far as their emotional texture is concerned, we would expect that in any society the relationships among all of the dyads comprising the family would be characterized by strong ambivalence, and that children would develop both an Oedipus complex [Spiro 1982b] and sibling rivalry. That these expectations also hold for East Asian families is abundantly evidenced in the chapters of this volume—those at least that deal with the social relationships of the family.   That these characteristics are symbolically expressed in the religious systems of East Asian cultures is no less evident from these reports.   I shall return to these points later in my discussion.

These general observations concerning the cross-cultural regularities in the human family have important implications for our understanding of its variability. For if these observations are correct, the biological characteristics enumerated in the foregoing discussion comprise a set of parameters, or invariant conditions, which all societies have had to cope with in the historical development of their family systems.

On the one hand, therefore, these invariant conditions might be said to account for the cross-cultural regularities in human family systems. On the other hand, however, the variability that is found in these systems—variability, for example, in principles of recruitment to the domestic group, the classification of kintypes, the norms which govern social relationships within the family, the rules which determine the distribution of inherited property, and so on—may be said to represent a limited range of institutionalized solutions to the problems, both sociological and psychological, created by those same invariant conditions. In sum, it might be argued that certain invariant biological conditions (bisexual reproduction and prolonged biological dependency) produce certain invariant sociological consequences (the biparental family and its caretaking functions) from which there flow certain invariant psychological consequences (such as ambivalence to parents and siblings), and that these consequences lead to variable cultural responses (norms and rules) which regulate the potentially disruptive effects of both dimensions—love and hate—of these ambivalent relationships.

I shall now argue that the invariant conditions that account for the cross-cultural regularities in family systems are no less important for the understanding of family behavior than are the culturally variable rules and norms that govern family relationships. I am not arguing, I hasten to add, that these rules and norms are merely epiphenomena—superstructure, as Marxists say. I am arguing, rather, that the emotional and motivational dispositions of family actors that require the elaboration of cultural rules and norms for their regulation continue to operate in these actors even after they acquire those rules and norms, and that their behavior, therefore, is a product (in the algebraic sense) of the simultaneous influence of both of these determinants.

Take, for example, filial behavior. Whatever the cultural values regarding parents might be, children's sentiments and attitudes regarding their parents are not formed exclusively by these culturally variable values. They are formed as well by their invariant, albeit socially acquired emotions of the type discussed earlier; and their filial sentiments and attitudes represent an interaction of these two sets of determinants. To be sure, to the degree that filial emotions conflict with cultural values, we would expect filial *behavior* to comply not so much with the actors' emotions as with their cultural values which, expressed in rules and norms, govern their duties and obligations to parents. When emotions conflict with values, the former must be repressed. Inasmuch, however, as the parents remain their unconscious targets, these emotions are as powerful as they ever were, but they are now expressed in various disguises—some more, some less disruptive in their social consequences.

In conclusion, if social relationships are governed by the attitudes and sentiments an actor has toward some Alter, and if these attitudes and sentiments are produced not only by culturally acquired values, but also by emotional and motivational dispositions acquired by the actor in his social experience with Alter, it is as foolish to ignore the emotional as it is to ignore the cultural determinants of their relationship. This is especially so in the case of family relationships, for many attitudes and sentiments which children hold toward parents and siblings are based on conceptions of them that are formed much before their acquisition of language—hence, before the acquisition of the cultural values which comprise the normatively expected conceptions of parents and siblings.   That is, these attitudes and sentiments are formed on the basis of their personal experiences with their parents and siblings, experiences which, as was argued above, arouse conflicting emotions of love and hate, of attachment and resentment, and the like. Since, moreover, these emotions are usually reinforced by later experiences with parents and siblings, they inevitably play a significant role in the development of the attitudes and sentiments that inform their social relationships with them.

RELIGION AND THE FAMILY

How, now, to turn to the second aspect of the theme of this volume, does the discussion of the family relate to religion?   As students of religion we can never know directly the superhuman beings postulated by religious belief systems; we can only know them indirectly, i.e., by means of the conceptions that religious actors have of them. Indeed, with few exceptions—for example, mystical experience and trance possession—the religious actors themselves do not claim to have direct knowledge of them. They, too, know them only indirectly—as they are represented in the collective representations of their culture, in their own mental representations of them, and in the rituals by which they attempt to relate to them.

If, then, we take these three sets of data as our evidence for the conceptions which religious actors have of superhuman beings, it seems safe to say on the basis of a great deal of comparative research that these conceptions are more or less isomorphic with the conceptions, unconscious as well as conscious, which, as family actors, they form of their family members, and more particularly the conceptions which as children they form of their caretakers, usually their parents, in their personal encounters with them.   It also seems safe to say that the rituals by which they attempt to relate to these superhuman beings express, and sometimes gratify, the wishes that are instigated by the emotions which those caretakers arouse in them, most especially the emotions of dependency and love, of fear and hatred.   Thus, if the child's dependency needs, for example, are gratified by a nurturant mother, it is not unlikely that as an adult he will worship a mother-like superhuman being(s) from whom he anticipates the gratification of his wish for continuing childlike dependency.   Similarly, if certain of his childhood needs are frustrated, for example, by an authoritarian father, whom he consequently learns to fear or hate, it is not unlikely that as an adult he will propitiate a fatherlike superhuman being(s) so as to avoid the wrath which he fears, or he will express his hostility to him (which he seldom does, at least not overtly).

In short, I am suggesting, that whatever the "objective" characteristics of his parents might be when seen through the lens of a camera, the child forms various mental representations of them which, given the fact that the child's lens is neither objective nor realistic, distort and exaggerate their characteristics. I am suggesting, further, that these parental representations, partly conscious, partly unconscious, constitute the *anlage* or conceptual schemata for the mental representations which he later forms of superhuman beings. I am suggesting, finally, that the psychological reality of superhuman beings, like that of the parents, is in no way affected by their physical reality. Thus, even if their parents have died and are no longer in the physical world, they continue to exist for their children in the latter's representational world—i.e., in their mental representations of them—and it is in the latter world that, even when they are alive, they have their important, i.e., their psychological reality. This condition also holds, *pari passu*, for gods, ghosts, and ancestors, to use Jordan's felicitous designation for the superhuman beings of East Asia [JORDAN 1972].

With this conceptual orientation to the relationship between the family and religion, we may now turn to the chapters of this volume in order to examine the extent to which this schema applies to the East Asia materials. If, in this examination, I emphasize some chapters more than others, it is not because the latter are any the less important or significant for the general theme of this volume, but because I was charged with examining the relationship between the family and religion in East Asia from a psychodynamic perspective. I should also note that if much of the focus of my discussion is on male actors, it is because the material herein has been typically presented from that perspective. It should finally be noted that some of the formulations in what follows were rather rigorously challenged during the discussion at the conference preceding this publication. Although I found many of the challenges both illuminating and provocative, I have nevertheless retained these formulations with only some few changes.

FAMILY TENSIONS IN EAST ASIA

In order to confine my discussion to reasonable boundaries, I have decided to focus on lines of tension in the East Asian family. Since, however, filial piety and family solidarity have always received a great deal of attention in discussions of the East Asian family, such a focus may perhaps contribute some new dimensions to the subject.

From the material presented in the conference papers, one might expect the following lines of tension to be most salient in the families of East Asia. First, given the extraordinary relationship of nurturance and dependency characteristic of the mother and the son, most especially, so it seems, in Japan, I would expect considerable tension to develop between the father and the son: on the father's part because of the wife's obvious emotional preference for the son, on the son's part because his father is a most important competitor for his wish for the mother's exclusive attention. If nothing else, it is the father—not the son—who has a monopoly on the mother's sexuality. Moreover, since the father-husband is an especially important authority figure, both for the wife and the children, one whose jural, if not personal, authority requires obedience and respect, one would expect that this would constitute an equally important source of tension in the father-son relationship.

It must be noted here that although the mother-son relationship is described in several chapters, none of them addresses the father-son, father-daughter, or mother-daughter relationships, nor, except in passing, the relationship among siblings. That this disregard of the latter relationships would not occur in a conference dealing, for example, with South Asia or the Middle East only serves to underscore the pivotal emotional, though not jural, importance of the mother-son dyad in the East Asia family system. (It also means that my comments will be incomplete and somewhat distorted).

Given the subordination of children to both parents, as well as the duties and obligations that the former owe the latter (which are summed up in the key concept of filial piety) and which continue even after their death, I would also expect considerable tension to develop not only between father and son, but also between mother and son. But there is an additional—and more important—reason that I would expect tension to develop in the latter relationship. Although the mother is extraordinarily nurturant to the son and attentive to his needs—which, of course, leads to the loving and dependent attachment to her that is stressed in all the papers—that very attentiveness can be expected to lead to three types of tension.

First, the mother's devotion, conceived as a "'perfect' act of perpetual selfless sacrifice" to quote Tanaka (Chapter 15), may produce a "deep feeling of guilt and indebtedness" in the son, and such a feeling can only lead to profound (though probably unconscious) resentment. Second, the young son's intimate and persistent physical contact with the mother—he sleeps with her, is bathed by her, and so on—most probably arouses erotic feelings for her which, however, are necessarily frustrated, and, I assume, ultimately repressed. It is for that reason, I would assume, that the mother-son relationship is characterized, to quote Tanaka again, by "the continuous presence of unresolved libidinality." Third, the dependent attachment to the mother, which she herself encourages, is in conflict with the child's need for autonomy, including psychological separation and individuation [MAHLER et al. 1975].

I would also expect considerable tension to develop in the husband-wife relationship: on the husband's part because of his subordinate place to the son in the wife's emotional life; and on the wife's part because, as Tanaka puts it, of the "unrecognition of sexuality in the marital relationship." Now if, as Tanaka also points out, the wife's nurturant relationship to her husband recapitulates that of the mother to her son, that is highly gratifying for the husband, since he can gratify his erotic needs outside the marriage—hence, have his cake and eat it too—but it can only be frustrating to the wife whose erotic needs, however much she may sublimate them in her relationship with her son, are nevertheless frustrated in her marital relationship in which (to quote Tanaka again) "sexuality is much downplayed." Indeed, I would argue that it is precisely because her sexual needs are frustrated in her role as wife that the woman invests such great affect in her role as mother, her nurturant relationship to her son being a sublimation of her frustrating erotic relationship with her husband.

I would argue, too, that the husband's relative disinterest in his wife as an erotic object is the last link in a feedback loop in which, having recoiled as a boy from the incestuous implications of his attachment to his highly affectionate mother, he marries a woman who in so many respects represents the mother. In Japan, for example, the husband not only calls his wife, "mother," following the birth of their first child, but since her relationship to him is, as Tanaka puts it, "not essentially different from her relationship to her young children"—implying that it is little different from his mother's relationship to him when he was a child—he comes to perceive her, so I would suggest, as a mother. In short, since the wife-husband relationship and the mother-son relationship are "dangerously similar" (to use Tanaka's words), it is hardly surprising that the wife becomes a non-erotic object for her husband.

The dynamics of that process are encapsulated in Freud's pithy comment concerning a class of males—the males of East Asia, of course, were far from his mind—concerning whom he writes, "Where they love they do not desire and where they desire they cannot love. They seek objects which they do not need to love, in order to keep their sensuality away from the objects they love" [FREUD 1912: 183]. For such males, the wife is classified with the class of females who, like the mother, are viewed as asexual, and they are distinguished from the class of females (including prostitutes, concubines, and mistresses) who are viewed as sexual. The former class, being pure, are worthy of love; the latter, being impure, are worthy only of sex.

I would suggest, then, that the Neo-Confucianist view of marriage, according to which, to quote Tu (Chapter 7), "mutual responsibility rather than romantic love" ought to characterize the conjugal relationship, is more a reflection of than a model for the actual relationship between the spouses. In either event, for the wife to be treated by her husband, as Ch'eng I reports his father to have treated his mother, with "full respect" and "reverence," or for that same wife to live with her husband in "tranquillity and correctness," and not to be the object of "indecent liberties and improper intimacies,"—all these quotations are taken from sources quoted by Tu—such a wife, I would suggest, is not only sexually frustrated, but in the context of East Asian society she is all the more resentful (perhaps unconsciously) because though *she* is not the object of her husband's "indecent liberties and improper intimacies," she knows that other women—concubines, mistresses, or whatever—are.

A fourth line of tension, as I see it, develops between siblings. Although the papers contributed to this volume stress the continuing involvement of the mother in her son, it seems reasonable to assume that the birth of a new child, especially a son, means that the elder child is, to some degree, displaced by the younger as the focal attention of the mother. In Korea this displacement is both symbolized and actualized in the sleeping arrangements in which, as Lee (Chapter 12) describes it, the elder sibling is extruded from his parents' bedroom following the birth of a younger sibling, and is sent to sleep in the room of his paternal grandmother. But even in Japan, where such extrusion does not occur, the rivalry between siblings for maternal love has its effects, so that it is little wonder that in the *Kojiki* myths analyzed by Sofue (Chapter 14), 12 of the 15 myths which deal with the relationship between brothers entail competition and rivalry, and that in 8 of these 12 the rivalry culminates in fratricide.

Given such strong indications of sibling rivalry, it is little wonder, too, that both in Japan and Korea the domestic unit comprises a stem, rather than extended family. Moreover, although Lee contrasts the Japanese and Korean stem family households with the extended family household in China, in fact the situation in China [HSU 1971; YANG 1969] is very little different from that in Japan and Korea, and for the same reason: following the death of the father, friction between married siblings leads to the segmentation of the extended family and their formation of independent households.

FAMILY TENSIONS AND RELIGION IN EAST ASIA

In the following sections I wish to examine some possible links between the putative tensions in the East Asian family discussed in the previous section and certain aspects of East Asian religion. Before examining these links it is important to emphasize two points. First, I am not suggesting that religious beliefs and rituals can be "reduced" to sociological or psychological variables. I am suggesting, rather, that social relationships, cognitive orientations and motivational dispositions both inform and are reflected in belief and ritual system, whether sacred or secular. Second, in focusing on the relationship between family tensions and religion, I am not suggesting that the solidaristic dimension of the family is not reflected in religion. Rather, that dimension is not the subject of my inquiry.

Ancestor Worship and the Father

Although ancestors are most often viewed as benign, it is also the case that sometimes they may be punitive. Although Fortes may have somewhat overstated his case in claiming that in East Asia, as well as West Africa, "the feature that stands out most conspicuously in all varieties of ancestor worship...is their punitive character" [FORTES 1977: 145], some of the chapters in this volume also noted (without emphasizing) their punitive dimension. Thus, in Korea, the dead (including the ancestors and ghosts) are dangerous, so Kendall (Chapter 3) remarks, "simply because they are dead...and their touch brings illness or affliction." This is especially true in the case of ancestors who died with "unfulfilled desires." Restless ancestors, as well as ghosts and angry household gods, cause not only illness, but financial loss and domestic strife, as well. Similarly, Lee (Chapter 12) observes that if the ritual service for an ancestor is not performed, the ancestor spirit becomes a wandering ghost; and although, he further observes, ghosts have no power to punish their descendants directly, this implies, I would assume, that they do have power to punish them indirectly.

In his treatment of ancestor worship in China (Taiwan) Suenari (Chapter 11) does not deal with the punitive dimension of ancestors, but it is implicit in his emphasis on (what he calls) the "economic reciprocity" characteristic of family relationships, including that with ancestors. Like their relationship with the gods, the

Chinese relationship with their ancestors is "contractual," which implies that the latter's punitive or non-punitive action is contingent upon the offering or withholding of gifts by their descendants. This implication is explicit in the work of Emily Ahern on ancestor worship in Taiwan. According to Ahern's findings ancestors are not infrequently blamed for such serious misfortunes as insanity, serious infirmity and death [AHERN 1973: Chapter 12].

The situation in Japan is no different. Thus, Morioka (Chapter 13) observes that for the lower class, at least, the function of ancestor worship is to avert disaster which would be caused by ancestors if their worship were neglected. Carmen Blacker makes the same point, restricting it, however, to the lower class. Thus, if "the ancestral dead are not correctly treated by their descendants, if the offerings or the obsequies necessary to their nourishment are neglected, then with frightening suddenness their nature will change. The kindly old grandfather, the sympathetic father, the loving mother will turn in an instant into a vicious and capricious tyrant, punishing the neglectful family with curses" [BLACKER 1975: 47–48].

In order to understand these findings, it is important to consider some other data offered in the accompanying chapters. First, approximately 50 percent of Japanese families, according to Morioka, continue to practice ancestor worship even when the *ie* system has collapsed. Second, in Korea, according to Lee, the ancestor tablet is kept in the ancestral shrine only until the fourth ascending generation, following which it is buried in the grave, which implies that the ancestor remains individuated only for a relatively short time, after which he is assimilated to the generic class of "ancestor."

Now although in ancestor worship, rites are performed for all one's ancestors, these findings suggest that the *cognitively salient* ancestors are not the genealogically remote ancestors, but rather the genealogically close and immediately dead ancestors—i.e. the parents and grandparents. The remote ancestors, of course, are important both jurally (to establish claims on property, to enhance the prestige of a clan line or to legitimize its rights) and politically (to inculcate respect for authority, beginning with the family and ending with the centralized state). But for the average individual, I would suggest, these corporate functions are second in importance to their "religious" functions. In the latter regard, an ancestor (like anyone else) is cognitively salient for a religious actor only to the degree that he has a clear and vivid mental representation of him, and the ancestors concerning whom he has the clearest and most vivid mental representations are his deceased parents and grand-parents—those whom he himself has personally encountered. Hence, even though in ancestor worship the actor in principle attends to all of his ancestors, it is his immediate ancestors, especially his parents, whom, I would suggest, he has most in mind, or whose mental representation forms the template for his conception of the other ancestors. Fortes [1961: 187] put it most succinctly in his remark that "ancestor worship is primarily the religious cult of deceased parents."

These claims are supported by Morioka's findings that (a) although traditionally a Japanese "ancestor" is the ancestor of the *ie*, with the collapse of the *ie* in urban families, "ancestor" has increasingly come to designate the "deceased bilateral kindred" (which most importantly means, I would suggest, the ascendance of the mother to the status of a cognitively salient ancestor), and (b) the "private" meanings of ancestor worship have superceded its "public" meanings. Consistent with my previous hypothesis, however, I would suggest that these private meanings were always foremost in the worshipper's mind (although the public meanings were, no doubt, the important formal meanings), and that the collapse of the *ie* merely permits their centrality to be acknowledged.

Even more important, however, is Morioka's finding that although many urban families do not own a *butsudan*, the rate of ownership dramatically increases with the death of a parent, and that in extended family households (in which, presumably, the *ie* is still somewhat important) it increases significantly in households with widows. These two findings suggest once again that the cognitively and emotionally salient ancestors are the immediate dead. Moreover, taking Morioka's findings concerning widows into account, the ancestors need not even be linear ancestors so long as they have been household members with whom the actor has sustained important social relationships.

If this is so, then inasmuch as ancestors are not only revered—an extension of filial piety—but also feared, I would suggest that both attitudes are a function of the mental representations that, as children, the actors had formed of their immediately deceased ancestors, most especially, but not exclusively, the father. The latter attitude, which is the one we are concerned with here, might be explained in the first instance by Fortes' hypothesis that it is the "authority component" of the father that is elevated to ancestorship. If, then, in addition to his positive feelings toward the father, one would expect—given the over-arching value of filial piety—that he would probably repress these feelings, or at least not exhibit them in overt behavior. That upon his death the father—now an ancestor—is viewed as a potentially dangerous figure, capable of inflicting harm on his descendants, is then susceptible of two, complementary interpretations.

First, the repressed hostility which was felt for the father when he was alive can now find an outlet in the culturally-constituted belief that ancestors are potentially dangerous. Specifically, that belief allows the child to project his erstwhile hostility toward the living father onto the dead ancestor, thereby transforming him from an ordinarily oppressive authority figure into a potentially dangerous one. The second interpretation is more complex. Clinical evidence indicates that hostility toward some person may generate death wishes (if only as an unconscious fantasy) toward him, and should that person die, the actor, given that the "omnipotence of thoughts" is one of the characteristics of unconscious mentation, may unconsciously experience his death as resulting from his death wishes toward him. Given, then, that the principle of *lex talionis* informs not only many legal systems, but unconscious mentation as well, the belief that the deceased father is potentially dangerous might be explained by the unconscious conviction of the child that the former might harm him in retaliation for the 'harm' that he (the child) had inflicted on the father.

Goddesses, Religious Specialists and the Mother

Since the most notable feature of the mother-son relationship in East Asia is the mother's nurturance and the son's dependence, we would expect that dimension of the mother-son relationship to be reflected in East Asian religion. The extraordinary nurturant-dependent nature of the mother-son relationship in East Asia, at least in Japan, is stressed in the chapters by Tanaka and Sofue. A "good mother," Tanaka observes, "is believed to care for and worry about her son eternally." Hence, the son's dependency (*amae*) on the mother persists not only over her lifetime, but even after her death when, as an ancestress, she is still supposed to be watching over him. As a measure of what he calls the son's "very strong continuing dependency need" in regard to the mother, Sofue points to the fact that it is the favorite theme of Japanese popular culture. For him, therefore, this need comprises a "mother-complex." Whatever that expression may denote, it certainly connotes the formation by the son of a mental representation of the mother as extraordinarily loving and nurturant, one who can be expected to do anything in her power in the service of his welfare.

Such a maternal representation is too good to give up. Hence, it is little wonder that when the mother becomes an ancestor the son continues to expect that he can rely on her assistance. It is little wonder, too—though I would not have predicted it—that with the introduction of Buddhism to China, and thence to Japan, the infinitely compassionate Hindu god, Avalokitesvara, was transformed into the goddess, Kuanyin (China) or Kannon (Japan). That the *amae* relationship with the mother is transferred to Kannon—probably the most popular deity (actually Bodhisattva) in Japan—and that the benevolent dimension of the maternal representation is reflected in the collective representation of Kannon (just as the authority dimension of the paternal representation is reflected in the collective representation of the male ancestor) can be seen in the following statement of Teruko Furuya (the translation is by Yohko Tsuji):

"Kannon's concern is not directed toward heaven or a utopia, but toward this world (in which many people still suffer). Kannon is benevolent and omnipotent. She never punishes us, nor gets angry with us. On the contrary, consistently and promptly she answers our selfish prayers, such as a desire to have an attractive child, a desire to pass an entrance examination for a prestigious school, a desire to get promoted at work, and so on. She is just like an *amai* mother who always listens to the desires of an indulged child..."

Like the mother, Kannon is not only infinitely compassionate, but she has another quality that the mother does not have: she is also all-powerful, as the following quotation from Blacker [1975: 94] indicates: "A man only has to think of the Bodhisattva Kannon to be saved from every conceivable calamity. A man hurled into a fiery pit has but to think of the Kannon for the fire to be quenched. A man floundering in an ocean of sea monsters has but to think of Kannon and he will neither sink nor drown. A man bombarded with thunderbolts has but to think of Kannon and not a hair of his head will be hurt. A man beset by goblins, demons, ghosts, giants, wild beasts or fearful fiery serpents has but to think of Kannon for these creatures to vanish." Power of this magnitude, of course, is never found in any human being but it *is* found in the mental representations that a young child forms of his parents. In the child's eyes the parent, who literally has the power of life or death over him, is indeed omnipotent. Hence, when the omnipotence of the maternal representation of the Japanese child is conjoined with its benevolence, the result—I would suggest—is a maternal representation that is projected in the adult's collective representation of Kannon.

But the relationship between the religious devotee and Kannon is not the only manifestation of the child's *amae* relationship with the mother on the religious plane. It is also manifested, as Tsuji [1980] has suggested, both in the relationship between client and shaman (*miko*)—and here, I would include Korea as well as Japan—and in that between the members and founders (*kyoso*) of the new religions.

In Japan and Korea, though not in China, shamans are almost exclusively female, and the rare male shaman performs his role as a transvestite. In Korea, according to Kendall, the shaman (*mansin*) is used to help the household overcome the afflictions—illness, financial loss, domestic strife—that are brought about by restless ancestors, ghosts, and angry household gods, as well as to help young women overcome infertility. According to Blacker, similar functions are served by the Japanese *miko*, as well as by her modern counterpart, the *kyoso*, who is usually also female. So far as the latter is concerned, Davis observes that the "great majority" of those who join a new religion hope "to receive some practical benefit—cure of disease, solution to some personal problem, support for some psychological difficulty, etc.—from their affiliation" [Tsuji 1980: ms]. In short, in both cases when faced with adversity, the adult re-establishes the dependency relationship with a *female* religious specialist that as a child he had experienced with his mother.

Just as the devotees' relationship with these female religious specialists is best understood by reference to the mother-child relationship—as a recapitulation of their early experience with the mother—the recruitment of these women to their religious vocations is also best understood by reference to the husband-wife relationship—to their experience as wives in a sexually frustrating relationship. Thus, in Korea, Kendall tells us, shamans are usually recruited to their calling in middle age, after suffering a "run of ill luck" as a result of possession by a god. In Japan, Sasaki (Chapter 4) writes, there are two ways of becoming a shaman: "One is through divine calling and the other by self-searching." In the former case, the woman suffers from some mental and physical abnormality, including visual and auditory hallucinations, trance, decrease in appetite, severe palpitations of the heart, sleeplessness and loss of weight. If her condition is not improved by resort to modern medical specialists, she will visit a shaman to discover the cause of her affliction. Should it be diagnosed as resulting from spirit possession, the most important means for overcoming her afflictions is for her to become a shaman herself, and to serve the spirit or god who has possessed her. (In Okinawa, this often means agreeing to marry him.) After agreeing to become a shaman, her "abnormality" gradually disappears.

These women, according to Blacker, exhibit in their personal histories a "curiously uniform pattern." "Nearly all of them in their early life betray symptoms of what could be called 'arctic hysteria.' They are sickly, neurotic, hysterical, odd, until a moment comes when exacerbated by suffering, these symptoms rise to a climactic interior experience of a mystical kind. A deity, by means of a dream or a possession, siezes them and claims them for his service. Thenceforward they are changed characters. Their former oddity and sickliness give way to a remarkable strength and magnetism of personality, which is conferred on them, together with various supernormal powers, by the deity who has possessed them" [BLACKER 1975: 129].

The characteristics of these women—which are almost identical with the characteristics and mode of recruitment of Burmese shamans whom I investigated in the 1960's [SPIRO 1978]—are the classical symptoms of conversion hysteria, a condition that is typically brought on by the repression of frustrated sexual needs. In this case, I would suggest, these frustrated needs are symbolically gratified by means of trance possession—i.e. by a hallucinatory experience—in which they are finally claimed by the most potent male of all, a god. If, then, the East Asian woman, like her counterpart in South and Southeast Asia, is often frustrated by her unfulfilled libidinal attachment to her father, as Roy [1975] observes in the case of India; if moreover, her unfulfilled desires continue to be frustrated in her sexually unsatisfactory relationship with her husband as occurs, so Tanaka suggests in Chapter 15 and Koh suggests in Chapter 16; and if, finally, the sublimation of her repressed libidinal desires in her relationship with her son is not entirely effective; if all this is true, then it is hardly surprising, as Blacker observes, that the women who become shamans or founders of new religions represent merely the tip of an iceberg. Nor is it surprising that some of the women—usually lower class and not highly educated—should find an outlet in these religious callings, especially since possession by a god serves not only to gratify their frustrated libidinal needs, but their status needs as well. From a position of subordination and relative powerlessness in the formal social structure, they suddenly become the medium for the gods themselves, so that their personality undergoes a transformation of corresponding magnitude [BLACKER 1975].

Buddhist Monasticism and the Parents

As a final example of the relationship between tensions in the parent-child relationship and religion in East Asia, I wish to turn to Buddhist monasticism. From the perspective of this paper and from that of Lancaster's too (Chapter 9), the crucial feature of Buddhist monastic recruitment is found in the carrying out of the Buddha's injunction that in order to achieve the Supreme Goal of Buddhism it is necessary—in the words of the *Mahavagga Sutta*—that "family men go forth from home into homelessness."

Now what was peculiar to Indian civilization at the time of the Buddha, as Dutt [1962: 43] observes in his magisterial history of Buddhist monks and monasteries in ancient India, is not that India produced saints and ascetics who renounced family and the world for a higher goal—religious manifestations of that type were also found in other civilizations as well—but that in India the "goers-forth" formed a community. Lancaster also stresses this point in regard to East Asia, but with an important twist that we shall note below. In ancient India, moreover, this community was "recognized as such not only by the people, but also by the State"—something which continues to be true of the Buddhist societies of Sri Lanka and Southeast Asia [SPIRO 1982]—whereas in East Asia the Sangha has most frequently met strong opposition from the people and the State alike.

The State aside, opposition to the Sangha is entirely understandable in the case of East Asia where "leaving home" is the ultimate act of filial impiety because as Lancaster observes, it means giving up the family name, removing oneself from the ancestral lineage by not having children, producing no descendants for the continuation of ancestor worship, and—on a more mundane note—causing trouble after death because monks leave no descendants to worship them.

It may also be remarked that, beginning with the Buddha himself, "leaving home" has meant abandoning not only parents, but also—since some "goers-forth" have been married when embarking upon their quest for Enlightenment—wives and children as well. The *locus classicus* is the *Vessantara Jataka*, the most famous Buddhist myth in Theravada Buddhist societies (*The Jataka* 1957: vol. 6). The Prince Vessantara, an earlier incarnation of the Buddha, abandoned his beloved wife and children in order to seek Enlightenment. To attain his quest he even gave his children as servants to a cruel Brahmin, and his wife to yet another. When his children, beaten and oppressed by the Brahmin, managed to escape and find their way back to Vessantara, he was filled with "dire grief"—his heart palpitated, his mouth panted, blood fell from his eyes—until he arrived at the insight that "All this pain comes from affection and no other cause; I must quiet this affection, and be calm." Having achieved that insight, he was able to abandon his children.

Such an attitude, as Ozaki reminds us (Chapter 6), was already found in East Asia prior to the arrival of Buddhism, being present in Taoism as well. The following story of Lu Hsiu Ching, which I take from Ozaki's chapter, indicates that very clearly. Lu Hsiu Ching retired from the world to the mountains where he studied. He left the mountains for a while to look for some medicine. When he passed through his native place he stayed at his house for a few days. At that time his daughter began to run a fever all of a sudden and fell into a critical condition. The family pleaded with him to cure her. But Hsiu Ching left, saying: 'Having abandoned my family, I am in the midst of training. The house I stopped by is no different from an inn to me.'[1]

In both cases, Buddhist and Taoist alike, the attitude of the perfect "goer-forth"

---

1) That the pursuit of the religious life requires the rejection of family ties is, of course, not restricted to the salvation religions of Asia. Early Christianity (as the attitude of Jesus, both to his ties with his own family as well as to family ties in general, reveals) required an equally powerful rejection (cf. Mark 3: 31ff, Luke 9: 59ff, Luke 14: 26).

is best described in the famous injunction of the *Sutta Nipata*. "Having left son and wife, father and mother, wealth, and corn, and relatives, the different objects of desire, let one wander alone like a rhinoceros" (*Sutta-Nipata*, verse 26 of the *Khaggavisana Sutta*). But, of course, for the typical Buddhist monk, "leaving home" does not entail wandering alone like a rhinoceros; instead, everywhere he enters a community of like-minded "goers-forth," a monastery.

Unless, as Lancaster perceptively observes, we recognize the "appeal of the monastery life, it is difficult to account for the fact, that, despite the monks' violation of the sacred duty of filial piety, Buddhist monastic organizations thrived and became one of the most important features of the religious, economic and social life of China, Korea, and Japan." In his discussion of monastic recruitment, Lancaster is entirely correct in stressing the appeal of the "pull" factors, as migration theorists call them, that attract young men to the monastery—special dress, ritual, mystical practices, and the like; but for the purposes of this paper, I should like to stress the "push" factors that motivate them to "leave home."

In attempting to understand these "push" factors it is important to stress that when the young man "goes forth," he does more than leave home—that is much too passive a term to characterize this process, especially in the societies of East Asia in which filial piety is an overriding value. Rather, he *abandons* home, that is, he actively severs his ties with his parents and siblings, and he refrains from forming expectable ties with a wife and children. It is the *wish* to sever the former ties and to refrain from forming the latter which constitutes, I am suggesting, the "push" factor in his "leaving home." This suggestion is supported by the fact that (as has already been noted) "going forth" does not mean wandering alone like a rhinoceros, but rather substituting a voluntary community, based on religio-mystical ties, for an involuntary one, based on biological-kinship ties. When it is considered, moreover, that the voluntary community, the monastery, has many of the characteristics of the family—indeed, in China, as Lancaster observes, the monastery became an actual family surrogate, even including fictive father-son relationships, fictive lineage formations and fictive ancestral tablets—it becomes all the more obvious that it is not living in a family-like structure as such that the "goer-forth" rejects in "leaving home," but rather living in his own biological family.

And make no mistake about it. "Leaving home" *is* a rejection of the latter family, despite the monks' attempts to rationalize it, and thereby cope with the guilt induced by this act of filial impiety, by claiming that by transferring merit to deceased parents, and thereby promoting their otherworldly welfare, the monastic vocation is in fact an expression of filial piety. This is tellingly demonstrated, for example, in Lancaster's data which show that 70 percent of the Korean monks he interviewed entered the monastery against the wishes of their parents, that they persist in their decision despite the fact that for as long as ten years their families begged them to return home, that the resentment of their siblings for having to assume the burden for caring for their aged parents is well-known to them, and that their lingering guilt for having abandoned the parents is evidenced by their resistance to discuss this matter in their interviews.

The recognition that monastic recruitment violates the norm of filial piety—and the attendant psychological consequences of guilt, remorse, and rationalization attendant upon this violation—is clearly evident as well in the autobiographies of the five Korean nuns that Koh summarizes in her chapter (Chapter 16). To be sure, other "push" factors in the nuns' motivation to enter the monastery—the traumata attendant upon such experiences as the death of a lover, the failure of a marriage, frustrated childlessness, the remarriage of a father, the death of a mother, etc.—were even stronger. Nevertheless, their recognition of their violation of the duty of filial piety, more especially since they have been importantly influenced by the Confucian ethic, is equally evident. Thus, one nun characterized her decision as "this unfilial act," but then immediately rationalized the decision by saying that as a Buddhist nun she could more effectively fulfill her filial duties. Another nun, though her father was a Christian minister, made the same claim. Their rejection of the family, their guilt, and their rationalizations are all evidenced in the fact that, as Koh observes, they all experienced "sorrow" about leaving home without their families' permission, and yet they nevertheless carried out their decision over the strong opposition of their families, and in the full realization that the latter would suffer "tremendous social stigma." Now, it may also be true, as Koh claims, that their decision, given their "sentimental" and "deep attachment" to family members, is a measure of their self-reliance, but it is also a measure (I would argue) of their willingness, if not wish, to abandon their families.

Since, however, the nuns' decisions to enter the monastery were traumatically motivated, I shall return to the monks in order to address the problem that is by now rather obvious: what "push" factors could possibly account for the fact that a young man, reared in a culture which places such strong emphasis on filial piety, is nevertheless motivated to violate his filial duties in such an extreme fashion?

The answer—or at least one of the answers—is to be found, I would suggest, in the wish to escape the tensions that, as discussed at the beginning of this chapter, are endemic in East Asia (but not only East Asia) in the relationship between the boy and the other members of his family. These tensions include the fear and resentment engendered by the father, the incestuous and dependency anxiety aroused by the mother, and the rivalry induced by male siblings in his family of origin. They also include the Oedipally-induced fears concerning the formation of a sexual relationship with a woman other than the mother, as well as the anxiety about giving up his dependency orientation, both of which are aroused in anticipation of establishing a family of procreation. All of these tensions, I would submit, are experienced in some sense by most young men in East Asia. (For a Southeast Asia parallel example, compare SPIRO 1977.)

In most cases these tensions are of a magnitude that can be handled and overcome. In some few cases, however, they are too powerful to sustain in continuous and ongoing relationships with members of the family—especially since most of these tensions continue to be experienced interminably as the result of living in stem and extended family households in East Asian societies. For such men the monastery is a marvellously contrived institution which, inasmuch as it is religiously sanctioned, permits them to avoid family relationships while at the same time providing cultural legitimicy for their violating the duty of filial piety by interpreting it as motivated by a higher duty. Indeed, I would suggest that the resort to such an extreme solution, in spite of the sacred duty of filial piety, is convincing demonstration of how painful those family tensions are.

But we don't have to turn to those few who seek a solution in monasticism to assess the strength of family tensions even for the majority that are able to cope with them. Thus, it is not accidental, I believe, that when they have the chance, even those who do not enter a monastery seize the opportunity to leave their natal family for the city. And once there, rather than forming stem or extended family households, most of them establish nuclear family households, as Tanaka and Lee have shown for Japan and Korea respectively. It is for that reason that I disagree with Lee's interpretation of the modernization of the Korean family and religion as an extension of traditional familism. The traditional sentiment may still remain—after all we are still witnessing the first generation of this phenomenon—but the difference between the persistence of the sentiment of familism and its expression in the formation of a stem household is a difference that, as William James puts it, makes a difference.

I wish now to conclude this chapter with the mother-son relationship, the theme with which it began. I want to suggest that of all the tensions that motivate home-leaving, whether it be for a celibate life in the monastery or a married life in the city, the most important is the tension the son experiences in his relationship with the mother. Let us consider the choice of the monastery—because we can learn most from the more extreme case.

Since the monastery can be viewed, as we have already seen, as a kind of non-biological family, it is not inaccurate to say about Buddhist monasticism everywhere—as Lancaster says about Buddhist monasticism in China—that the monk can "join the new group (the monastery) and break the binds of the family system and yet find within Buddhism a re-creation of the family." That is not, as I said, inaccurate, but it is not entirely accurate either, because although the monk can re-create in the monastery a relationship with a "father," "sons," and (male) "siblings," there is one relationship that he cannot re-create, that with a "mother"! And it is that pivotal relationship of the East Asian son, I would suggest, that the monk especially wishes to avoid by joining the monastery. For despite its highly pleasurable aspects, the young boy's relationship with the mother, as I have already stressed, has two potentially frightening dimensions, as well: a sexual dimension, on the one hand, and a symbiotic one [MAHLER et al. 1975] on the other.

Thus, if the highly attentive mother is "seductive" in her relationship with the son, the intensity of the libidinal dimension in their relationship can become frightening for him because of its incestuous implications. Similarly, if, rather than being seductive, the mother is overprotective toward him, the exaggeration of his dependency on her can become frightening for the son because it signifies a regressive pull to the symbiotic state of early infancy in which the psychic differentiation between self and mother has not yet been achieved. If either alone can be frightening, the combination can be terrifying. In becoming a monk, then, the son not only escapes these frightening dimensions of his relationship with the mother, but he also—because of the monastic rule of celibacy—avoids their re-creation in a relationship with a wife. (For a more detailed analysis of these and other motives for monastic recruitment in Southeast Asia, see SPIRO 1982a.) I am suggesting, then, that the monastery is attractive to those few men for whom the relationships with mother and wife are too threatening to sustain. It allows them to escape the former and avoid the latter.

BIBLIOGRAPHY

AHERN, Emily
    1973   *The Cult of the Dead in a Chinese Village.* Stanford: Stanford University Press.
BLACKER, Carmen
    1975   *The Catalpa Bow.* London: George Allen and Unwin.
DUTT, Sukumar
    1962   *Buddhist Monks and Monasteries of India.* London: George Allen and Unwin.
FORTES, Meyer
    1961   Pietas in Ancestor Worship. *Journal of the Royal Anthropological Institute* 91: 166–191.
    1977   Custom and Conscience in Anthropological Perspective. *International Review of Psychoanalysis* 4: 127–154.
FREUD, Sigmund
    1968 (1912)   On the Universal Tendency to Debasement in the Sphere of Love. *The Standard Edition of the Complete Psychological Works of Sigmund Freud*, Vol. 11. London: Hogarth Press.
HSU, Francis L. K.
    1971   *Under the Ancestors' Shadow.* Stanford: Stanford University Press.
JORDAN, David K.
    1972   *Gods, Ghosts, and Ancestors: Folk Religion in a Taiwanese Village.* Berkeley and Los Angeles: University of California Press.
MAHLER, Margaret S., Fred PINE and Anni BERGMAN
    1975   *The Psychological Birth of the Human Infant.* New York: Basic Books.
ROY Manisha
    1975   The Oedipus Complex and the Bengali Family in India (A Study of Father-Daughter Relations in Bengal). In Thomas R. Williams (ed.), *Psychological Anthropology.* The Hague: Mouton.
SPIRO, Melford E.
    1977   *Kinship and Marriage in Burma.* Berkeley and Los Angeles: University of California Press.
    1978   *Burmese Supernaturalism.* Second expanded edition. Philadelphia: I.S.H.I.

1982a *Buddhism and Society: A Great Tradition and Its Burmese Vicissitudes*. Second expanded edition. Berkeley and Los Angeles: University of California Press.

1982b *Oedipus in the Trobriands*. Chicago: University of Chicago Press.

TSUJI, Yohko

1980   *Females in Japanese Religion* (ms.).

YANG, C. K.

1969   *Chinese Communist Society: The Family and the Village*. Cambridge: MIT Press.

Pali Texts (Translations)

1957   *The Jataka*. E. B. Cowell, ed. London: Luzac and Co.

1881   *Sutta-Nipata*. Translated by V. Fausboll. Oxford: Clarendon Press.

Part II

Shamanistic Features in Indigenous Religions

Chapter 3

Korean Shamanism: Women's Rites and a Chinese Comparison[1]

LAUREL KENDALL

INTRODUCTION: THE UBIQUITY OF SHAMANIC PRACTICE

The series, "Confucianism, Buddhism, Taoism, and shamanism" recalls from distant memory a college board examination question: "Which of the items in this series is *least* appropriate?" I would necessarily answer with my own area of interest, "shamanism." The other three "isms" are anchored, however loosely, in a corpus of written text and orthodox ritual as they float about in geographic diffusion. "Shamanism" is a researcher's category, a heuristic tool for comparing analogous practices in diverse societies (Cf. [PETERS and PRICE-WILLIAMS 1980]). We do find shamans in China, Korea,[1] and Japan, but we also find them in Siberia, Southeast Asia, Oceania, Africa, and the Americas. Outside Europe, we would be hard pressed to find an area of the world that did not have some form of shamanism.[2]

For some religious historians, shamanism implies a single and ancient religious tradition diffused from Siberia (Cf. [ELIADE 1964]). In this tradition, scholars do speak of "Korean Shamanism" as a discrete religion and historical stratum. Yim Sokchae and his students have discussed the limitations of this approach: The term "*mudang*" 巫堂 indicates both the hereditary priestess and the inspirational shaman. As in Okinawa, shaman and priestess perform many of the same ritual functions, a distinction obscured by the blanket use of the term "shamanism" or the indigenous title "*mudang*." "Shamanism," as an ancient north Asian faith, intimates "primitivism" and obscures the development and complexity of Korean religious traditions [YIM 1970: 215–217; CH'OI 1978: 12–30]. In this paper, I will use the term "shama-

---

1) My field work in Korea was supported by the International Institute for Education, the Social Science Research Council, and the National Science Foundation. I wrote this paper during my tenure as a National Institute of Mental Health Post-Doctoral Fellow in the Department of Psychiatry at the University of Hawaii.

This paper owes inspiration to George DeVos's suggestion that I say something about Chinese shamans and Taoist priests, and to Arthur Wolf's insightful remark that Korean women's active role in various rituals would be unthinkable in Chinese society. This paper owes much also to Homer Williams's editorial suggestions. I alone am responsible for its shortcomings.

2) See [KENDALL 1981a] for a survey of English-language sources on East Asian shamanism.

nism" to indicate the rituals professional shamans (*mudang, mansin*) 萬神 perform for families and households.   I use the term "shamanism" to indicate a cross-culturally comparable religious phenomenon, not a regional or historical "religion."

Anthropologist William P. Lebra provides a useful working definition of shamans: Shamans hold recognized supernatural powers that they use for socially approved ends, and shamans have the capacity to enter culturally acknowledged trance states at will (Lebra n.d. cited in [HARVEY 1979: 4]).   By this criterion, the Korean *mansin*, Chinese *tâng-ki* 童乩, and Okinawan *yuta* have a solid claim to the title. Throughout East Asia, shamans have established a working relationship with gods, ghosts, and ancestors.   Through possession trance, *tâng-ki, mansin, yuta,* and *itako* make manifest in their own persons entities that would otherwise exist only as religious abstractions (Cf. [AHERN 1978] for China).   The dead vent their needs and desires through the shaman's lips as shaman and client dramatize "Buddhist" and "Confucian" concern for the soul's well-being.   Shamans are also possessed by powerful gods who exorcise, chastise, bestow largess, or engender fertility. Many of the gods step down from "Buddhist" or "Taoist" pantheons.

Although the Korean *mansin* speaks with the authority of gods and ances-tors, she is more than a simple conduit of divine will. The *mansin* engages the supernatural. She lures gods into dwellings, exorcises malevolent beings, and cajoles and bargins with the gods (KENDALL 1985]. In all of this, the *mansin* conducts her own show; she does not collaborate with a priestly religious specialist, although this arrangement holds for some other East Asian shamans.   Some Japanese mediums work in partnership with temple priests or receive tutelary *kami* invoked by a sutra reading [BLACKER 1975].   In the Chinese spirit-medium cults of Singapore, a nonshaman assistant interprets the spirit language of a *tâng-ki* in trance [ELLIOTT 1955: 67].   Not only does the Korean *mansin* trance without the orchestra-tion of a non-shaman interlocutor but she herself performs the priestly business of exorcism, blessing, and prayer.

Another noteworthy feature of Korean shamanic practice is the prominence of women. Not only are most *mansin* women but they are, for the most part, ritual specialists for women.   Housewives consult shamans and housewives sponsor the rituals performed by shamans.   The crowd of spectators at a shaman's night-long *kut* is overwhelmingly female.   Here, men hover in the shadows, ogling the dancing shamans, or a few men, emboldened by drink, will make occasional dancing forays onto the lighted porch.   The rare male shaman (*paksu mudang*) 박수巫堂 performs *kut* 굿 dressed in women's clothing down to the baggy pantaloons that hide beneath a full Korean skirt.   *Paksu* draw large crowds to their *kut* for the novel sight of a man performing a woman's role.

SHAMANISM AND WOMEN'S STATUS IN KOREA

Women hold this corner of religious life in an overtly Confucian society where, in general and as my male informants often reminded me, "man is respected and woman lowly" (*namjon, yŏbi*) 男尊女卑. Neo-Confucian philosophers did see virtue in a compatible connubial relationship and deemed mothers the significant first teachers of children (Tu (Chapter 7)). Even so, the "Confucianization" of Korean society between the fifteenth and seventeenth centuries had an overwhelmingly negative impact on the status of Korean women as daughters, wives, and shamans. The full breadth and depth of the Confucian transformation of Korean society, however, remains a topic of continuing scholarly debate. As social historian Martina Deuchler (1983) suggests, women are an excellent focus for considerations of social change. In her own work, she describes how, in an older Korea, women lived uxorilocally in the first several years after marriage. Women joined their husbands' kin as mothers, often as matrons in charge of their own households. They inherited a share of their own parents' wealth and sometimes assumed, or saw their husbands or sons assume, responsibility for their own parents' ancestor tablets. Being without a son was not a liability, nor was the birth of a daughter reason for lamentation [DEUCHLER 1977, 1980; PAK 1974; K. YI 1977: 289–292].

In the early centuries of the Yi Dynasty, neo-Confucian reformers redefined the family as an exclusive continuity of sons. Only a son, or a genealogically appropriate male substitute, could offer rice and libations to the family's ancestors; only a son could inherit the ancestral house and lands. Daughters left their own homes and villages as brides who would serve in a house of strangers and bear sons in their midst. The young woman, ignorant of the customs of an alien house, now was trained and disciplined by her potentially hostile mother-in-law. This scenario reads like a replay of Chinese family life, although as we shall see, it leaves us with an incomplete accounting of Korean women.

Confucianization also set more rigorous standards of feminine modesty and chastity. Women, with the exception of slaves, now went abroad in veils, and upper class women were almost totally sequestered [DEUCHLER 1977]. The *mudang*, both shamans and hereditary priestesses, could not but pique the ire of the Confucian. These women sang and danced in public, performing what were for the Confucian "obscene rituals" (*umsa*) 淫祀. Moreover, paternalistic officials considered these activities fraudulent and sought to protect the credulous from exploitation. Reformers attempted, at various times and in various places, to ban the *mudang*'s activities, to discourage clients from patronizing *mudang*, and to transform *mudang*-centered community rituals into Confucian-style sacrifices (*che*) 祭 [N. YI 1976].

The female shaman's staying power and her popularity among Korean women has been interpreted, with a twist of irony, as a consequence of women's vulnerability within the patrilineal, patrilocal Confucian family. The birth of a son is a daughter-in-law's first success, but a woman must raise up healthy children to anticipate a secure old age and an ancestor's immortality. Thus, we are told, women under duress will resort to all manner of bizarre practices to secure, through mystical means, the conception, safe birth, and long life of sons. Akamatsu and Akiba thus dubbed Korean women's rituals "motherly observances" (*Bosei chūshin no gyōgi*) 母性中心の行儀 [AKAMATSU and AKIBA 1938: v. 2, 187, 193; KIM 1949: 145–146].

By this interpretation, the Korean *mansin* ministers to the needs of women within what anthropologist Margery Wolf calls the "uterine family." In rural Taiwan, the uterine family is an in-marrying woman's primary reference group. It includes her children and eventually, her married sons' children. It excludes her husband and all other members of her husband's household. The interests of her uterine family outweigh a woman's dubious loyalty to the larger domestic group, the *chia* 家 into which she has married. It is only through her own sons that a woman attains security and a modicum of oblique authority within the male-centered Chinese kinship system [WOLF 1972: 32–41].

On Taiwan, as we shall see, female shamans do minister to the "uterine" concerns of Chinese women. These female *tâng-ki* are the mediums of low-ranking deities and ghosts, while male *tâng-ki* are possessed by powerful high gods. Male *tâng-ki* perform public rituals surrounded and assisted by Chinese men. Male *tâng-ki* provide many of the services that are, in Korea, the province of a female *mansin*. The different attributes of male and female shamans in these two otherwise so similar societies suggest basically different perceptions of the power and authority of men and women, the dominion of Chinese women and Chinese female specialists being far more limited. A Chinese comparison suggests the lingering religious authority of women within the Confucianized Korean family and challenges the standing interpretation of Korean shamanism as an expression of women's structural vulnerability.

With this introduction, let us consider the various services Korean *mansin* provide for their female clients, then compare this profile with Taiwanese material collected by several ethnographers. I will describe Korean *mansin* and their clients as I observed them in and around a rural community in central Korea, summarizing material I have presented elsewhere in more detail [KENDALL 1985]. Observations are based on my field experience in "Enduring Pine Village," Kyŏnggi Province, Republic of Korea, during 1977 and 1978. In this region, shamans provide the following services: divination, conception rituals, rituals for the health and well being of children, healing rituals, household revitalization rituals, and rituals to settle problematic dead. Insofar as my observations are limited to the shamans of central Korea, I use the more precise term "*mansin*" rather than the more widely known term "*mudang*." In other parts of Korea, hereditary priestesses, also called *mudang*, perform analogous functions. Throughout Korea, monks and non-shaman diviners provide some similar services, including divinations and prayers for children and the sick.

SHAMANS IN ENDURING PINE VILLAGE: AN ETHNOGRAPHIC ILLUSTRATION

"Enduring Pine Village" is a rural community of one hundred and thirty-six households on the periphery of Seoul. Buses running along paved roads connect the village to the market town and the capital. Traditional straw roofs have been replaced by slate tile or tin, and several of these new roofs boast television antennas. Rice production for subsistence and surplus is no longer the most significant means of livelihood in Enduring Pine Village.   Seventy households, more than half the total, do not grow rice although they may own or rent vegetable plots and raise livestock. Some of the village men work at the local military installations or in the town as semi-skilled laborers—taxi drivers, factory workers, carpenters, and stone masons. Two men from the village took contracts as drivers for a Korean construction project in Saudi Arabia.   By the villagers' own definition, this is not "real country." The relative prosperity of this community in both recent and traditional times, when it was an administrative seat located at an important crossroads, have fostered an elaborate tradition of shaman ritual.

In household ritual, men honor the family's ancestors (*chesa*) 祭祀 and women make periodic offerings to the household gods (*kosa*) 告祀.   Men's dealings with the ancestors are solemn and polite, periodic rites performed with a careful eye to the ritual manual.   Women also deal with the dead, but under less friendly circumstances. Restless ancestors and ghosts and angry household gods bring affliction to the home— illness, financial loss, domestic strife.   The *mansin* provides a direct link between her clients and their household gods and ancestors.   Through divination and possession, she determines the source of present trouble.

Certain families have particularly powerful gods in their household pantheons— ancestors who held high position, ancestresses who rigorously served the spirits, Mountain Gods and Seven Star Gods who gave the family sons.   Capable of good or ill, these gods demand periodic homage.   Neglect brings trouble.

The dead—ancestors and ghosts—are dangerous simply because they are dead. They do not mingle well with the living and their touch brings illness or affliction. Even the compassionate touch of sympathetic ancestors brings illness to their children and grandchildren.   More dangerous are familial dead who died with unfulfilled desires (*han*) 恨: grandparents who did not live to see their grandchildren, a first wife who was superseded by a second wife, a father who labored to provide for his family but died before he could taste his labor's fruit, young men and women who expired before they could marry and have children.   If ancestor worship is a static show of respect, this darker side of the familial ideal makes family history a dynamic process. Longing souls mingle with the fate of the living until a shaman brings resolution.

If a housewife suspects that the supernatural lurk behind a nagging illness or a run of bad luck, she consults a *mansin*.   She either goes to her own "regular" (*tan'gol*) 丹骨 *mansin* or to someone a kinswoman or a neighbor recommends.   Some women consult the *mansin* during the first two weeks of the lunar new year, then perform simple rituals at the first full moon to protect vulnerable family members from anticipated supernatural malaise during the year.

Mansin, like the Chinese *tâng-ki* and many shamans in many other societies, receive their calling when the gods descend, possess, and claim them, usually in middle life and amid a run of ill luck.   The gods inspire aberrant behavior in their chosen one until her concerned kin acknowledge the divine message and a senior *mansin* initiates the woman [HARVEY 1980].   The new *mansin* can now summon gods and ancestors at will and conjure divination visions.   She performs divinations and simple exorcisms as clients begin to seek her services. Apprenticed to her initiating *mansin*, she learns the *mansin's* elaborate ritual lore and gradually builds a network of regular clients.

A divination session (*mugŏri*) 巫臣里 is the first step in the *mansin's* therapy, the diagnosis. The *mansin* performs the simple divination seated on the floor of her own main room. She tosses coins and fumbles grains of rice and, as visions rise up before her eyes, she asks increasingly specific questions: "Is there a distant grandfather in your family who carried a sword and served inside the palace?" "Did someone in your family die far from home and dripping blood?" She circles in on the supernatural source of her client's problems and suggests an appropriate ritual to mollify a greedy god's demands or send a miserable and consequently dangerous soul "away to a good place." If a housewife would evaluate the skill of an individual *mansin's* diagnosis, she must know the supernatural history of her husband's family and her own kin. And if the *mansin* is convinced that there was "a grandmother who worshipped Buddha," or "a bride who died in childbirth," she tells her client, "Go home and ask the old people, they know about these things."

As a foreigner, I was hopeless. When a *mansin* asked me if I had "an aunt or uncle (*samch'on*) 三寸 who died young," I wrote home hoping to unravel a bit of family history. No such ghost, my mother wrote, "unless one of your grandmothers had a secret life." The *mansin* I worked with said, "We don't know how you foreigners do things in America." When I brought a Chinese-American friend for a divination, this same *mansin* acknowledged their affinity as "East Sea People" (*Tongyang Saram*) 東洋사람 and would not let unclaimed ghosts slip by. The *mansin* asked if there was someone in my friend's family who died away from home? Someone who died in childbirth? An ancestor who was an official? My friend explained that her father had been kidnapped as a boy in China and raised by foster parents, that he knew nothing at all about his own family.

The *mansin* would not accept a dead end. "When you're home for a visit, ask your mother. When the two of you are sitting around chatting, she'll tell you these things." My friend again explained that her mother had already told her all she could about the family. Her father's origins were a mystery. Now the *mansin* grew concerned, appalled that a Chinese mother could send her married daughter off to set up housekeeping in a foreign land without telling her about the family ghosts and ancestors.

I offer this anecdote because it illustrates a *mansin's* insistence that women are responsible for the supernatural well being of their own and their children's households. Supernatural history is knowledge a housewife uses to protect her family. But are the housewives' concerns an attribute of status or of vulnerability?

Some of the rituals *mansin* perform for their female clients are, indeed, "motherly observances" for the conception and rearing of healthy children. Brides unable to conceive seek out the *mansin*, either on their own initiative or led by an anxious mother or mother-in-law. The *mansin* invokes the Birth Grandmother (*Samsin Halmŏni*) 三神할머니 and lures this god into a gourd dipper full of grain [KENDALL 1977]. The woman who would become pregnant holds the dipper in her hands until it begins to shake, indicating the Birth Grandmother's presence.   She carries it home and places it in the room where she sleeps with her husband, the room where she will conceive and give birth.

The Birth Grandmother also protects infants.   For three days after a birth, the attending mother-in-law or, occasionally, the woman's own mother offers seaweed soup and rice to the Birth Grandmother.   On the *mansin's* advice, the family might make a special offering to the Birth Grandmother (*Samsin Me*) 三神메 during the final stage of pregnancy.   If the infant is sickly, the mother or grandmother makes a similar offering at the shrine combined with an exorcism to drive off afflicting ghosts.

The Seven Stars (*Ch'ilsŏng*) 七星 protect growing children and help them progress in life.   Women continue to enlist their aid on behalf of grown sons.   When a *mansin* divines that a child has a short life fate, she suggests "selling the child away" (*p'arabŏrida*) 팔아버리다 to the Seven Stars.   The child's mother or grandmother dedicates a length of white cloth (*myŏngdari*) 命다리 at the shaman's shrine.   The child now calls the *mansin* "mother" and the *mansin* jokingly refers to the child as "my adopted son."   Once a woman has dedicated a child, she should visit the *mansin's* shrine and honor the Seven Stars on the seventh day of the seventh lunar month. The *mansin* invokes the Seven Stars who divine for and promise blessings to each member of the woman's family.   Women make similar offerings during the first two weeks of the lunar year (*Hongsu Megi*) 横數메기.   Worship at the shrine on Seven Star day and in the lunar new year implies a special relationship (*tan'gol*) between a woman, who represents her household and her household gods, and a *mansin*, who maintains a shrine.

Illness attributed to hovering ghosts can be cleaned up with a simple exorcism, and some housewives exorcise family members without consulting a shaman.   "Parents have to be half shamans (*pan mudang*) 半巫堂 to raise up their children," my landlady told me when she deemed her daughter's cough and fever worthy of aspirin and an exorcism.   My landlady flourished a kitchen knife at invisible baleful forces in the air above her daughter's pillow, then lured them into a gourd dipper filled with millet.   She carried the dipper a safe distance from the house and cast the contents out.   A *mansin's* exorcism follows this same form but with more drama; the offending shades speak through the *mansin's* lips and vent their grievances.

Persistent illness implies that individual affliction is merely symptomatic of a deeper malaise within the house.   In the *mansin's* words, "The ancestors are hungry and the gods want to play."   The family should sponsor an elaborate shaman ritual, a *kut*, to feast and entertain them.   Financial loss, domestic quarrels, and illness can inspire a *kut*.   This ritual addresses more than a woman's uterine concern for healthy children; through *kut*, the housewife seeks prosperity, health, success, and tranquillity for the entire household: children, husband, parents-in-law, daughters-in-law, and grandchildren.

A *kut* revitalizes the house.   First the *mansin* purify the dwelling, then they invite the gods and ancestors inside.   They exorcise sick or unlucky family members. Throughout the night, gods and ancestors appear throughout the house and possess costumed shamans. They vent their grievances, provide divinations, and shower blessings on each member of the family. At the end of the *kut*, the *mansin* casts lingering ghosts far away in the fields beyond the house gate.

Some communities sponsor village-wide *kut* to honor the tutelary gods and purge the community of baleful forces (*Sŏngwang kut*, 城隍굿 *Todang kut* 都堂굿.) The *kut* follows the form of a household *kut* with the tutelary god replacing the House Lord who lives in the roofbeam of each house and appears in household *kut*. Ancestors from any village house can be summoned up to speak through the *mansin*. Women represent each village household, petitioning the village gods as they would petition their own gods in a household *kut*.

In some communities, men, not women, honor the tutelary god by making offerings in a solemn, Confucian-style ritual (*Sansin che*, 山神祭 *Tong che* 洞祭). Scholars consider these male rites a product of Korea's Confucianization during the last dynasty [N. Yi 1976; Dix 1980: 32-33]. In Enduring Pine Village, women and *mansin* hold a *kut* for the tutelary god (*Todang kut*) and men honor the Mountain God (*Sansin che*).

Ghosts are a common source of affliction. The family's own ghosts bring trouble as a sign of their own netherworldly discomfort. Seeking to pacify all of its supernatural denizens, a family might send its unquiet dead to paradise in a special ritual appended to the end of a *kut*. For an extra fee, shamans escort souls out of hell and along the road to the Lotus Paradise (*Kungnak* 極楽). While performing an act of devotion and succor, the family also distances the dead, sending their potentially dangerous influence away from the house.

This quick and cursory sketch suggests that in and around Enduring Pine Village, "shamanism" implies a professional *mansin* who invokes and is possessed by the gods, ghosts, and ancestors of client households, and a housewife, usually the senior woman in the household, who deals with the supernatural on behalf of her house. Housewives honor the household gods and occasionally exorcise the sick. They monitor supernatural malaise through a *mansin's* divination and confront their own gods and ancestors when a *mansin* conjures them up in ritual. Recall my landlady's remark, "Parents have to be half shamans to raise up their children." Shaman and housewife perform analogous tasks for the same spirits. Possession trance is the *mansin's* special skill; she uses it to contend with the gods, ancestors, and ghosts of several client households. "Shamanism," in this context, can be considered a professional elaboration upon the beliefs and rituals contained in Korean household religion as described by Kwang-kyu Lee (Chapter 12, below).

Rituals for conception and for the successful rearing of children do seem to reflect the "uterine" concerns of a mother or a grandmother who must buffer her position in a patrilocal kin group through the loyalty of sons and grandsons (Cf. [WOLF 1972]). But the full range of ritual tasks Korean women perform with shamans suggest a matron's broader ritual authority within the household. Women's rituals revitalize the whole house and everyone who dwells within; sometimes women's rituals revitalize the entire community. Women tend the family's gods and send the family's restless dead to the Lotus Paradise.

This system bears comparison with Okinawan religion (see Sasaki, Chapter 4), where housewives perform priestly functions within the home, consult shamans who divine the cause of supernatural malaise, and hire shamans and priestesses to hold healing and revitalizing rituals for households and communities. In traditional Okinawan society, each administrative unit had a reigning priestess who was the administrative chief's sister. Okinawa provides a clear dichotomy of sex roles. Men, as household heads and rulers, wielded temporal political authority. Women of equivalent status held, in complement, unambiguous religious authority in household, community, and kingdom [LEBRA 1966]. In Korean families and lineages, the senior male heir performs ancestor worship as an attribute of his special status among agnatic kinsmen. Other men participate as an attribute of their status as "sons." Formal ancestor worship, once consciously encouraged as a vehicle for Confucianization, is the only component of Korean family religion to have been accorded both official encouragement and public esteem. Other ritual tasks, the activities of housewives and shamans, have therefore seemed less important to the scholarly observer and have readily been interpreted as no more than the particularistic concerns of women. A comparison with the more limited role of women in Chinese family religion should suggest that Korean women do hold considerable ritual authority within the Korean family.

RITUAL AND STATUS: A CHINESE COMPARISON

Chinese religion strikes familiar chords. As in Korea, the Chinese shaman is one among a variety of divination specialists. Possessed by powerful gods, the *tâng-ki* exorcise and heal. Possessed by ghosts and ancestors, they negotiate reconciliations between the living and the dead. Here, too, shamans deal with problems that arise in the context of household and community religion. But within this scheme, we find the ritual roles of men and women rearranged. In Chinese households on Taiwan, men honor the "high gods," the kitchen god who governs the household and the village tutelary or local cult divinity. Women supervise the ancestors' day to day care, feeding them as women feed the rest of the household. Women also "traffic with the residents of the world of the dead" as observers or mediums in seances.[3] They deal with "low ranking supernatural spirits" like the Bed Mother (*Cu-si: Niu-niu*) 註生娘娘 who brings sons or cures a sickly child. Women's minor goddesses thus minister to the self-interested "uterine" preoccupations of mothers and grandmothers within the larger family [AHERN 1975: 205; FREEDMAN 1979: 283; JORDAN 1972].

Students of Chinese society have interpreted this division of ritual tasks as an expression of the relative authority of men and women in Chinese households.

3) Ahern [1975], Elliott [1955], Freedman [1979:311–312], Potter [1074], and Wolf [1974] are among those who have discussed Chinese women's prominence in soul raising.

Women, a potentially divisive force within the family, are brought under the ancestors' dominion. Honoring the kitchen god, men represent the household before a supernatural authority associated with "domestic discipline" [FREEDMAN 1979: 283]. The emperor's analogue within the home, the male head presumes to address Heaven indirectly via the kitchen god [FEUCHTWANG 1974: 118]. In Chi'nan, Ahern notes, "Unless they are menstruating, women are not barred from worshipping...(at the high gods' festivals) and they sometimes participate if the men of the household are absent. But men almost always make it their business to be home at those times" [AHERN 1975: 205].

The allocation of men's and women's roles in household ritual is reflected in the different services provided by male and female *tâng-ki*. According to Jordan, "There seems to be a tendency...for female *tâng-ki* to be associated often with purely local divinities who answer individual petitions at private altars in the medium's home, whereas male *tâng-ki* seem usually to operate by visiting the family of the petitioner or guiding village affairs in the village temple. The distinction is not hard and fast and exceptions occur in both directions" [JORDAN 1972: 69 fn.]. The gods who possess the predominantly male *tâng-ki* are the powerful deities of local cults who give divinations and defend the family and village from malevolent ghostly incursions. Most of the female *tâng-ki* seem to be the mediums of "little maids" or "little gods," local or undistinguished ghosts who demand acclaim by seizing their own *tâng-ki* [JORDAN 1972: 54–86, 166]. Many of these *tâng-ki* are kin to their possessing goddesses [JORDAN 1972: 166]. Similarly, in the Hong Kong New Territories, the Cantonese *mann saeg phox* 問醒姿 is assisted by her own dead children [POTTER 1974: 226–228]. Not only are the little gods' *tâng-ki* primarily women but they serve a female clientele. "The term little god...is used to refer to divinized spirits of local people, whose oracles are consulted primarily by women for information on the rearing of children and other of the family's affairs that are entirely or largely under the government of women" [JORDAN 1972: 141 fn.]. Among their tasks, they divine the source of ghostly affliction and arrange "ghost weddings" for souls who die unwed and are thus eternally unsatisfied [JORDAN 1972: 140–141, 169–170].

But if women bring their "womanish concerns" to the little god *tâng-ki* and other female specialists, they seem to consult other *tâng-ki* when the problem merits more powerful supernatural intercession. Conception is most immediately women's concern, and Wolf reports, "In every *tâng-ki*'s session...there is always a worried looking middle-aged lady who has come to ask what to do about a daughter-in-law who is not showing signs of pregnancy." In the northern Taiwan community where she worked, a male *tâng-ki* was reputed to be particularly good at solving problems of infertility "in pigs and brides" [WOLF 1972: 149–150]. A female healer, a *Sian-si:-ma* 先生媽, calls back startled children's wandering souls, and mothers sometimes perform the same ritual for their own children [AHERN 1975: 206 fn., 1978: 27]. In Chaochuang, northern Taiwan, if a mother deems a child's complaint more serious than "soul loss," she may bring the child to the high god's *tâng-ki* [GOULD-MARTIN

1976: 107, 122]. High gods have more power and high gods tend to possess male *tâng-ki*.

In rural Taiwan, men represent their households in most other dealings with the high gods' *tâng-ki*. Jordan reports that in Bao-an, men assist the male *tâng-ki* and Taoist priest (*âng-thâu-â*) 紅頭仔 in celebrating the cult god's birthday, purifying cult members' houses, and defending the community against malevolent ghostly incursions [JORDAN 1972: 53–57, 120–128]. Similarly, men hold the divinely-animated god's palanquin (*kiō-á*) 轎 in divination sessions and ghostly battles. Jordan remarks, "Women do not perform this task in Bao-an or in any seances that I have seen elsewhere. Other lines of evidence suggest to me that this is probably not because they are prohibited from doing so, but rather because in some sense it is men's work, rather like building cabinets or fixing plumbing in America" [JORDAN 1972: 64 fn.]. But these same tasks—seeking divination and participating in rituals for the supernatural defense of home and community—are in Korea the concern of women and female shamans much as pickling cabbage is women's work. Similarly, the *mansin*'s intercession on behalf of souls in the underworld is, on Taiwan, a task performed by the male Taoist priest. Although Chinese women converse with souls in seances, the recent dead need a different, more powerful sponsor to see them safely through the perilous nether regions. According to Ahern, "Because the road to the underworld is beset by dangerous monsters and unknown obstacles, the deceased might succumb to some fatal disaster long before arriving unless he receives help" [AHERN 1973: 223]. The priest bargains with the earth god and guides the soul, just as in Korea women and *mansin* bargain with the Death Messenger (*Saja*) and lead the dead out of hell.

In short, two categories of Taiwanese *tâng-ki* accomplish the work of one Korean *mansin* in Enduring Pine Village: possession by powerful gods who drive off malevolent supernatural entities, bestow blessings, and issue pronouncements, and possession by ancestors and ghosts who have urgent business with the living. Another possible generalization, Chinese women seem to use *tâng-ki* to further the interests of their own uterine families while Chinese men join forces with *tâng-ki* and male Taoist priests to perform other significant ritual tasks in the interest of home and community, tasks that are, in Enduring Pine Village, the work of women and female *mansin*.

Ahern suggests that in the Chinese scheme, pollution beliefs provide a symbolic rationale for women's subordinate ritual and social status. Menstruation and birth pollution render women ritually "unclean," and unclean women deal most directly with unclean spirits, with dead souls and "little low goddesses" who are tainted by association with childbirth or death. She notes, "The common relegation of women to the worship of the low, unclean end of the hierarchy is appropriate because women are so frequently unclean themselves. Conversely, the near-monopoly by men of the clean, high end of the hierarchy is appropriate because they are much less often unclean" [AHERN 1975: 206–207]. Ahern concludes that pollution beliefs are consistent with women's place in the Chinese kinship system. Death, birth, and menstruation as a "minor birth" pollute because they rupture the integrity of bodies and families. Women's greater perceived uncleanliness is a function of women's position in families "It is because the kinship system is focused on male lines of descent that women are depicted on the boundaries breaking in as strangers. It may be events that are polluting rather than women *per se*, but polluting events are events that intrude new people or remove old ones in a male-oriented kinship system" [AHERN 1975: 213].

Korea again poses a contrast. Here, too, women intrude as strangers into a male-oriented kinship system. Here, too, menstruation, birth, and death pollute, and pollution imposes a temporary ban on ritual activity. Women do not worship the household gods or make offerings in the shaman's shrine when they are menstruating or when they have had recent contact with childbirth or funerals. Neither do households sponsor *kut* after a recent birth, when they are in mourning, or when one of the women is menstruating. Menstruation offends Korean gods: a particularly good *mansin* will, when possessed, denounce a "dirty woman" for presuming to appear at a *kut* in a state of pollution. But menstrual and birth pollution are temporary conditions, not an inherent sullying. When they are not immediately polluted, Korean women worship the gods and female *mansin* are possessed by them [KENDALL 1981b].

While pollution beliefs undoubtedly reinforce the ritual dichotomization of the sexes in Taiwan, pollution beliefs, in and of themselves, do not provide an explanation sufficient to account for a contrasting arrangement of ritual roles in Korea. The social assumptions that underlie the pattern of pollution beliefs and ritual roles in each of the two societies will provide a more solid basis of comparison.

The Chinese consider women "narrow-hearted" and fractious; to further the interests of their own children, wives tug against the familial loyalty of brothers [WOLF 1972: 164–167]. While brothers, and not brothers' wives, may actually initiate household division (*fen-chia*) 分家, brothers' wives are commonly perceived to be the source of domestic strife [FREEDMAN 1979: 21f., 46f.]. Ahern suggests that Chinese pollution beliefs cast a negative shadow over women's capacity to bear sons, the source of her power and danger within the Chinese family [AHERN 1975: 123–124].

Korean household division carries less potential volatility. The senior heir inherits the house and a major share of the household lands. Secondary sons establish independent households on or soon after their marriages. Family division is gradual, sequential, and inevitable. The scheming wife has no part in the process; she is neither a necessary catalyst nor a ready scapegoat. Following Ahern, if Korean women lack Chinese women's ascribed negative powers, Korean women need not bear Chinese women's onus of dangerous pollution. Conversely, we might now ask whether Korean women's ritual activities imply a positive perception of women's power and authority in families. Here are some alternative possibilities.

Korea might simply be the mirror image of China, with men's and women's roles rearranged but the relative significance of men's and women's rituals preserved intact. Ancestor worship is esteemed today as an expression of filial piety; the ritual practices of women and shamans are an embarrassing superstition. But who levels this judgment? In the tradition of East Asian literati, the Chinese elite have scorned Taoist priests, *tâng-ki* and Buddhist monks no less than the Korean elite have scorned Buddhist monks and *mansin*. Elite disdain fosters local defensiveness. People in Bao-an were no more comfortable with Jordan's initial inquiries about *tâng-ki* than Enduring Pine Villagers who giggled with embarrassment through my early interviews (JORDAN 1972: 69; KENDALL 1985: x–xi]. Yet both Chinese and Koreans hire shamans to deal with gods, ancestors, and ghosts. At issue is Korean women's special prominence in these activities.

We might consider women's gods equivalent to the baser "little gods" or "little maids" of Taiwan, not on a par with the powerful gods that possess Chinese male *tâng-ki*. A few of the *mansin*'s gods do, indeed, resemble the "little gods." *Hogu* is an envious maiden who died before or immediately after her marriage. *Tongja* 童子 or *Tongja Pyŏlsang* 童子別星 are children of the house or wives' siblings who died in childhood, commonly of smallpox or measles.[4] By force of mischief, some of these otherwise insignificant beings win a place in the family pantheon and gifts of bright clothing, pocket money, and treats to pacify their caprice. They appear in the *mansin*'s *kut*, but they make only cameo appearances amid a battery of more powerful, gods. *Mansin* claim the full range of spirits the high and little god *tâng-ki* of Taiwan divide among themselves. Powerful gods in the *mansin*'s pantheon heal, revitalize, and defend the house. The General (*Changgun*) 將軍 and the Warrior (*Sinjang*) 神將 drive out ghosts and noxious influences with a flourishing of knives and a pelting of millet. The Birth Grandmother (*Samsin Halmŏni*) 三神할머니 inspires conception in a reluctant womb. The gods' greed, a part of the drama and comedy of a full dress *kut*, is an attribute of the gods' power—power to repel malevolent incursions and power to work good or ill in the house. The gods sing songs of self praise while they demand yet more tribute at a *kut*, "I'm so wonderful, I just can't say."

These may be empty boasts, though, for are not the ancestors and ancestor worship far more important in Korean religious consciousness than these greedy, flamboyant gods? A simple dichotomy of men and ancestors versus women and gods flounders on the notion of restless ancestors and ghosts. The Janellis remind us that in Korea, as elsewhere in Asia, the term implies not only proper patrilineal forebears and their wives but also a range of dead relatives including maternal, collateral, and affinal relations [JANELLI and JANELLI n.d.]. Any among these ancestors may grow restless and potentially dangerous [KENDALL 1985: 156–157]. The Janellis found that men and women share notions of ancestral malevolence and methods of propitiation

---

4) A few of Barbara Young's urban inspirational diviners claimed the aid of Child Gods (*tongja*) and one informant gave her a grisly account of how a would-be diviner secures a dying child's soul to do her bidding [YOUNG 1980]. A similar account may be found in Kim Tongni's popular novella, *Ŭlhwa*. Diviners who use childrens' souls as messengers seem similar to the little gods' mediums on Taiwan and to the Cantonese *mann saeg phox* who is assisted by her own dead children [POTTER 1974: 226–228]. But the diviners in Young's study do not claim to be *mansin* nor do they provide the *mansin*'s range of services.

although women are inclined to view the ancestors as malevolent [JANELLI and JANELLI 1982:148–176]. Dealing with restless ancestors and ghosts is women's work. Women consult *mansin*. *Mansin* summon up the ancestors to expiate their grievances. *Mansin* muster the gods to protect the family, household and community from ghostly malevolence. Women and *mansin* protect the ancestral soul in hell and lead the soul to the Lotus Paradise. *Mansin* perform the combined functions of high and lesser god *tâng-ki* and Taoist priests in Taiwan. Utilizing female specialists, the women of Enduring Pine Village perform not only "motherly observances" but undertake those ritual tasks which in Taiwan would be the prerogative of a male household representative and a male specialist.

It would be naive to ignore the tremendous moral weight of Korean ancestor worship as the quintessential expression of filial piety and rationale for such homilies as "man is respected and women lowly." Social historians remind us, however, that these sentiments took root in Korea only in recent centuries. Women lost status and prerogatives with the loss of daughter inheritance and the shift to patrilocal residence. The Korean bride was now as vulnerable as the Chinese bride. But when brides alone are considered, the foregoing discussion of shamans and housewives makes no sense at all. The women who worship household gods, consult shamans, and sponsor *kut* have passed through the ordeal of young womanhood to become the matrons and managers of their own homes, and they have attained this position without the trauma of Chinese family division.

In Korean families, the heir's wife is chosen with particular care, since she will one day be mistress of the main house. She should be a good manager and a scrupulous housekeeper. She should also be even-dispositioned and patient since she will serve her mother-in-law until the senior matron's death or retirement. Secondary sons' wives establish their own households on or soon after their marriages. The managerial acumen and behind-the-scenes assertiveness of the Korean wife, once she acquires her own household, is acknowledged in both early missionary and traveler accounts and in more recent ethnography. It is as the female head of an independent or successor household that a woman begins to make offerings to her own house gods and to consult *mansin* for herself, her husband, and her children.

CONCLUSION

The Confucian overlay is the most obvious and most often studied aspect of Korean religious life, but the foregoing discussion suggests that in Enduring Pine Village, the Confucianization of family life and family ritual is incomplete. Women's ritual concerns betray a greater range of authority and responsibility in household and family life than the motherly preoccupations of their Chinese cousins. Nor have pollution beliefs so completely relegated women and female shamans to exclusive dealings with the tainted and low ranking supernatural. These differences can be attributed to differences in family structure and to different perceptions of the role of women in family dynamics. A more detailed consideration of women might further enhance our appreciation of the distinctive features of Korean family life.

BIBLIOGRAPHY

AHERN, Emily M.

1973 *The Cult of the Dead in a Chinese Village.* Stanford: Stanford University Press.
1975 The Power and Pollution of Chinese Women. In M. Wolf and R. Witke (eds.), *Women in Chinese Society*, Stanford: Stanford University Press, pp. 193–224.
1978 Sacred and Secular Medicine in a Taiwan Village: A Study of Cosmological Disorders. In A. Kleinman, P. Kunstadter, *et al.* (eds.), *Culture and Healing in Asian Societies*, Cambridge: Schenkman Publishing Company.

AKAMATSU, Chijo and Takashi AKIBA

1938 『朝鮮巫俗の研究』東京：大阪屋號書店。
(*Research on Korean Shamanism*, Tokyo: Osakayago Shōten.)

BLACKER, Carmen

1975 *The Catalpa Bow.* London: George Allen and Unwin.

CHANG, Chugŭn

1974 「民間信仰」李　杜鉉，張　籌根，李　光奎共著『韓國民俗學概説』，서울：民衆書館，pp. 128–197。
(Folk Beliefs. In T. Lee, C. Chang and K. Yi, *Introduction to Korean Folklore*, Seoul: Minjung Sŏgwan, pp. 128–197.)

CH'OI, Kilsŏng 崔　吉城

1978 『韓国巫俗의研究』, 서울：亞細亞文化社。
(*Research on Korean "Mu" Practices.* Seoul: Asia Munhwasa.)

DEUCHLER, Martina

1977 The Tradition: Women during the Yi Dynasty. In S. Mattielli (ed.), *Virtues in Conflict: Tradition and the Korean Woman Today*, Seoul: Royal Asiatic Society, pp. 1–48.
1980 Neo-Confucianism: The Impulse for Social Action in Early Yi Korea. *The Journal of Korean Studies* 2: 71–112.
1983 Preface. In L. Kendall and M. Peterson (eds.), *Korean Women: View from the Inner Room*, New Haven: East Rock Press, pp. 1–3.

DIX, Griffin M.

1980 The Korean New Year's Village Offering: Social Function and Continuity. Paper presented at the Conference on Korean Religion and Society, Mackinac Island, Michigan, August 25–29.

ELIADE, Mircea

1964 *Shamanism: Archaic Techniques of Ecstasy.* New York: Pantheon.

ELLIOTT, Alan J. A.

1955 *Chinese Spirit Medium Cults in Singapore.* London: L. S. E. Press.

FEUCHTWANG, Stephen

1974 Domestic and Communal Worship in Taiwan. In A. Wolf (ed.), *Religion and Ritual in Chinese Society*, Stanford: Stanford University Press, pp. 105–129.

FREEDMAN, Maurice

1979 *The Study of Chinese Society: Eassys by Maurice Freedman.* G. W. Skinner (ed.), Stanford: Stanford University Press.

Gould-Martin, Katherine
   1976   Women Asking Women: An Ethnography of Health Care in Rural Taiwan. Ph. D. Dissertation, Rutgers University.
   1978   Ong-ia-Kong: The Plague God as a Modern Physician. In A. Kleinman and P. Kunstadter *et al.* (eds.), *Culture and Healing in Asian Societies,* Cambridge: Schenkman Publishing Company.

Harvey, Youngsook Kim
   1979   *Six Korean Women: The Socialization of Shamans.* St. Paul: West Publishing Company.
   1980   Possession Sickness and Women Shamans in Korea. In N. A. Falk and R. M. Gross (eds.), *Unspoken Worlds: Women's Religious Lives in Non-Western Cultures,* New York: Harper and Row, pp. 41–52.

Hori, Ichiro
   1968   *Folk Religion in Japan.* Chicago: Chicago University Press.

Im, Sokchae
   1970   「韓国巫俗研究序説」『亞細亞女性』9: 73–90, 161–217.
          (Introduction to the Study of Korean 'Muism'. *Asian Women* 9: 73–90, 161–217.)

Janelli, Roger L. and Dawnhee Yim Janelli
   n.d.   Ancestral Malevolence in a Korean Lineage Village.   Unpublished ms.

Janelli & Janelli
   1982   *Ancestor Worship and Korean Society.* Stanford: Stanford University Press.

Jordan, David K.
   1972   *Gods, Ghosts, and Ancestors: Folk Religion in a Taiwanese Village.* Berkeley and Los Angeles: University of California Press.

Kendall, Laurel
   1977   Receiving the *Samsin* Grandmother: Conception Rituals in Korea. *Transactions of the Korea Branch of the Royal Asiatic Society* 52: 55–70.
   1981a Review Article: Supernatural Traffic—East Asian Shamanism. *Culture, Medicine, and Psychiatry* 5(2): 171–191.
   1981b Wood Imps, Ghosts and Other Noxious Influences: The Ideology of Affliction in a Korean Village. *The Journal of Korean Studies* 3: 113–145.
   1985   *Shamans, Housewives, and Other Restless Spirits: Women in Korean Ritual Life.* Honolulu: University of Hawaii Press.

Kim, Tuhŏn
   1949   『朝鮮家族制度研究』, 서울 : 乙酉文化社。
          (*Research on the Korean Family System.* Seoul: Ŭlyu Munhwasa.)

Kim, Tŭkkwang
   1963   『韓国宗教史』, 서울 : 에펠출판사사。
          (*History of Korean Religion.* Seoul: Ep'el Ch'ulp'ansa.)

Lebra, William P.
   1966   *Okinawan Religion: Belief, Ritual and Social Structure.* Honolulu: University of Hawaii Press.

Lee, Kwang-kyu
          see Yi Kwanggyu

Pak, Pyŏngho   朴 秉濠
   1974   『韓国法制史攷』, 서울 : 法文社。
          (*Reflections on Korean Legal History.* Seoul: Pŏbmunsa.)

PETERS, Larry and Douglas PRICE-WILLIAMS
  1980 Toward an Experiential Analysis of Shamanism. *American Ethnologist* 7(3): 397–419.
POTTER, Jack M.
  1974 Cantonese Shamanism. In A. Wolf (ed.), *Religion and Ritual in Chinese Society*, Stanford: Stanford University Press, pp. 207–231.
WOLF, Margery
  1972 *Women and the Family in Rural Taiwan.* Stanford: Stanford University Press.
  1974 Chinese Women: Old Skills in a New Context. In M. Z. Rosaldo and L. Lamphere (eds.), *Women, Culture and Society*, Stanford: Stanford University Press.
YI, Kwanggyu
  1977 『韓国家族의史的研究』, 서울 : 一志社。
        (*Historical Study of the Korean Family.* Seoul: Ilchisa.)
YI, Nŭnghwa
  1976 『朝鮮巫俗考』(李在崑의번역), 서울 : 백룩。
        (*Musings on Korean Shamanism.* C. C. Yi ed. and transl. into modern Korean. Seoul: Paengnuk.)
YIM, Sokchae
        see IM Sokchae
YOUNG, Barbara
  1980 Spirits and Other Signs: An Ethnography of Divination in Seoul, R. O. K. Ph. D. Dissertation, University of Washington.

Chapter 4

Spirit Possession as an Indigenous Religion in Japan and Okinawa

Kokan Sasaki

INTRODUCTION

This chapter deals with one form of magico-religious phenomena in Japan and in the Ryukyu Islands south of Japan, known as Seirei-Hyoi, "spirit possession". These occurrences are to be considered within the wider context of shamanistic beliefs and practices that maintain their socio-cultural meaning for contemporary Japanese. It is to illustrate the conspicuously animistic or "manaistic" character of Japanese folk religion that I have selected this topic. Spirit possession has persisted from very ancient times to the present day. It is prevalent among those who live in urban areas as well as in isolated settings [HORI 1968: 13–48].

Self appointed magico-religious specialists are adept at such related practices as exorcism, divination, interpretation of oracles or curing ceremonies. Many of these specialists deal with the troubles caused by spirits. Contact is established by becoming a medium or working with a medium who becomes possessed. These practices represent an animistic substratum of belief among the Japanese masses and are to be contrasted with the very sophisticated attitudes toward religion found in other elements of Japanese society.

It is impressive to note that according to a recent report issued by the Headquarters of the Sōtō Zen Buddhism Sect [SATO 1978] among those who claim to belong to Sōtō Zen Buddhism are many who call on shamanic specialists called *Kitoshi* or *Gyoja* to gain mystical advice, rather than visiting a Zen temple to sit in meditation. For example, in Miyagi Prefecture, in the northeast, only 6.7% of the people who claimed to be Sōtō Zen Buddhists knew the names of the Buddha Sakyamuni or the two founders of the sect. Only 10.2% of them had any experience of sitting in Zazen. On the contrary, 71.5% knew local shamans and 38.7% had visited a shaman. It is evident that local Japanese in their religious life keep contact with spirit possession as a continuation of animistic belief. Without understanding this continuity, it would be impossible to grasp the true continuity of expression of Japanese religious life.

VARIETIES OF SPIRIT POSSESSION IN JAPAN

What is spirit possession? According to Professor Raymond Firth [1959],

75

"Spirit possession is a form of trance in which behaviour actions of a person are interpreted as evidence of a control of his behaviour by a spirit normally external to him". This definition is brief and to the point and has been widely accepted; but it is not without problems. The definition needs modification in order to apply it to Japanese phenomena. Generally speaking, all the conditions under which "spirit possession" is postulated by Japanese do not necessarily involve trance behavior. Frequently, for example, illness can be judged to be a form of possession; yet the possessed are far from being in trance [Lewis 1971: 44-48].

Japan can be regarded as a country that manifests many unique kinds of spirit possession, constituting a very large and wide category of complicated phenomena. Let me cite a few typical examples to illustrate this:

1. Spirit Possession of Divine Priestesses

In the *Izaiho*, a grand festival held on Kudaka Island, Okinawa, every twelve years, all women above the age of thirty are expected to observe abstinence in a sacred forest called *Izaiyama* for four days and three nights, breaking off all relations with the outer world [Sakurai 1980]. During this period it is believed that the novices, staying in small improvised huts covered with holy leaves, are visited by deities from the outer world. They are possessed by *Seji*, a divine spirit. They are, for the first time as divine priestesses, entitled to perform magico-religious rituals in order to enhance the prosperity and happiness of both their families and their communities. In this case, spirit possession takes place without evidence of trance.

Similarly in Japan proper, there are many magico-religious practitioners who are believed to possess some divine powers or spirits in themselves, or who are able to control directly mystical powers and spirits at will, although they never go into trance states when they perform rituals. This may be the reason why in Japan it is very difficult contextually to distinguish between a priest and shaman or "spirit medium."

2. Shamanic Spirit Possession

Generally speaking, there are two ways of becoming a shaman reported in modern Japan. One is through divine calling and the other by self-searching. In the former, a person gradually or suddenly begins to suffer from mental and physical abnormality frequently accompanied by visual and auditory hallucinations as well as trances and special dreams. At first, she (females being predominant) visits doctors or hospitals but the sufferer comes to believe that her abnormality cannot be diagnosed nor treated. She then calls on a shaman to determine whether her abnormality is physical in nature or the result of divine influence involving spirit possession. If the cause of her abnormal condition is found related to the supernatural, usually she is instructed to take one of the following ways to free herself from her sufferings:

    a.   Exorcism by a shaman
    b.   Restoration of a lost soul through the aid of a shaman

    c.   Becoming a shaman herself in accordance with divine will

    d.   Postponement of shamanization through the supplication of the super-
        naturals

It goes without saying that if a person who is suffering from a critical affliction caused by divine calling accepts the divine will and becomes a shaman, her abnormality will gradually disappear. In this case, those who are physically handicapped, especially the blind, usually apprentice themselves to local senior shamans, often on the advice of their families so that they can establish themselves as shamanic mediums. Under senior shamans, they generally spend two or three years learning how to become a shaman. The most important thing they have to learn is how to find their tutelary spirits while they are in trance. After two or three years of apprenticeship, they become qualified to participate in a ritual called *Kamitsuke*, a ritual in which they may be possessed by a divine spirit. In this ritual, when the person concerned falls into a state of mental dissociation, the senior shamans ask them by what kind of god they are possessed. The god reveals its name through their mouths. This god is hereafter thought to be their tutelary spirit, helping them in their shamanic activities when necessary.

3. Spirit Possession in Everyday Life

    Although the Japanese of today enjoy an advanced standard of civilization, their belief systems and practices still reveal a deeply rooted tradition of indigenous religion, including spirit possession. In ordinary speech Japanese will often use expressions such as "I am possessed today" or "You are now possessed" whenever they happen to have good luck or success. On the contrary, if they make mistakes or are unlucky, they will say, "I am not possessed today" or "You are not possessed now". Although the original conscious meaning of these expressions has been lost, the logic still manifest in these expressions suggests that it is due to a possessing spirit that the person concerned has found good fortune, or that because of the loss of a helping spirit he has experienced a sudden reverse. Although I have been describing possession by a "spirit", spirit is merely a hypothetical term. It is very difficult for us to decide at this stage of research whether the possessing entity Tsukimono is "anima", a spirit, or "mana", a magical power.

    Let me cite here a few examples of spirit possession which I have collected in my field work:

    a.   A junior high school boy in Tokyo was ill with a slight fever. His mother took
        him to a national hospital. A doctor diagnosed his case as influenza, and gave
        him medication; he took it, but showed no improvement. He visited the hos-
        pital numerous times but showed no signs of recovery. His parents became
        impatient, for their son was preparing for the entrance examination of a senior
        high school. Due to the insistent advice of his grandmother, his parents
        finally made up their minds to take their son to a medium living in the downtown
        section of the city. The medium, in trance, suggested that the boy had been
        possessed by *Inari*, identified as the fox-god of a small neighborhood shrine.

She exorcised the god from him by waving the *Gohei*, a sacred staff to which are attached cut white paper strips. Soon thereafter, he recovered. It is important here to note how the traditional concept of spirit possession and exorcism had been transmitted from grandmother to the parents and now further to the son. It must also be noted how *Inari* is a Shinto concept only vaguely understood by most Japanese. In some versions of belief the fox is simply a messenger of an agricultural fertility deity or deities.

b.   A fisherman in Goto, Nagasaki, suddenly one day while he was fishing aboard a ship felt his whole body being oppressed by some heavy object. A doctor, who diagnosed him, said that he had no physical ailments at all. However, in the Goto District, such a personal condition is interpreted as the "Meeting with the Bad Wind" or "Possession by the Wind". It is said that the "wind" in this context means the influence of the spirit of some person who died at sea or the spirit of Yako, a wild fox. The fisherman called on a *Honin*, or shaman, who gave him a divine message saying that he met with the spirit of a person who had died at sea. In accordance with the advice of the specialist, he propitiated the dead spirit, offering rice, fish, fruit, and vegetables on an altar which was prepared for it. Soon his abnormal condition disappeared.

c.   In villages one still finds that a certain family is regarded by the villagers as a possessor of the spirit of some specific animal—a fox or a dog or other beast. Members of the concerned family are the object of fear and contempt, and endure various forms of discrimination. For example, in a village of Tokunoshima, a certain family is looked upon as the possessor of the dog spirit which is considered by the villagers to have been inherited through the family line. It is believed that if another family were to bring in a daughter from this possessed family, they too would become possessed. Therefore, this family tends to be avoided, especially in respect to marital relations. While it is considered possible for a possessed person to have a spirit expelled by exorcism, it is impossible for a possessed family to chase away a possessing spirit because liberation from spirit possession means the abolition of the family itself. A family regarded as a possessor of spirits is often a family who has migrated into a village later than most of the other families but, by some chance of fortune, has become wealthier than their neighbors. The villagers believe that when a socially vulnerable family becomes wealthy and successful it is due to spirit possession. It is quite clear that concepts of spirit possession may be used to explain certain dualities in the Japanese view of life, i.e., rich and poor, good and ill health, success and failure, etc.

SOCIO-CULTURAL MEANINGS OF SHAMANIC SPIRIT POSSESSION

Although there are other types of spirit possession to be found, I would like to focus upon "shamanic" spirit possession especially in regard to its socio-cultural meaning. As I have already observed, every form of possession is not always accompanied by trance, and it is obvious that all manifestations of spirit possession will not necessarily involve a personality change in the change from human nature to incarnate spirit.   In this regard, I can agree with Professor Firth's definition concerning spirit mediumship and spirit possession.   He describes that, "...in both, a person's actions are believed to be dictated by an extra-human entity which has 'entered' his body or otherwise 'affected' him" [FIRTH 1969].   On the basis of his definition, we can consider that spirit possession has two different spiritual functions: one is the spirit's entrance or intrusion, and the other is its effect or influence.   In the former, a spirit which has entered (possessed) a person will speak in the first person through his mouth.   In the latter, however, a person who has been affected (possessed) by a spirit may speak in the second person, in his own words but in accordance with the inspirations sent by the spirit.   It seems possible for most Japanese shamans to contact (directly) the supernaturals by either means.

Recently, anthropologists tend to characteristically distinguish between spirit mediums and prophets.   It is pointed out that while a spirit medium uses "oratio recta" (direct narration), a prophet uses "oratio obliqua" (indirect narration); therefore, we can see that Japanese shamans are ordinarily mediumistic as well as prophetic in character because they can speak the words of the dead using direct narration or they can give divine messages by means of indirect narration.

One can explain the socio-cultural meaning of shamanic initiation by examining "divine calling".   As I have already described, the first symptoms of shamanization usually begin in various personal abnormalities, e.g., decrease in appetite, severe palpitations of the heart, sleeplessness, fatigue and gradual loss of weight.   These physical symptoms are apt to be accompanied by mental disturbances, e.g., visions, hallucinations, and dreams in which appear strange and uncanny men wearing *Hakui*, a white Japanese ceremonial kimono.   In Okinawa, people who are suffering from such abnormalities are sure to be suspected by their families as being victims of *Kamidari*, a trouble caused by gods or spirits.   *Kamidari* is considered as one form of spirit possession because the concerned persons have been put in a state of bondage by the gods and spirits. The gods and spirits often visit in visions or in dreams, show them the gods in heaven, ancient kings and queens, or bring them to divine heavenly palaces or ancestral graveyards.   Sometimes they urge a form of spirit marriage.   It is customary for a prospect to visit a *Yuta*, a shamanic medium, to get advice concerning the contents of their mysterious experience.   If the cause of the abnormal condition is made clear by the *Yuta*, then they must follow the advice of the *Yuta* in order to recover; and, if the supernaturals want them to become *Yuta*, they must consent. The more resistance they show to becoming *Yuta*, the more aggravating will be their *Kamidari*.   Thus they must pay numerous visits to the *Yuta* to learn how to use spirit possession and inspiration in seances.   It is also believed that they can be instructed directly by the supernaturals in further visions or in trances. Okinawans eagerly anticipate the birth of a *Kaminoko*, child of god, and gather at the house of anyone possessed. It is quite likely that someone considered possessed will eventually become celebrated as a shaman.

What kind of person becomes a shaman?   Those who have come to suffer from *Kamidari* have experienced some critical affliction beforehand, such as sudden death in the family, divorce, a husband's fickleness, a sudden change in environment, extreme poverty, failure, prolonged illness or bad physical health from an unknown cause [Lebra 1974: 111; Ohashi 1980]. Susceptible individuals, helpless in their distress, will gradually begin to show symptoms of *Kamidari*. As previously mentioned, the Japanese often believe that good and bad fortune is somehow related to the world of the supernatural; therefore, it should be quite easy for those meeting personal adversity to attribute their condition to supernatural causes. Needless to say, this belief is constantly strengthened by the *Yuta*. *Kamidari* is sometimes called *Kamigurui*, "divine insanity". Thus, having been made insane by the gods and spirits a person meeting adversity will be able to readapt to society without actually being considered insane in secular terms. Speaking broadly, spirit possession in this sense may be considered as having the important function of dissolving personal frustration and, at the same time, maintaining social order. Some examples, which I have collected, will be cited here to make clear cause and effect in spirit possession.

a.   A housewife troubled with extreme poverty for a number of years fell into a state of "possession". She had no appetite and grew thin and weak. Every night she dreamed strange dreams in which a nobleman or a woman dressed in gorgeous costumes appeared. She went to a shaman who told her that her ancestors were of a noble family in the Ryukyu Dynasty, and she was expected to become a shaman. She is now a rich *Yuta* and when she performs rituals, wears elaborate costumes which were peculiar to the nobility during the Ryukyu Dynasty. It is clear that this woman has been able to realize symbolically in possession and her profession as a shaman what she could not obtain in ordinary family life.

b.   A housewife suddenly started to show symptoms of divine insanity when she learned that her husband was keeping a concubine. From early in the morning, she began trancelike dancing, loudly crying out prayers and strongly beating a drum. Her husband who ran a grocery store was forced to close his shop due to her behavior. He visited a shaman and learned that she was possessed by the spirit of her paternal ancestress who was also a shaman. She became a medium by using her ancestral spirit as a tutelary spirit. Soon her husband left his concubine. This case shows that the spirit possession of a housewife can symbolize both her strong antagonism against her husband's sexual conduct and, by sanctioned disruption, bring to bear heavy pressure upon him. Here spirit possession becomes a communally condoned moral sanction. There are many similar examples cited in various parts of Japan.

c.   A seventeen-year-old girl from an isolated island came to a big city, and lived in her paternal uncle's house as a maid. After two months, she became afflicted with an undiagnosed illness. At about five o'clock in the morning she used to be haunted by a vision of an old man with white hair and beard, dressed in a white kimono. This old man, whom she believed to be a god, ordered her to go to shrines and holy forests. If she disobeyed his order, she was struck by intense pain, and felt as if her whole body were being struck by innumerable needles. When she set about to obey his orders, her pain soon disappeared. She came to understand why she was suffering from this unknown illness when a shaman, by divine message, told her that she too was destined to become a shaman. She entreated the god to postpone the time to become a shaman for three years. Her affliction was then lessened but she had to visit a shrine daily [SASAKI 1978]. This example demonstrates how belief in the spirit possession of a young girl functioned to transform personal maladjustment into a means of changing her relationship to her paternal uncle's family.

We can learn from such examples that the persons concerned have first sublimated their present stressful condition by attributing it to the work of gods, and secondly achieved forms of personal liberation from their conditions by "obeying the will" of the gods. Thus, it follows that, "...the link between affliction and its cure as the royal road to the assumption of the shamanistic vocation is thus plain enough in those societies where shamans play the main or major role in religion and where possession is highly valued as a religious experience" [LEWIS 1971: 70]. In this sense, Japanese society and culture can be said to still give evidence of the saliency of belief in possession.

SPIRIT POSSESSION IN WOMEN

How should we interpret the fact that in Japan those possessed by gods and spirits are, for the most part, women? In Japanese folk beliefs, women are considered more easily possessed or influenced by the supernatural than are men. It is mostly women who are positively concerned with both Buddhist and Shintoist services or rituals in mainland Japan; but it is in Okinawa that one finds the closest relation between women and the supernatural.

There are such expressions in Okinawa as "Seji (Shiji) Dakai" (meaning spiritually strong) or "Seidaka Umari" (meaning to be endowed with divine character). Such expressions are most likely to be applied to women, not to men. Those who are destined to become *Yuta* or exhibit *Kamidari* are commonly the women who are *Sejidakai* or of *Seidaka Umari*.

The *Sejidakai* woman is regarded as one who has been endowed with far stronger and higher spiritual or magical power than common Okinawan women who have also been given spiritual character by nature. In Okinawa the status of women generally has remained higher than in mainland Japan. Okinawan personality and culture was much less influenced by feudalism than mainland Japan (cf. HARING 1953, 1956). In Okinawa, it is only the women who can mediate between the supernatural and human beings either in their immediate family or in *Monchu* (a kind of patrilineal descent group). They are expected to be much more acquainted with religious matters than are the men.

There is a kind of division of labor in Okinawan society in that the women are to be concerned with sacred matters and the men are to be concerned with secular pursuits. Women have been trained from infancy to be sensitive to magico-religious events including ancestor worship.

Usually, it is women who are very sensitive in regard to how to build graves, how to worship the ancestral tablets and how to deal with gods. It is they who believe that ghosts and ancestor spirits are very influential in what happens to their descendants, and are sure to bring grief and disaster upon them if they fail to deal properly with them. In this sense, spirit possession is recognized as a sign of supernatural desire as well as dissatisfaction. It is the women who observe various festivals for their families or *Monchus* in accordance with ancestral ways dating back to more remote ages. If they cannot satisfy their dead or ancestor spirits, the family order, the Monchu, and even the village might be destroyed by their wrath. Thus, women's magico-religious status and their expected role behavior are said to provide for the safety of Okinawan society.

In Okinawan society a dependence on religio-cultural beliefs makes it easy to attribute mental and physical abnormalities to supernatural causes. Moreover, Okinawans are apt to suffer from supernatural abnormalities when they are confronted with persistent grief or sudden disaster.

At one period in ancient Japan, it was the men who carried on secular government but with the spiritual assistance of their wives. There are recorded instances found both in the ancient dynasties of the mainland and in Okinawa. Referring to *Himiko*, a shaman queen of ancient Japan, Professor Hori stated, "It seems to me important that this highly shamanic and charismatic girl was enthroned in order to meet a social crisis presumably caused by civil war in a transitional period of revolutionary political, economic, social and cultural change at the juncture of the Yayoi and Kofun Periods" [Hori 1968: 191].

It is clear in the tradition of Japanese shamanism from ancient times that the women were considered more easily susceptible to symptoms of mental and physical abnormalities whenever they met a personal or family crisis.

CONCLUSION

Belief in spirit possession remains present in Japanese life in both abstract and concrete terms. It continues to be part of, not only a solid substratum in Japanese religion generally, but also serves as a strong constituent of many so-called new religions in Japan. The Japanese visit Buddhist temples and Shinto shrines as public believers and devotees but, at the same time, they privately visit spirit mediums in order to obtain divine information concerning problems in their daily lives. Some people even say that while Buddhism and Shintoism are the religions of the *Omote*, "the front", spirit possession and shamanism remain the religions of the *Ura*, "the back". Actually, in a variety of situations, both religions are found to be complementary in function. In various parts of the country funerals are being performed by the cooperation of both Buddhist priests and shamanic mediums. While the former ceremony supposedly leads the soul of the dead to the other world, the latter can, upon occasion, bring it back to this world.   There are even cases reported where the husband functions as a Buddhist priest and his wife as a shamanic medium.   It is well-known that many founders of new religions in Japan are conspicuously shamanic in character.   The founders of such big religious associations as Tenrikyo, Omotokyo and the Rissho-koseikai are regarded as typical female shamans who had experienced violent forms of spirit possession.

As an important element of indigenous religion in Japan we must not overlook the worship of those dead who manifested some particular form of power.   According to Professor Noboru Miyata [1970] Japanese worship of human beings is two-fold: that of the powerful living and that of the powerful dead.   He cites in his book many interesting examples of how living persons regarded as being possessed by abnormal qualities including spirits have been deeply respected and worshipped.   I think that the worship of and belief in living persons as gods included the Emperor and the various founders of new religions.   Such beliefs have to be discussed in connection with Japanese belief in spirit possession and shamanism.   Furthermore, I must add here that the worship of living persons might have a close connection with the animistic worship of nature which includes worship of mountains, oceans, animals, etc. Many Japanese have trained themselves on holy mountains or turned to the sea, where they sought to find the power of the supernatural.   Thus we can contend that spirit possession, the worship of human beings, and the worship of nature are mutually interrelated in Japanese thought and constitute the basic elements of Japanese indigenous religion.

BIBLIOGRAPHY

FIRTH, Raymond
    1959   Problems and Assumptions in an Anthropological Study of Religion. *Journal of the Royal Anthropological Institute* 89(2): 129–148.
    1969   Forward. In J. Beattie and J. Middleton (eds.), *Spirit Mediumship and Society in Africa*, London: Routledge & Kegan Paul.
HARING, Douglas G.
    1953   The Naro Cult of Amami Ōshima: Divine Priestess of the Ryūkyū Islands. *Sociologus* 3: 108–121.
    1956   Japanese National Character: Cultural Anthropology, Psychoanalysis and History. In D. G. Haring (ed.), *Personal Character and Cultural Milieu*, Syracuse: Syracuse University Press, pp. 424–437.
HORI, Ichiro
    1968   *Folk Religion in Japan: Continuity and Change.* Chicago: University of Chicago Press.
LEBRA, William P.
    1974   *Okinawa no Shūkyō to Shakai-kōzō* (translated into Japanese by K. Sakihara & M. Sakihara). Tokyo: Kobundo. (Original English edition: *Okinawan Religion: Belief, Ritual and Social Structure*, Honolulu: University of Hawaii Press, 1966.)

84 K. SASAKI

LEWIS, I. M.

1971 *Ecstatic Religion*: *An Anthropological Study of Spirit Possession and Shamanism*. New York: Penguin Books, Ltd.

MIYATA, Noboru

1970 *Ikigami Shinko.* Tokyo: Hanawa Shobō. (*The Belief in the Living Gods.*)

OHASHI, Hideshi

1980 On the Initiation Process of Shamans in Okinawa: Social-Psychological Approach. *The Bulletin of the Faculty of Letters, Tohoku University* 30: 232–280.

SAKURAI, Tokutaro

1980 Shinnyo no tanjō: Okinawa Kudaka Jima no Izaihō. *Gekkan Bunkazai* No. 2, pp. 18–30. (The Birth of the Divine Priestesses: The Izaihō in Kudaka Island, Okinawa.)

SASAKI, Kokan

1978 Kamidārī no shosō: Yuta-teki shokunōsha no initiation. In T. Kubo (ed.), *Okinawa no Gairai Shūkyō*, Tokyo: Kōbundō. (Varieties of Kamidari: On the Initiation of Yuta. *Foreign Religions in Okinawa.*)

SATO, Noriaki

1978 Dan-shinto kara mita jiin to Sōtō-shū. *The Sōtō Shūhō* 517: 298–303. (The Temple and the Sōtō Sect as Seen by Believers and Devotees.)

Part III

The Influence of the Great Traditions

Chapter 5

Elite and Folk: Comments on the Two-Tiered Theory

LEWIS R. LANCASTER

In the previous two chapters we have begun examining the interaction of family roles and functions with traditions. We must differentiate between performance of ritual by an elite or specialized professional group of elders or clerics as contrasted with what is done or believed by lay or folk practitioners. This distinction between two tiers of religious activity has long been a part of the study of Christianity. In recent years the attempt to sort out an abiding folk level of religious beliefs as distinct from the elite traditions has also become an important part of comparable research in East Asia. Earlier the study of Asian religions by Westerners emphasized the philological analysis of the works which made up the classical canons of Buddhist and Confucian writings. The Taoists were studied primarily by reference to the philosophical treatises attributed to Lao Tzu and his successors. When the result of this type of historical study was applied to contemporary living practices found in Asia, it was apparent that the elite tradition as contained in accepted and recognized texts was not adequate for describing actual folk activities. Conversely, when ethnographic reports began to circulate in the literature of anthropology and sociology it was obvious that direct study of the folk level of religious performance did not produce sufficient information about the special beliefs and practices of the elite/ literate group of professionals and clerics. These two tiers remain separate and require methods of study appropriate to each. In this general volume on family and religion in East Asia, we include examples of different approaches brought to view when we describe folk practice in the two previous chapters or the philosophical contentions of literate elites as described in chapters which follow.

There are two major ways of studying a popular approach to the religious life as contrasted with the approach described in the textual sources of the classical canons: one is through field work and direct observation of current practice and the second is through the study of texts which may be excluded from the accepted canons due to their special content. These latter texts may have no place in the accepted canon or, even if included, may be suspect by virtue of containing 'heterodox' material. Study which is open to data derived from observation or from texts not approved by the traditionalists gives an added depth to our understanding of the fullness of the religious life of people. Increasing attention to this approach has raised serious questions about limitations or deficiences inherent in studying any culture, especially one in East Asia, using only texts which time and tradition have sanctified. A scholarly approach benefits by making use of so-called 'folk' material or suspect texts filled with the unorthodox. Their appropriate analysis can make a considerable contribution to a deeper understanding of the Asian religious life. Conversely, exhaustive studies of folk practices by themselves cannot arrive at an understanding of how or why a 'great' tradition continues to exert its influence. The failure of an exclusive approach of either 'folk' or 'great' to furnish convincing description of the other attests to an essentially irreducible disparity of content and approach. The division into the 'great' and 'folk' remains a real one. The religious life of East Asian societies cannot be described as any syncretic unitary entity.

The notion of a two-tiered system of religious life is not a new one in western scholarship. Hume [1875: 334] describes in his *Natural History of Religion* the difference existing between trained professionals and the lay community with its popular patterns of belief. The problem of the two systems goes back long before Hume; we see in the writings of Church fathers such as Jerome (Fremantle 1893) and Augustine of Hippo (Brown 1967) concern over the fact that the influx of new converts was accompanied by practices considered 'pagan'. In a more recent study, Peter Brown in the *Cult of the Saints* [1981] points out that Latin Christianity was beset with this very problem of how to interpret and deal with two tiers of organization. Brown has some timely warnings for those who attempt to deal with this duality. First, he reminds us forcefully that we cannot rely on any 'elite' description of the 'folk'. He further indicates a frequent misunderstanding held by some who deal with this issue, namely the idea that the 'folk' tradition represents an unchanging substratum of culture which emerges from time to time to challenge or impinge on 'elite' structure. It is important to keep in mind that the 'folk' side of the religious life of society is just as susceptible to change as any other part of the culture and must be viewed as a continuously dynamic element rather than a passive one resistive to change.

Buddhism is usually considered to be a 'great' tradition but this leads to some problems, especially if we fail to define what we mean by Buddhism. A tradition so complex and multi-faceted cannot be adequately described or studied as if it were a homogeneous movement. It is, for example, essential to deal with a monastic system as well as with lay activity, since the belief systems followed in the two are often quite divergent. And within the lay and monastic communities, we also find several problems of approach, depending on whether the 'folk' is taken in equal part with beliefs that have their origin within the Buddhist core of teachings or whether the balance is shifted either toward the Buddhist ideas or those of the 'folk'. Thus the investigation of the Buddhist lay community may require that local non-Buddhist elements be studied alongside Buddhist ones. If we consider the Korean case as an example, such issues are made more evident.

When Buddhism was introduced into the peninsula it came into contact with rich and varied religious life. Over the centuries, Buddhism with its firmly established monastery system has come to exist side by side with the *mudang*, who are often referred to under the generic name of shamans. It is tempting to say that

Buddhism represents the 'great' and the mudang the 'folk', but such simple definitions must be avoided, since, as has been pointed out, Buddhism cannot be considered as a single system any more than the mudang tradition can be taken as a unitary entity.   Most Korean scholars will argue that Buddhism is completely enmeshed with shamanism and that it is impossible to make a clear separation of 'great' and 'folk'.   If we attempt to compare the mudang with the Buddhist community, then it is essential to be very specific about what elements are being compared.   On the Buddhist side the Chogye Order monastery life may be considered one aspect of Buddhism and the non-professional lay life as another.   Since the lay people are in close contact with the mudang, most comments about the relationship of Buddhism to shamanism deal only with that situation in which there are lay women who follow both the traditions of the mudang and Buddhism.

Having made the point that there are at least two tiers within the Buddhist side of the equation, one can then make more specific comparisons, as for example comparing the Chogye Monastery activity, rather than lay life, with that of the mudang. At first glance a visitor to a Korean Chogye Monastery (the country's major organization of Buddhist monks and nuns) will be tempted to agree with the appraisal which holds that Buddhism and shamanism have become intertwined not only at the lay level but in the monastery as well.   There are to be found shrines dedicated to the Mountain Spirit and Constellation Deities.   Further proof of the impact of shamanism is said to be seen in the paintings decorating the walls and eaves of the buildings, paintings of tigers, roosters, etc., all of which play a role in the rituals of the mudang.   In the storage rooms of the monasteries there are costumes worn by the monks when doing dances which have affinity to the gyrations of the mudang.   No building is constructed without geomancy being performed to make certain the location is an auspicious one.   Monks are involved with healing ceremonies and on occasion will perform the ritual to give aid to some ailing person; the ritual consisting of throwing red beans at the altar, signifying the burning up of the illness and the causes of it. While this is a telling array of practices, all pointing to the encounter of the elite Buddhist tradition as found in the Chogye Monastery with the folk system native to Korea, research which focuses on the life and training of the monks and nuns provides us with quite a different picture.   It is a surprise to find how little the monastic dwellers have to do with the mudang.   The lighting of incense in the shrine hall of the Mountain Spirit is an age old procedure which has a very small part to play in the daily life of the monastic community.   The lack of interest in or the appropriation of mudang-like factors within the monasteries of the Chogye Order raises a number of important issues. How is it possible for the Order to be so separated from the practices which surround it?   It might be that appearances are misleading and that underneath all of the Buddhist distractions there is the hidden inclusion of the whole world of spirits which are shared with the mudang in her trances.   From actual field experience, this mix of monastic life and the mudang cannot be documented, and it appears to be true that Chogye Order monks and nuns are virtually free of an interest in or participation in the rituals and procedures of the mudang.   This is difficult to reconcile with the fact that the mudang dominates much of the life of the lay women, a group from which the Buddhists must secure recruits and support.

It is here that we must turn to the family to provide us with some reference for an understanding of how the 'elite' is separated from the 'folk'. In the work of Kendall [1985] we have a detailed account of the mudang's ceremony and there we find a combination of Buddhism and non-Buddhist elements. We can conclude that the Chogye Order monastery represents an aspect of Buddhism which is highly resistant to the inclusion of shamanic elements. While these monasteries may be free of the dances and rituals of the mudang, in those very rituals performed outside of the monastery, Buddhist notions abound. The amount of lore which has passed from Buddhism to the mudang is impressive, for the mudang in her performance of the trance ritual undergoes possession by a sequence of spirits and deities; among these are a number that have been borrowed from Buddhism. The Buddhist Sage comes to her body and she dresses in white costume; alongside the Sage is the Buddhist Monk Sage who speaks when she is wearing gray. In addition to these Buddhist sages, Maitreya appears as does Avalokitesvara and Bhaisajyaguru, all possessing for a time the mudang as she placates and consults the repertoire of spirits. During certain rituals, the mudang helps lead the dead through the agonies of the ten hells, the ten realms of the nether world, an idea brought into East Asia by the Buddhists. The King of the Hells comes to the mudang and gives information about the situation of the family members who are undergoing judgments in the nether world, and it is usually the King of Hells who informs the living that the dead have escaped finally from the torments there. As the released souls journey out of hell they are led by the mudang to the road which reaches the Lotus Land, a type of Buddhist paradise. The shrine used by the mudang for the rituals in her home is called the Poptang (Hall of the Dharma) and the ritual performed at the shrine is given the name of Pulgong (Buddhist Service).

The work of sorting out the Kut with its cast of characters has given us a new vision of the way in which Buddhism and shamanism as practiced by the mudang have interacted. The Chogye Order monastery community with its rules of conduct, intense training in meditation, a large canon of scripture, carefully preserved in written form, and a model for the role of the monks and nuns constitutes the 'great' tradition. It is in the monastery that we find the community which depends on the classical texts. This monastic community holds itself aloof from the mudang, but the same cannot be said of the lay women who consider themselves to be Buddhists. Hume's description of the two-tiered structure of religion based on the professional priests and the lay followers seems to have application in Korea. It is among the lay group that we find involvement with the mudang, the mudang who has no resistance to Buddhist ideas, personages or concepts of hells and paradises, and indeed welcomes such entities into her system. With shrines that bear the name of Buddhism, possessed in her trances by Buddhist deities, the mudang appears as a pseudo-Buddhist. In the mudang we find the 'folk' element, followed by lay women who consider themselves to be Buddhists.

The distinctions are not limited to Buddhism but exist for the Confucians as well. The male dominated Confucian rituals can be termed a 'great' tradition with a textual canon and clearly defined rules and regulations, but as noted in the chapters by Kendall and Lee, the wife and mother of any Confucian may well be followers of the mudang and spend time and money in trying to find out the reasons for sickness, bad luck or conversely attempting to bring about prosperity and health. Here the division between the 'great' and 'folk' is related to sex, status, and training, the higher status male as representative of the 'great' and his female family members being involved with the 'folk'. Just as Jerome in European Christianity separated himself and his fellow clerics from the lay people, especially the lay women, who had hints of the pagan in their practices [BROWN 1981: 28], so Korean Buddhist and Confucians with their seniors and professionals are set apart from the 'folk' practices which are dominated by the women.

In this discussion of the relationship of the 'great' and the 'folk' religions, one cannot avoid including the integrative role of the family. While traditions such as the Buddhist monastery or the Confucian rituals may remain separated from other aspects of religion in the society, the family is related to both the 'great' and the 'folk' and the involvement of an individual in a religious activity may depend on the status of that individual within the family. The Korean model for the levels of religious life and the importance of family in determining the role of an individual is helpful in looking at the rest of East Asia, but it is not a model which can be applied indiscriminately to either China or Japan. In both of these other areas, the 'folk' and the 'great' interact in particular fashions which are culturally distinctive. Nevertheless, there do exist some similarities which can assist us in this search for an understanding of how the 'elite' and 'folk' relate to one another in a family context. In all three areas, we must be aware that the Buddhist tradition is not unitary, and that differences between the lay community and those who live in the monastery are quite significant. This raises a question of whether monastic Buddhism can be termed an elite movement while the lay alone belong to the 'folk'. Caution must be advised for those who wish to make such a clean cut distinction; some monks are involved with elements which can only be termed 'folk' and some lay people are trained in the higher doctrines of the faith.

In a general sense there are non-Buddhist movements such as Taoism and shamanism which are more 'folk' in nature and tend to stand off against the Buddhist system which is, depending on the particular aspect being studied, both 'elite' and 'folk'. Ozaki in the following chapter documents how Taoist attitudes about family were at some historical periods different from the Buddhist tradition.

When compared with non-Buddhist groups, Buddhist lay people are less distinctive than the monastic dwellers. Again, we can turn to the Korean model for an example. In Korean Buddhism there are devout women called Posals (Bodhisattvas), who are to be seen within the confines of the monasteries of the Chogye Order doing a number of tasks: cleaning, sewing, mending, assisting with the cooking, while taking time to do prostrations and lighting of incense in the halls. These women are carefully distinguished from the nuns by dress, hair style, training and practice. The nuns carry on a life style which is nearly the duplicate of the monks and as such can be said to fully participate in the 'elite' aspect of Buddhism; the Posals live as lay women with family obligations and a complete life within secular society. While monks and nuns usually stay in the monastery and do not frequent the lay homes, the Posals often perform an important teaching function among other lay adherents. Some Posals dance in the same manner as the mudang and are capable of doing divination; they use a different shaped drum and wear different clothing but the activity is quite similar. It is the Posal who visits in the homes and many monks and nuns will say that their first lessons in Buddhism came from these women. Here, in the lay community we see an individual holding a place in the family as mother, wife and senior female, who plays an important role in the spread and teaching of Buddhism. She may not be deficient in some of the more abstract doctrines of the Buddhist 'elite' system and will teach the interested young about karma, rebirth, and even the notion of 'emptiness'. At the same time, as described later in Lee's chapter, she is, like the other women of her standing, involved with the world of the spirits and the welfare of the people around her as determined by the forces of those spirits. It is in the person of the Posal that we can find 'elite' and 'folk' in the activities of a single individual. Throughout East Asia, there are such examples of devout lay people who are versed in the textual aspects of Buddhism but who also teach and pursue non-Buddhist practices. Thus we have in the Buddhist lay group, tiers of teaching and comprehension which indicate that the lay people are not all equally ranked. A discussion of the 'elite' and 'folk' traditions among this segment of the population requires the scholar to construct some outline by which the relative weight given to either the classical 'elite' or the 'folk' material can be judged. Lay followers who do not know the two traditions as separate, but rely on the myriad teachings of both folk and elite as if they belong to a single cohesive entity, are in a different class from those who do recognize a difference. Lay followers who lack sophistication in these matters are the ones who shock and amaze scholars who attempt to define Buddhism strictly on the basis of the sutras and commentaries. These 'Buddhists' who profess to beliefs that are a mixture of 'folk' and 'elite' have a religious life that contains within it many contradictions of the 'classical' Buddhist teachings. At the same time, when we separate the professional monks from the lay community, it must be said that monks and nuns themselves come from the community and often the belief patterns of a life-time continue to be a part of their life. It is one of the recognized tasks of the monastery to train novices fresh from the homelife to accept a new structure and to internalize the teachings of the 'elite' texts. The results, while mixed, tend to move the monastic dweller into a lifestyle and a pattern of beliefs which are quite distinct from those of their home and the world of the lay believers. It is difficult to conceive of the 'elite' tier of Buddhism separated from the monastery and the controlled life which the monastery is able to maintain. The removal of the monk from the home is considered in the traditional Buddhist setting to be essential for the promulgation and continuation of practices held to be of primary importance in the religion. This highlights the fact that the family is one of the primary centers for 'folk' and as such the monk and nun must be removed from that family unit in order to learn and live by a different code. As discussed by Koh in the final chapter of this volume, the competition of the monastery and the family for the allegiance of the monk and nun is not surprising under these circumstances.

In Japan, the matter is complicated since the family of the married priest looks to the temple as a source of support and the continuation of the tradition means much to that family not only in spiritual matters but in monetary ones as well. When the family and temple are partners, the situation is quite different from that found in either China or Korea where monastery and home were separated. Interestingly enough in Japan the 'elite' teachings are carefully maintained by the temple priests and it is only there that Buddhism in East Asia was able to bring about a reconciliation of doctrines derived from the Indian yogic system of meditation and the needs and interests of the homelife. The force of this tie between family and the temple is nowhere better seen than in the pressure placed on the eldest son to assume his place as the temporal and spiritual leader. No discussion of Japanese Buddhism is sufficient without reference to this unique combination of temple and home.

The family is a unit in which elite and folk come into contact with one another, and part of the reaction created by this encounter relates directly to religious matters. With their monastic institution in China and Korea, the Buddhists create a new community which separates the monks and nuns from the belief patterns of their childhood. This causes tensions between Buddhism and the family and these tensions are the subject of no small part of the 'elite' canons of the Buddhists and the Confucians.

The problems between religious activities and the home are not limited to the monastic situation of the Buddhists, as we have seen in the case of the Confucian male's response to the mudang. The followers of the classical tradition of this lineage of teaching give high praise to the values of the family and the necessity of following the regulations which govern human relationships. At the same time, as higher status males they express disdain for, or at the very least disinterest in, the mudang even though from an objective point of view the mudangs play a major role in family life, for it is among the women who follow this tradition that many family problems are handled, such as health and success of children. The Confucian tradition in this case is antagonistic to a 'folk' tradition which focuses its activities only on the home life and the welfare of those within the home. Here we have another example of the 'great' tradition that is resistant to being drawn into a close tie with a 'folk' practice, even when the two are attempting to provide for similar human needs. The discussion of the contact of 'elite' and 'folk' must take into account that this encounter does not occur in some vacuum, nor does it occur exclusively in a temple or in public rituals of the folk practitioners. Rather, it is within the family that many of the significant events are to be observed.

In other chapters on Confucianism which follow, an 'elite' description of the family is critically documented. The actual functioning of the family as a social unit may not accord with the ideal description of the family in the 'elite' texts. Nevertheless, the 'elite', especially the Confucian tradition, bases a major part of its view of life and society on the image of the family as presented in its teachings. The family members in turn attempt to act in ways that can be considered appropriate when judged against the admonitions of the texts. We cannot understand the Confucians without some comprehension of this teaching any more than we can deal with Buddhism without giving careful consideration to the statements about the family which occur within its canons. The descriptions and the comments about the family in the 'elite' texts cannot be used to describe the family as found within a given situation; neither can a description of that family in turn be used to provide an account of the ideal orientation of behavior similar to the 'elite' text. We have here a major distinction between what is said about a social entity in idealized religious rules of conduct and what can be observed about that unit in a contemporary setting. The situation seems to be that neither the descriptions based on observing the family nor the picture of the ideal family of the texts is a sufficient one; both must be examined. The family as a unit is bound by kinship ties but those ties alone do not encompass the complete aspect of the family. The actions of people within society can be based on principles which are applied by only some individuals in their judgment of a proper way to act. It is one thing to observe the act but of equal importance to a full understanding of the events must be a comprehension of the internalized belief systems which influence the thinking and decision process of the members of the social unit. Just as religion must be studied on the basis of at least two tiers, so the family can be viewed from the point of view of the 'folk' and the 'elite'. At the 'folk' level we find one side of the family involved in magic and dependence on divination and shamanic healing powers, and at the elite level we see the senior male attempting to act in accordance with the teachings of his texts. The family cannot adequately be studied by reference to only one of its facets, for while practice may not always be in accord with the regulations of the ideal, neither can it be said that the family is susceptible to study without reference to the elite canons of Buddhists and Confucians. The conclusion must be that the family and religious involvements can only be studied by looking at both daily life and elite idealized descriptions, for both give important dimensions to our study of human behavior which as Spiro suggests is inextricably familial and religious.

BIBLIOGRAPHY

BROWN, Peter
    1967 *Augustine of Hippo.* Berkeley and Los Angeles: University of California Press.
    1981 *The Cult of the Saints: Its Rise and Function in Latin Christianity.* Chicago: University of Chicago Press.
FREEMANTLE, W. H., trans.
    1893 *St. Jerome: Letters and Select Works.* New York: Christian Literature.
HUME, David
    1875 *The Natural History of Religion (Essays: Moral, Political, and Literary).* London: Longman Green.

KENDALL, Laurel
  1985   Shamans, Housewives, and Other Restless Spirits: Women in Korean Ritual Life.
         Honolulu: University of Hawaii Press.

Chapter 6

The Taoist Priesthood: From Tsai-chia to Ch'u-chia

MASAHARU OZAKI

INTRODUCTION

During the approximately 1800 years from the latter half of the later Han Dynasty (25–220) to the fall of old China, Confucianism, Buddhism and Taoism remained the major Chinese religions. No mention is necessary of how much Taoism learned from the other two, especially Buddhism, and how much it was influenced by them in the process of forming and developing itself. As we are well aware, Confucianism is a *shih-chien tao* 世間道 (a path within society), and Buddhism is a *ch'u shih-chien tao* 出世間道 (outside the social order), and hence opposite in nature. Buddhism had to withstand rigorous criticism from Confucianism before it became accepted within Chinese society. One such point of contention was the question of *hsiao* 孝, filial piety. From a Confucian viewpoint leaving home to become a priest (*ch'u-chia* 出家) is clearly an un-filial act.

As it happened, Confucian ideology declined greatly during the political confusion that occurred from the latter half of the Later Han through the Wei Chin and Northern and Southern Dynasties. As a result, during this period, Buddhism had a good opportunity to permeate into Chinese society, while Taoism was becoming more formalized as a definable religion.

Is and was Taoism intrinsically a *shih-hsien tao* (within the family), or is it a *ch'u shih-hsien tao* (leading away from family life), or did it follow a unique path that combined the two? These have become extremely interesting questions now that the recent academic climate is re-examining the definition of Taoism. Without requisite research on the multi-faceted aspects of Taoism we cannot expect easy answers. Therefore, I shall approach this issue here through the historical question of whether or not Taoists practiced *ch'u-chia* and retired from family life during the first half of the T'ang Dynasty.

TAOISTS DURING THE NORTHERN AND SOUTHERN DYNASTIES

First, let me briefly refer to the actual practices of Taoists that can be presently observed in Taiwan and Hong Kong as well as of those reported by our predecessors in pre-war China. As far as I know there are no "*ch'u-chia*" Taoists living apart in present-day Taiwan: all Taoists are leading family lives and those considered priests simply preside over religious rites in a broad sense. This seems the same in Hong

Kong also [Ōfuchi 1980: 753–754]. One Taoist with whom I am acquainted is a *T'ien-shih Tao* 天師道 Taoist from Fu-chou 福州 now living in T'ai-nan 台南. His family have been Taoists for over ten generations since the Ch'ing Dynasty, from which we can infer that they have continuously lived married lives. In Pei-ching in pre-war China, however, the *T'ien-shih Tao* Taoists located there seem to have led lives of *ch'u-chia* priests, like the *Ch'üan-chen Chiao* 全真教 Taoists [Yoshioka 1975: 418–420]. Another example is that of the Chang T'ien-shih 張天師 sect whose family line has continued for about 1800 years from the first *Tien-shih* 天師, Chang Ling 張陵 of the later Han Dynasty, to T'ien-shih Chang Yüan-hsien 天師張源先, who is of the sixty-fourth generation now based in Taiwan. In short, there seem historically to have been from the earliest period on two types of Taoists—*ch'u-chia* 出家, or non-secular, and *tsai-chia* 在家, or lay.

Taoism lacks a so-called founder. Its origin is generally considered to be so-called "Primitive Taoism", or folk cults such as *T'ai-p'ing Tao* 太平道 and *Wu-tou-mi Tao*. 五斗米道. Until the emergence of the *San-tung* 三洞 theory, in the first half of the fifth century, the various Taoist sects scattered throughout China were formed and developed more or less separately. There was some communication among them but there were no feelings of special solidarity or fellowship uniting the various groups. There were no recorded tendencies for the various sects to unite.

Whether the Taoists during this period were prevailingly *ch'u-chia* or *tsai-chia* cannot be fully known, but we know that at least *Wu-tou-mi Tao* Taoists were married. For example, three generations of Changs, Chang Ling 張陵, Chang Hêng 張衡, and Chang Lu 張魯, are often referred to as the San Chang 三張, or three Changs. They were clearly blood kin, and the position of leader was hereditary within the family. We can also infer from the description in *Lao-chün yin-sung chieh ching* 老君音誦誡経 (*Tao-ts'ang* 道蔵 vol. 562) that *T'ien-shih* Taoists in the later periods also practiced primogeniture. This scripture is a remainder of the twenty volume *Yün-chung yin-sung hsin-k'ê chih chieh* 雲中音誦新科之誡 which was given to the priest K'ou Ch'ien-chih 寇謙之 (365?–448) of the Northern Wei Dynasty by T'ai-shang *Lao-chün* 太上老君 in October of the second year of Shen-juei 神瑞 [Yang 1956: 17–18]. It contains Ch'ien-chih's own views under the pretext of being those of Lao-chün and is one of few precious materials describing the actual situation of Taoism in Hua-pei (North China) 華北 in about 400 A.D.

Ch'ien-chih's Taoism is called the *New T'ien-shih Tao* 新天師道. He considers the first T'ien-shih to be T'ai-shang Lao-chün, Chang Ling the second, and himself as the third T'ien-shih, which indicates quite clearly that there was no blood relationship among the three. Furthermore, Ch'ien-chih criticizes the common practice of the priest's son inheriting the father's position after his death, and strongly asserts the need to adopt the policy of respecting ability rather than birth. This, then, would indicate that T'ien-shih Taoists in the Hua-pei area during this period took wives but did not approve of the priesthood being passed on as part of inheritance.

Among the collected works that play an important role in the study of Taoism are the *Tao-ts'ang* and the *Tao-ts'ang chi-yao* 道蔵輯要, from which we can extract a considerable number of scriptures written in the Chiang-nan 江南 area during the Six Dynasties. These are where the term "*ch'u-chia*" is found. A minor qualification is necessary. We cannot find the term among those that were written early in the Six Dynasties, such as *Ku shang-ch'ing ching* 古上清経 and *Ku ling-pao ching* 古霊宝経, but we begin to see the term in writings appearing toward the end of the Six Dynasties. One example of this is the twenty volume *Tao-hsüeh chuan* 道学伝 written by Ma Shu 馬枢 of the Ch'en Dynasty (557–589). Although the entire collection is not extant, it is quoted not only in Taoist books but in many others. Ch'en Kuo-fu 陳国符 once made tremendous effort to collect the lost text [CH'EN 1963: Appendix 454–504]. In it we find specific mention of 14 Taoist priests and nuns. These priests and nuns whose activities are relatively well known were all active in the Chiang-nan area during the Liang (502–557) and Ch'en (557–589) Dynasties. We can infer from this that they did not have clear *ch'u-chia* consciousness in the fourth and fifth centuries. Such consciousness of specific priesthood became clear in the sixth century. This contention would explain the fact that the term *ch'u-chia* cannot be found in prior works like *Ku shang-ch'ing ching* and *Ku ling-pao ching*.

There were, however, Taoists who were practically leading a *ch'u-chia* life even before the term actually appears in the texts. One such example is Lu Hsiu-ching 陸修静, who was active during the Sung Dynasty (420–479). There is a description of him in the *Tao-hsüeh chuan* 道学伝 quoted in chapter two of the Chao Sung Dynasty author Ch'en Pao-kuang's 陳葆光 *San-tung ch'ün hsien lu* 三洞群仙録 (*Tao-ts'ang* vol. 992). "He left his wife and children, removed himself from his worldly responsibilities, and day and night strove solely to acquire the teachings". Also a famous work by Ma Shu (*Tao-ts'ang* vol. 780) includes an anecdote in which his family pleaded with him to cure his daughter who had suddenly become ill. He declined by saying, "Having abandoned my family, I am in the midst of training. The house I stopped by is no different from an inn and is a passing point to my destination. How can I not abandon my love toward my family?" This is a clear case of *ch'u-chia* since Hsiu-ching had left his family in order to search for the Way.

Does this imply, then, that Taoists in Hua-pei were *tsai-chia* and those in Chiang-nan were *ch'u-chia*? Or did they vary from sect to sect? In order to clarify this it is necessary to specifically examine the situation of the T'ien-shih Taoists in the Chiang-nan area, because by the period of the Northern and Southern Dynasties *T'ien-shih Tao* was influential in that region.

Chang Yü 張裕, who was active in Chiang-nan during the Liang Dynasty, is said to be a twelfth generation descendent of Chang Ling. It is clear that he retreated from family into *ch'u-chia*, but there is no document to our knowledge that indicates he was actively enlightening the masses. This makes us wonder how faithful he was to the teachings of *T'ien-shih Tao*. A converse example is that of a T'ien-shih Taoist during the Liu Sung Dynasty, Liu Ning-chih 劉凝之. He apparently brought his wife and children to the mountains (*Tao-ts'ang* vol. 780).

Taoism, like Buddhism, in Hua-pei was strongly influenced by the state and was very practical, whereas in Chiang-nan it was influenced by the nobility and was logical

[OZAKI 1979: 66–67]. Therefore, one can observe a strong tendency for Taoism in Hua-pei to be *tsai-chia* Taoism, and in Chiang-nan to be *ch'u-chia* Taoism, although there is some variation depending upon the tradition of different sects. Granted that it is dangerous to judge on the basis of the one example of Liu Ning-chih, it seems that T'ien-shih Taoists in the Chiang-nan area were *tsai-chia* on the whole, even though they were influenced by other Taoist sects, like the Mao Shan 茅山.

TAOISTS DURING THE FIRST HALF OF THE T'ANG DYNASTY

The two major types of priests in the Northern and Southern Dynasties changed during the T'ang Period as a world empire was gradually being formed.

Let me begin with a six volume Taoist text entitled *Tung-hsüan ling-pao san-tung fêng-tao k'ê-chieh ying-shih* 洞玄霊宝三洞奉道科戒営始 (*Tao-ts'ang* vols. 760–761). There are many dates given for its completion: none is generally accepted as convincing. I would like to suggest that it was written sometime during T'ai-tsung's 太宗 reign (626–649). One can clearly tell, however, that the version available at present is not the authorized one, by comparing it against the Tun-huang 敦煌 manuscript (ŌFUCHI 1978: 115–121]. In *Fêng-tao k'ê-chieh ying-shih* quoted in "Ming-k'ai tu 明開度, *I-ch'ieh tao-ching yin-i miao-men yu-ch'i* 一切道経音義妙門由起 (Tao-ts'ang vol. 760), we find a description of Taoists.

> Taoists are those who are not concerned with worldly responsibilities but rather strive to serve the ever-unchanging Tao. They all are courteous as Taoists, should be and are completely different from the lay people in their spirit and behavior. Therefore they do not worship the emperor and the nobles. The Taoists of today are Taoist priests (*ch'u-chia*) and they should not attempt to acquire wealth by coming into close contact with those with power.

Here they say clearly, "The Taoists today are Taoist priests written *ch'u-chia*, "out of home"", which is extremely important to us. If we were to investigate this literally, there were no lay (*tsai-chia*) Taoists during the reign of T'ai-tsung and all the Taoists were (*ch'u-chia*) priests. In other words, there may have been lay (*tsai-chia*) Taoists in the society of that time, but they were operating sub rosa, so to speak, and were not authorized by the sects. We may note that this text is not something that was prepared from the perspective of a single sect, as the term *san-tung* in the title indicates.

As mentioned earlier, there is no specific founder in Taoism. Although Lao-*tzŭ* 老子 is often mentioned as such, it is simply a measure with which to compete against Śākya-muni-buddha 釈迦牟尼仏 of Buddhism, and the Taoists did not consciously think of Lao-tzŭ as their founder. Diverse sects were not unified until the end of Eastern Chin Dynasty (317–420). At this time a large number of Buddhist scriptures were being translated into Chinese. The nobles found Buddhism attractive which contributed to its spread in the Chiang-nan area. Taoists began to realize that single sects could not meet this challenge. Various sects of the Chiang-nan area who shared relatively similar scriptures began to unite around the *Shang-ch'ing* 上清 sect. This is the beginning of the San-tung theory, a major event in the history of Taoism.

San-tung in a narrow sense includes Tung-chen 洞真, Tung-hsüan 洞玄 and Tung-shen 洞神. The basic scriptures are the *Shang-ch'ing ching* 上清経 for Tung-chen, the *Ling-pao ching* 霊宝経 for *Tung-hsüan*, and the *San-huang wen* 三皇文 for Tung-shen. Although it was still in a very primitive form, we can consider that the Tao-ts'ang of Taoism as I-Ch'ieh Ching 一切経 was formed here. This is when the Taoists began to have a certain sense of comradery, and each group can be understood as a religious sect. Later orders with long tradition, such as the *T'ien-shih Tao* 天師道 and the *T'ai-p'ing Tao* 太平道 and their scriptures, were incorporated into one organization.

San-tung in a broader sense refers to all the sects, all the scriptures, and ultimately Taoism itself. Some examples of this are a ten chapter collection compiled by the early T'ang Taoist, Wang Hsüan-hê 王懸河 entitled *San-tung chu-nang* 三洞珠嚢 (Tao-ts'ang vols. 780–782), and the *San-tung fêng-tao k'ê-chieh ying-shih*. That the term was used in a broader sense is indicated by the fact that the major sects from the Six Dynasties are all grouped into one system in Chapter 4, "Fa-tz'ǔ i 法次儀" and Chapter 5, "Fa-fu t'u-i 法服図儀". All these indicated that during T'ai-tsung's reign all the Taoists were priests, including the T'ien-shih Taoists.

By this time they had tried to classify Taoists into the seven categories of *T'ien-chen* 天真, *Shen-hsien* 神仙, *Yu-i* 幽逸, *Shan-chü* 山居, *Ch'u-chia* 出家, *Tsai-chia* 在家 and *Chi-chiu* 祭酒 in *Miao-men yu-ch'i hsü* 妙門由起序. The seven category system first appears in *T'ai-shang tung-hsüan ling-pao ch'u-chia yin-yüan ching* 太上洞玄霊宝出家因縁経 (*Tao-ts'ang* vol. 176). This is considered to have been written before the *Miao-men yu-ch'i hsü* but after *San-tung fêng-tao k'ê-chieh ying-shih* (quoted by "Ming-k'ai tu", *I-ch'ieh tao-ching yin-i miao-men yu-ch'i*), in which the category *Yu-i* is missing.

In the explanation of Taoists given in the *Miao-men yu-ch'i hsü* the seven categories are further divided into two groups, the first one being from the first *T'ien-chen* to the fifth *Ch'u-chia*, and the second being the sixth *Tsai-chia* and the seventh *Chi-chiu*. Taoists in the former group were pure priests, being completely separated from the lay world. Those in the latter group did not lead a normal lay life as do the Taoists in present day Taiwan and Hong Kong, but rather were considered to be students who were seeking the way through such activities which brought them lay benefits such as curing illness, while they lived among the lay people. These Taoists were regarded as lower than those in the former group, although nonetheless as one form of genuine Taoists. It has been said that this type of Taoism was popular in Chiennan 剣南, (the area south of Chien-kê 剣閣, Ssǔ-ch'uan 四川 Province) and Chiang-piao 江表 (the area south of the Yang-tzǔ 揚子 River), which indicates that it was probably Taoism of the *T'ien-shih Tao* type.

SOME RE-EXAMINATION

Having pointed out that during the first half of the T'ang Dynasty Taoists were classified into six or seven categories and that all Taoists were considered to be non-secular priests, I shall now try to examine these points from other perspectives by referring to some curious records and questions.

First, let me begin with an example from a text in which a Taoist refers to himself as a "*ch'u chia*": Pelliot no. 4659 of the Tun-huang manuscripts is a segment of a text with the subtitle, "*T'ai-shang (tung)-hsüan ling-pao tzŭ-jan chih-chen chiu-t'ien shêng-shen chang*" 太上（洞）玄靈宝自然至真九天生神章. This piece is the last part of *Tung-hsüan ling-pao tzŭ-jan chiu-t'ien shêng-shen chang ching* contained in the current version of the *Tao-ts'ang* vol. 165. It is a chapter that makes up the so-called *Ku ling-pao ching*. The curious thing about it is that there appears in the colophon of the Tun-huang manuscripts the sentence, "*ch'u-chia* Taoist priest Wang Fa-ch'ien 王法遷 respectfully finished copying on the third of May in the year of Ping-wu 丙午". As far as I know there is no other example of this among the Taoist texts in Tun-huang manuscripts.

The term "*ch'u-chia*" has two meanings: In the broad sense it means non-secular, *ch'u-chia* in contrast to *tsai-chia* or lay; a man has left his family to seek the way, living away from the lay world; in the narrow sense it means a specific category of Taoists. Since Wang Fa-ch'ien's accomplishments are not known it is unclear just what the text really meant. One possible interpretation, however, is: According to Dr. Ōfuchi [1978: 19] that this version was copied in Tun-huang. The year of Ping-wu is calculated to be the twentieth year of Chen-kuan 貞観 (646). If so, this date was very close to the time when the *San-tung fêng-tao k'ê-chieh ying-shih* was finished, and when the seven fold categorization was done for the first time. In this vein we could interpret the term in the narrow sense, as a category of Taoists. This, of course, is only one possible interpretation, and whether it is correct or not is another matter.

The writing of "*ch'u-chia* Taoist priest" in the colophon is indeed peculiar. The common practice was to write "temple name, name of the priest", also a practice of Buddhist monks. The difference is that Taoists used their lay names before becoming priests.

As mentioned earlier, this is the only extant example to use the term "*ch'u-chia* Taoist priest*". This, however, does indicate that the Taoist thought of himself as a *ch'u-chia* priest. Obviously, further examination is necessary as to the content and the degree of consciousness for being *ch'u-chia* on the priest's part as well as the question of how such a designation differentiated Taoists from Buddhist priests.

In *Fêng-tao k'ê-chieh ying-shih* 奉道科戒営始 (quoted in Ming-k'ai tu 明開度, *I-ch'ieh tao-ching yin-i miao-men yu-ch'i* 一切道経音義妙門由起) there is a list of names of two Taoists in each class along with explanations:

T'ien-chen Taoist priests:	Kao Hsüan	高玄
	Huang Jen	皇人

Shen-hsien Taoist priests:	Tu Ch'ung	杜沖
	Yin Kuei	尹軌
Shan-chü Taoist priests:	Hsü Yu	許由
	Ch'ao Fu	巢父
Ch'u-chia Taoist priests:	Sung Lun	宋倫
	P'êng Ch'en	彭諶
Tsai-chia Taoist priests:	Huang Ch'iung	黃瓊
	Chien K'êng	錢鏗
Chi-chiu Taoist priests:	Li Tung	李東
	Kan Shih	干室

Although the accomplishments of all these twelve Taoists are not known, our purpose here is to examine the difference between the first four and the last two types. For this we will compare Sung Lun, a *ch'u-chia* Taoist; Chien K'êng, a *tsai-chia* Taoist; and Kan Shih, a *chi-chiu* Taoist. We have to keep in mind here that we need to examine them not historically but as individuals who had become idealized.

According to legend, Sung Lun had acquired a technique of apparition; sometimes he lived among the people, and when the mood struck him he cured people's illnesses. However, people did not know who he really was. It would be safe to say he was a *ch'u-chia* priest, keeping quite apart from the human world (*Tao-ts'ang* vols. 140, 605, 639, 698, 992).

Chien K'êng was not always in the human world, and not much of his active engagement with the lay world is reported. He was half-lay, half-immortal. He had designed a health regimen, *yang-shêng chia* 養生家, and had acquired various special techniques for lovemaking or *fang-chung* 房中, breathing, or *fu-ch'i tao-yin* 服気導引 and taking pills, or *fu-shih* 服食. In his answer to a question by a courtesan he clearly distinguishes an immortal, or *shen-hsien*, from one who has attained the way, or *tê-tao chê* 得道者. He himself strove to attain the way and live long *ti-hsien* 地仙. According to the *Fêng-tao K'ê-chieh ying-shih*, a lay Taoist, *tsai-chia* is someone who concentrates his mind on the way but places his body in human society and quietly follows the trend of the world around him, without seeking fame or displaying his wisdom. In this sense K'êng is a most appropriate person to represent this type of Taoist (*Tao-ts'ang* vol. 139; *Shen-hsien chuan* chap. 1).

Kan Shih 干室 always lived in the human world, and his strong relationship with lay people is emphasized. Therefore, he is not given high credit as an immortal, *shen-hsien*, by people in the later period. However, people in Chiang-nan served him as if he had been a god, and Shih cured their illnesses with dispatch, with magic water of *fu-shuei* 符水. This is a good indication of what kind of teaching he employed (*Tao-ts'ang* vols. 143, 700, 994).

When we compare these three biographies, there are common areas but the differences between Sung Lun, Chien K'êng and Kan Shih in regard to whether or not they lived a lay life are considerable. These differences, however, do not contradict too much the description in the *Miao-men yu-ch'i hsü*.

Lastly, if we accept that the Taoists were non-secular, we must re-examine the uninterrupted family line of the T'ien-shih since Chang Ling of the Later Han Dynasty because it is only natural to think that if the family line had not been disrupted then they must have been married. However, this supposition counters the fact that Taoists during T'ang were all *ch'u-chia* priests. Thus we have to examine the way the *T'ien-shih* actually lived during the T'ang.

The earliest existing document which makes full use of the biographies of all the *T'ien-shih* is the *T'i-tao t'ung-chien* 体道通鑑 (*Tao-ts'ang* vols. 139–148) by Chao Tao-i 趙道一 (Yüan). According to Chao's introduction he utilized then existing materials fully and did not construct a biography based on his own opinion. While this attitude as an editor is commendable, it would not be safe to assume that biographies are made up of historical facts alone, and one should expect a considerable number of articles of faith as well.

Although not extant, a text that precedes this and touches upon the T'ien-shih Taoists during the Suei and T'ang Dynasties is the *San-tung ch'ün-hsien lu* (*Tao-ts'ang* vols. 992–995) edited by Ch'en Pao-kuang, a Chêng-i Taoist. (Chêng-i Taoism is the later form of T'ien-shih Taoism.) The introduction to this book, written in the Southern Sung, Shao-hsing 紹興24 (1154, A.D.), describes three T'ien-shih, quoting the *T'ien-shih chuan* 天師伝 and the *T'ien-shih nei-chuan* 天師内伝: the tenth generation Chang Tzŭ-hsiang 張子祥 (Suei); the twelfth generation Chang Chung-ch'ang (Kao-tsung 高宗 period, T'ang: appears as Chang Hêng 張恒 in *Han t'ien-shih shih-chia* 漢天師世家 and the fourteenth generation Chang Tz'ŭ 張慈: appears as Chang Tz'ŭ-chêng 張慈正 in both *T'i-tao t'ung-chien* and *Han t'ien-shih shih-chia*.

As mentioned earlier, this text does not exist today, but it was probably written after the fifteenth generation T'ien-shih Chang Kao 張高, who is said to have been active during Hsüan-tsung's 玄宗 reign (712–756), because there is a passage about the immortalization of the fourteenth T'ien-shih. As far as I know, *T'ien-shih* (*nei-*) *chuan* is only quoted in the *San-tung ch'ün-hsien lu*. It probably was not much popularized. Or it may be that it was intended mostly for internal use, and Ch'en Pao-kuang could get hold of it because he was a Chêng-i priest. It is probably correct, however, to think that it was written when the genealogy of the past T'ien-shih had been organized and made clear. Then again, it may be that it was written out of necessity, because of political and social changes occuring in society. The *T'ien-shih* (*nei-*) *chuan*, only segments of which exist today, is significant since there is very little material on the generations of the T'ien-shih which preceded the *T'i-tao t'ung-chien*. It should also be noted that the descriptions of the T'ien-shih are limited only to those three mentioned above in the *San-tung ch'ün-hsien lu* and that all three are based on the *T'ien-shih* (*nei-*) *chuan*.

There is a statement in the introduction of Sun I-chung's 孫夷中 *San-tung hsiu-tao i* 三洞修道儀 (*Tao-ts'ang* vol. 989) that each one of the ancestors of T'ien-shih, who were the Chang family at Mt. Lung-hu 龍虎山 in Hsin-chou 信州, was recorded and known. Sun I-chung seems to have lived during the Later Chou of the Five Dynasties period, when there was a family on Mt. Lung-hu who claimed to be descended from Chang Ling. In this connection we should turn our attention to the biography of Chang Hsiu 張修 (*Tao-ts'ang* vol. 142) which cites *Ling-yen chi* 靈驗記. In this is a description of Liu Ch'ien 劉遷, a wealthy merchant in Chiang-hsi 江西, who was given *Tu-kung fa-lu* 都功法籙 by the nineteenth T'ien-shih: after his death he revived and entered Mt. Lung-hu to respect and serve the T'ien-shih as his teacher. Whether this story is true or not is unimportant here. But that T'ien-shih is enumerated up to the nineteenth generation, although his name is not mentioned, and that the T'ien-shih based himself in Mt. Lung-hu are of extreme importance to us for the following reason: although there are descriptions about a T'ien-shih's entering Mt. Lung-hu in the previously mentioned sources, we should not believe these descriptions without careful examination because they were all compiled in later periods. But it is also incorrect to assume that older materials have more truth in them. What we have to do is try to look for the oldest possible materials, with which we should compare the materials from later periods for the purpose of verification. It is in this connection that the *Ling-yen chi* is very important. The *Ling-yen chi* corresponds to twenty chapters of the *Tao-chiao ling-yen chi* 道教靈驗記 written by Tu Kuang-t'ing 杜光庭 which is recorded in *Sung-shih* 宋史, chapter 205, "I-wen chih 芸文志". It is also included in the current version of the *Tao-ts'ang* (vols. 325–326) in chapter 11 in which the above story is recorded in full. Tu Kuang-t'ing, the author of the *Ling-yen chi*, lived from Ta-chung 大中 4 of Hsüan-tsung 宣宗 of T'ang (850) to Ch'ang-hsing 長興 4 of Chuang-tsung 莊宗 of the Later T'ang (933), according to chapter 40 of the *T'i-tao t'ung-chien*, that is, he lived during the end of T'ang into Five Dynasties. We do have to acknowledge that by that time the T'ien-shih was already based in Mt. Lung-hu, and that the genealogy of the past T'ien-shih was fairly well organized. However, we cannot find any materials about the T'ien-shih older than this one.

There is no trustworthy description of the T'ien-shih during the T'ang Dynasty either in the general sources, representative of which is *Chêng-shih* 正史, or in Taoist sources. Even the description in *T'i-tao t'ung-chien* is very brief. This leads us to suppose that even in the Yüan Dynasty the materials were scarce. This is probably because, we may conjecture, the T'ien-shih during the T'ang did not have much power, let alone the power to unify the *T'ien-shih Tao* sects all over China, and was merely a local power among many. There remain many unanswered questions: Was it because it was so small the government allowed them to continue the family line as an exception because it had continued so long? Did they become powerful when government control weakened during the second half of the Dynasty? Furthermore, what was the relationship with Chang Ling? In the remainder of this section I will describe a T'ang Dynasty T'ien-shih that appears in the *T'i-tao t'ung-chien*.

The position of T'ien-shih was handed down basically by primogeniture. The first sons did not always get special education from birth and continue their life-long training to immortalization at Mt. Lung-hu. Sometimes the son entered the Mountain (to become a priest) at the mid-point of his life. For example, the eighteenth T'ien-shih, Tzŭ-yüan 子元, is recorded to have studied the Tao 道 for the first time in his forties; the twentieth T'ien-shih, Ch'en 諶 is said to have liked the

Tao and avoided eating grains.   Often in old age when they entered the Mountains
some took their wives with them and some did not.   All in all, the image of the T'ien-
shih, though it may be vague because of lack of information, cannot be turned into
that of individuals practicing strict asceticism.

CONCLUSION

Although our attempt to acquire detailed information about Chang T'ien-shih
張天師 during the T'ang Dynasty may not have been too successful, we did learn
with confidence that as a basic rule Taoists were supposed to become priests during
this period.   In concluding, I would like to fill in a few points that I have not yet
discussed.

First, why did all the Taoists have to become priests (*ch'u-chia*)?   At present,
there is no material that would indicate any internal reasons within the Taoist sects,
which makes me suspect that there were outside reasons.   It may be possible to
ascribe it to the intervention of the state with the organization of Taoist sects.   The
relationship between the Taoist sects and the government has been touched upon
in well-researched studies written from the Buddhist point of view.   Therefore,
I shall attempt a brief discussion based on such previous studies.

Throughout the T'ang Dynasty Buddhism and Taoism were both generally
respected.   One could say that Taoism had practically achieved the position of a
national religion in those times when the political climate favored using religion for
the enhancement of the imperial position and state unification, which, conversely,
meant that when a religious sect became a hindrance to the state it was suppressed.
Taoist sects as well as Buddhist sects grew steadily from the Six Dynasties on despite
many such suppressions.   However, this brought about the inevitable deterioration
of the quality of Taoist practitioners.   A fair number of them became Taoists simply
because they had the advantage of tax exemption.   This sometimes led to the issuing
of certificates of ordination (tu-tieh 度牒) by the government to questionable Taoist
"priests".   For example, in as early as May of the ninth year of Wu-tê 武德 (626)
Kao-tsu 高祖 issued an edict to discern who were worthy Buddhist monks and
Taoists for the reason that many of the Buddhist and Taoist temples in the capital
were considered impure. The government thereby allowed for three Buddhist and
two Taoist temples in the capital and one each in other prefectures to be established
by the state, where only those who studied seriously and observed the rules could
live.   They were to be fed and clothed by the government, in addition to which they
were to receive treatment comparable to state employees. If anyone violated the rules
he risked losing his status as a priest and being sent to his home town. This
edict, however, was never carried out because Kao-tsu resigned (626) after the up-
heaval at Hsüan-wu men 玄武門.   The T'ang policy toward religions was continued
with little change thereafter. As far as this edict was concerned, it did not specify
the necessity for Taoists to become priests. However, it is possible to interpret
the equal treatment given to Taoist as well as Buddhist priests and nuns, with violators

being sent home, as meaning that they would be returned to the lay life. Judging from the spirit of this edict, it is not unlikely that Taoists were also required to become priests (ch'u-chia). Furthermore, it may not be too wrong to see that there were advantages to be gained when Taoists chose to become priests.

Even though one assumes that direct state intervention in religion caused all the Taoists to become priests, it still remains as only an outer factor. It is necessary first to examine those developments within Taoism that made it feasible for the government to treat Taoists as basically the same in nature as Buddhist priests, and a Taoist sect as similar to a Buddhist sect. As I have said, some Taoists in the fifth century were practically leading a separate priestly (ch'u-chia) life. It was also mentioned that toward the end of the sixth century, such Taoist priests were more in evidence. It is easily imagined that Taoists became priests because they were influenced by the practices of hermits and Buddhist monks. It is generally said that Ling-pao Chiao 霊宝教 and Shang-ch'ing Chiao 上清教 are strongly influenced by Buddhism. However, when compared with Taoism during the T'ang, Taoism during the Northern and Southern Dynasties shows much less such influence. This makes it necessary for us to look at, albeit schematically, the Taoist idea of leaving the lay life (ch'u-chia) during the period from the last half of the Northern and Southern Dynasties to the Suei Dynasty. Unfortunately, however, we are not fully prepared to discuss this in detail except to offer a very interesting reference: ten volumes of the T'ai-hsüan chen-i pen-chi ching 太玄真一本際経 according to the second chapter of Hsüan I's 玄嶷 (T'ang) Chen-chêng luen 甄正論 recorded in Taishō Daizōkyō 大正大蔵経 vol. 52. The first five chapters were written by Liu Chin-hsi 劉進喜 of Suei, and the other five were added by Li Chung-ch'ing 李仲卿. At this point the two parts cannot be discerned clearly, but chapter two, Fu-chu p'in 付嘱品 (Tao-ts'ang vol. 758), for now is assumed to belong to the first group. In this chapter one finds two further meanings given to "chia 家" or house: one is "love of the family", and the other is "all existence". Furthermore, leaving love of parents and wives and children to strive to study is considered as elementary ch'u-chia, and leaving all existence is considered as ultimate ch'u-chia. This is clearly a Buddhistic influence, from which we can infer that they attempted a rather theoretical study of ch'u-chia. This helps us to infer that by the Suei, ch'u-chia was an expected course of behavior in certain sects and met very little resistance.

Finally, I will point out the differences between the Buddhist monks and Taoist priests to whom the term ch'u-chia was equally applied. The first difference was that Taoists did not shave their heads. Despite the strong similarity, which sometimes elicits such remarks as that Taoists imitate Buddhists in many respects, Taoists kept their hair. Shaving of the head was one of the central issues in the debates between Confucianism and Buddhism because it violated the teaching the Classic of Filial Piety, Hsiao ching 孝経, the most respected classic: "One's body, hair and skin are given by your parents. It is the first step to filial piety not to damage these." Although it is possible to think that this teaching of filial piety was powerful enough for the Taoists to keep their hair, a more direct reason would be a Taoist teaching that says that a spirit resides in every part of one's body. For example, in "Shen-shen p'in 身神品" Chapter 5 of *Wu-shang pi-yao* 無上秘要 (*Tao-ts'ang* vol. 768), cited in *Tung-chen tsao-hsing tzŭ-yüan êrh-shih-ssŭ-shen ching* 洞真造形紫元二十四神経, there is a sentence, "the spirit of hair, its name is Hsüan wen-hua 玄文華., its style-name is Tao-hsing 道行". This scripture is contained in *Tao-ts'ang* (vol. 1064) as *T'ai-wei ti-chün êrh-shih-ssŭ-shen huei-yüan ching* 太微帝君二十四神回元経 and was compiled by the end of the Six Dynasties. Thus it is probably more likely that the direct reason for Taoist priests to maintain their hair was that there is a spirit in the hair.

The second difference is a question of surnames. Until Tao-an's 道安 (314–385) time in the Former Ch'in Dynasty Buddhist monks carried over their teachers' surnames like An 安, K'ang 康, Po 帛, Chu 竺, etc. Tao-an declared that priests should use Shih as their surname, since monks were those who believed the teachings of Śākya-muni-buddha 釈迦牟尼仏. He subscquently called himself Shih Tao-an 釈道安. From this precedent Buddhist monks generally have followed this practice. On the contrary Taoists, with some exceptions, continued to use their lay surnames even after becoming priests. Also we should note that when the Taoists prayed they used *ch'en* 臣 vis-à-vis the immortals. All Taoist spirits in heaven possess different surnames, and their status and official rank are clearly distinguishable. The world of spirits is a reflected image of the real world.

Another possible reason for this distinction in names may be because there was no specific founder recognized in Taoism as was true for Buddhism. However, a more realistic reason may be that Taoism, unlike Buddhism, was indigenous to Chinese culture and therefore could not completely separate itself from a Chinese way of thought. Taoists could not leave "chia" completely in the spiritual sense though they could become "ch'u-chia".

In the foregoing I have presented and attempted to present evidence for a shift from the presence of both *tsai-chia* and *ch'u-chia* during the Northern and Southern Dynasties to the dominance of *ch'u-chia* during T'ang.. Obviously I could not exhaust all the issues in this matter, especially the point which was raised by Lewis Lancaster, that is, that it is necessary to examine the relationships between Taoism and the wide spread of the *Wei-mo ching* 維摩経 and the popularity of Buddhism among the devotees of (chü-shih 居士 Buddhism). I shall have to save this consideration, along with many other issues, for future work.

BIBLIOGRAPHY

Ch'en, Kuo-fu
    1963   Tao-hsüeh chuan chi-i. *Tao-ts'ang yüan-liu k'ao, Appendix 7*, Peking: Zhonghua
           Shungju, pp. 454–504. (Collected Documents of Tao-hsüeh chuan chi-i. *Origin
           and Development of Tao-ts'ang, Appendix 7.*)
Ōfuchi, Ninji
    1978   *Tonkō Dōkyō Mokuroku-hen.* Tokyo: Fukutake Shoten. (*Catalogue of the Taoist
           Scriptures at Tun-huang.*)

1980 Hong Kong no Dōkyō Girei. *Oriental Studies: Essays and Studies Presented to Dr. Ikeda Suetoshi in Honor of His Seventieth Birthday*, Tokyo: Ikeda Suetoshi Koki Kinen Jigyōkai, pp. 753–769. (Taoist Rituals in Hong Kong.)

OZAKI, Masaharu
1979 Kō kenshi no shinsen shisō. *Tōhō Shūkyō* 54: 52–69. (Kʻou Chʻien-chih's Idea About Hermits.)

YANG, Lien-sheng
1956 Collation and Annotation of the Taoist Text Entitled Lao-chün yin-sung chieh-ching. *Bulletin of the Institute of History and Philology, Academia Sinica* 28: 17–54.

YOSHIOKA, Yoshitoyo
1975 *Dōkyō no Jittai*. Kyoto: Hōyū Shoten. (*Actual State of Taoism.*)

Chapter 7

On Neo-Confucianism and Human Relatedness

The primary purpose of Neo-Confucian learning is "for the sake of one's self" (*wei-chi* 為己).[1] One learns to be human not to please others or to conform to an external standard of conduct. Indeed, "learning to be human" (*hsüeh tso-jen* 學作人) is a spontaneous, autonomous, fully conscious and totally committed intentional act; an act of self-realization. It gives its own direction, generates its own form and creates its own content. Virtually all root precepts in Neo-Confucian thought, both in the Ch'eng-Chu 程朱 and the Lu-Wang 陸王 traditions, take self-realization as a background assumption. Ch'eng I's 程頤 "Self-cultivation requires reverence; the pursuit of learning depends on the extension of knowledge"[2]; Chu Hsi's 朱熹 "dwelling in reverence and fathoming principle"[3]; Lu Hsiang-shan's 陸象山 "establishing first that which is great in us"[4]; Wang Yang-ming's 王陽明 "full realization of one's primordial awareness"[5]; and Liu Tsung-chou's 劉宗周 "effort of vigilant solitariness"[6] are paradigmatic examples. Yet, even though Neo-Confucianism

---

1) The idea occurs in the *Analects* (14:25) and is accepted as an underlying assumption by virtually all schools of Neo-Confucian thought beginning in the 11th century.

2) This phrase, *"han-yang hsü-yung ching ching-hsüeh tsai chih-chih,"* 涵養須用敬進學在致知 is characteristic of the Ch'eng-Chu approach to moral self-cultivation. See Wing-tsit Chan, *A Source Book in Chinese Philosophy* (Princeton: Princeton University Press, 1963), p.562.

3) The idea of *"chü-ching ch'iung-li"* 居敬窮理 can be taken as Chu Hsi's interpretation of Ch'eng I's method of education. Wing-tsit Chan notes: "Like Ch'eng I, Chu Hsi struck the balance between seriousness and the investigation of things in moral education. He said that seriousness is the one important word transmitted in the Confucian School, that it is the foundation in Ch'eng I's teachings, and that it is Ch'eng's greatest contribution to later students." See Chan, *A Source Book*, p. 607. It should be noted that the word *"ching"* is rendered as "reverence" or "respectfulness" in this essay, whereas Chan has chosen "seriousness" to convey its many-sided meanings.

4) It is commonly known that Lu Hsiang-shan builds his moral philosophy on the Mencian idea, *"hsien li-hu ch'i ta-che,"* 先立乎其大者 *Mencius*, 6A : 15.

5) *"Chih liang-chih"* 致良知 has been variously rendered as "extension of innate knowledge," "extension of conscientious consciousness," "extension of knowledge of the good," and "extension of intuitive knowledge." In this essay, *liang-chih* 良知 is rendered as "primordial awareness" and *chih* 致 as "full realization." See *Mencius*, 7A : 15.

6) Liu Tsung-chou's teaching of *shen-tu* 慎獨 is based on the *Great Learning* and the *Doctrine of the Mean*.

asserts that the center of creativity in the ethicoreligious realm is human subjectivity, it is neither subjectivistic nor individualistic.

For one thing, the self in Neo-Confucian thought, instead of being the private possession of an isolated individuality, is an open system. It is a dynamic center of organismic relationships and a concrete personal path to the human community as a whole. This essay intends to explore the ethicoreligious significance of this insight by addressing some of the perennial issues of religion and family from the perspective of Neo-Confucian philosophical anthropology.

A defining characteristic of Neo-Confucian thought is its re-enactment of the classical Mencian learning of the mind as a ceaseless process of deepening and broadening self-knowledge. This involves an ontological justification for the enterprise of personal cultivation and an existential description of how to pursue it. In Neo-Confucian terminology, learning for the sake of one's self involves two inseparable dimensions: "original substance" (*pen-t'i* 本體) and "moral effort" (*kung-fu* 工夫). On the level of original substance, the justification for learning of the mind is predicated on the Neo-Confucian perception of humanity as "sensitivity."[7] Human beings, like any other modalities of being in the cosmos, are endowed with the reality known as the "principle" (*li* 理). Human beings are thus an integral part of the "chain of being," encompassing Heaven, Earth and the myriad things. However, the uniqueness of being human is the intrinsic capacity of the mind to "embody" (*t'i* 體) the cosmos in its conscience and consciousness; through this embodying, the mind realizes its own sensitivity, manifests true humanity and assists in the cosmic transformation of Heaven and Earth.[8]

Far from being an unbridled romantic assertion about the unity of all things, this Neo-Confucian commitment to the unlimited sensitivity of the mind is a deliberate attempt to accord human nature a kind of godlike creativity. In theological terms, although Neo-Confucians do not believe in the transcendent personal God which is sometimes characterized as the "wholly other," they have faith in the ultimate goodness and all-embracing divinity of human nature, which is decreed by Heaven to be fully realized through the conscious and conscientious activity of the mind. An obvious background assumption here is what may be called the idea of the "continuity of being" [FANG 1981: 446-469]. The reality of Heaven so conceived is by no means radically alien and therefore incomprehensible to human rationality. Rather, it is in principle accessible to the willing, feeling and knowing functions of the mind. The mind may never understand the subtlety of the workings of Heaven through its intellectual faculty alone, but the nourished and cultivated mind, like the attuned ear, can perceive even the most incipient manifestations of the voice of God. Of course, Neo-Confucianism, being significantly different from any style of theologi-

---

7) See Ch'eng Hao's essay, "Understanding Humanity" ("Shih-jen" 識仁), in *Erh-Ch'eng i-shu* 二程遺書, 2A : 3a-b.

8) This is based on the anthropocosmic vision in the *Doctrine of the Mean*, chap. 22. See Tu, 1976, Chapter IV.

zing, depicts the course of Heaven as devoid of sound and fragrance.[9] Furthermore, following the Mencian tradition, it insists that Heaven sees as the people see and Heaven hears as the people hear.[10] This mutuality of Heaven and Man defines Neo-Confucian religiosity.

Wilfred Cantwell Smith [1964], in his seminal study on the meaning and end of religion, makes a helpful distinction between "a religion" as an institution characterized by a set of objectifiable dogmas and "being religious" as spiritual self-identification of the living members of a faith community. Accordingly, the problem of whether Neo-Confucianism is a religion should not be confused with the more significant question: what does it mean to be religious in the Neo-Confucian community? The solution to the former often depends on the particular interpretive position we choose to take on what constitutes the paradigmatic example of a religion, which may have little to do with our knowledge about Neo-Confucianism as a spiritual tradition; the question of being religious is crucial for our appreciation of the "inner dimension" of the Neo-Confucian project. For the sake of expediency, being religious in the Neo-Confucian sense can be understood as being engaged in *ultimate self-transformation as a communal act* [Tu 1979a]. Since the self, as already mentioned, is an open system, this process entails a continuous enlargement of the self.

We can perhaps envision the enlargement of the self diagrammatically as a series of constantly expanding concentric circles which symbolize the unplumbed sensitivity of the mind to embrace Heaven, Earth and the myriad things. To enlarge oneself is therefore to purify, enlighten and bring to fruition the ultimate capacity of the mind to "embody" the cosmos. The self so conceived is not a static structure but a dynamic process. It is a *center* of relationships, not an enclosed world of private thoughts and feelings. It needs to reach out, to be in touch with other selves and to communicate through an ever-expanding network of human-relatedness. Yet, even though the Neo-Confucian self can be understood very well in terms of social roles, it is primarily an ethicoreligious idea with far-reaching cosmological and ontological implications.

The concrete path to actualizing human nature through the learning of the mind involves a dynamic interplay between contextualization and decontextualization. This unique feature of Neo-Confucian ethics and religiosity can be characterized as a dialectic of structural limitation and procedural freedom which emerges at each stage of self-cultivation. The necessity of recognizing the interrelated conditions, the context, in which the self as a center of relationships initiates its own realization, is based on the aforementioned "continuity of being." Self-transformation is by definition not simply a departure from but is also a return to one's "locale." It is not a quest for pure spirituality nor is it a liberation from the flesh, the mundane or

---

9) This is also based on the *Doctrine of the Mean*, chap. 33. However, the idea originally came from the *Book of Poetry*, no. 235.

10) *Mencius*, 5A : 5. It should be noted that this "democratic" or "populist" idea is found in the *Book of History*. See James Legge, trans., *The Shoo King* in the *Chinese Classics*, vol. 3 (Oxford: Clarendon Press, 1865), p. 292.

the profane. The dichotomy of secular and sacred, or for that matter of body and mind, is rejected as heuristically misleading. The real task, perceived by the Neo-Confucians, is to manifest the ultimate meaning of life in ordinary human existence [Tu 1979b].

The Neo-Confucian universe is certainly not without locale and date. Time and space experienced by the "self in transformation"[11] provide an inalienable context— thus the centrality of primordial ties in Neo-Confucian self-definition. Surely, the sense of being situated in a definite place at a particular moment involves more than the awareness of one's physical presence. The human mind may resemble a *tabula rasa,* but a person is always born to a complex social network. The self, not as an abstract concept but as a lived reality, must be aware of the others around it as integral parts of its own existence. The situatedness of the self requires not only a passive acceptance but also an active recognition. Once the fact of human relatedness is recognized, one can begin to assume personal responsibility for one's social role. The structural limitation that we are inevitably contextualized need not be perceived mainly as an external imposition on our freedom of choice; it also provides us with the nourishment for survival, the environment for growth and the symbolic resources for creativity.

In a deeper sense, however, the meaning of the self in Neo-Confucian thought cannot be determined by the social roles that contextualize it. At any particular juncture of development, no matter how coercive one's structural limitation is or is perceived to be, there is always an authentic possibility for transcending it and overcoming its negative influence. The self is situated, but neither enclosed nor enslaved, in its sociality. The texture of the dyadic relationships that define its social roles is never fixed. It has to be constantly interwoven with the changing configuration of disappearing and emerging threads which the self encounters in its life situations. To be sure, there are underlying permanent webs, such as the father-son relationship, that must endure all contingencies. Even there, however, the self is by no means fixed because as it shapes other relationships, it is also being shaped by them. The interaction of a variety of dyadic relationships generates the dynamism for personal integration earlier referred to as procedural freedom.

To pursue this further, the enlargement of the self, with its eventual union with Heaven as the most generalized universality, travels the concrete path of forming communions with a series of expanded social groups. The *locus classicus* for this ethicoreligious insight is the *Great Learning*:

> When the personal life (*shen* 身) is cultivated, the family (*chia* 家) will be regulated; when the family is regulated, the state (*kuo* 國) will be in order; and when the state is in order, there will be peace throughout the world (*t'ien-hsia* 天下).[12]

11) An expression borrowed from the title of Herbert Fingarette's thought-provoking book, *The Self in Transformation: Psychoanalysis, Philosophy and the Life of the Spirit* (New York: Basic Books, 1963).

12) *Great Learning,* chap. 1.

The Neo-Confucian reading of the text, true to the spirit of learning for the sake of self-realization, puts great emphasis on the issues directly relevant to the cultivation of one's personal life. Thus, much hermeneutic effort is focused on the "inner dimension" of the enlargement of the self. This consists of "investigation of things" (*ko-wu* 格物), "extension of knowledge" (*chih-chih* 致知), "sincerity of the will" (*ch'eng-i* 誠意) and "rectification of the mind" (*cheng-hsin* 正心).[13] A kind of archaeological digging, with the expressed purpose of acquiring a deep understanding of the self, is featured prominently in the writings of virtually all major Neo-Confucian thinkers.

The Neo-Confucian faith in the perfectibility of the self is extended to the family, the state and the world. Cultivation of the self as the "root" (*pen* 本) conveys not only personal but also social, political and religious import. The corollary to this belief in the great transformative potential of the self is an awareness of the necessary form for its manifestation. Implicit in the statement that "when the personal life is cultivated, the family will be regulated" is an assertion that, so long as the family is not yet regulated, the cultivation of the personal life must be continued. By analogy, if the body politic is not yet in order or if peace has not yet pervaded all under Heaven, the effort of self-cultivation should not be interrupted. Learning (*hsüeh* 學), in the Neo-Confucian sense, requires an ultimate and a continuous commitment.

Writers like Robert N. Bellah have argued that Neo-Confucian religiosity is limited by the lack of transcendent leverage in Confucian symbolism. As a result, "there is no basis for a structurally independent religious community" [BELLAH 1976: 91]. Since there is little in the Confucian position which justifies going beyond socially sanctioned norms, the authentic possibility for creative social innovation is often "precluded by the absence of a point of transcendent loyalty that (can) provide legitimation for it" [BELLAH 1976: 95].

Recent scholarship has significantly revised this broadly conceived Weberian interpretation of Confucian ethics. Thomas Metzger, for example, argues with energy that there is indeed a functional equivalent of the Puritan ethic in Neo-Confucianism [METZGER 1977: 29–47, 198–204]. Max Weber's claim that the spiritual orientation of Confucianism is adjustment to the world, rather than mastery over the world, is no longer tenable. Nor is his overall assessment of the Confucian life-orientation:

> A well-adjusted man, rationalizing his conduct only to the degree requisite for adjustment, does not constitute a systematic unity but rather a complex of useful and particular traits... Such a way of life could not allow man an inward aspiration toward a "unified personality," a striving which we associate with the idea of personality. Life remained a series of occurrences. [WEBER, 1964: 235].

However, even though Weber was misinformed when he insisted that in the Confucian ethic "there was no leverage for influencing conduct through inner forces freed

---

13) *Ibid.*

of tradition and convention" [WEBER 1964: 236], his basic thesis still merits our attention, namely that by harmonizing the conflict between self and society, Confucian ethics lacks:

> any tension between nature and deity, between ethical demand and human shortcoming, consciousness of sin and need for salvation, conduct on earth and compensation in the beyond, religious duty and socio-political reality [WEBER 1964: 235–236].

Whether or not the Neo-Confucian masters themselves managed to overcome the conflict between their commitment to moralizing politics through spiritual self-transformation and the autocratic demand for loyal participation in the political order, it was not conceivable to them, as it was taken for granted in Christianity, that "every particular pattern of social relations was in principle deprived of ultimacy" [BELLAH 1976: 95]. And, historically, it is undeniable that under the influence of highly politicized Confucian symbolism, "filial piety and loyalty became absolutes" [BELLAH 1976: 95]. The inability of even the most brilliant minds in Confucian China to develop a soteriology beyond politics clearly indicates that the idea of transcendence, as radical otherness, was not even conceived as a rejected possibility in Neo-Confucian thought.

To criticize Neo-Confucian symbolism for lack of transcendent leverage is to impose a Christian and, therefore, alien perspective. It would be indeed difficult for modern Confucians to appreciate fully the idea of the "wholly other," the sentiment of absolute dependency, or the justification for total faith in an unknowable God. However, within the symbolic resources of the Neo-Confucian tradition, the authentic possibility exists for developing a transcendent leverage which can serve as the ultimate basis for an intellectual community, or the community of like-minded followers of the Way, structurally independent of the political order and functionally inseparable from the lived realities of society and politics. Despite the difficulty of conceptualizing transcendence as radical otherness, the Confucian commitment to ultimate self-transformation necessarily involves a transcendent dimension. The idea of going beyond the usual limits of one's existential self so that one can become true to one's Heavenly endowed nature entails the transformative act of continuously excelling and surpassing one's experience here and now. This transformative act is predicated on a transcendent vision that ontologically we are infinitely better and therefore more worthy than we actually are. In the ultimate sense we, as persons, form a trinity with Heaven and Earth. From this transcending perspective, it is not at all inconceivable that every particular pattern of social relations is only instrumentally important and is therefore deprived of ultimacy.

We can perhaps restate Neo-Confucian religiosity in terms of a twofold process: a continuous deepening of one's subjectivity and an uninterrupted broadening of one's sensitivity. Ultimate self-transformation as a communal act, in this connection, entails a series of paradoxes. The cultivation of the self assumes the form of mastering the self; for the self to realize its original nature, it must transform its self-centered structure. Accordingly, to deepen one's subjectivity requires an unceasing struggle to eliminate selfish and egoistic desires. By inference, just as the cultivation of the personal life impels us to go beyond egoism, regulation of the family, governing the state and bringing peace throughout the world impel us to transcend nepotism, racism and chauvinism. The Neo-Confucians may not have been as sensitive to the bigotry of these limited and limiting collective consciousnesses as we are in our pluralistic global village. Yet, it is vitally important to note that, in their perception, broadened sensitivity should also enable one to rise above anthropocentrism. To them, the real meaning of being human lies in the mutuality of Heaven and Man and the unity of all things.

From this anthropocosmic perspective, the Neo-Confucian idea of the family is laden with ethicoreligious as well as social and political implications. Chang Tsai's 張載 (1020–1077) *Western Inscription*, which Wing-tsit Chan 陳榮捷 describes as "the basis of Neo-Confucian ethics," speaks directly to this:

> Heaven is my father and Earth is my mother, and even such a small creature as I finds an intimate place in their midst.
> Therefore that which fills the universe I regard as my body and that which directs the universe I consider as my nature.
> All people are my brothers and sisters, and all things are my companions [CHAN 1963: 497].

The family and, by extension, the state and the world are integral parts of the "fiduciary community" where organismic connections unite all modalities of being in a common bond. A natural application of this anthropocosmic vision to human society is to recognize:

> Even those who are tired, infirm, crippled, or sick: those who have no brothers or children, wives or husbands, are all my brothers who are in distress and have no one to turn to [CHAN 1963: 497].

However, as Chu Hsi (1130–1200) points out, the underlying assumption in Chang Tsai's all-embracing humanity is not undifferentiated "universal love," but the Neo-Confucian thesis: "unity of principle and diversity of its particularizations" (*li-i fen-shu* 理一分殊) [CHAN 1963: 550].[14] Without going into the technical issues, this thesis means that, from the perspective of the "original substance," organismic unity pervades everything. There is absolute equality among things, and the mind's sensitivity can and should embody all of them without discrimination. From the functional viewpoint, on the other hand, the exertion of "moral effort" necessitates a concrete analysis of a given situation. As a result, the diversity in which the

---

14) This phrase is often rendered as "principle is one and its manifestations are many." In this essay, I follow Wm. T. de Bary's translation. See de Bary, *Neo-Confucian Orthodoxy and the Learning of the Mind-and-Heart* (New York: Columbia University Press, 1981), p. 144.

principle is particularized becomes the central concern. Since it is thought to be humanly impossible for one to care for a stranger in the same degree and to the same extent one cares for one's closest kin, a proper way to express one's sensitivity requires a differentiated manifestation.

The "five human relations" (wu-lun 五倫), understood in this light, point to five structurally and functionally distinct dyadic relationships.[15]   A sense of priority or an order of hierarchy can be assigned to the five relations.   The prominence of the father-son dyad seems indicative of a prioritied or hierarchical pattern which underlies all the relationships.   It is misleading, however, to suggest that the father-son dyad provides a model for the other four.   Rather, each has a uniqueness which cannot be reduced to or subsumed under any other.   A common mistake in interpreting traditional Chinese political culture, presumably under the influence of Neo-Confucianism, is to assume that the ruler-minister relationship is modeled on that of the father-son. The father-son or, generally speaking, the parent-child relationship is a primordial tie, absolutely binding and inescapably given.   While one cannot choose one's parents, the freedom not to enter a ruler-minister relationship and the choice to sever a political obligation is always available.   Thus, the guiding principle between father and son is "affinity" (ch'in 親), whereas the governing virtue between ruler and minister is "righteousness" (i 義).   It may be more appropriate to understand the ruler-minister in terms of the father-son and the friend-friend relationships combined.

Another common mistake in analyzing the five relations is to exaggerate the importance of asymmetry in all the dyads.   This gives rise to the general impression that the "three bonds" (san-kang 三綱),[16] emphasizing the one-dimensional dependency of the minister to the ruler, the son to the father and the wife to the husband, are defining characteristics of Neo-Confucian ethics.   Historically, Neo-Confucianism as a political ideology may have contributed to despotic, gerontocratic and male-oriented practices in premodern Chinese society; however, the value that underlies the five relations is not dependency but "reciprocity" (pao 報) [YANG 1957].   The filiality of the son is reciprocated by the compassion of the father, the obedience of the minister reciprocated by the fair-mindedness of the ruler and so forth. Friendship, in this connection, is a reciprocal relation par excellence.   It is mutuality rather than dependency that defines "trust" (hsin 信) between friends.

---

15)   The locus classicus for this is again Mencius: "According to the way of man, if they are well fed, warmly clothed, and comfortably lodged but without education, they will become almost like animals.   The sage (emperor Shun) worried about it and he appointed Hsieh 契 to be minister of education and teach people human relations, that between father and son, there should be affection; between ruler and minister, there should be righteousness; between husband and wife, there should be attention to their separate functions; between old and young, there should be a proper order; and between friends, there should be faithfulness." (3A : 4).   See A Source Book, pp. 69–70.

16)   The "three bonds" are those binding the ruler with the minister, the father with the son, and the husband with the wife.   The Han 漢 philosopher, Tung Chung-shu 董仲舒 (c. 179-c. 104 B.C.) discusses these relations in terms of moral education.   The idea of one-dimensional dependency is a highly politicized interpretation of the whole matter; A Source Book, pp. 277–278.

The fiduciary community which friends enter into is not a "trust" created to achieve a narrowly defined economic or social goal. The modern idea of a religious fellowship, rather than a professional association or an academic society, comes close to the Neo-Confucian "way of the friend" (*yu-tao* 友道), which is intimately connected with the "way of the teacher" (*shih-tao* 師道). Friendship as well as the teacher-student relationship is for the sake of communal self-transformation. Its purpose is moral education:

> Master Lien-hsi 濂溪 (Chou Tun-i 周敦頤, 1017–1073) said: Righteousness, uprightness, decisiveness, strictness, and firmness of action are examples of strength that is good, and fierceness, narrow-mindedness, and violence are examples of strength that is evil. Kindness, mildness, and humility are examples of weakness that is good, and softness, indecision, and perverseness are examples of weakness that is evil. Only the Mean brings harmony. The Mean is the principle of regularity, the universally recognized law of morality, and is that to which the sage is devoted. Therefore the sage institutes education so as to enable people to transform their evil by themselves, to arrive at the Mean and to rest there [CHAN 1967: 260].

This idea of moral education "for the sake of one's self" is also featured prominently in the relationship between brothers. Application of the principle of reciprocity in pursuit of self-knowledge involves altruism as well as fairness. The pervading spirit is empathetic understanding of the other which implies considerateness and forgivingness (*shu* 恕).[17] The idea of vengeance is diametrically opposed to the Neo-Confucian value of reciprocity. To the question: "Suppose the older brother is respectful toward his younger brother but the younger brother is not reverent toward the older brother. Should the older brother imitate his brother's lack of reverence and stop being respectful?" Chu Hsi emphatically stated, "The older brother should be respectful to the highest degree." This behavior, he insisted, is the true meaning of the verse in the *Book of Odes*: "Brothers should be good to each other but should not imitate each other" [CHAN 1967: 181–182].

It would be misleading to suppose that self-sacrifice or a simple psychology of detachment is the message here. A fiduciary community means that the moral well-being of each member is the personal concern of all. In a specific dyadic relationship where an obvious asymmetry occurs, as with the younger brother's lack of reverence, conscious effort is required of the righteous (the older brother) for his own self-cultivation to help the other (the younger brother) to resume his course of moral learning. The *locus classicus* for this is the Confucian *Analects*: "In order to establish oneself, one helps others to establish themselves; in order to enlarge oneself, one helps others to enlarge themselves."[18] Therefore, in the light of self-education, the reciprocal relationship is always a two-way communication. The ruler, the parent,

---

17) *Analects*, 4 :x5 reads: "The Way of our Master is none other than conscientiousness (*chung* 忠) and altruism (*shu* 恕)." See *A Source Book*, p. 27.

18) *Analects*, 6 : 28.

the teacher, the senior friend and the older brother are as much involved in making themselves obedient, faithful and dedicated to the shared values of the community as are the minister, the child, the student, the junior friend and the younger brother.

It is conceivable that occasionally one may have to find a way to help one's parent and, by implication, one's teacher (not to mention one's ruler, who often falls short of a minimum standard of rulership) to behave properly. The necessity and desirability of doing so are taken for granted, but the actual style adopted to bring about the necessary and desirable result requires careful deliberation and, of course, finesse. Commenting on the line from the *Book of Change*: "In dealing with troubles caused by one's mother, one should not be too firm," Ch'eng I (1033–1107) said:

> In dealing with his mother, the son should help her with mildness and gentleness so she will be in accord with righteousness. If he disobeys her and the matter fails, it will be his fault. Is there not a way to obey with ease? If one goes forward with his strength and abruptly resists or defies her, the kindness and love between mother and son will be hurt. That will be great harm indeed. How can he get into her heart and change her? The way lies in going backward, bending his will to obey, and following his mother so that her personal life will be correct and matters well managed. The way for strong ministers to serve weak rulers is similar to this [CHAN 1967: 171–172].

This concern for the irreparable damage to the amiable relationship between mother and son caused by the son's blunt confrontation in order to right the wrongs of the mother is a concern for the moral wellbeing of the mother as well as the harmony of the family. Voluntary change of attitude is preferred; an arbitrary imposition of an external standard, despite its possible heuristic value for self-discipline, can never bring about genuine self-transformation. Thus,

> In teaching people, Confucius "would not enlighten those who are not eager to learn, nor arouse those who are not anxious to give an explanation themselves."[19] For if one arouses them without waiting for them to become eager to learn and anxious to give an explanation themselves, their knowledge will not be firm. But if one waits for them to be eager and anxious before arousing them, they will learn irresistibly like the rush of water. A student must think deeply. If he has thought deeply but cannot understand, it will then be all right to tell him [CHAN 1967: 266].

On the surface, the conjugal relationship seems to be a significant departure from the principle of reciprocity. The common impression that the wife and daughter-in-law in a male-oriented society have no "rights" of their own is, however, a misconception of how the normative system actually works in Neo-Confucianism. It is true that, in response to the loaded question: "In some cases the widows are all alone, poor, and with no one to depend on. May they remarry?" Ch'eng I, apparently

---

19) *Analects*, 7 : 8.

troubled by the questioner's intention to establish the strong claim that remarriage is sometimes necessary if not desirable, stated in an unusually stern manner: "This theory has come about only because people of later generations are afraid of starving to death. But to starve to death is a very small matter. To lose one's integrity, however, is a very serious matter" [CHAN 1967: 177]. This uncompromising articulation of faith in the sacredness of marriage as a total commitment probably in Ch'eng I's mind applied equally to husband and wife. Furthermore, it was meant to be a critique of a common practice which seemed to have taken too lightly the true meaning of matrimony by using a simple economic justification. The very fact that Ch'eng I cited approvingly his father's decision to marry a widowed relative as a manifestation of kindness [CHAN 1967:179] indicates that, while he was in principle against remarriage, he did not make a dogma out of it.

Ideally, in the Neo-Confucian order of things, the conjugal relationship is the most fundamental of all human relations. The Neo-Confucians argue that it is from husband and wife that all other familial ties are engendered.[20] Failure to establish genuine reciprocity between husband and wife destroys domestic harmony, indeed social stability. Therefore, in underscoring its importance their emphasis is on mutual responsibility rather than romantic love. Injunction against devoting too much attention to the affective aspect of conjugal relationship is readily available in Neo-Confucian literature:

> Tranquillity and correctness are the ways to enable husband and wife to live together for a long time, whereas indecent liberties and improper intimacies result in disrespect and cause husband and wife to drift apart [CHAN 1967: 173].

Reciprocity in the conjugal relationship is often characterized by "respect" (ching 敬). A common expression in describing a proper husband-wife relationship is that they treat each other respectfully as guests. For example, Ch'eng I summarized his mother's relationship to his father as follows: "she and father treated each other with full respect as guests are treated. Grateful for her help at home, father treated her with even greater reverence. But mother conducted herself with humility and obedience" [CHAN 1967: 179].

Like all other forms of dyadic relationships, the idea of mutual respect between husband and wife conveys a profound ethicoreligious import. Although it is basically correct to interpret the Neo-Confucian perception of conjugal relationship in terms of social values such as the creation, maintenance and perpetuation of the family, the mutuality of husband and wife should also be taken as an integral part of the self-education of both of them. One wonders if Ch'eng I did not somehow simplify the complexity of the actual situation in his praise of the virtue of his mother as wife:

---

20)   The underlying philosophy of this assertion is to be found in the *Book of Change* where it states: "The great characteristic of Heaven and Earth is to produce." See Chan, 1963: 268.

"She was humane, altruistic, liberal, and earnest. She cared for and loved the children of my father's concubines just as she did her own. My father's cousin's son became an orphan when very young, and she regarded him her own" [CHAN 1967: 179]. Nevertheless, despite the male-centeredness of the culture, the active participation of the wife in shaping the form of human relatedness in the family is fully recognized and strongly encouraged. The division of labor between the inner (domestic) and the outer (public) realm of responsibility makes it functionally necessary for the wife to assume a major role at home. Thus, Ch'eng I's mother's preference in consulting her husband even in small matters was noted as an indication of extraordinary considerateness [CHAN 1967: 179]. Needless to say, the ultimate self-transformation of the wife-mother, like that of the husband-father, provides a standard of inspiration for the family and the society at large.

The Neo-Confucian conception of what constitutes proper conduct of the wife may have differed significantly from the accepted standard of behavior in premodern China. Therefore, the popular belief that the rise of Neo-Confucian culture in the 11th century signaled a significant decline in the status of women in Chinese society deserves a more focused investigation. Although no convincing evidence has been found to establish a causal relationship between Neo-Confucian ideology and such appalling social practices of the period as footbinding, the Neo-Confucian masters, either by conscious choice or by default, subscribed to a hierarchical order of the human community in which man is superior to woman. It is likely that male supremacy in this particular connection was more a reflection of the sociopolitical reality of the time than of a clearly articulated intellectual stance. Nevertheless, the total absence of any active participation by women in shaping the spiritual direction of the Neo-Confucian project impels us to reexamine its universalistic claim that every human being (in the sense of the sexually neutral term *jen* 人) has the potential to form a unity with Heaven, Earth and the myriad things. Does this simply mean that only through the moral influence of the Confucian sages, worthies and "gentlemen" can women and, by implication, the majority of the uneducated masses have a chance of becoming fully human? One wonders if Chu Hsi or, for that matter, Wang Yang-ming could have entertained the thought of the transformative influence of women on society as a whole. They could certainly see the educational importance of the mother and the harmonizing effect of the wife, and they would probably have encouraged girls as well as boys to learn to read and write. It would have been an entirely different matter, however, for them to speculate on the possibility that women could also become Confucian masters. If they did, they surely did not make any effort to train women as their successors.

To criticize Neo-Confucian ideology as male-oriented is to introduce a modern feminist viewpoint which is beyond the realm of imagination in most traditional discourses, East and West. Yet, if Neo-Confucian thought is to be not merely an historical phenomenon but also a mode of thinking that has relevance to us, it must be able to respond to the challenging questions of our age. As far as practice is concerned, the historical record is far from encouraging, but within the symbolic resources of the Neo-Confucian tradition there is a wellspring of insights to nurture the idea of true mutuality between man and woman. Chinese society, while still male-dominated, has abandoned the conventional division of labor between domestic and public affairs. It has become less male-oriented than North America in such critical areas as higher education and business. The "liberation" of the Chinese woman is the result of decades of struggle against the so-called "feudal" past of which Neo-Confucianism has been the main target. Nevertheless, this struggle may have been aided by the fact that within Confucian moral metaphysics, there is no justification for excluding women from the community of like-minded followers of the Way. Furthermore, we encounter no theological or scriptural difficulty in stressing the necessity and desirability of the participation of women in influencing, shaping and leading the Confucian Way in the future. Chu H•i and Wang Yang-ming may not have entertained the possibility that women could also become Confucian masters, but it is vitally important for their modern interpreters to realize that such a possibility exists.

I have suggested that, in the perspective of Neo-Confucian thought, human-relatedness is an essential dimension of religiosity. As the ultimate self-transformation, religiosity entails being actively engaged in a communal act. Religious consciousness so understood is a quest for the identity and continuity of one's communality as well as one's selfhood. Paradoxically, for the self to be ultimately transformed, it must travel the concrete path defined in terms of its primordial ties such as parentage, ethnicity, locale, historical moment and so forth. Strictly speaking, if the self fails to transform the primordial ties into "instruments" for moral cultivation, it can only be contextualized and structured to assume a predetermined social role. Yet, its creativity as a moral agent cannot be manifested merely by transcending the context and the structure that determines its center of relationships. The authentic approach is neither a passive submission to structural limitation nor a Faustian activation of procedural freedom but a conscientious effort to make the dynamic interaction between them a fruitful dialectic for self-realization. Learning for the sake of one's self is ethicoreligious because it takes as its root idea the inseparability of the ethic of human relatedness and the religiosity of the quest for personal knowledge.

Characters

Chang Tsai	張載	*ching*	敬
cheng-hsin	正心	Chou Tun-i	周敦頤
Ch'eng-Chu	程朱	Chu Hsi	朱熹
Ch'eng I	程頤	*chü-ching ch'iung-li*	居敬窮理
ch'eng-i	誠意	*han-yang hsü-yung ching chin-hsüseh tsai*	
chia	家	*chih-chih*	涵養須用敬進學在致知
chih	致	Hsieh	契
chih-chih	致知	*hsien li-hu ch'i ta-che*	先立乎其大者
ch'in	親	*hsin*	信

hsüeh	學		*pen-t'i*	本體
hsüeh tso-jen	學作人		*san-kang*	三綱
i	義		*shen*	身
ko-wu	格物		*shen-tu*	慎獨
kung-fu	工夫		"Shih-jen"	識仁
kuo	國		*shih-tao*	師道
li	理		*shu*	恕
li-i fen-shu	理一分殊		Shun	舜
liang-chih	良知		*t'i*	體
Lien-hsi	濂溪		*t'ien-hsia*	天下
Liu Tsung-chou	劉宗周		Tu Wei-ming	杜維明
Lu Hsiang-shan	陸象山		Tung Chung-shu	董仲舒
Lu-Wang	陸王		Wang Yang-ming	王陽明
Lü Tsu-ch'ien	呂祖謙		*wei-chi*	為己
pao	報		*wu-lun*	五倫
pen	本		*yu-tao*	友道

BIBLIOGRAPHY

BELLAH, Robert N.

1976   Father and Son in Christianity and Confucianism. In *Beyond Belief: Essays on Religion in a Post-Traditional World*, New York: Harper & Row, pp. 76–99.

CHAN, Wing-tsit

1963   *A Source Book in Chinese Philosophy*.   Princeton: Princeton University Press.

1967   *Reflections on Things at Hand: The Neo-Confucian Anthology Compiled by Chu Hsi and Lü Tsu-ch'ien*, trans., Wing-tsit Chan. New York: Columbia University Press.

DE BARY, Wm. Theodore

1981   *Neo-Confucian Orthodoxy and the Learning of the Mind-and-Heart*.   New York: Columbia University Press.

FANG, Thomé H.

1981   *Chinese Philosophy: Its Spirit and Its Development*.   Taipei: Linking Publishing Co.

FINGARETTE, Herbert

1963   *The Self in Transformation: Psychoanalysis, Philosophy and the Life of the Spirit*.   New York: Basic Books.

LEGGE, James

1865   *The Shoo King*. In *The Chinese Classics*, trans., James Legge, vol. 5. Oxford: Clarendon Press.

METZGER, Thomas A.

1977   *Escape from Predicament: Neo-Confucianism and China's Evolving Political Culture*.   New York: Columbia University Press.

SMITH, Wilfred C.

1964   *The Meaning and End of Religion*. New York: Macmillan Company.

TU, Wei-ming

1976   *Centrality and Commonality: An Essay on Chung-yung*. Honolulu: University Press of Hawaii.

1979a Ultimate Self-Transformation as a Communal Act: Comments on Modes of

Self-Cultivation in Traditional China. *Journal of Chinese Philosophy* 6: 237–246.

1979b The Neo-Confucian Concept of Man. *Humanity and Self-Cultivation: Essays in Confucian Thought*. Berkeley: Asian Humanities Press, pp. 71–82.

WEBER, Max

1964 *The Religion of China*. Trans. from the German and ed., Hans H. Gerth. New York: Free Press.

YANG, L.S.

1957 The Concept of 'Pao' as a Basis for Social Relations in China . In J. K. Fairbank (ed.), *Chinese Thought and Institutions*. Chicago: University of Chicago Press, pp. 291–309, 395–397.

Chapter 8

Confucian Thought During the Tokugawa Period

MASAHIDE BITO

INTRODUCTION

At the beginning of the Tokugawa Period (1603–1868 A.D.), the School of Chu Hsi was respected as the orthodox school of Confucianism. However, from the middle of the 17th century, questions and criticism were raised by Nakae Toju, Yamaga Soko, Ito Jinsai and Ogyu Sorai, all of whom attempted to establish new theories. Although their theories reflected various other differences, they shared one common attitude or approach in that they all tried to deny the most basic proposition in the school of Chu Hsi, "*Hsing* is *Li*". (*Hsing* is original or true nature of the human heart, and *li* are moral rules or their original principles governing one's mode of social living.) To say these two are identical means that moral principles are inherent in the true nature of man; therefore people innately possess the ability to judge behavior as morally sound or not on the basis of the original nature of their hearts.

Different though they were in their tenets, what was common to all the above-mentioned scholars is that they denied this basic proposition of the Chu Hsi School. This denial seems to be related to a fundamental difference between the Chinese and Japanese family system. Whereas the Chinese family is purely a paternal kinship organization, the *ie* as a unit of social organization in Japan is not always based on true kinship, but rather displays the characteristics of a fictive corporate organization formed to preserve a family name by artificially ensuring succession to the family business so as to maintain its prosperity. A person does not qualify as a member of society just by being born into a family. Rather he can become a full member of society only after achieving a proper position in an *ie* structure. In China, on the other hand, a boy born into a family automatically receives the rights and obligations of a family member. These become the basis of his social activities, and it is up to each person individually to choose an area of activity.

This difference is probably one of the reasons why the Japanese have lacked a concept of individual morality and why the theory of Chu Hsi, which forwarded this characteristic of individualism, met resistance in Japan. Japanese scholars imbued with the notion of *ie* as an integral group, and the state as an aggregate of *ie*, sought to explain that the true basis of morality lies in role performance within such units.

HISTORICAL ANTECEDENTS

Confucianism as a major system of thought and knowledge in pre-modern Japan underwent tremendous development during the long and peaceful Tokugawa Period (1603–1868 A.D.). Accompanying Confucianism was *kokugaku* 国学, or study of the "Japanese" classics, and such branches of natural science as mathematics and medicine. However, those pursuing other forms of knowledge were not completely free from Confucianism, which was the mainstream of Chinese literary learning. *Kokugaku*, for example, was strongly influenced by Confucianism in its method of study, and in the process of establishing itself as a system of thought took Confucianism as its thesis to create an antithesis. Other sciences, like medicine, were largely dependent on Chinese materials until the end of the 18th century, the time when western learning was introduced into Japan through the medium of Dutch. In particular, many scholars and philosophers used the Confucian classics as their basic material for the contemplation of social morals and political issues. On the one hand this promoted the scholastic understanding of these texts, and on the other helped the formation of a Japanized Confucian thought that indicated desirable states of morality and politics adjusted to the Japanese context. This adaptation provides important material for historical research, in that it reflects the sense of life of the people who lived during the Tokugawa Period.

The reason that Confucianism gradually replaced Buddhism, which had been the mainstream of thought until the middle ages (ca. late 12th century—15th century), seems to be the fact that the social structure of this period shared some similarities with the centralized bureaucratic system in China [BITO 1968a]. The last half of the 16th century—the Oda-Toyotomi Period (1568–1600 A.D.) just prior to the establishment of the Edo Shogunate by the Tokugawas in 1603—saw the foundation of a new unified regime with the warriors or *samurai* as the executors of political power.

The bureaucratic structure of the nation, which had been established around the 7th century, being modeled after the T'ang system for which the social foundation was still premature, rapidly changed its nature and shifted to a system in which major members of the national power structure, such as the nobility, large temples, various government offices and even the imperial family itself, used the *shōen* 荘園 system—the land owning system that allowed large private holdings based on the division of national power—as their economic basis. This shift undermined the administrative ability of the central government. To complement this situation warriors or *samurai*, who had power in local communities, emerged and gradually increased their power within the central government, starting around the end of the 12th century. The *shogun*, or leader of the warriors, established a military government in Kamakura. The centralizing power of the nation further deteriorated in the course of political and military disputes between the court nobility and the warriors, and between various alliances among the warriors. On entering the period of continuous wars, known as the *Sengoku* 戦国 Period, from the end of the 15th century to the 16th century, the warriors' regimes that had by then emerged in many places deprived the nobility of their power-base by abolishing the *shōen* system, which had heretofore provided the warriors themselves, as well as the nobility, with an economic foundation. Instead, they mobilized political power to govern their local areas. This was the *daimyo* system. By aligning these local powers with themselves the Toyotomi and Tokugawa families re-established centralized power in the nation. In the process of this unification the *samurai* were gradually separated out from the farmers throughout the country [BITO 1981]. The warriors were called in to live in the castle towns which were their lords' headquarters. Thus they lost direct contact in governing the rural areas and became somewhat similar to bureaucrats. A similar centralizing shift can be seen operative among the lords acting as administrators. This centralizing shift is the main reason why Confucianism—the orthodox learning for the ruling class in China— became of interest to the warriors, the *shogun* and *daimyo*. Confucian social thought was something they could refer to when thinking about their own lives or about ways of government.

While the social mode of existence of the warriors came to share certain characteristics with that of the Chinese bureaucrats, it was something that naturally emerged from Japanese society through a long historical process. Thus, throughout this time Japanese social life displayed many characteristics that remained unique to the Japanese context. For example, the structural relationships between the *shogun* and the *daimyo* and between the *daimyo* and their retainers were feudalistic in nature, in that the *daimyo* and the retainers were obligated to provide military service in exchange for a fief that they received from the *shogun* or the *daimyo* respectively. This master-retainer relationship remained hereditary. Such feudalistic relationships were not found in China, but they are similar to what appeared in European feudalism to a degree. A basic difference from the European model was due to the fact that the retainers who served a *daimyo* were regarded as members of the *daimyo*'s clan, reflected in such terms used in reference as *kachu* 家中 or *kashin* 家臣. Japanese type feudalism cannot be fully understood without referring to the human relationships based on the *ie*, a notion or institution unique to Japan. The internal social structure and human motivational relationships of classes other than the *samurai*, such as farmers and townspeople (i.e., merchants and craftsmen who were living in cities), were also based on the institution of *ie*. The differences between the Japanese and the overall Chinese social structure as illustrated above, must have limited the extent of Japanese acceptance of Confucianism, and must have stimulated thinking as to how Japan could adjust Confucianism to Japanese society.

Another condition that made it difficult for Confucianism to be accepted unreservedly was that there was no institutional foundation to make Confucianism a necessary education for administrators. In China, the bureaucrats were chosen on the basis of examinations, a basis for institutional Confucianism since at least the Sung Dynasty. In Japanese *samurai* society one's ranking was first determined on the basis of military capability, ranking was then passed on through generations, and there was very little room for something like the Chinese examination system.

During the first half of the Tokugawa Period there were only a few schools in *daimyo* territories (*han*) to educate *samurai* in any organized manner.   It was only after the middle of the 18th century or the beginning of the 19th that more schools were set up by the *han* or the Edo shogunate.   This indicates that in the earlier part of the Tokugawa Period it was not necessary for the *samurai* to study Confucianism, and those who had a special interest in learning, or those who wanted to be scholars, studied Confucianism individually.   However, since the early period many of the higher administrators, like the *shogun* and *daimyo*, following the traditions of the ancient nobility, valued Confucian education, and appointed Confucian scholars as their private teachers.   In this sense, therefore, it could be said that studying Confucian thought was useful for acquiring a position, but that the position was not an administrative one, unlike that which would be obtained by passing the examination in China.   Rather it was a scholar's position, which was irrelevant to actual politics. Confucianism in the Tokugawa Period, therefore, was something that developed under very different social conditions from those prevailing in China.

INDIGENOUS RESPONSES TO THE TENETS OF CHU HSI

The main stream of Confucianism during the early period of Tokugawa was the school of Chu Hsi [BITO 1961].   The circle was a small one, consisting of a few professional scholars.   Its scholastic standards were relatively high, having inherited the traditions and fruits of learning from the aristocratic society of ancient times as well, as drawing upon the active Chinese scholarship pursued in the Zen temples during the medieval periods.

The first Confucian scholar to be appointed by the Edo shogunate was Hayashi Razan 林羅山 (1583–1657 A.D.).   Razan was at first a monk at the Kenninji 建仁寺, a Zen temple in Kyoto.   In 1604, when he was 22 years old, he became a pupil of Fujiwara Seika 藤原惺窩 (1561–1619). Razan presented a list of Chinese books that he had read by then, which included 440 titles, to Seika.   Seika himself was a member of a noble family and had studied at a Zen temple, the Shokokuji 相国寺.

There were two reasons Seika and Razan devoted themselves to the school of Chu Hsi: first, the theories of Chu Hsi incorporate many influences from Buddhism, mainly the Kegon 華厳 sect, which was relatively easy to understand not only for Zen priests but also for the ordinary people of the post-medieval period, who had been under the strong influence of Buddhism.   Second, in contemporary China (the Ming Dynasty) and Korea (the Yi Dynasty) the school of Chu Hsi was respected as the orthodox school of Confucianism, and was the standard used for the examination system.   During the medieval period the Zen temples had served as windows through which Chinese and Korean cultural features continued to be introduced.   Therefore, it was natural for the priests to accept the Chu Hsi school as orthodox.

It is commonly believed, that the school of Chu Hsi was adopted as an official discipline by the Edo shogunate after Hayashi Razan received an official appointment.   But this is contrary to the facts.   Tokugawa Ieyasu appointed Razan simply as a secretary for literary affairs because he recognized that Razan was very learned, and not because he accepted the value of the school of Chu Hsi or understood the content of Razan's thought. This sort of appointment was not unique to Ieyasu, but, rather, was quite common among the administrators of the shogunate and local han during the early Edo Period. Therefore, the vogue enjoyed by the school of Chu Hsi among the scholastic circles does not necessarily mean that it had any strong direct connection with the political powers.

As the school of Chu Hsi became popular it also began to stimulate questions and criticism. The important thing here is that criticisms were raised not by scholars and educators, who simply accepted the theory of Chu Hsi, but by those who attempted to understand it through actual experiences as functioning members of society [BITO 1961]. The first of such criticisms was raised by Nakae Toju 中江藤樹 (1608–48 A.D.), who abandoned the school of Chu Hsi and switched to "Yomei gaku," the school of Wang Yang-ming. Following Nakae, around 1662, Yamaga Soko 山鹿素行 (1622–85 A.D.) and Ito Jinsai 伊藤仁斎 (1627–1705 A.D.) independently began to question the thought of the Chu Hsi School and attempted to establish new theories of their own. Although the content of their theories differed [BITO 1968b, 1971], they shared a common attitude of approach; they both tried to reach back to the original spirit of Confucianism (or so they believed) by reading such classics as *The Analects* themselves, without depending on the commentaries by later scholars, like Chu Hsi. Later Ogyu Sorai 荻生徂徠 (1666–1728 A.D.), who was active in the early 18th century, also advocated a similar procedure of study [BITO 1979]. Sorai, along with Yamaga Soko and Ito Jinsai, is often referred to as *kogaku* 古学 or the Old Learning. *Kogaku* is a school of Confucianism that developed independently in Japan, although one might find similarities to the school of textual explication of the Ch'ing dynasty. One of the differences is that whereas the *kogaku* group tried to read and understand the original meaning of the classics without the assistance of any commentaries, the Ch'ing scholars relied heavily on the earlier Han period commentaries in order to understand the classics.

It can easily be imagined that passages of the ancient classics are prone to various interpretations. This possibility may have become even more exaggerated when Japanese scholars, for whom Chinese was not the native tongue, read them without any commentaries. They must have found a great deal of room for free interpretation. In fact, the main advocates of the *kogaku* school were proud of the objectivity of their interpretation of the classics compared to those by the school of Chu Hsi, which were regarded as strongly subjective. Although Jinsai and Sorai accomplished much in the area of objective study of the ancient language, their systems of thought as a whole remained undeniably Japanese.

Thus *kogaku* was formed through criticizing the thought of Chu Hsi. One can also observe modifications of Japanization of the thought of Chu Hsi by changes in the emphasis given his system. Such modification was apparent among the faithful followers of the school, one of whom was Yamazaki Ansai 山崎闇斎 (1618–82 A.D.) and his associates.

That such criticism or modification of the school of Chu Hsi had taken various shapes before the end of the 17th century seems to indicate that the thought of Chu Hsi contained some characteristics which could not be adapted, readily or entirely, to the reality of Tokugawa society.   In the following section I would like to compare some Japanese modifications with Chu Hsi's teachings in order to examine their characteristics. (Parenthetically, Japanese Confucianism after the 18th century can be understood, for the most part, as a composite of or further development of, the various schools of thought to which I have just referred.)

The essence of the thought of the school of Chu Hsi is expressed in the basic proposition—"nature is principle" 性即理.   *Hsing* 性 is the true nature of the human heart (original nature), and *li* 理 are the moral rules or their original principles in terms of social life.   It follows that to say these two are identical means that moral principles reside in the true nature of man, and therefore an individual innately possesses the ability to judge whether behavior is morally sound or not on the basis of the natural inclination of one's heart (mind).   We can understand this theory as implying respect for an individual's independence or autonomy in regard to morals. However, it would be an ideal situation for an individual to be able to carry out such a perfectly autonomous life.   In order to reach such a state one should make a continuous effort to clarify the true nature of one's own heart.   There is, in fact, a necessary effort to inquire into the question of what is the principle in one's heart; therefore one gives heed to the so-called "penetrating principle" 窮理.   The actual procedure operative in the "penetrating principle" is that of "investigating phenomena" 格物 as appears in *The Great Learning*, that is, it is necessary to investigate the *li* of each phenomenon thoroughly.   The *li* of each phenomenon can be interpreted as the principle of various acts of individual social behavior.   For example, a person, as a lord, establishes a lord-retainer relationship with his retainers, and as a father maintains a father-son relationship with his children.   In this manner one establishes relationships with others depending on one's role in society, and it is considered a morally just way of life to carry out what is appropriate in each social relationship.   It is thought that there exists a principle that governs how one should "be" in each relationship, such as lord-retainer or father-son.   In other words, principles that govern moral behavior are highly situation-specific.   Because they are situation-bound they are diverse in content.   When, however, they are traced to an original principle, they turn out to be simply its particular manifestations.   The reason for this unitary base is that principles for moral behavior, after all, derive from the *li* of each individual's heart.   As a performer of behavior, one exhibits concrete manifestations of the *li*.   In the terminology of the school of Chu Hsi this is expressed as "the principle is unitary, the manifestations are particular," 理一分殊 (that is, although the *li* is one, its manifestations in each specific situation are diverse).   In order to master the principles of moral behavior in all its variety one must follow the teachings of the ancient sages and other predecessors and submerge oneself in the patterns of model behavior.   This discovery of precedent is "investigating phenomena."   Training itself is heterogeneous.   It is the diverse means through which one can experience the principles of moral behavior.   Furthermore, with the accumu-

lation of particular experiences "understanding will suddenly dawn on one," 一旦豁然
貫通 (*Supplement of the Great Learning*); i.e., the time will come when one's view
becomes completely clear and all the abiding principles of moral behavior become
self-evident. This is the perfected state of the "penetrating principle," by which one
perfects the moral personality that allows him automatically to perform morally
just acts on his own initiative under any circumstances. Sages are those who have
reached this stage, which any one can reach through effort. This is what is meant
by the Chu Hsi school when they say "all men can become sages."

Such an emphasis on respecting the autonomy and equality of individuals in the
logical structure of the Chu Hsi school was its strong point over the other schools.
At the same time, however, in reality it could not avoid confining people to a way
of life that forced them to follow the social norms, by demanding very strict training
in "investigating phenomena." Furthermore, the intellectual self-control demanded
often accompanied the suppression of one's natural emotions and desires; all of these
weak points are well-known.

These shortcomings were often the target of criticisms of Chu Hsi made by such
people as Lu Hsiang-shan 陸象山, Chu Hsi's contemporary, and Wang Yang-ming
of the Ming Dynasty in China. The same type of criticisms were to be found in
Japan as well. However, it should be stressed that criticism of Chu Hsi by Japanese
scholars went beyond pointing out such shortcomings and came to include denying
the basic theory of the school of Chu Hsi itself.

Nakae Toju had the clearest understanding that the main issue of the theory of
the school of Chu Hsi lay in its respect for the individual's autonomy in regard to
morals, and he tried to practice it faithfully. In his *Okina Mondō* 翁問答 (1640
A.D.) [BITO 1961] he states: "if the luminous virtue of one's heart is clear, the judgment as to what ought to be done in a given situation comprising time, place and social
position (時處位), one's responsibility as a person, one's fate and other things, all
become as clear as if they were reflected in a mirror." He also elucidated that it is
an ideal state for a person to live autonomously, free from moral formalities.

Toju practiced this free way of life himself: when he was 27 years old he left his
position as *samurai* in Ozu 大洲 Han, Shikoku, without his lord's permission, and
returned to his native farm village in Omi (Shiga Prefecture). This act was his
actualization of the Chu Hsi school teaching that one should respect "departing and
residing, advancing and retreating" 出處進退; and that when one should serve a lord
he should do so, and other times he should be among the people. Toju was also
faithful to the teaching of "investigating phenomena": while he was serving as a
samurai he performed his duties as a retainer faithfully, and when he went home he
served his mother earnestly. Despite all this, however, he could not attain peace of
mind, and he suffered psychologically. At the age of 37 he encountered Wang
Yang-ming's writing and became a faithful follower of his tenets. However, his
thought during the last four years of his life came to differ from that of the school of
Wang Yang-ming. He sought only "peace of mind" and abandoned his previous
interest regarding the ideal state of behavior in society. These features of his latter

thought one must judge as rather strongly Buddhistic in nature. The path taken by Toju's thought suggests that he failed to carry out the "penetrating principle" in the manner advocated by the school of Chu Hsi. Although he devoted himself to the school of Chu Hsi, regarding it as a theory that provides a way to reconcile the discrepancy between autonomous individual behavior and that considered socially just, he nevertheless failed to realize such theory in his own life and was forced to retreat to a hermit-like existence in the end. Toju's efforts did not die out however. His ideals were carried on by his student Kumazawa Banzan 熊沢蕃山, and by Arai Hakuseki 新井白石 who began his study of Confucianism by reading Toju's *Okina Mondō*.

That aspect of the Chu Hsi school that respects the autonomy of an individual remained influential to some extent, since it was similar in some aspects with traditional spiritual attitudes held by *samurai*. However, the fact that Toju, who wrestled with the theory squarely, failed to reconcile the "individual" and his social role in coping with the various social conditions of the time, eventually caused further criticisms of the school of Chu Hsi among the next generation of scholars.

What is common to the scholars of *kogaku*, such as Yamaga Soko and Ito Jinsai, is that they all deny the basic proposition of the Chu Hsi school that *hsing* is indeed *li*. As Soko defined the *hsing* of man's heart, it is innately irrelevant to moral good or evil, but is simply equipped with an ability to "know," that is, the ability to recognize things and matters objectively. What one ought to "know" using this ability is that one should master the principles of "things" and "matters" following "the investigation of phenomena and pursuit of knowledge" 格物致知 in *The Great Learning*. The *li* of things and matters are rules that define the ideal relationships between various people in society, which is what Chu Hsi argues as well. What is different between Soko and the Chu Hsi school is that whereas Chu Hsi maintains that the rules of various patterns of behaviors are the manifestations of one *li*, which is expressed in "the principle is unitary, the manifestations are particular," Soko sees no need to contemplate the one *li*, and the objects of recognition are solely the rules of diverse human relationships. When a person masters the rules, he can obtain a standard of judgment as to how one should live as a lord, as a retainer, or as a father or a son, according to "the station" given to him. This is, to Soko, what learning is and what a man should know. Furthermore, as is well known, this was the underlying guideline for compiling the *Buke Jiki* 武家事紀, which is essentially an encyclopedia for *samurai*. This work stresses that *samurai* should respect their professional responsibility and teaches *bushido* 武士道 or the way of *bushi* as the norm for everyday life. It is also a compilation of what was considered necessary knowledge for a *samurai*, such as military affairs and history.

Similarly, Jinsai also denies the proposition "*hsing* is *li*," and states that morals do not wait upon the existence of particular individuals. They exist in themselves; that is, they exist whether a person exists or not [Bito 1968b] (Dojimon 童子問, part 1, chapter 14). Jinsai indicates that the nature (*hsing*) of a person's mind is simply specific to an individual whereas morals are social properties; therefore, the

latter cannot be deduced from the former.   Like Chu Hsi, Jinsai also accepted
Mencius' theory that nature is good, and acknowledged that the nature (*hsing*) of
human mind is innately equipped with a possibility or a tendency toward good.
However, it is merely a possibility and he does not consider that man's nature (*hsing*)
is completely equipped with moral principles, as Chu Hsi averred.   Therefore, after
one's birth, education is regarded by Jinsai as a necessary medium through which one
learns what morals are.   Morals here mean the norms that men must observe as long
as they are social beings, which is expressed as "morals do not exist outside man, and
man does not exist outside morals" (*Ibid.* pt. 1, ch 8). This might seem contradictory to the previous statement that "morals" exist independently of man. "Man"
here, however, is defined as "lord-retainer, father-son, man-wife, brothers and
friends," which suggests that "man" is a being who assumes a role in a specific social
relationship.

   Jinsai, however, is not interested in diverse relationships themselves, as Soko was,
but focuses on "benevolence." This may seem to indicate that Jinsai, like the Chu
Hsi school, also lays the basis of morals in the function of man's heart. The definition of "benevolence" 仁 by Jinsai, however, is simply "love" 愛, while it is
"the principle of love" 愛之理 in the school of Chu Hsi.   The significance of this
difference can be clarified through Jinsai's notion of "benevolence."

   The perfected form of "benevolence" is: first, one's heart is filled with compassion; second, the other(s) will receive "benefit and favor" as a result of his love.
"One's heart is filled with love" probably means that only other people's welfare
occupies his mind.   Furthermore, "benevolence" is very close to "empathy" 恕.
He states: "when one performs what is 'empathy' on an occasion, he will gain in
'benevolence' at the same time" (*Dojimon*, pt. 1, ch. 58). "Empathy" is "to
surmise another's feelings"; that is, when one associates with someone, he has to
surmise what the other person likes and dislikes and tries to understand him by, as
Jinsai puts it, "taking his feelings as your own and taking his body as your own"
(Gomojigi 語孟字義, Shu 恕). Beautiful as this is, it has to be pointed out that this
teaching of love and tolerance lacks a view of humanity that ties the self, as the performer of love, to the other.

   In the school of Chu Hsi "empathy" is defined as "to project one's self" 推己
which is, as explained by the words of *The Analects:* "one should not do things to
others that he himself does not like to have done to him." Jinsai does not accept
this interpretation.   That is to say, Jinsai's teaching of love and tolerance can be
summarized as an act of serving others with an awareness of his position in relation
to them, or performing one's role in relation to others.   It is different from love and
tolerance in the sense that self and others are equal individuals.   An act of love
emerges out of love for oneself or on the basis of one's sense of consideration for
others.

   Opposed to Jinsai, who focused on how an individual's state of mind should
be (as did the school of Chu Hsi in that sense), Ogyu Sorai shifted his focus to how
society and state should be from a perspective emphasizing how society affects an

individual's attitude toward life [BITO 1979]. Sorai defined "nature" as something that contains the ability to love, to be friendly and to afford mutual support as well as an ability to perform some task of social utility. This latter ability manifests great variety because each individual differs in his social utility, depending on his personality and his talent at birth. And it is only harmful, not beneficial, to control this diversity by the uniform teaching of morals. "Rice is useful as rice and beans are useful as beans." (Tomonsho 答問書). Therefore, it is necessary for individuals as well as for the society as a whole to create the social conditions that allow people to demonstrate their relative abilities. And this is a question of politics and not of morals. Therefore, "the way" 道, Sorai advocates does not refer to morals but to the way to govern in order to realize a peaceful society.

More concretely, "the way" is represented in the form of various political institutions, or "rituals, music, punishments and institutions of government" 禮樂 刑政,; these were established by the sages who were the ideal lords in ancient China. Therefore, to Sorai, learning is to study what "the way" is through reference to the Chinese Confucian classics. "The way" is something that was created from the viewpoint of politics for the society as a whole, and is not something that can be judged in terms of the minds of individuals. This implies that the theory of the school of Chu Hsi, the principle of "the way" lying in the *li,* that is, "nature" of one's mind, is incorrect.

Thus *kogaku* scholars like Soko, Jinsai and Sorai denied the proposition of the school of Chu Hsi that "nature" is "principle," and Yamazaki Ansai, who succeeded the school of Chu Hsi, modified the thought of Chu Hsi by shifting the emphasis from "penetrating principle" to "reside in reverence" 居敬. "To reside in reverence" or to continue to be in the state of "reverence" means to bring one's mind under control and to maintain a state in which one's mind is concentrated, which is valued as a precondition to performing "penetration of principle" in the school of Chu Hsi. But Ansai explains that "residing in reverence" accomplishes all of one's moral training, by which he tried to teach a way of life, through "investigating phenomena" without utilizing the "penetrating principle"; that is, one should unconditionally devote oneself to given social expectations.

Different though they may be in their approach, what is common to all these scholars is that they all deny a basic proposition of the Chu Hsi school. If this is a characteristic of Japanese Confucian thought generally, to what can we ascribe the reason? I would now like to consider this shift in Confucian thought in Japan by relating it to the traditional form of the family.

THE INFLUENCE OF THE FAMILY IN JAPANESE CONFUCIAN THOUGHT

Except for some minor historical changes, the Japanese family as a social institution did not change in its basic characteristics from about the eighth century on. The system of *ie,* discussed in detail by Yanagita Kunio [1963] and Ariga Kizaemon [1967], was already the prevalent system in eighth-century Japan

[NAKADA 1943]. Nakada noted that in the Japanese legal system, which was based on the T'ang legal system, some amendments were made in regard to inheritance. This view is carried further and developed by such scholars of legal history as Ishii Ryosuke [1980] and Shiga Shuzo [1967]. Whereas the Chinese family (as well as the kinship group) is purely a paternal kinship organization, the *ie* as a unit of social organization in Japan is not always based on kinship, but rather displays the characteristic of an artificial social organization ostensibly formed to preserve the family name and to ensure successful succession of the family business and its property. It is possible for a non-kin to succeed to the *ie*. There are even cases where the legitimate son of the head of the household is given none or a very small part of the family business or property. The condition requisite to being regarded as an appropriate heir is not the fact of birth, but the possession of unique individual qualities appropriate to a satisfactory continuation of the business. It is obviously an advantage to be born as the first son, which is part of such uniqueness, but it is not an absolute asset. There have been many cases where the first son loses his position to his younger brothers or to non-kin members. When the *ie* is prosperous either at the present or likely to be in the future, it is passed on in parts, normally in uneven parts, with an emphasis on the main house. This is an effort to maintain the family name and business through the main household.

Under such a system of *ie* a family based on kinship is simply a building block to the construction of an *ie*. Furthermore, a person does not acquire the qualifications of a member of the society by just being born as a family member. He can be a full member of society only after assuming a position in an *ie* structure by some route, be it becoming the successor of the head or the protégé of the *ie*, creating a new *ie* using a small inheritance, or becoming a subordinate (often called a *kenin* or *kerai*) of another *ie*.

In China, on the contrary [BITO 1968a], a boy born to a family is given rights and obligations as a family member, which become the basis of his social activities. They do not have the notion of family business, and it is up to each individual to choose an area of activity. The results of the activity, however, become the family asset shared by the family as a cooperative body consisting of his father and his brothers. After the death of the father the male siblings have the right to divide and inherit the asset with absolute equality. The obligation as a member of such a cooperative body is understood as his obligation to obey his father, its representative. This is expressed by *hsiao* 孝. This, however, does not mean to obey people in higher positions as it is often misunderstood, but it probably meant to respect the relationship where an individual is respected as a human being and not by virtue of his ability or qualifications. Such a relationship, they considered, appeared first between a father and a son. The moral system that is unique to the Chinese in which *hsiao* is the basis of all morals can be understood only in this context.

Hsiao is a foreign loan-word in Japanese. Since there was no comparable native Japanese word there is only a Sino-Japanese reading *ko* for this even today, which implies that the original meaning of *hsiao* was a difficult one for the Japanese to grasp. Tsuda Sokichi, who was a prominent scholar of the history and thought of East Asia, argues [TSUDA 1938: Chapter 1] that the reason the Chinese people regard *hsiao* as the basis of morals is because they view all morals as based on the relationship between individuals. He also contrasts this with the Japanese view where there is more emphasis placed on an individual's relationship with the group than on those between individuals.

Tsuda's point was that the Japanese concept was more "modern," and the Chinese concept was considered to be inferior. I would rather infer, however, that the Japanese lacked a concept of morals based on the individual. Furthermore, one can say that because the theory of the school Chu Hsi espoused an individualistic characteristic, that is, the principle of morality is contained in each individual's "nature," it met resistance in Japanese culture which constrained scholars to use the notion of *ie* as a group, or the state as a composite of *ie*, to explain that the basis of morality lies in the performance of one's role.

BIBLIOGRAPHY

ARIGA, Kizaemon
  1967 *Hōken-isei to Kindaika.* Tokyo: Miraisha. (*Feudalistic Tradition and Modernization.*)
BITO, Masahide
  1961 *Nihon Hōkenshisōshi Kenkyū.* Tokyo: Aoki Shoten. (*Study of Feudalistic Thoughts in Japan.*)
  1968a *Nihon no Bunka to Chūgoku.* Tokyo: Taishukan Shoten. (*China in Relation to Japanese Culture.*)
  1968b Itō Jinsai ni okeru gakumon to jissen. *Shisō* 524: 66–79. (The Theories and Practices of Ito Jinsai.)
  1971 Yamaga Soko no shisōteki tenkai. *Shisō* 560: 22–37, 561: 82–97. (Developmental Changes in the Concepts of Yamaga Soko.)
  1979 Ogyu Sorai no shisō. *Tōhōgaku* 58: 154–168. (The Concepts of Ogyu Sorai.)
  1981 Society and Social Thought in the Tokugawa Period. *The Japan Foundation News Letter IX:* **1-9.**
ISHII, Ryosuke
  1980 *Nihon Sōzokuhōshi.* Tokyo: Sobunsha. (*History of Inheritance Law in Japan.*)
NAKADA, Kaoru
  1943(1926) Tōsōjidai no kazoku kyōsansei. *Hoseishi Ronshu* 3: 1295–1360, first published in *Kokka Gakkai Zasshi* 40: 1–33, 28–58. (Communal System of the Family in T'ang and Sung Era.)
SHIGA, Shuzo
  1967 *Chūgoku Kazokuhō no Genri.* Tokyo: Sobunsha. (*Principles of Family Law in China.*)
TSUDA, Sokichi
  1938 *Jukyō no Jissen Dōtoku.* Tokyo: Iwanami Shoten. (*The Practical Philosophy of Confucianism.*)
YANAGITA, Kunio
  1963(1946) *Ie Kandan.* Tokyo: Chikuma Shobō, first published by Kamakura Shobō. (*Essays on the Family.*)

Chapter 9

Buddhism and Family in East Asia

LEWIS R. LANCASTER

INTRODUCTION

Buddhism brought many new ideas to East Asia, innovations, some of which provoked criticism and resistance on the part of the peoples who were inheritors of long established patterns of social behavior and religious beliefs. No institution of Buddhism had more far reaching effect than the monastery with its inhabitants who took a vow of celibacy and separated themselves from their families. This career of Buddhist monk and nun constituted an alternative life style to the universally accepted belief that one of life's major duties was that of fulfilling obligations to the living parents as well as to the lineage of ancestors extending back through the generations. Since the Buddhist monastery was filled with those who had 'left home,' given up their family name, shaved their heads and deliberately removed themselves from the ancestral lineage by not having children, thus granting the *sangha* a greater call on their loyalty than the extended family, a tension was created between this religious tradition and East Asian society. Generations of Buddhist opponents have directed their criticisms at the monastic life which they characterized as the epitome of unfilial action.

The problem of family life as contrasted with the monastic one was not limited to East Asia. In India, the family was no less a part of the social fabric and the accounts of the early life of Sakyamuni are vivid descriptions of the trials and obstacles encountered by one who choose the life of the wandering ascetic over the responsibilities and rewards of the householder life. The story of young Sakyamuni deserting his father, wife and infant son in order to pursue his search for enlightenment is one which Indians still find unsettling and even unforgivable.

THE MONASTIC LIFE

"Leaving home" came to describe the process of initiation and inclusion in a monastic community; it was the advent of this monastic tradition in East Asia which was seen as a serious challenge to the extended family system. Those who were following this regime of 'leaving home' were not adopting the path of individualism, if by individualism we mean a separation of the person from community. Buddhism did not bring a model of behavior based on the idea of an anchorite existence; rather, it introduced a form of community not based on blood lines of familial relationships. The emergence of a powerful new group within China articulating new ideals of social behavior made it necessary for those who joined it to redefine their concept of self and society. The Buddhist monk and nun were not isolated individuals in a mountain wilderness; they were practitioners in a campus of monastic buildings, part of a group conforming to life pattern set forth in the Buddhist code of conduct (*vinaya*). For those who entered the consciously chosen community that had no tie to family or clan their life goals and purposes came to be defined within the ideals of the new community. There are ways in which this growth of the monastery in East Asia can be compared to the 12th century in Europe, an era that has often been described as a time when individualism developed [MORRIS 1972]. Recent scholarship questions the premise that the older form of European culture gave way in the 12th century to the 'individual.' More important to this period was the "burgeoning thought . . . of new norms of communities with new rules" [BYNUM 1980: 2]. This is a good description of the time when Tao An (4th century) set up common rules of conduct for monasteries and changed every resident's name to the Buddha's clan name of Sakya. He, like the 12th century Europeans, was establishing a new mode of life centered on a community in which individualism was not the primary goal [CH'EN 1964: 100]. Hsu suggests that the Buddhists introduced the Indian idea of the *gotra*, an association of people not based on kinship but on rules and teachings [HSU 1972: 534]. It was the *gotra* that contrasted with the intricate kinship patterns which dominated Chinese life. The *gotra* in China had one form—the organization and structure of the monastery with its residents.

It was the discovery of the new group and the redefinition of self within the context of the monastic community that attracted so many East Asians. Without recognition of this appeal of the monastery life it is difficult to account for the fact that even though 'leaving home' did damage to the most sacred of social functions in East Asia, Buddhist monastic organizations thrived and became one of the most important features of the religious, economic and social life of China, Korea and Japan. The appeal of these various communities with special dress, demeanor, rules of conduct, ritual, religious teaching and yogic practices of meditation was sufficient to attract people even when joining was viewed by many as an unfilial action toward the family.

PARENTAL IMAGES

Buddhism appealed to certain of the faithful to give allegiance beyond the kinship ties, but at the same time it had to seek accommodation with local customs and in particular to have an acceptable relationship with the family. Buddhism is, after all, an institution which must secure its support from donations and it alienates the lay population only at the peril of becoming extinct. We see in the Buddhist canon as it is preserved in the Chinese language version, that parents receive a good deal of attention. In many of these scriptural passages the praise of the parents and the enumeration of the obligations due to them would satisfy the most vehement proponent of ancestral worship.   In the *Madhyamāgamasūtra* (T. 26: 641a) a son is told to revere his parents in five ways:

(1)   increase their wealth
(2)   take care of their affairs
(3)   provide for their wishes and needs
(4)   give up his own personal desires
(5)   offer everything owned to them.

In turn parents are told to be mindful of their son in five ways:

(1)   give loving care when he is an infant
(2)   always provide sufficient food
(3)   keep him from falling into debt
(4)   arrange a good marriage
(5)   leave all possessions to him.

A son who follows these proscriptions can be assured of good karma, great success and material prosperity.   A number of texts go further in the glorification of the family.   There are, say these texts, two people who can never be repaid the debt which is owed to them: the father and the mother (*Ekottarāgamasūtra* T. 125 : 601a; *Subāhuparipṛcchā* T. 895 : 729a).   Even if one were to carry the father on the right shoulder and the mother on the left for eons of time, the debt to them could not be repaid.   The reward for revering the parents goes beyond worldly success.   The son who honors his parents can be assured of a future life in heaven (*Ekottarāgamasūtra* T. 125 : 601a). An important eighth century text, the *Ta ch'eng pen sheng hsin t'i kuan ching* (T. 159 : 297a) goes into great detail about the role of the mother and the debt which is owed to her. She has carried the son in her own body for ten months; there the fetus has lived feeding off her blood and when born the child sucks her milk.   No life could occur without this giving of sustenance and shelter on the part of the mother.   Therefore the obligation to the mother is so great that doing homage to her brings more merit than giving homage to the greatest of brahmins or sages. A son who turns his back on his mother can expect to be condemned to one of the three evil rebirth destinies and will be born as a hell-being, a hungry ghost or an animal.   A son or daughter, continues this text, could cut off a portion of their flesh three times a day for a *kalpa* of time and present it as an offering to the mother but could not in all of these extreme acts of asceticism repay one day of her kindness. Saving the life of a parent is an act which results in great rewards.   The son who drowns while saving his mother and holding her up in the water, even though it means his own death, receives rebirth as a king. Therefore, concludes the text, on the day of the death of a virtuous mother, one should weep.

The *vinaya* texts of the monastic discipline of the Buddhists even while setting forth the rules for living apart from the family, provide solace to the sensibilities of the family oriented East Asians.   The *Sarvāstivādavinaya* (T. 1435: 152c), the *Mahāsaṅghikavinaya* (T. 1425: 421b), the *Vinayavastu* (T. 1444: 1035a, b) are specific in setting forth the rule that no son should enter the monastery and leave home without the permission of his parents.   Those who enter the monastery without parental consent commit a great sin.

Parents are given a status that ranks them with the highest beings.   A mother's loving kindness can be compared to the Buddha's compassion which prompts him to create Buddha realms for sentient beings (*Ta ch'eng pen sheng hsin t'i kuan ching* T. 159 : 297c). A son who quarrels with his mother creates the same situation as when kings fight with kings or nations attack nations; in every case there is destruction and suffering (*Madhyamāgamasūtra* T. 26 : 585a). Tantric texts equated parents with kings. The *Yü ch'ieh chin kang ting Su tzu mu p'in* of Amoghavajra (T. 880 : 338a) describes the ritual homage due to parents and the Four Guardian Kings. The *Chin kang ting ching yu ch'ieh shih pa hui chih kuei* (T. 869 : 284b) provides us with a list of merits attained through performing rituals for the king, parents and relatives.

Bad karma results from treating parents in the wrong way.   The *Mahāprajñā-pāramitāśāstra* (T. 1509 : 120a) points out that one who smashes images of the Buddha or of his parents will be reborn in a deformed body without limbs and with parts of the body missing. Subhakarasimha's translation of the *Subāhupariprccha* (T. 895 : 729a) accounts for rebellious behavior toward parents by noting that one who acts in such a contrary manner does so because of past action and the karma accumulated in the former life. In rebelling against the parents, the son is thought to have committed the heinous crime of killing an arhat. By hostile acts in the present life traced back to that murder, the evil son will in the future suffer terrible punishment and be reborn in hell.   On the other hand the son who wants to have the love of his parents can assure this acquiring the good karma which results from revering the Prajñāpāramitā texts (*Pañcaviṁśatisāhasrikaprajñāpāramitāsūtra* T. 223 : 289a).

From these examples of the praise which was heaped on the parent in a variety of texts, some translated from the Sanskrit and others probably compiled within China itself, it is clear that the Buddhists attempted to give support to the family. Even so, there are an equal number of passages which express the ambivalent nature of the Buddhist view of parents.   The *Śatasāhasrikāprajñāpāramitāsūtra* (T. 220 [vol. 5]: 251a; [vol. 7]:466a) warns the monks that Mara the tempter may come in the form of a parent and this 'parent' will tell the Bodhisattva not to be too hard on himself, not to practice so as to achieve ultimate enlightenment but rather to take the easier road of the Hinayana.   In other texts the glorification of the mother is replaced by descriptions which demote her to the level of being an ordinary sensuous woman. The *Mahāprajñāpāramitāśāstra* (T. 1509 : 199a) describes the womb as an impure spot, sitting in a pit filled with feces and urine; if a child chooses to enter that womb it is an example of the perverted views which are held by all whose destiny it is to seek rebirth. The *Mahāratnakūṭa* (T. 310 : 323a ff.) gives the details of the thirty-eight weeks of pregnancy and sees birth as the child's freedom from the horrors of the womb.   The *Yogācarabhūmiśāstra* (T. 1579 : 617a) speaks of the act of copulation as the time when parents are carried along on the wave of their passion and in the moment of conception the frenzy of the senses sends the sperm down the track of urine and out of the father's body into the same path and up into the womb of the mother. Since the body is produced by passion and originates in the defilements of the male and female body it is considered to be little more than a stinking and rotting corpse. Parents who have played their role in this rebirth cycle are not worthy of praise because they have bequeathed to their child an impure body that is to be a life long source of pain and suffering. From this perspective there is little reason to honor parents or thank them for the gift of life and body.

It is obvious that the two types of passages were intended for different audiences: the monastic celibate taught to feel revulsion for the mother and father, to turn away from the process which brings about birth while at the same time the tradition urged that all sons should revere the parents and treat them as if they were higher than the kings and on an equal with the Buddha. Textually we can note that accommodation to the family was attempted and passages in praise of parents were used to counter the attacks which were directed against the monastic career that seemed to support unfilial acts. In many ways, the opponents of Buddhism were right; the monks and nuns did turn away from their parents, they did 'leave home,' they did burn their scalps and shave their heads, thus desecrating the body given to them, they did fail to fulfill their responsibilities to the ancestors by taking a vow of celibacy. It is not surprising that Buddhists were never able to completely avoid censure on account of their monastic life.

RELATIONS WITH THE ANCESTORS

As indicated in these attacks, family was not limited to the living parents but extended backwards for seven or nine generations of ancestors. The dead family no less than the living needed and demanded attention. There were a series of ritual activities centered around the ancestors. Serving them required that they be buried in a proper and auspicious place which was determined by divination; they had to be given assistance for some generations to assure that they did not suffer. This was interpreted to mean that food and gifts were to be provided to the dead by the living at appropriate times. The key to assuring that these ritual acts were performed for the requisite number of generations was to have an unbroken line of family lineage with sons who carried the name of the family, assumed the obligations of the kinship ties and in turn produced a son to perpetuate the system. The Buddhist career of monastic life ran directly counter to this duty because the monks removed themselves from the lineage and were consequently accused of unfilial attitudes with regard to the dead. The degree of feeling on this matter can be judged by the pressure on individuals which occurs today (see also Koh, Chapter 16). Continuing the family line is such a major part of life that those who do not participate are excluded from ritual remembrance. In China children who died young were considered to have committed an unfilial act by this early death. A boy in the Taiwanese town of Ch'inan who dies is held to be an incarnation of someone to whom the parents owed a debt and that person is thought to have returned to live with the couple only until the debt is paid [AHERN 1973: 125]. In Japan one who has no descendants cannot become an ancestor but lives in the state of being a ghost (*gaki*) and the children who die without issue are called the *muenbotoke*, those toward whom one does not have an obligation [YONEMURA 1976: 178]. In Taiwan the ancestral spirits may become unhappy ghosts (*preta/gaki*) if not properly remembered and cared for and in this state are a source of potential trouble to the family [JORDAN 1972]. If there is such strong feeling and so little hope for the young and unmarried who die without producing sons, one can imagine the strong resentments aroused toward monks who removed themselves from the lineage. The Buddhists had to address themselves to this issue because it was of equal importance to the debt owed the living parents. In some ways the Buddhists were more successful in answering the complaints about their treatment of the ancestors than they were in the situation regarding their relationship to the family and parents. In the pre-Buddhist ancestral cults it appears that the dead were thought to live near their graves or in near-by mountains. During the seasonal rituals these ancestors would gather and receive the offerings [YONEMURA 1976: 180]. While this tradition has never been completely surplanted, the Buddhists did bring a new notion to the area, that of the underworld and the eight or ten hells into which the dead descended there to be punished for sins committed. These hells proved to be of great interest and much attention was paid to them and the drama of judgment and meted out punishment. As Ahern points out in her study of the Taiwanese village, there is not always a clear view of the underworld but villagers do have compassion for their dead and want to help them escape from the punishment which awaits [AHERN 1973: 225]. Having introduced the East Asians to the idea of the hells and the torments being suffered by ancestors who had committed evil deeds, the Buddhists removed the ancestors from the grave site and the mountains and placed them far away in the depths of the underworld or in heavens above. Such ancestors, as hell-beings, required different treatment than the usual grave-centered rituals, and so the Buddhists put themselves in a position to perform a signal service for these dead. In the T'ang dynasty tales of assisting such dead ancestors were widespread. Most famous of the legends was that of Maudgalyayana, a disciple of the Buddha who was famous for his magical power. He could travel to distant world systems as a result of this power and made the decision to visit his parents in heaven. Transporting himself to heaven he located his father but was dismayed to find that his mother was not in that blissful realm; she was in one of the lower hells undergoing terrible torture for her misdeeds. Maudgalyayana immediately flew down to hell and found his mother hanging upside down and starving. Distressed by this suffering he took food and tried to feed her but it turned to ashes and she could not eat it. Unable with all of his famed power to accomplish the feeding he sought out the Buddha and asked how he might aid his mother. The Buddha told him that the only way to assist her was to present food on the day when rainy season retreat ended and monks were allowed to come out of the monastery. On that day the food could be presented to the monks and they could dedicate it to the ancestors and even a mother in hell could be fed. The popularity of this tale and its implications should not be overlooked. It was a Buddhist solution to the problem of their relationship to the dead ancestors. By the introduction of the idea of the hells, the Buddhists had created a situation in which only they held the key to securing food and assistance. Monks who had left the lineage and removed themselves from the normal pattern of providing assistance to the ancestors who lived at the graves, could now claim the ultimate act of filial attention for those ancestors who were being judged in hell.

Buddhism in East Asia achieved a working relationship with the family system by praising living parents and creating for them good karma; in addition, the Buddhists were seen to care for the ancestors in a way that was unique and unmatched by any of the previous rituals. While accommodation was going forward, the monks and nuns were weaned away from filial responsibilities of the sort commonly practiced by the laity and these ordained members transferred loyalty to the Buddhist community in which no kinship ties existed. Although the monastery was set up as a counterpart to the family, it could not be totally separated from the social patterns of life. In China many monasteries began to mimic family organization. Across China public monasteries were supplemented by thousands of 'Father-Son' ones in which two or three monks might live with the oldest playing the role of 'father.' In these living units, the monk would adopt a young boy as his 'son' and would pass on to that 'son' the hermitage in which they practiced. For some of these monastery families, ancestral tablets were kept and appropriate rituals were performed by the monks who were adopted into the lineage, even though no blood line kinship existed between the members of the group. In this way even the celibate monks could expect to have the advantage of care and remembrance after death. The large public monasteries played a dominant role in the history of Chinese Buddhism, for they were the places of ordination, training and scholastic programs, but the 'Father-Son' hermitages were of equal importance. In China one could join the new group and break the bonds of the family system and yet find within Buddhism a re-creation of the family.

JAPANESE ADAPTATIONS

In Japan there were developments which gave Buddhism a distinctive form with regard to the family; the Japanese established sectarian divisions within the *sangha* and started the practice of married monks. With regard to sectarian development, Korea and China had held only one ordination for monks. Even though there were 'schools,' these never became sects in the sense of being restrictive about membership. Joining one of the sects is the only way to become a Buddhist in Japan and entering the clergy is specifically related to a particular group. Along with this division of Buddhism into a number of distinct units, the Japanese added the practice of having monks marry and produce families of their own. These married priest/monks established themselves as heads of households and following the mores of the society began to pass on the family occupation from father to

eldest son. The filial piety was expressed when the eldest son accepted his responsibility and continued the family tradition by assuming his place as head of the
temple/monastery. 'Leaving home' was changed to 'staying home' for the Japanese
priests who lived this life of householder and cleric. Obviously the tensions between
family and monastery life were removed and Buddhism became family centered even
within the living units of the meditators.

Having done away with the monastic celibate life and establishing family as a
recognized part of the sects of Buddhism, the Japanese were faced with the question of
dealing with the ancestors. Just as in the rest of East Asia, Buddhism created for
itself a unique and significant role in the situations which related to the dead. In
every home the ancestor worship was carried on by veneration and daily offerings on
the Buddhist altar where the dead one was referred to as 'Buddha' (hotoke). The
dead became the major business of Buddhism in Japan. A symbol of this relationship between the living and the dead can be seen in the difference between Shinto and
Buddhist shrines. The two names which are given to every individual, the birth name
(zokumyō) and the death name (kaimyō), are written on different tablets; birth
names find a place on the Shinto shrine and the death names on Buddhist ones. The
ancestral tables (ihai) and mortuary tables (toba) have the death name and both are
associated with Buddhist rituals. The family reveres its hotoke and ancestors by daily
offerings at home, visits to the grave in the spring and autumn and observation
of the obon festival. There are, in addition, the special memorial services for the
dead: the 3rd, 7th, 21st, 33rd, 49th and 100th death day celebrations. All of these
events are said to be performed for the purpose of acquiring merit (kudoku) for the
ancestors [OOMS 1976: 78]. In Nichirenshōshū, we can observe the practice of the
recitation of the sutra specifically for the peace which it can bring to the dead.

As strong as funereal functions are at present in Japanese Buddhism, they may
have been of even more importance in the past. Takeda expresses the opinion that
the popular temples of Buddhism in the pre-Tokugawa period were established primarily for funereal events; it was Tokugawa policies which tended to establish the
uniform Buddhist temple style known today [TAKEDA 1976: 135]. Takashi Maeda
sees in Buddhist practices the remains of a more ancient method of worshipping
ancestors. He points out that the practice of obon in Japan, while connected to
the Ullambanasūtra [CH'EN 1964: 282] and the story of Maudgalyayana which had
such influence in China, nevertheless reflects a theme more ancient than the text.
In obon, the ancestors are not in the Buddhist hells but are residing near by and come
to the festival to join in the entertainment and receive offerings [MAEDA 1976: 140].
In this case the Buddhists have maintained the idea of feeding the dead at the specified
time of the rainy season but they have located the ancestors outside of the hells
described in the sutra.

In Japanese Buddhism we can see that the family was dealt with in several ways.
First, the living family becomes a part of the organization of Buddhism as married
priests remain within the kinship system and create a regular family life centered on
the continuity of the father-son control of the temple. In addition to this establish-

ment of family life within the temple, the Buddhists of Japan have taken over a major role of caring for the ancestors and the dead.   The priests find in this service to society a filial role for Buddhism that is both religious and economically essential for the support of the temples.   There can be little conflict today between the family and Buddhism except in those cases where the son does not wish to fulfill his duty by assuming his position in the operation of the temple.

KOREAN CONTINUITIES

Korea provides us with a very different model of East Asian Buddhism.   In Korea the traditional form of monastic life has been maintained, even though the nation and Buddhism have suffered from proscriptions, wars and invasions.   During the Yi dynasty, King Injo (1623–1649) issued a decree that Buddhist monks could not enter the city of Seoul [PARK 1964: 7].   This was but one example of the supressions instituted by the Confucian ruling group.   The Buddhists were seen as being a destructive element in Korean society and the rulers of the dynasty did much to destroy the place which Buddhism had held during early periods.   King Hyonjong (1659–1674) would not allow anyone to become a monk and destroyed monasteries located in the capital or converted them to Confucian halls. In 1765, King Yongjo struck a blow at the Buddhist role of handling death ritual by demanding that all ancestral tablets be removed from the monasteries.   King Chongjong (1776–1800) again denied the monks admission to Seoul and his proscription lasted until the end of the 19th century [YOSHIKAWA: 1920: 46].   These strictures on Buddhism in Korea caused the monasteries to shrink in number of residents as well as in their importance within the cities.   Yoshikawa attributes the survival of Buddhism under these hostile rulers to the fact that the women of the royal house and the upper classes remained devout believers and gave it support.   Around the city walls of Seoul there were small hermitages housing monks who performed prayers for the women who came to the monastery asking to receive forgiveness for whatever sin had caused them to be born as women [YOSHIKAWA 1920: 47].   While the men gave their full support to the Confucian tradition and its rules of living within the family and nation, the women found Buddhism to be more attractive.   This meant that many of the Korean families were split with regard to religious allegiance.

When Japan took over control of the government of Korea in 1910, the role of the celibate monks and nuns took on a political significance.   The Japanese gave support to Buddhism and saw in it an institution which had the potential for creating a cultural bond between the two nations. It soon became apparent that if this role was to be realized, something had to be done with the situation of married priests in Japan and celibates in Korea.   As long as the rules governing the Buddhist groups of Japan were in conflict with those of Korea little in the way of cooperation was possible.   Pressure was put on the Korean *sangha* to follow the form of married clergy so it would be in step with Japanese groups.   It was ruled that monks in positions of leadership should have wives and later decrees indicated that only married monks could receive support. For a time it appeared that Korean Buddhism would become similar to Japanese with the married group taking the place of the celibates. The end of Japanese rule in 1945 left the Korean *sangha* with the major problem of what to do with the married monks. The battles which were fought over this matter were bitter and at times marked by physical violence. President Yi Sung-man tried to settle the legality of the question by issuing a statement in 1954 that all married monks should leave the monasteries. He also decided that only celibates could hold major positions of authority and have control over finances and policy decisions. While power was shifted to the unmarried monks, the anguish of rejecting the married ones continues even today, although the unmarried group completely dominates the *sangha*. As the monastery has returned to the ancient rules of conduct, it now faces the problems of tensions between the family and those who 'leave home.' There are more than 20,000 monks and nuns in South Korea occupying nearly 7,000 monasteries and hermitages and they are often in conflict with families that are oriented to the Confucian ethics of family responsibilities and the role of father-son models.

From 1976–80, I conducted extended interviews with 128 monks and nuns representing a variety of age groups and backgrounds. Out of those interviews came a definite pattern of friction between the families and those who had been ordained in the monasteries. Ninety (70%) of those interviewed indicated that they were in the monastery against the wishes of their families. This opposition on the part of the family ranged from expressions of unhappiness from parents to active attempts on the part of family members to remove the monks and nuns from their chosen life. Many of the residents (51%) recounted wrenching experiences of having family members come to them to beg that they return home. Sometimes these arguments erupted into physical wrestling as brothers or cousins tried to get them to leave the life and take up a regular position in the family. One of the primary complaints expressed to them by their siblings was that they owed a debt to their aging parents which was not being met. Quite often these scenes took place in the kitchen areas where the young novices are normally engaged in cooking and working during their first months in the monastery. But the contact was not limited to the young or the new recruits; many of the interviewed group who had been in the monastery for more than ten years (40% of this group) still had visits from unhappy family members. One of the most important and senior meditation teachers in Korea told of his family coming to see him thirty years after he had 'left home.' They had had no knowledge of his whereabouts and some had thought him dead until he achieved fame and his picture appeared in the newspaper. When they came as a group to the monastery, he preached them a sermon and asked them to support Buddhism. Because of his position, they accepted his commitment to remain a monk. Some of the novices (20%) go to the monastery without the permission of parents, even though it is officially required. But consent may not be a true response considering the concern shown by parents and family toward the career. In a small number of cases (20 of 128), the monks and nuns had approval and support of their families for the choice of becoming a Buddhist mendicant. Fifteen of the twenty who told of this parental support also indicated that the support was given because they had a childhood marked by illness and chronic poor health.   When the parents sought the advice of shamans they had been told that the only hope for survival or long life of the young person was to put them into a monastery.   All of these who had come to the monastery for health reasons said that they no longer had problems and their decision to remain was based on wanting to practice and study.   Three did admit that they suspected their health would decline if they left the life.   Only three of the 128 (2%) said that their parents were devout Buddhists who had urged them to consider the monastic career for religious reasons.

Admittedly, this is a very small sample of the monastic community of Korea, but it does suggest that there is conflict between the family and the monastery.   One of the impressive aspects of interviewing the monks and nuns was their resistance to answering any questions regarding the family.   They often (85%) complained that my questions about the family were disturbing to them because having 'left home' they no longer wanted to be concerned about it.   Using questionnaires proved to be ineffective because so many would refuse to answer or if they did so would give random 'yes' and 'no' responses that had no relationship to facts.   Some gave deliberately misleading information as a means of teaching the interviewer that such an interest in the family was of no value.   It was only possible to secure what appears to be reliable information from interviews that lasted in some cases for several days and involved time spent in discussing Buddhist doctrine.   While dealing with doctrinal matters, they often could be led to deal with the implications of the family life, a life they were always anxious to characterize as inferior to the state where one could have time and energy for meditation.

CONCLUSION

From the survey of some of the encounters that have occurred in East Asia between family members and the Buddhist monks and nuns, we see how complex the relationship is between the family and Buddhism.   The Buddhists alternately praise parents and denigrate them; copy the family organization and reject ties to the family; absorb the family framework into their rules and ridicule such relationships. Householders, Confucians, Taoists, Shintoists, laymen, non-Buddhists (and Buddhists themselves) have a similar mixed reaction to Buddhism, criticizing it on occasion and on others using it to secure such things as assistance for ancestors, giving monasteries significant support while issuing proscriptions against the celibate life. Time, place and situation create the context in which Buddhism and the family have interacted.   Of one thing we can be assured, neither has been able to ignore the other or maintain an unchanging attitude.   It is the dynamics of this interchange which promise much to the disciplines that have scholars willing to investigate the relationship of these two social institutions.

BIBLIOGRAPHY

AHERN, Emily A.
1973   *The Cult of the Dead in a Chinese Village.*   Stanford: University Press.
BYNUM, Caroline W.
1980   Did the Twelfth Century Discover the Individual? *Journal of Ecclesiastical History*
       31: 1.
CH'EN, Kenneth
1964   *Buddhism in China.*   Princeton: University Press.
HSU, Francis L. K.
1972   *Psychological Anthropology.*   Cambridge, Mass: Schenkman.
JORDAN, David
1972   *Gods, Ghosts and Ancestors: Folk Religions of a Taiwanese Village.* Berkeley and
       Los Angeles: University of California Press.
MAEDA, Takashi
1976   Ancestor Worship in Japan: Facts and History. In W. Newell (ed.), *Ances-
       tors,* The Hague: Mouton.
MORRIS, Colin
1972   *The Discovery of the Individual 1050-1200.*   New York: Harper & Row.
OOMS, Hermar
1976   A Structural Analysis of Japanese Ancestral Rites and Beliefs. In W. Newell (ed.),
       Ancestors, The Hague: Mouton.
PARK, Chong-hong
1964   Buddhist Influence on Korean Thought. *Korea Journal* 4: 5.
TAKEDA, Choshu
1976   Recent Trends in Studies of Ancestor Worship in Japan. In W. Newell (ed.),
       Ancestors, The Hague: Mouton.
YONEMURA, Shoji
1976   Dōzoku and Ancestor Worship in Japan. In W. Newell (ed.), *Ancestors,* The
       Hague: Mouton, pp. 177–203.
YOSHIKAWA, Buntaro
1920   *Chōsen no Shūkyō.*   Tokyo: Keijo.   (*Religion in Korea.*)

CANONIC TEXTS CITED

Chin kang ting ching yu ch'ieh shih pa hui chih kuei   (T. 869)
       Translated by Amoghavajra between the 5th year of T'ien Pao and the 9th year of
       Ta Li, T'ang dynasty (A.D. 746–774).
Ekottarāgamasūtra   (T. 125)
       Translated by Gautama Saṅghadeva in the 1st year of Lung An, Eastern Chin dynasty,
       (A.D. 397) in Lu-shan.
Madhyamāgamasūtra   (T. 26)
       Translated by Gautama Saṅghadeva between the 1st and 2nd year of Lung An, Eastern
       Chin dynasty (A.D. 397–98) in Tung-t'ing Monastery.
Mahāprajñāpāramitāsāstra   (T. 1509)
       Translated by Kumārajīva between the 4th and 7th year of Hung Shin, Later Ch'in
       dynasty (A.D. 402–406) in Hsiao-yao Garden.

Mahāratnakūṭa (T. 310)

A compilation and translation made by Bodhiruci between the 2nd year of Shen Lung and the 2nd year of Hsien T'ien, T'ang dynasty (A.D. 706–13).

Mahāsaṅghikavinaya (T. 1425)

Translated by Buddhabhadra and Fa-hsien in the 12th year of I Hsi, Eastern Chin dynasty (A.D. 416) in Tao-chang Monastery.

Pañcaviṁśatisāhasrikāprajñāpāramitāsūtra (T. 223)

Translated by Kumārajīva in the 6th year of Hung Shih, Later Ch'in dynasty (A.D. 404).

Sarvāstivādavinaya (T. 1435)

Translated by Puṇyatara and Kumārajīva during the years of Hung Shin, Later Ch'in dynasty (A.D. 399–413). The last two *chuan* were translated by Vimalākṣa after Kumārajīva died (A.D. 413) in Shih-chien Monastery, Shou-ch'un.

Śatasāhasrikāprajñāpāramitāsūtra (T. 220 (1))

Translated by Hsüan-tsang between the 4th year of Hsien Ch'ing and the 3rd year of Lung Shou, T'ang dynasty (A.D. 659–663) in Yu-hua-kung Monastery, Fang-chou.

Subāhuparipṛcchā (*sūtra*) (T. 895)

Translated by Śubhakarasiṁha in the 14th year of K'ai Yuan, T'ang dynasty (A.D. 726) in Ta-fu-hsien Monastery, Tung-tu.

Ta ch'eng pen sheng hsin t'i kuan ching (T. 159)

Translated by Prajñā in the 6th year of Chen Yuan, T'ang dynasty (A.D. 790).

Vinayavastu (T. 1444)

Translated by I-ching between the 1st year of Chiu Shih and the 2nd year of Ching Yün, T'ang dynasty (A.D. 700–711).

Yogacarabhūmiśāstra (T. 1579)

Translated by Hsüan-tsang between the 20th and 22nd year of Chen Kuan, T'ang dynasty (A.D. 646–648) at Hung-fu Monastery.

Yu ch'ieh chin kang ting Su tzu mu p'in (T. 880)

Translated by Amoghavajra between the 5th year of T'ien Pao and the 9th year of Ta Li, T'ang dynasty (A.D. 746–774).

Part IV

Ancestor Worship Within a Cultural Context:

Past and Present

Chapter 10

Founder Worship in Kamakura Buddhism

MASAO FUJII

INTRODUCTION

Japanese Buddhism can be regarded in some respects as an indigenous religion rather than one simply introduced from China and Korea. Historically of major importance in the development of Japanese culture, it continues to function in the contemporary period as an in integral part both of spiritual as well as daily life. The Buddhism of Japan is classified with other forms of Mahayana Buddhism, the form in which the teachings of Buddha traveled north and east to play their role in the cultural achievements of Tibet, Mongolia, China, Vietnam, Korea and Japan. The older Theravada form of Buddhism has played a similar role in Sri Lanka, Burma, Thailand, Laos and Cambodia.

The practices of the original forms of Buddhism were gradually modified during their transmission throughout Asia by their inclusion of local native beliefs and practices. This phenomenon was well manifest both in China and Korea before Mahayana Buddhism was introduced to Japan. The Japanese, too, combined local religious practices and gradually transformed Buddhist performance and administrative structure toward more accommodation with other features of Japanese culture. In this way, Japanese Buddhism diverged into forms indigenous to Japan differing considerably from those first introduced from China and Korea.

The original form of Indian Buddhism which had begun as a philosophy of life was gradually recast into various schools after Shakyamuni's death. By the time of its introduction into Japan there were in China a number of major "sects" such as the Kegon, Tendai and later, the Zen sects of Rinzai and Sōtō. The usual meaning given the word "sect" by contemporary sociologists of religion gives reference to a relatively small group of opponents to a governing church. At the beginning of the Kamakura Period it is therefore proper to use the term sect as I do, whereas when these groups later stabilized, as some did by the modern period, it is more proper to call them "denominations".

Sect Buddhism in China had developed quite strong scholarly characteristics and there were intensive debates on the justifications of each sect. But Chinese Buddhism gradually changed its scholarly character after its introduction to Japan in the sixth century A.D. It first combined with state power and one ultimate goal was to help secure the state structure as it existed during the Nara and Heian Periods. By the time of the Kamakura Period, at the latter part of the 13th century, Buddhism had become a vital part of daily life inseparable from Japanese thought. During the Kamakura Period Buddhism became progressively more Japanese in content and organization. While Kamakura Buddhism remained a "sect" Buddhism on the Chinese model, it shifted from the strong scholarly character of Chinese Buddhism toward a religion more centrally concerned with salvation. Adoration of sect founders became part of practices aimed at assuring one's personal salvation in an afterlife.

New sects of "Japanese" Buddhism were established through recording the founder's particular religious experience and particular doctrines. Deification of the founder was common as was true for powerful Kami in Shinto (see Chapter 4). Belief in him was further strengthened based on a Japanese cultural analogy to father-son blood lineage relationships, a fundamental principle of Japanese corporate family structure.

Such founder worship is especially evident in every sect of Kamakura Buddhism. However, prior precedents can be found. A particularly noteworthy example of founder worship dates back to the Heian Period when Kōbō-daishi founded the Shingon sect. Later sect founders who lived during the Kamakura Period, such as Hōnen (1133–1212) of the Jōdo sect, Shinran (1173–1262) of the Jōdo-shin sect, Nichiren (1173–1262) of the Nichiren sect, and Ippen (1239–1289) of the Ji sect never visited China for purposes of study. Dōgen (1200–1253), of the Sōtō-Zen sect and Eisai (1141–1215) of the Rinzai Zen sect became exceptional cases, but all sect founders before Hōnen established new sects based on their scholarly experiences in China. This new trend in leaders without overseas experiences verifies that sects which became dominant during the Kamakura Period were organized and established in accord with the prevailing Japanese cultural patterns rather than in reference to Chinese practices.

VARIOUS ATTRIBUTES OF FOUNDER WORSHIP

Present-day Japanese Buddhism could hardly exist without founder worship. Sect founders are regarded almost on a par with Buddha. Various ritual services are to adore both the virtues of Buddha and the sect founder. Such ceremonies comprise the majority of a sect's annual events. Kanbutsu-e, marking the birth of the Buddha, is the most popular event and, regardless of sect, is generally commemorated on April 8. The first record on this event is found in *Shokunihongi*, which mentions that the first such event was conducted in 840 A.D. by Emperor Ninmyō at Seiryō Palace. Also, according to *Nenchūgyōjihisho*, the event was publicly established by Kōben, high priest of the Kegon sect in 1225 A.D. It became more popular and developed as a general custom after the middle of the Muromachi Period. By then it was accompanied by various popular folk practices such as: the practice of attempting to improve a person's writing technique by using ink prepared with tea poured over an image of Buddha on Buddha's birthday. Damage by vermin was to be controlled by utilizing a poem stating that "April 8 is the happiest day and all vermin are exterminated". This poem was written on a piece of paper fastened to a house pillar. Thunder damage would be avoided if the phrase "eight great dragon tea" was written on a piece of paper stuck to the ceiling. April 8 has been celebrated jointly among all sects as the "Flower Festival" on a nation-wide scale since the beginning of the Meiji Era. Other events pertaining to Buddha and common to all sects are "Jōdō-e", which celebrates his enlightenment on December 8, and "Nehan-e", which commemorates his death on February 15.

Annual events pertaining to sect founders of each sect vary. There is "Tendai-daishi-e", "Shusotanjō-e", and Sange-e" of the Tendai sect; "Miei-gu", "Tanjō-e", "Resso-ki" of the Shingon sect; Shūso-gotan-e, "Gyōki-e", "Kōsoki", and "Kishu-ki" of the Jōdo sect; "Hōon-Kō", "Goshō-ki", "Rikkyōkaishū-hōyō", Gotan-e, Rennyo-ki" of the Jōdo-shin sect; "Daruma-ki", of the Zen sect; "Ryozan-ki", of the Sōtō sect; "Rinzai-ki" and "Takuan-ki" of the Rinzai sect; and "Oeshiki", "Gotan-e", "Rikkyōkaishū-e", "Ryūkō-hōnan-e", Izu-hōnan-e", and "Sado-hōnan-e" of the Nichiren sect. Generally, all sects hold a special feast every 50 years for the three annually celebrated events of their founders—his birthday, the day he established the sect, and his death. In 1980, at Hsi-an, the Jōdo sect, for example, performed a special ritual service to commemorate the 1300th anniversary of the death of the Chinese high priest Shan-tao, known as Zendō-Daishi (613–681 A.D.) who has been worshipped as a founder or "Kōso". Furthermore, each temple, regardless of sect, conducts a special service with its parishioners to commemorate the anniversary of the temple founder's death.

Founder worship is reflected in the architecture of main temples. The *Soshi-dō* or *Kaisan-dō*, a special hall used to commemorate the founder, is usually contained on the premises. Hieizan Temple, headquarters of the Tendai sect, for example, has a hall, "Yogawa-daishidō" which was constructed to honor the memory of Ryōgen (912–985 A.D.) who founded the temple. Ryōgen, known as Ganzan-daishi, was the object of a popular vulgar belief utilizing an amulet bearing his printed image, called *Tsuno-daishi*. This amulet was thought to have miraculous effects.

The same type of hall was constructed also in many other large temples, like the Hōryu-ji temple of the Shōtoku sect, the Shitennō-ji temple of the Wa sect, the Kōya-san temple of the Shingon sect, Chion-in temple of the Jōdo sect, and the Higashi-hongan-ji temple and the Nishi-hongan-ji temple of the Jōdo-shin sect. In all cases the hall occupies a central location and clearly reflects the importance of the founder. In smaller temples that lack an independent hall to commemorate the founder an important space in the main hall is reserved for the purpose.

Worship of the sect founder is also concisely expressed in the components of the Buddhist family altar. An image of Buddha, a mandala chart, and the Buddhist names of ancestors are common items occupying the center of any family altar, regardless of sect. Along with these items, an image or picture of the sect founder is enshrined in the center, in a position varying according to the sect. For example, the object of worship of the Chizan Shingon sect is Mahāvairocana-tathāgata. An image of Kōbō-daishi is located to the right, facing the altar, whereas an image of

Kōgyō-daishi (1095–1143 A.D.), Kakuban, the founder of the Shingi-shingon sect, is set to the left.

The object of worship of the Jōdo sect is *Amida* Buddha. A scroll with the image of Zendō-daishi is hung on the right side facing the altar whereas an image of Hōnen is hung to the left. The composition of an altar of the Nichiren sect has an image of Nichiren in front of the mandala chart, which is the object of worship. In general, the lower levels of an altar are usually occupied by memorial tablets bearing the ancestors' posthumous names, regardless of sect. This is not true for the Jōdo-shin sect, for in this sect one never puts such tablets on the altar but instead hangs a scroll bearing the posthumous name on the altar only on the occasion of a memorial service for an ancestor.

Founder worship is the very core of the fundamental principles of every sect. This is verified by the fact that the slogan "to return to the founder", was a chant reiterated to combat the inevitable secularization that developed during every reform movement. Eminent examples of recent reformation movements are *Dōhōkai-undō* (the believers' association movement) and *Monshintokai-undō* (the followers' association movement) of the Shin sect which started in 1962. They have had quite an impact on other sects and led to various reformation or reorganization movements. The main theme of the reformation movements conducted by the Shingon sect since 1967 has been unification of the object of worship. Formerly the sect worshipped various images of Buddha according to the principle that Mahāvairocana Buddha is the dharma-kaya-Buddha with all virtues and each aspect of the virtues materialized in Amida Buddha, Kannon Bodhisattva etc. A variety of images were replaced by Kōbō-daishi under his title, dharmakaya Dainichi. He had mastered the main doctrine, "Henjokongō", as the sect founder. The meaning of the belief in Mahāvairocana Buddha became easier to understand and more concrete as the result of this replacement. The chanting sutra of the sect, "Namu-henjo-kongō" (lit. "reliance shines upon us like a diamond") was also reformed as "Namu-daishi-henjo-kongō" (lit. "reliance goes to the Great Master who is shining upon us like a diamond"). The Buzan school of the sect has been distributing a hanging picture with three images of Mahāvairocana-tathāgata, the Mantra of Light, and Kōbō-daishi to the followers as the principle object of belief, whereas the same picture with only one image of Mahāvairocana-tathāgata has been distributed by the Chizan school of the sect. The Tendai sect has been involved in a reformation movement under the slogan "to revive the doctrine of Dengyō-daishi and make use of it in our daily life". An image of Dengyō-daishi has been distributed to the followers as the object of belief. The Sōtō sect began a reformation movement to worship three images. Probably it was initiated to reduce the rivalry between the two main temples, Eihei-ji and Sōji-ji, which had been vying for superiority. Consequently, three images, both founders of the sect Dōgen-daishi and Keizan-daishi and Shakyamuni Buddha have been worshipped in a political compromise.

In this way, contemporary ancestor worship has been established based on three types of closely interrelated founder worship: worship of the founder of Buddhism, worship of the sect founder, and worship of the family founder.

A PROTOTYPE OF FOUNDER BELIEF

The prototype of all founder worship in Japan is that of Kōbō-daishi. This usage represents the most popular form taken. The process by which founder worship became established can be traced through an analysis of how the gradual Japanization of Buddhism took place within a social context which made it possible.

Buddhism in Japan has developed particular features which came to characterize it during each historical period since its first introduction in the sixth century. It was only within the Kamakura Period, however, that Buddhism became organized by reformers as a popularily established religion. Under these reformers sect Buddhism became the predominate characteristic of the Kamakura Period.

The Chinese character used to write the Japanese word Shū (sect) was quite close to the original Sanskrit word, "Siddhānta" (lit. "ultimate truth", "the zenith of accomplishment"). Belief in Buddhism became a simple reliance on each founder's conversion. The Kamakura Period was this turning point in the history of Japanese Buddhism as "Japanization" aimed at personal deliverance and salvation by introducing creativity and subjectivity into Buddhism.

The introduced Buddhism of the Nara Period had been a scholarly form, whereas that of the Heian Period after 800 was characterized by both a scholarly approach and by incantation accompanying ascetic practices. These early forms are categorized as "Ancient" Buddhism which, as state policy, was spread widely in accordance with an increase of central power. Ancient Buddhism was developed mainly for aristocrats under the strict control of the state. All temples were constructed as national temples, and all priests and nuns were given official ranks according to regulation. The *Soniryo* (lit. "priests' and nuns' ordinance") was promulgated by Emperor Monmu in 701 A.D. The number of priests and nuns was regulated. They were exempted from paying tax, and their rank and status were guaranteed by the state.

State-sponsored Ancient Buddhism contained undeniable contradictions from the very start because it prohibited the idea of personal salvation which became the very core of Buddhism as a popular universal religion. This contradiction became clearer as Buddhism spread out from the capital throughout the nation. In some localities private priests challenged a scholarly doctrine with the support of powerful local families.

Gyōki (668–749 A.D.) provides a good example. He became a priest at the age of 15 and studied the *Hossō-shūgi* doctrine. His mother's death, however, afforded him a chance to depart completely from the scholarly life and to involve himself with the enlightenment of ordinary folk throughout the country. He devoted himself to programs for social betterment such as road and reservoir construction by leaders enlightened by Buddhist precepts. Such social activities had been prohibited for priests by the *Soniryo*. His conduct was later approved, however, by the Emperor

Shōmu, who promoted him to archbishop and awarded him the name of great bodhisattva.   In this way Gyōki, who was also made famous by his creation of the *Gyōki-zu,* the oldest illustrated map, later became an object of founder worship and was revered as Gyōki bodhisattva.

Priests during the Nara Period belonged to either the scholarly schools of national temples or the family temples of powerful local families.   There was also a group of priests which conducted ascetic practices at the Hiso-ji temple, located deep in the mountains of the Yoshino Region [SONODA and TAMURA 1962].   This is worthy of consideration because it was a group that used incantation as far back as the Nara Period.   The idea of personal salvation in Kamakura Buddhism depended on a reestablishment of incantation which had been officially excluded from Ancient Buddhism.

The difference between Nara and Heian Buddhism, which are both categorized as Ancient Buddhism, is a matter of location.   The center of Nara Buddhism was the capital, the symbol of the secular world, whereas Heian Buddhism retreated to the mountains far from the secular world, as both the Hieizan temples founded by Saichō (767–822 A.D.) and the Kōyasan temple of Kōbō-daishi, illustrate.   The shift of religious center was an epoch-making event in Ancient Buddhism as Buddhism sought to separate the religious from the secular world.

Heian Buddhism contained a strong incantation factor but it was basically a religion for aristocrats.   Its believers were limited generally to members of the royal family itself and other aristocratic families.   However, a certain spreading out of Heian Buddhism was accelerated owing to the increasing number of priests drawn from these privileged families for whom new temples were constructed further afield.   Conflict over succession rights following sect founders was another negative aspect of Heian Buddhism.   For example, there was political strife between the two main temples, Kōyasan and Tou-ji, as to who would gain the initiative after the death of Kōbō-daishi.   This conflict became more involved by the end of the ninth century, owing to the lack of any decisive leadership appearing after Kōbō-daishi.   The strife within the Shingon sect was resolved only by splitting it into smaller schools.

The Tendai sect, which had only one headquarters—the Hieizan temples—was also split into two groups, the Sanmon group and the Jimon group, again over the succession right of the founder.   The Sanmon group, which regarded Jikaku-daishi-Ennin (794–864 A.D.), the third successor, as its leader, never admitted Yokei from the Jimon group as the new successor, in 989 A.D.   The Jimon group regarded Chishō-daishi-Enchin (814–891 A.D.), the fifth successor, as its leader.   The veto of the Sanmon group exercised against Yokei obligated him to give up the successor position within three months.   Strife between these groups, which started with a dispute over personnel affairs, developed into more severe skirmishes in 993 A.D., when the Jimon group attacked the Sekizan-zenin temple, which had a special meaning for the Sanmon group because of its connection with their leader, Ennin.   Without delay, the Sanmon group took its revenge by counter attacking against the Senjuin temple, the center of the Jimon group.   Nearly 1,000 members of the Jimon group who were purged from the Hieizan temples after the skirmishes established their own headquarters in the Onjō-ji temple, and confrontation between the two groups continued without interruption.

This conflict within and between sects, which was quite often accompanied by armed confrontations involving monk-soldiers, accelerated the spread of the concept of *Mappō-shisō*. This was a widespread pessimism due to the Buddhist theory that mankind was in the latter days of a Karmic cycle. People clearly sensed a decline due to a series of natural and man-made calamities which were occurring one after another. The concept of *Mappō-shisō*, which existed also in China, first appeared in Japan during the Nara Period, but it was at the end of the Heian Period that it seemed to be a real possibility, especially if one looked upon the contemporary social situation.

This pessimistic philosophy derived from an historical view of Buddhism which divided the entire period after the Buddha's death into three periods: "Shōbō" (righteous law), "Zōbō" (imitative law), and "Mappō" (last law). The first period, Righteous Law, was the period when Buddhist doctrine, practices and enlightenment became dominant. The second period, Imitative Law, was the period when both doctrine and practices still continued but when there was no longer any genuine enlightenment. The third period, that of the Last Law, was when doctrine alone remained alive. After these three periods, the doctrine itself was to vanish.

There are various views as to the duration of the first two periods. In Japan, it had been widely believed that the first two periods continued for 1,000 years each before the last Mappō period, which was to continue for 10,000 years. *Fusōryakki*, a historical record compiled at the end of the Heian period, declared that the Mappō period had started in 1052 A.D., based on the calculations mentioned above.

The sociological reason for the pervasiveness of Mappō-shisō at the end of the Heian Period was the uneasy atmosphere throughout the nation caused by the rise of the warrior class and by the tyrannical conduct of monk-soldiers. Psychologically, Japanese religious thought of the time which regarded even a trivial incident as a bad omen accelerated this pessimistic interpretation of history.

The only spiritual relief for the population that had been suffering and despairing of their daily life was a desire to be born again in paradise. It was at the beginning of the eleventh century when a place of retreat, called "Bessho", was established on the grounds of major temples like those of Hieizan or Kōyasan and in the Tōdai-ji temple compound. These retreats were mainly concentrated in the Kinki district, but 64 such places were scattered in western Japan (from Ōmi in the east to Ōsumi in the west), according to Takagi's study [1973]. People living in these places were called "Hijiri" (holy) groups. Such groups consisted of various types of individuals such as ex-priests of Heian Buddhism, who parted from it due to its corruption and secularization, mountain-dwelling ascetics, other wandering ascetics, and many others wishing to be born again in paradise. Gorai [1965] characterized the Hijiri groups as comprised of: 1) hermits; 2) ascetics; and 3) wanderers. There were also those seeking to master some sort of incantation. They hoped to cure both physical and spiritual uneasiness through becoming hermits developing ascetic practices or wandering from place to place.   Belief was to be measured by the quantity of good works.   There would be promotion of virtue through group activities such as temple construction.   They advocated understandable sermons, preaching with pictures and chanting along with dance as practical methods of promoting virtue.

Activities of such Hijiri groups were considered to exemplify "Honjisuijaku-setsu" (a theory explaining that Shinto gods are manifestations of original Buddhist deity) and "Shinbutsu-shūgō" (lit. Buddhism and Shinto in harmony).   These ideas were in operation as part of the Japanization of Buddhism.   These groups also preached a form of personal salvation based on "Jōdo-shisō" (paradise philosophy).   Incantation was a means to induce salvation.

There were two types of Jōdo-shisō: "Miroku-jōdo-shisō" (Maitreya paradise philosophy) and "Gokuraku-jōdo-shisō" (*Amida* paradise philosophy).   The first one spread widely through the nation and became the core belief advocated by Kōbō-daishi, whereas the latter developed into sects of Kamakura Buddhism (Jōdo, Jōdoshin, Ji, and Yūzūnenbutsu).

The sanctification of Kōbō-daishi was a product of "Shinbutsu-shūgō" spread widely by the activities of Hijiri groups.   Belief in Kōbō-daishi was established as the result of combining contemporary Japanese Buddhist theory, which regarded Kōyasan temple as the "promised place" where the expected Maitreya would be born, and a Japanese characteristic attitude of welcoming newcomers.   This attitude re-flected an idea prevalent in ancient Japanese folk religion that God continues wander-ing to bless people everywhere.   The *Toji-kanchiin-monjyo* and *Shokunihonkoki* recorded that Kōbō-daishi died in March 835 A.D. and his remains were cremated.   Contrary to this historical fact, "Nyūjō" legends regarding Kōbō-daishi maintained he still was alive.   The legend that he had only put his body into a temporary trance to devote his spirit to meditation in order to wait and welcome the expected Maitreya-bodhisattva first appeared in the *Nihonkiryaku*.   According to that book, the remains of Kōbō-daishi showed no signs of death, and his hair continued growing notwithstanding the decayed condition of his robes.   Kangen (853–925 A.D.) had opened his grave in 921 A.D., 87 years after his death, to dedicate an imperial letter which notified the Emperor's admission of his honorable name, Kōbō-daishi, and present him priestly garments from Emperor Daigo.   An image of Kōbō-daishi, especially his young image as a priest Kukai when he conducted severe ascetic practices in various mountains to master mysterious power had become an object of worship soon after his death.   People associated his ascetic practices with the ancient Japanese religious idea of a wandering God blessing people.   This worship was also connected with the contemporary national mood eager for the Messiah which had been accelerated by the popular belief of "Miroku-gesho".

Belief in Kōbō-daishi, which regarded a real human being as the incarnation of Maitreya-bodhisattva, had spread widely throughout the country.   Legends about Kōbō-daishi, quite often accompanied by stories of miracles, appeared accordingly at various places.   With the passage of time, Kōyasan temple, where his grave is still located, was idealized as the paradise of Maitreya, and the popular custom arose of using the temple grounds as the most suitable place to inter the ashes of the dead. The innermost shrine of this temple is surrounded by graves, mainly dating from the medieval period, but the earliest ones go back to the end of the Heian Period.

As is clear from the case of Kōbō-daishi, founder worship in Japan is basically composed of associating a real human religious leader and the idea adopted from ancient Japanese local religions of a wandering God who blesses people everywhere. Therefore, every human being worthy of respect who conducted any religious activities had a chance of becoming an object of founder worship as an incarnation of God. Belief in Shōtokutaishi (574–621 A.D.) is another good example.

Founder worship in Japan usually is connected with a given region such as Jikaku-daishi-Ennin, in the Tōhoku district, Shinran, in the Hokuriku district, Chishadaishi (538–591 A.D.) and Ganzan-daishi, in the Kantō and the Tōhoku districts, Taichō-daishi (683–768 A.D.), in the Hakusan area of the Hokuriku district and so on [MIYATA 1970]. The exceptionally widespread popularity of the belief in Kōbō-daishi, compared to these other cases of more limited areal extent, is thought to be the result of the nation-wide proselytizing of Hijiri groups who impressed on people the sanctity of the Kōyasan temple.

BLOOD THEORY IN FOUNDER WORSHIP

The common factor shared by the six "Daishi" priests of the Kamakura Period was their reformist attitudes toward the scholasticism of Ancient Buddhism. All these priests except Ippen studied at the Enryaku-ji temple in Mt. Hieizan which was then regarded as one of the sacred places of Buddhism. Although the duration of their studies differed, each tried to find the real meaning of Buddhism in his own way after leaving the temple. Hōnen established a hermitage at Kurodani-bessho in Kitadani; Shinran also studied in Hieizan and then became Hōnen's student. Ippen did not study in Hieizan but was influenced by Hōnen. Eisai and Dōgen went to China, whereas Nichiren visited various temples of Ancient Buddhism in Japan and conducted ascetic practices until he finally established his own Buddhist theory of salvation.

Believers in Mappō shisō pessimism about the world, these founders commonly claimed the necessity of three practices for any secular person to enter nirvana: "Senchaku" (selection, one from either "Nenbutsu", "Zen", or "Daimoku"), "Senju" (devoted practice), and "Igyō" (simple practice procedure). These became the characteristic features of Kamakura Buddhism. The premise of world negation had become the very source of founder worship which had spread widely, even to the very bottom of the social structure of that time. This premise erased the secular control of official Ancient Buddhism which inevitably had developed in connection with state power.

This negation of official Buddhism also brought a new but very original interpretation of Buddhism to the surface. These founders simply wished to pursue religious truth based on negation of this world.

Nevertheless, religious sects, as they became "popular", although they pursued religious truth, were inevitably vulnerable to secularization since for the most part their members were ordinary people. The religious truth of each sect had to be carried by those who maintained ordinary occupations. This dilemma became another source of founder belief.

Each Buddhist sect called succession of their doctrine by prelates either "Shishi-sōjō" or "Kechimyaku-sōjō". The meaning of "Shishi-sōjō" is transmission of doctrine from master to disciples. Such transmission resembles family transmission from father to son through bloodline and is therefore called "Kechimyaku-sōjō", which means blood vessel transmission (see M.B.D. 1960).

Blood-vessel genealogy had already been adopted in China during the T'ang Dynasty to clarify Bodhidharma's succession and the succession of the Tendaihokke sect. The Chinese custom became the basis of the Tendai and Shingon sect traditions of preparing blood-vessel genealogies to verify the righteousness of their "Shishi-sōjō". The importance of "Shishi-sōjō" was paramount. This was the obvious reason for Saichō's parting from Kūkai. It was caused by Kūkai's rejection of Saichō's request to see the most basic doctrine contained in the *Rishushakkyō*. From Kūkai's point of view, their relationship never had the conditions of "Shishi-sōjō" although they had maintained a close friendship. Kūkai was willing to show to Saichō all the documents of esoteric Buddhism that he had brought from China, except this doctrine (see Shōreishū 1910).

The lawful religious lineage of the sect founder was also a serious problem of Kamakura Buddhism as it was during the age of Ancient Buddhism. The Jōdo sect, started by Hōnen and which became the first of the Kamakura Buddhist sects, worshipped both its founder Hōnen and Zendō-daishi, to cover for Hōnen's lack of direct connection with China. He had neither been in China nor had a transmitted blood-vessel genealogy from a high priest there. The law of transmission was realized only in his dream; dreaming had a special meaning as certification at that time. It was Shōgei (1341–1420 A.D.), during the early Muromachi Period, who clarified the transmission of the sect theoretically in his writing *Jōdoshinshū-huhōden*. He established the idea of transmission through three nations from India to Japan via China in the work, and systematized the idea into "Shu-myaku" (sect founder's lineage) and "Kai-myaku" (Shakyamuni Buddha's lineage). "Shu-myaku" is transmission of sect doctrine by the founder's successors. "Kai-myaku" is the systematized procedure used to verify every followers' religious connection back to Shakyamuni Buddha. Sect followers were usually given an individually named document from their direct missionary, who was called either "Dentō-shi" or "Denkai-shi". The document mentioned righteous lay lineage from Shakyamuni to the missionary and thus the personally named document with the seal of the missionary verified each follower's connection to Shakyamuni Buddha.

The idea of blood succession from father to son is symbolized in Buddhism as the relationship between a religious founder and his followers. Shakyamuni is Great Father and all Buddhists are his sons. Kōashōken (1265–1345 A.D.) published

Sanbu-kanasho to explain this relationship quite concisely by using "Kana" characters, which were easier to understand than the Chinese characters, whose use was limited to scholars of the higher classes. In the part of the work entitled "Fushisōgō" ("mutual welcome between father and son"), he explained the relationship as follows: "Amida Buddha and mankind were born in the same house. The house means heaven and the father is Amida. After long ascetic practices, Amida has returned to the house where he was born, but mankind remained astray and wandered to other places. The father sincerely wishes all mankind to return to the house, too, though we cannot even approach the premises. The only possible way for us to return to the house is to chant *Nenbutsu* seriously to purify our spirit". Kōashōken, in this way, recommended the performance of *Nenbutsu* was the only way of self-salvation.

It was the Hongan-ji temple group which adopted blood succession, or, in other words, a hereditary lineage succession. However, this was exactly what the founder tried to avoid. Shinran's strict order to his followers was to throw his remains away in the Kamo River. His statement indicated he wanted no repetition of an infamous incident known as "Karoku-no-hōnan". Disciples of Hōnen had sought to protect their master's remains by removing them from his original grave at Higashiyama Ōtani prior to the intended raid from Hieizan. Monks of the Enryakuji temple planned to throw the remains into the Kamo River since they symbolized the source of conflict existing between temple groups. This incident, which Shinran himself witnessed, made him wish to prevent any similar conflict regarding his own remains in the future. His order also clearly reveals an absence of any idea of hereditary lineage succession in Shinran himself, although he had a wife and children. The sect center of the Jōdo-shin sect after Shinran's death was the founder's commemoration hall, constructed in 1272 A.D. An image of Shinran carved by himself in 1243 A.D. when he was 71, was enshrined in the hall as the main object of worship. Kakushin, the youngest daughter of Shinran, for whom he carved the image originally, was guardian of the hall. The worship of Shinran's image resembled what happened to Hōnen. His image carved by Kuwabarazaemon was enshrined at his grave site. The use of a founder's commemoration hall and the founder's image were used to sanctify and organize ceremonies of worship in both cases.

Nun Kakushin was entrusted with her position as guardian by the common consent of all sect followers; but no monopoly by the family for the position of guardian was implied. Nevertheless, Kakue, son of Nun Kakushin, succeeded to the position after her death. Conflict regarding succession to the position had already arisen between Kakue and his stepbrother Yuizen, who took away the founder's ashes and carved image and enshrined them in a new commemoration hall, which he constructed at Tokiwa, in Kamakura. This conflict made sect followers realize the dangerous possibilities which could result from the guardianship being automatically assumed by any descendant of Shinran. They, therefore, resisted the automatic succession of guardianship by Kakunyo, the eldest son of Kakue. Kakunyo, who finally succeeded to the position after the resolution of the dispute, devoted himself to certifying his righteousness of blood-vessel transmission by writing *Kudensho*. The main purpose of this work was to establish his righteous lineage, starting from Hōnen and Shinran. He especially stressed the legitimacy of his succession by the lawful procedure of direct transmission of teaching from Nyoshin, son of Zenran, who had been banished by Shinran. Kakunyo's claim was vulnerable. He was only a grandson of Shinran's youngest daughter.

Kakunyo had a new image of Shinran carved seven years after publishing his work, and enshrined it instead of Shinran's image, which had been taken off to Kamakura by Yuizen. The original head, however, was later taken away by Eizan, grandson of Yuizen. Zennyo, who succeeded Kakunyo, ordered the carving of a new head and joined it to the body of the image. Special treatment was used to apply lacquer, mixed with the remaining ashes of Shinran, on the joined part, ensuring its authenticity. The restored image has been worshipped as the main object of belief of the sect ever since [YAMAORI 1973].

The founder's commemoration hall was put to use as a temple by Kakunyo who set up a wooden plaque entitled "Hongan-ji Temple" in the hall. Blood-vessel transmission by hereditary lineage succession within the founder's family gradually gained admittance, but it was not until Rennyo (1415–1499 A.D.), the eighth successor of Shinran, that the sect established its fundamental organization as a modern religious order.

CONCLUSION

Analysis of the development of founder worship in Japanese Buddhism shows the existence of two patterns. The first is represented by the case of Kōbō-daishi. The belief in Kōbō-daishi was established as the result of a folk belief "Shinbutsu-shūgō", the idea of a "wandering God". The second pattern is represented by Kamakura Buddhist sects which endeavored to establish legitimacy of transmission through a form of father-son blood lineage succession.

The Jōdo-shin sect of Kamakura Buddhism is the best example of this latter pattern. The founder, Shinran, had a wife. Both his doctrine and his lineage have continued as a family succession. "Blood" was imbued with the same meaning as sect doctrine through the course of time, and transmission of doctrine was consequently transformed into the belief in blood itself. In other words, founder worship by "Shishi-sōjō" has maintained a clear blood lineage that permits a direct tracing back to the founder from today's leadership. The blood lineage of Hongan-ji Temple is culturally comparable with that of the Imperial Family.

A new trend in religious transmission resulted from a new law issued at the time of the Meiji Restoration of 1868 which permitted priests to eat meat and to marry. It marked a change of Buddhist sect character from "Shukke" (priesthood) order to "Zaike" (laity) order. The earlier transformation of the founder worship of the Jōdo-shin sect from a transmission of doctrine to one of blood succession, made apparent how Japanese social and cultural characteristics have made such transformations possible within Japanese Buddhism. There is no doubt that the component principles of the corporate family organization of Japan bears direct relationship to the development of Buddhism in Japan.

BIBLIOGRAPHY

GORAI, Shigeru
  1965 *Kōyahijiri.* Tokyo: Kadokawa Shoten.
MIYATA, Noboru
  1970 *Miroku Shinkō no Kenkyū.* Tokyo: Miraisha. (*Study of the Belief in Maitreya.*)
M. B. D.
  1960 Kechimyaku. *Mochizuki Bukkyō Daijiten,* 3rd edition. Tokyo: Sekai Seiten Kankōkai. (Blood-Inheritance Succession. *Mochizuki's Dictionary of Buddhism.*)
SHŌREISHŪ
  1910 Eizan no Chōhōshi no Rishushakkyō o motomuru ni tōsuru sho. *Shōreishū, vol.* 10. Tokyo: Yoshikawa Kōbunkan. (Reply to Saichō's Letter Requesting the Rishushakkyō.)
SONODA, Koyu and Encho TAMURA
  1962 Heian Bukkyō. *Kōza Nihon Rekishi: Kodai* 4. Tokyo: Iwanami Shoten. (Buddhism during the Heian Period.)
TAKAGI, Yutaka
  1973 *Heian Jidai Hokke Bukkyōshi Kenkyū.* Tokyo: Heirakuji Shoten. (*Study of the Tendai Sect of Buddhism during the Heian Period.*)
YAMAORI, Tetsuo
  1973 Kechimyaku Sōjō. *Nihon Bukkyó Shisōron Josetsu.* Tokyo: San'ichi Shobō. (Blood Succession. *Introduction to the History of Buddhism in Japan.*)

Chapter 11

The "Religious Family" Among the Chinese of Central Taiwan

MICHIO SUENARI

INTRODUCTION

In this chapter I have attempted to elucidate some basic principles relating the Chinese family and religion, using data from a village in central Taiwan. Some detailed materials are presented on various units of worship: the conjugal family, the household, temporal groups of households, the residential compound, and the lineage. I seek to illustrate the allocation of religious functions to these various units of belonging and to reveal some common features among them. First, religious units lie on a continuum, rather than being divided into contrasting categories. Kulp's term "religious family" [KULP 1925] should be re-evaluated in this context. Second, economic considerations are prominent in many of the religious relationships, including that between worshipper and gods. Third, there is a strong sense of "share holding" in most religious units in rural Taiwan which reveals much about religious practices. These features of Chinese religion might emerge even more clearly in a comparison with other Asian religious practices.

The term "religious family" seemed at first too ambiguous and confusing when I read Kulp's monograph on Phoenix village. He defines it as "the practical unit of ancestral worship" [KULP 1925: 145] including "all those persons who ordinarily come together for ancestor worship, whether of the moieties just beneath the sib in rank and size, or just above or identical with the economic groups" [KULP 1925: 146]. This definition seemed vague and covered units at various levels. Moreover, he added three other categories of family (natural, economic and conventional). I found, however, after having conducted field research among the Chinese in central Taiwan, that this first impression was derived partly from my bias as a Japanese.[1] In Taiwan I found that various functions are distributed among groups and categories on various

---

1) The village was chosen as a sample where lineage organization is clearly observable. As Chen [1975: 116] points out, it is an enigma why the foreign researcher in Taiwan chooses only villages where the lineage is weak or absent.

   The field work was conducted in the village for a total of four months (Jan. 8, 1976–April 7, 1976; December 22, 1976-January 7, 1977; August 20, 1977-September 8, 1977). I owe much to the kind help by scholars at the Institute of Ethnology, Academia Sinica, Nankang and to the generous support of villagers during my stay. I would like to express my gratitude to them.

levels, in contrast to Japan where the multi-functional *ie* (Japanese household) occupies the major part of social life. The questions raised by a Korean scholar might also be related to this same point, when he expressed some puzzlement at the similar title of another symposium, asking why religion would be paired with family instead of "individual" or other unit [Nakane 1972: 115]. Japanese participants, however, took the combination for granted and never dreamed of such a question.

In what follows, I shall attempt to describe what is the "religious family", based on field data, and in so doing, consider some basic principles that make up Chinese social organization. That is, I shall use the term not as a conceptual tool for analysis but rather as a concept expressing unique features to be analyzed. Since my interest is more sociological than ideological, I will concern myself with social aspects of religious practices rather than with the content of belief.

THE VILLAGE

"Bamboo Village" is a Fukienese hamlet in central Taiwan, located between Taichung and Chai. The fictitious name I have given the village is adopted from the landscape, wherein a compound of red brick houses is surrounded by thick hedges of green bamboo. Seen from a distance, the village looks like an island of bamboo floating in a sea of paddy fields. This hamlet is part of a traditional local administrative unit, now composed of four villages in Shetou *hsiang* (rural township), with a total population of 37,557 in an area of 35.8 square km. Though traditionally the administrative unit was totally a farming area, it now includes some parts close to commercial centers. Recently factories have been built among the paddy fields. The population of Bamboo Village itself was 5,602 (911 households) in 1975 up from 4,355 (721 households) in 1955. It has increased by about 20 percent (30 percent for

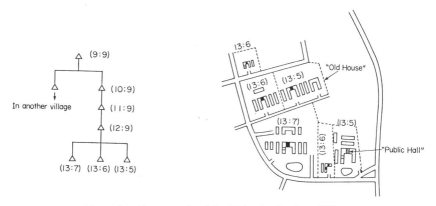

Figure 1. Compounds of the Hsiao in Bamboo Village.

LEGEND
■ : Big Room with the domestic altar
( ): The apical ancestor or the compound
(13:7): The compound of Rightsound

households) in the last 20 years. The natural increase itself has been greater, but many villagers have migrated to nearby cities. The average size of a household has remained almost constant, from 6.04 to 6.14.

Though the name of the township is associated with the aborigines, the present inhabitants, for the most part, are descendants of immigrants from Mainland China. The majority group is of the Hsiao lineage, which comprises 34.7 percent of the *hsiang's* population [CHEN 1975: 115]. Many of their ancestors are supposed to have come from Fukien Province a number of generations ago, around the early 18th century. The lineage members live clustered in compounds separated from one another by walls of bricks and hedges of bamboo.

As an example let us choose the 13th generation compound of "Rightsound" now inhabited by those who moved from the adjacent "Old House" (Figure 1).

THE COMPOUND OF RIGHTSOUND

The compound is composed of 23 households of which 10 live in cities or towns. Most of the urban dwellers have given up the right to their rooms to their brothers or people with other surnames. Only three of them still keep rooms vacant. Only the Big Room (大庁) is jointly owned, thus permitting some urban migrants to return for worship of their ancestors. In addition, three households have separated from the others, and have the ash of the incense pot of the "Big Room" brought to the altar of their own house.

The people of the compound say that their ancestors were poor when they came to Taiwan. It was the money earned by two menial servants that became the base of the present wealth of the Hsiao in this village. Therefore, they celebrate the Chinese All Souls' Festival (中元節) twice in order also to commemorate the souls of the faithful servants as well as soothing wandering ghosts in general. The Hsiaos became especially prosperous in the fifteenth generation, increasing their property as rice merchants and amassing more than 20 ha of paddy field.

When the first registration took place in 1909 the compound was jointly owned. The first division took place among the descendants of the two senior grandsons of generation 13 and was registered in 1944. This division was initiated by Generous-Charity. Mastering bone setting and being a man of benevolence, he became such a famous doctor that many patients came also from other townships. Living an assiduous and frugal life he added 30 ha of paddy field to his own property; he constructed another set of buildings at the back of the main buildings;[2] he constructed his own Deity Room (神明庁) but continued to join in worshipping the ancestral tablets in the Big Room of the compound. After the end of the Second World War a woman of strong personality quarreled with the others of the compound and went

---

2) Freedman [1958:49–50] points out this unequal segmentation of Chinese lineages. He [FREEDMAN 1966: 35] also stresses the importance of the study of the land holdings jointly held by segments beneath the level of the ancestral hall segment.

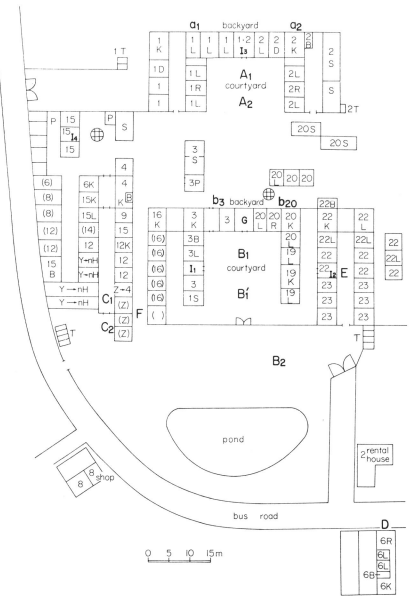

Figure 2. Room plan and the places for Rituals within the compound of
Right-sound (13: 7).

to court to demand definite division which led to the registration of the shares of the respective households comprising the compound.

Religious activities at the domestic level are held in several locations within the compound (Figure 2). A domestic altar is placed in the Big Room (G). There are four Deity Rooms ($I_1 \sim I_4$) for gods of higher levels. The yard is used for gods of lower levels and for the highest gods (天公). There is a distinction between who should be worshipped in the front and back yards, and inside and outside the compound. For example, the Gods of Heaven are celebrated in the courtyard inside the compound (A1, B1, C1), whereas the Gods of the Housesite are served food on a bench instead of an altar in the backyard (a1, a2, b3, b20). Wandering souls have been provided offerings outside the compound (B2, C2).

Residents often cooperate in worshipping gods and ancestors. Several levels in the formation of the units for worship can be distinguished: Firstly, a couple with young children may become a worshipping unit for the "Bed Mother" (床母), even though the couple belongs to a larger household unit. The goddess is believed to protect children, and the ritual is held on the evening of July 7. Though I did not find an example in which the deity is worshipped separately by several couples within a household, some informants admitted the possibility of such a case.

Secondly, a household sharing the fireplace and livelihood together worship the God of the Fireplace (灶君) in kitchens (k) and the God of the House-Site (地基主). The household is also the basic unit that prepares most of the offerings to the ancestors and high gods.

Thirdly, several households share the table of offerings outdoors and worship together, even though the offering dishes are prepared later and consumed separately. This joint worship by bringing one's share and taking it back is the unique feature which appears in many social activities of the Chinese. I shall call this the "bringing share" principle. This may be found, for example, in the worship of the God of Heaven, the Soldiers of Gods, and the Good Brothers (好兄弟).

Fourth, the whole compound worships together, utilizing the "bringing share" principle, at the ritual commemorating the death of Right-Sound, the founder of the compound. This ceremony is attended by a few household members who live in town. More women participate in most of the rituals of the compound than men. However, the rituals at the ancestral hall are supposed to be for men only. Even there, however, I saw a woman who brought the offerings on behalf of a particular segment.

LEGEND

number:	household number	S	: storehouse
( )	: vacant	T	: toilet
B	: bathroom	nH	: non-Hsiao family
D	: dining room	G	: Big Room
K	: kitchen	I_1, I_2, I_3, I_4:	deity room
L	: living & bed room	$A \sim F$	: places for rituals
P	: pigpen	#	: well
R	: room for guest		

The "bringing share" principle is involved in most cooperative religious activities within the compound.   I also note, however, another principle, "the rotation principle".   It is applied in the management of the Big Room of the compound.   Here the amount of responsibility assigned is proportionate to the share of the inheritance. This principle seems to be put into effect when some properties are owned jointly. We will be able to see this more clearly in the worship at graves and at ancestral halls.

GRAVE WORSHIP

Worship at the graves of ancestors annually occurs on the spring solstice, Ching-iming (清明), as well as on special occasions such as the birth or marriage of male descendants.   The presence of some basic property for worship is important for maintaining the graves of remote ancestors.   The grave of Right-Sound had 3.7 ha of paddy field as supporting property, but 3 ha of it was divided among the descendants before the end of the Second World War and now the remnant is rented.   The rent is used for the offerings at the grave and for the expenses of the domestic altar.   There are now only a small number of participants in grave worship.   Informants say that many descendants would take part were the property large enough to make as rich offerings as in older times.

The graves of subsequent generations are without basic property and are worshipped by the "bringing share" principle of offerings prepared in each household. For recent ancestors there are more worshippers.   Graves without property, however, tend to be obliterated as the generations pass. In a rare case an older descendant may make efforts to care for the graves of the more remote ancestors, offering only incense and covering them with yellow paper.

I witnessed one case in which it took nearly twenty minutes to identify in the public cemetery the grave of the second grandmother.   It can be inferred that many graves of remote ancestors were forgotten when there was no custom of inscribing names on the grave stone.

THE PUBLIC HALL

In Bamboo Village, there is a building called "public hall" which does not belong to either of the compounds (Figure 1) though descendants of one lineage live in both wings of the building.   The hall occupies the center of a U-shaped structure with almost the same appearance as the Big Room of ordinary compounds.   Like a domestic altar, a board-type tablet is placed on the altar with a pot of incense, containing 93 names of ancestors beginning with one of the 10th generation. Though the hall is somewhat more impressive, it would be impossible to distinguish it from a Big Room by outward appearance alone.

It is similar to an Ancestral Hall in the following points: financial trusts are attached, and rituals are financed by profit from the trust instead of utilizing the "bringing share" principle.   Many guests participate in its rituals.   The trusts are dedicated to a particular ancestor of the 9th generation although his name is not listed among the ancestors worshipped—which commence with one of those of the 10th generation. This prevented the inclusion of descendants of the 9th generation ancestor now residing elsewhere from possible participation. This instance brings out the intermediate form between the domestic altar room and the ancestral hall.[3]

THE HSIAO ON THE MAINLAND AND IN TAIWAN: PARTICIPATION DESPITE DISTANCE

According to genealogical records, the great grandfather of the founder of the present lineage segment came to Fukien Province as a high officer. His two grandsons established themselves at the local places which became the residential bases of the two major segments of the lineage. It was well after ten generations that some of their descendants moved to Taiwan. By this time there had been considerable segmentation of the lineage, judging from the halls built for the major ancestors. It is interesting to note how in Taiwan there developed the halls and trusts similar to those found on the mainland. A lineage like the Hsiao of Shetou might be compared to a tree grown from a cutting while the parent tree continues to grow in the homeland.[4]

Communication between these two segments of the lineage continued well until the end of the Second World War. Informants say that some trusts sent money for ancestral rituals held on the mainland and some even visited the mainland to participate in the ritual held at the ancestral hall. There were also visitors from the mainland who stayed on until they received money to "repair the graves and ancestral halls at home".

ANCESTRAL HALLS

The Hsiao of Shetou have eight halls. A hall is used to house memorial tablets for the ancestors and for commemorating rituals once or twice a year. A hall keeper, living in the side building, offers tea and incense daily. Some of these halls owned enormous amounts of paddy fields, the rent of which provided for large-scale rituals. The size of the hall and the richness of ritual were the symbols of the unity and the relative status of the segment of the lineage, as can be noted in the folk song about the ancestral ritual of the Hsiao [SUENARI 1977: 124–144].

If we judge only from wealthier examples we might consider ancestor worship

---

3) The ancestral hall in Ch'inan described by Ahern [1973] seems to resemble the Big Room in Shetou in several aspects [SUENARI 1978: 44]. Nelson [1974: 266–267] also discusses an intermediate form found in Hong Kong.

4) Professor Chen Chi-nan of the Academia Sinica suggested that such a lineage might be compared to a transplanted tree. Strictly speaking, however, this metaphor should be applied only to a case when the members of an entire lineage move to another place.

as uniform for all or as remaining stable through time.   A more careful examination, however, discloses the wide range of size and the radical rise and fall of ancestral halls. Before the end of the Second World War, some of the halls of this village held annual rituals, inviting hundreds of guests to performances of Taiwanese drama and to the feast that followed.   In the case of "B" hall, for example, on one occasion, they had forty tables for guests and prepared as many straw mats for children totaling nearly a thousand people in all.   Hall "A" was next in the size of ritual, whereas "D" and "F" were less notable and their activities were not well known even by the Hsiao of other segments.   "E" is said to have lost its property through poor management before the end of the Second World War.   Now their site is used for the community shrine of the god Kuan-ti.   Though "D" had a large hall with a pond to the south, their site now has been sold off and moved to a small hut at the foot of the mountain, managed by a descendant who had some success in business. After land reform in 1953 "B", "G", and "H" had little property left. I saw no worshippers on a festive day other than the managers of the hall trust.   Such variation and change is quite natural when one considers that care for the hall is affected by the politico-economic power of the descendants; ancestral halls reflect also the adversity suffered by descendants.

RESPONSIBILITY FOR PREPARING THE CEREMONY

Though rotation is the major principle in the activities at an ancestral hall with property, the independence of each segment is also seen in the process of the ceremony.   Each stirp, or branch lineage, composing a segment of the trust brings its offerings and displays to the hall. Feast tables are also assigned to each. These are determined by the property distributed to each segment. The principle of "bringing share" does not involve lower units such as households.

It is misleading to imagine a strong sense of reverence to a remote ancestor as just because there are sumptuous festivals held at the lineage halls.   Such feasts are feasible only when there is enormous property attached to the halls.   Maintenance of the hall is more related to other motives such as a display of economic or political power, rather than religious reverence.   If the presence of a hall reflects directly the strong sense of veneration of ancestors, then it is possible that an ancestral hall maintained without much economic base might also be memorialized by the "bringing share" principle just as is done for rituals held at the domestic altar. This does not happen at any of the halls maintained by the Hsiao. Such practice indeed was observed at a hall of another lineage, the Liu. In their hall members brought offerings that they had cooked in their households and that they took back after the ritual, just as is done at the ritual held at the Big Room of the Hsiao.

LINEAGE TRUST

A lineage trust is the joint property of the lineage or of a particular segment.   The property utilized usually is paddy land rented to its members or sometimes to out-siders. A trust is both a symbol of the unity of the segment and a potential source of conflict within the group.   In Shetou township, lineage land amounted to 766 ha, or 41.9 percent of the total arable land.   The Hsiao of Shetou owned about 73.4 percent of the lineage land (500 ha) [SAKA 1936: 666, 769–770].   The average size of farm land per household was 0.73 ha in 1932 [SHATO KOGAKKO 1932].   It is tempting to ask why such an enormous amount of land came to be owned collectively when there were so many landless farmers.

It is conjectured that the Hsiao trusts in Shetou began to be organized around the middle of the 18th century.   A survey shows 1744 as the year of origin for trust organization in Shetou, though the source document is not indicated [SHATO KOGAKKO 1932].   In this early period, immigrants participated in the ancestral rituals of an an-cestral hall only by sending money to the mainland.   However, once able to establish a permanent economic base for their life in Taiwan, they began to organize trusts and to construct halls.   The first date appearing in the preface of the memorandum of the Hsiao Eleven-units Trust is 1763.   They took their own share of the trust on the mainland and used it as a fund for the new trust organized in Taiwan.   The trust is further subdivided into junior level trusts.   An informant said that the segmentary composition of the trust is the same as on the mainland.   If this is true, we may infer that immigrants came almost evenly out of the parent population in the mainland.   Otherwise it would be difficult to maintain such an organization.   Each major stirp, or branch lineage, had at least a few immigrants who could represent them.

A trust may be started from a portion set aside for the cult of ancestors at the time inheritance is distributed, or from a sum contributed by descendants.   In the latter case stocks are established in the names of ancestors who have suitable positions in the genealogy which can represent the contributors.   Also, they can organize a new trust from the surplus of an older fund, giving it a different name but having the same group of members.   Why this is done is not always clear.   There may be quite a few trusts with different names organized by the same descendants.   I noted in one instance five trusts dedicated to the name of one ancestor.

Trusts were also re-organized due to fission, as some segment of a lower level became influential and independent from other segments of the same order.   On the other hand, there are relatively few cases in which several segments united to organize an upper level trust.   The only example that I could check out was the construction of the ancestral hall of "A".   Hsiao's trusts proliferated by one or another of these processes.   Saka [1936] reports that 147 trusts existed in 1929, although many trusts had already been liquidated as a result of conflicts and lawsuits among their members.   Informants say that the trusts were declining in the Taisho era (1912–1926) because there were so many lawsuits that the Japanese government had to make a new law to deal with them.   The court records have been one of the major sources of docu-mental data on the trust [SUENARI 1980a].   I have been able to check the names of 82 trusts and 42 ancestors to whom these trusts were dedicated.

The major function of a trust seems to have been to assure land to cultivate for the poor landless lineage members. In former times in Taiwan, before land reform, the demand for arable land was high owing to population pressure. Landowners occupied an advantageous position. The rent was high (often more than 50%) and the land could be given to another cultivator at the will of the owner. It was customary to bring a small gift to the landowner on the Moon Festival Day or on his birthday to ensure his good favors [GALLIN 1966: 89–93]. If the land belongs to the trust of the lineage there is no fear of eviction provided the rent is paid. Hence, a trust is a kind of a cooperative land association managed by the lineage.

Another important function might have been to defend the land against the encroachment by other groups. There is an interesting example of this.

> A man of Hsiao came from the adjacent county to settle in Shetou. When he bought a house and lot the seller required him to buy the pond at the same time. Fearing that robbers and other influential surname groups would mark him as a rich man and encroach on his property, he asked leaders of the big trusts of Hsiao to buy the pond jointly. Two trusts took a quarter-share jointly, and the other trusts took a quarter-share each. This trust is still managed as a fish pond by the man's descendants and the trusts.

The question remains why this trust is not regarded as a lineage trust even though it was organized by members of the Hsiao lineage. A typical lineage trust seems to have required an ancestor as a focal point: an idiom of ancestor worship is involved even if the major objective of the trust is economic or political. We can, then, see why ancestral halls without economic function are left to decay and only a few people are interested in the continuation of rituals. Idioms cannot survive by themselves. Closer ancestors are worshipped not *pro forma* but with more expressive emotional motivation involving personal memories or feelings of gratitude held by descendants valuing the gift of life or the inheritance of properties. Therefore, I infer that the Hsiao continue to worship their proximate ancestors on the domestic level by a "bringing share" method even when they lack common property. This contention supports Freedman's dichotomy of ancestor worship as functioning on a lineage level and on a domestic level. The dichotomy is useful for distinguishing the emotional sources of ancestor worship from other purposes. We should note, however, that this contrast is useful only in the abstract. A border cannot be so clearly demarcated in any continuum between household and lineage group functions. Even on the domestic level the sense of sharing is a basic principle unifying the group in all its purposes as is true for the lineage level.

The concept of sharing is cardinal to the formation and the management of a trust, and is closely associated with the distribution of goods. The profit from the trust is divided in one of three ways of calculation—per stirpes, or branch lineages; per capita; or by shares of stock. Freedman [1966: 51–54] discusses the distinction of "per stirpes" and "per capita", and notes that the former was often applied only at the time of formation, so that the descendants subsequently took their share per capita.

The first form of division follows after the principle of equal inheritance among sons; the second is the allocation of profit to each living male member; and the third means to divide the profit in proportion to the amount of stock in which the original members invested. Tai [1945: 233–369] applies this classification to different types of trusts, but I think these three ways can be combined and applied to the same organization for different purposes, for the stock may be owned jointly by the descendants of the original owner, and the trust may supply a grant-in-aid to a successful candidate. One informant said that he was able to attend and graduate from the higher normal school by such grants from the four trusts to which he was related.

A similar function is at work in a "respect-for-the-aged" grant which is paid irrespective of the stirps one belongs to or of the stock one holds. Judging from one example, it is not always clear which methods apply in the distribution of the assets. When one grant was dissolved in 1935, there arose a dispute regarding what principle should be used to divide the assets. The descendants of one brother formed the majority and insisted on the division per capita, whereas the descendants of the other wanted to adopt a per stirpes calculation. The latter constituted the minority and were voted down but they instituted a court case and succeeded to getting a share per stirpes. This case might indicate existence of an unstable balance between the per stirpes way based on the inheritance rule and the per capita way that reflects the actual population and power of various segments [SUENARI 1977: 109–111]. This tension between two principles could be a cause for the structural dispersion of trust groups in the long run.

The same imbalance between two principles may be also found on the household level. For example, differences between brothers in the number of sons, combined with the inheritance rule by stirpes, might lead to inequal economic status in the next generation. This would be counter to the solidarity of a family based on an equal status of those in the group (per capita principle). So, the Chinese "religious family" may be usefully analyzed as a unit on a continuum rather than as representing two distinct contrasting categories of membership.

FEATURES OF THE RELIGIOUS FAMILY

The following characteristics of the "religious family" of Central Taiwan emerge. First, religious units lie on a continuum from smaller to larger. A lineage trust may be organized for the ancestors of more proximate lower levels to more distant generational levels. The size of the trust can vary from small, with less than 1 ha of paddy land, to large with more than 100 ha. The number of worshippers at the grave may vary according to the generation of the ancestors and the nature of the gods. We may regard any of these units as a "family" in the wider sense of the word. Of course the lineage as a jural unit may also be contrasted with the family as a domestic unit. It provides a useful insight for understanding Chinese kinship. But, as far as the data from Shetou are concerned, it leaves some gaps between facts and theory [SUENARI 1978: 45–46, 49]. If the term is used too strictly, limiting it to the household unit, then we may overlook the dispersing of domestic functions to other units on various levels of inclusion which is, I think, one of the critical features of Chinese kinship. It would also be useful, therefore, to notice such a widening extension of terms in order to comprehend the local usage of the term "family" for wider units. The concept of "family" or "house" is often extended elsewhere to wider units as found in the usage of the Hsiao "family" (蕭家) for the Hsiao "lineage" or of the Liu "house" (劉厝) as applied to clusters of compounds of Liu, or "Old House" (故厝) from which new units are divided. We find such tendencies also recorded in the description by Ahern [1973: 61].

Second, one must note the prevalence of economic considerations in family relationships. Most relationships are formed and expressed in terms of economic reciprocity. One of the motives for ancestor worship is the sense of obligation for having obtained property through inheritance. There have been many studies of this function. For example, Ahern [1973: 144–147] writes that the presence of inheritance property is one of the major factors motivating worship by descendants. The "succession to the deceased" (過継) is practiced as a reciprocal obligation to continue the fire of incense in repayment for inheritance of the property rights of the deceased. Remote ancestors are worshipped with offerings only when there is basic property for it. Even the relationship between gods and worshipper is contractual: the latter gives the former a small offering as token of cognizance and prays for help promising to make offerings of a larger amount if the wish is fulfilled. Thus A. Wolf [1974: 162] writes, "If divination reveals that the god is not inclined to grant the petition, he then promises a more substantial gift, repeating the process until the god finally agrees." Such a sense of contractual economic reciprocity is more clearly seen in the relationship with gods of a lower level, since it is easy to bargain with them, even on immoral matters.

Third, a strong sense of conscious sharing is characteristic of Chinese social organization [WANG 1967, 1971]. Sharing is the basic concept utilized in many of the religious groups, business groups, or voluntary associations as well as trust groups or other units found within a compound. The three ways of calculating shares, however, sometimes leave room for choices that might be manipulated to adapt rights into uneven realities. On the household level, for example, a sense of inequality as to what is to be one's share is strongly felt before a possible division of a household. The cause for such a division is often the uneven contributions of male members, though, interestingly enough, such division is culturally attributed to the incorrigible egoistic nature of rivalrous women. The rivalry is actually between applying the principle of stock contribution versus the principle of per capita, the equal rights of members. Though income by each member is pooled and managed collectively in the household account, there is a sense of independent sharing rather than a sense of total immersion in the group.

A CONCLUDING COMPARISON

The above mentioned features of the Chinese religious family become clearer when compared with those operative in Japan and Korea.

Japan provides a case at the opposite extreme from that of China. The Japanese *ie* assumes most of the functions which are assigned to units of various levels in Taiwan. It is not only an economic unit but also a religious unit of worship of ancestors or gods, and also the unit of life crisis rituals and many of the other social activities. The *dōzoku* (a group of *ie* related by main and branch relationships within a hamlet) may be compared with the compound in Taiwan, but one notes quickly it is not characterized by differentiation at various levels, as in the latter. In northeastern Japan, ancestors of higher generations are worshipped at the main household, since they are regarded as ancestors only of that household. The descendants of the branch households send one person as a representative from each household to attend the ritual of the main household, but they do not view it as a ritual for their own ancestors. They participate in it as an event of the main household, just as a man of the main household takes part in the worship of the ancestors of the branch household who are not his direct ancestors. Though *dōzoku*, in some parts of western Japan, might worship an ancestor jointly, it is only the founding ancestor that is worshipped collectively by its members; the custody of worship of lower ancestors is assigned to the households to which they belonged in their lifetime [YONEMURA 1976: 186ff]. Relationships with ancestors or gods are based more on emotion than on contract [PLATH 1964]. Households worship ancestors even though no secular gains are promised or even if it is not prescribed by some Confucianism rule of behavior.

Although there is a rotation system to assign the responsibility of celebrating gods, the sense of sharing does not penetrate widely. Usually, offerings to gods at the festivals are prepared jointly. Expenses are collected from each community household and are pooled. After making the offering, members eat it together without taking it to each household.

The Korean case is, at first sight, very close to that of Japan. Their household (*chip* 집) is, ideally, composed of a stem family in which the eldest son remains with his parents and his younger brothers leave their natal household after marriage. The household is not only the economic unit, but also the unit of religious activities concerning folk deities, such as the Protecting God of Family or the God of House Site. Allotments of the expense of the village festivals are collected from each household. The names of the heads of the households are read when paper is burned in dedication to the village god at the community festival. But this is just one aspect of family as a worship unit. When we look at the activities involving ancestor worship generally, differentiation into various levels beyond the household emerges. Koreans also gather at the household of the eldest son for the ritual commemorating the anniversaries of the deaths of ancestors. The responsibility for those ceremonies is committed to the eldest. Though this may seem identical with the Japanese case, there is a sharp difference in the consciousness of the participants. The ancestor in Korea is "our ancestor" instead of the ancestor of the main household. Furthermore, segmentary gradation of the patrilineal lineage may be observed.

As for the relationship between ancestors and worshippers, Koreans seem to be more formalistic. This is not only seen in the manner of Confucian worship to ancestors, but also in the salutation of the children to their living grandparents [Janelli 1973: 180–187]. Confucian manners are observed even more faithfully among Koreans than among the Chinese of Taiwan [Suenari 1980b].

The "bringing share" principle is not so clear although Koreans organize associations in which membership is based on equal shares. Distribution is managed by the principle of rotation among members. Here an equalitarian principle of sharing is stressed except in some financial associations. During my field work in a fishing village in the east coast of Korea I gained the strong impression that although a sense of calculation is strong, the emotional incentive seems to be the more important element involved in group solidarity. Offerings to the gods, collected from the households, are consumed together, just as in the Japanese case.

In general I would conclude the Chinese "religious family" may be regarded as relationships existing on various levels, whereas the Japanese lack intermediate units beyond the *ie* level. The Korean case seem to fall between those operative in China and Japan.

BIBLIOGRAPHY

Ahern, Emily
    1973   *The Cult of the Dead in a Chinese Village.*   Stanford: Stanford University Press.
Baker, Hugh
    1968   *A Chinese Lineage Village: Sheung Shui.*   Stanford: Stanford University Press.
Chen, Chi-nan
    1975   『清代臺灣漢人社會的建立及基結構』[國立臺灣大學考古人類研究所碩士論文]
            (*The Formation and Structure of Chinese Society in Ch'in Period.* In Chinese.) [Master Paper for the Department of Anthropology at National Taiwan University.]
Choen, Myron
    1969   Agnatic Kinship in South Taiwan.   *Ethnology* 8: 167–182.
Diamond, Norma
    1979   *K'un Shen: A Taiwan Village.*   New York: Holt, Rinehart & Winston.
Freedman, Maurice
    1958   *Lineage Organization in Southeastern China.*   London: Athlone.
    1966   *Chinese Lineage Society: Fukien and Kwangtung.*   London: Athlone.
    1967   Ancestor Worship: Two Facets of the Chinese Case.   In M. Freedman (ed.), *Social Organization, Essays Presented to Raymond Firth*, Chicago: Aldine, pp. 85–103.
Freedman, Maurice (ed.)
    1970   *Family and Kinship in Chinese Society.*   Stanford: Stanford University Press.
Fried, Morton
    1970   Clans and Lineages: How to Tell Them Apart and Why with Special Reference

to Chinese Society. *Bulletin of the Institute of Ethnology, Academic Sinica* 29: 11–36.

GALLIN, Bernard
  1966 *Hsin Hsing, Taiwan. A Chinese Village in Change.* Berkeley and Los Angeles: University of California Press.

JANELLI, Roger L.
  1973 Anthropology, Folklore and Korean Ancestor Worship. 『文化人類學』 6: 175–190, Seoul. (*Cultural Anthropology.*)

JORDON, David
  1972 *Gods, Ghosts and Ancestors.* Berkeley and Los Angeles: University of California Press.

KULP, Daniel
  1925 *Country Life in South China: The Sociology of Familism, Volume I. Phoenix Village, Kwangtung, China.* New York: Columbia University Press.

KWAN, Hua-san
  1980 Traditional Houses and Folk Concepts in Taiwan. 『中央研究院民族學研究所集刊』 *Bulletin of the Institute of Ethnology, Academic Sinica* 49: 175–215.

LI, Yih-yuan
  1976 Chinese Geomancy and Ancestor Worship. In W. Newell (ed.), *Ancestors,* The Hague: Mouton, pp. 329–338.

NAKANE, Chie and Akira GOTO (eds.)
  1972 *The Symposium of Family and Religion in East Asian Countries.* Tokyo: Center for East Asian Cultural Studies. (*East Asian Cultural Studies* 11.)

NELSON, H. G. H.
  1974 Ancestor Worship and Burial Practices. In A. Wolf (ed.), *Religion and Ritual in Chinese Society.* Stanford: Stanford University Press, pp. 251–277.

PASTERNAK, Burton
  1972 *Kinship and Community in Two Chinese Villages.* Stanford: Stanford University Press.

PLATH, David
  1964 Japanese Household. *American Anthropologist* 66: 300–317.

SAKA, Yoshihiko
  1936 「祭祀公業の基本問題」『臺北帝國大學文政學部政學科研究年報』(Fundamental Problems on the Trusts for Worship. *Taihoku Teikoku Daigaku Bunseigakubu, Seigakuka Kenkyunenpō* 3: 485–793.)

SHATO KOGAKKO
  1932 『鄉土調査』 (*A Survey of the County Shetou.* In Japanese.)

SUENARI, Michio
  1969 書評・王崧興著『龜山島』 *Japanese Journal of Ethnology* 34(3): 284–286 (Book Review in Japanese). (Wang, Sung-hsing, *Kuei-shan Tao.*)
  1977 「漢人の祖先崇拝——中部台湾の事例より (1)」『聖心女子大学論叢』 (The Cult of the Ancestors in Taiwan: Part I. *Seishin Studies* 50: 86–153. In Japanese.)
  1978 「漢人の祖先崇拝——中部台湾の事例より (2)」『聖心女子大学論叢』(The Cult of the Ancestors in Taiwan: Part II. *Seishin Studies* 52: 5–55. In Japanese.)
  1979 「中国の家，日本の家」 飯島 茂編『アジア文明の原像』Tokyo: Japan Broadcast Publishing Co., pp. 107–110. (Chinese Family and Japanese Family. In S. Iijima (ed.), *Prototypes of Asian Civilization.* In Japanese.)

1980a 「漢人の祖先崇拝：資料篇」『聖心女子大学論叢』 (The Cult of the Ancestors in Taiwan: Appendix. *Seishin Studies* 56: 91–208. In Japanese.)

1980b Comparative Study of Memorial Tablets. (Paper read at the International Symposium on Asian Peoples and Their Cultures: Continuity and Change. Seoul: Korea.)

TAI, T.

1945 「臺灣の家族制度と祖先祭祀團體」『臺灣文化論叢』 (Family and Ancestor Worship Groups in Taiwan. *Taiwan Bunka Ronso* 2: 181–264.)

WANG, Sung-hsing

1967 『龜山島——漢人漁村社會之研究』 Nankang: Institute of Academia Sinica. (*Kuei-shan Tao: A Study of a Chinese Fishing Community in Formosa*. In Chinese.)

1971 *Pooling and Sharing*. (Unpublished PhD Dissertation for the University of Tokyo.)

WOLF, A. (ed.)

1974 *Religion and Ritual in Chinese Society*. Stanford: Stanford University Press.

YONEMURA, Shoji

1976 Dozoku and Ancestor Worship in Japan. In W. Newell (ed.), *Ancestors*, The Hague: Mouton, pp. 177–203.

Chapter 12

Family and Religion in Traditional and Contemporary Korea

KWANG KYU LEE

INTRODUCTION

The religious concepts and value system of the Korean people are directly reflected in the worship of household gods and ancestor worship on a family level, rather than in the theories and practices of higher religions such as Buddhism, Confucianism and Christianity.

My purpose in what follows is to elucidate the characteristics of the Korean family structure, and the value of the family, which are reflected in the belief system of traditional society.

There are usually about eight recognized gods per household: the Ancestor God, House Master God, Fire God, House Site God, God of Wealth, God of Long Life, God of Toilet, and God of Gate. Even though these gods have their own positions and names in the house, they are characterized by mutual independence, and some overlap of functions or duties. Their basic function is the promotion of family health and wealth.

Ritual services for house gods as well as ancestor worship reflect the sexual role segregation between husband and wife: the house gods are worshipped by the housewife and the husband engages in ancestor worship. Ancestor worship also becomes the main task of the eldest son. Succession to responsibility for worship is the base for the inheritance of property and for the formation of the main family and branch families.

The East Asian societies we are considering are all characterized by highly developed patrilineal family systems. Family in these societies is not only the basic unit of society but also affords the individual the most important social identity. An individual is subordinated to and lives for or, in extreme cases, sacrifices himself for the family. This value of familism was emphasized greatly in the past, and even today in Korea there are many sorrowful but admirable stories of young women who sacrifice themselves for their younger brothers after losing their parents. Some women give up their own education and even postpone marriage to work in factories to support and educate younger siblings.

The concept of family in Korea, as well as in China and Japan, includes not only a sociological meaning, such as a social unit of individuals and an economic entity,

185

but also the material culture such as house buildings, social status, and the customs and traditions of the family.

The state, "Kuk-ga", in Korean is a combination of two words, nation and family. It is not only a terminological expression, since in reality the filial piety of an individual to his parents is also considered as loyalty to the state. The state in feudal times emphasized the hierarchical social order of subordination of individual to family, family to patrilineal kin group, and kin group to state.

The subordination of the individual to the family can be seen also in the religious life of Korea. In other words, religious practice in Korea is not for the individual but for the family unit.

Local variations in the characteristics and functions of household gods in the traditional rural family of Korea occur in the Korean peninsula, but my presentation will focus on their more general aspects. The characteristics of household gods in Korea that I shall examine are the form or figure of the god, the location and function of the god, ritual performance and symbolic explanation of the god by believers.

The gods worshipped at home also include ancestor spirits. Ancestor worship is regarded as the most important aspect of religion at the family level. It is the fundamental basis of kinship organization and kinship activities in Korea. In the present context I shall examine ancestor worship only as it pertains to the ritual services performed within the household.

Religious activities of ordinary people in rural areas are not limited to the household god and ancestor worship. The village gods or certain features of mountains are objects or worship for the health, wealth and welfare of the family. But here I consider only the ritual services for the gods within the household.

While the religious thought of the Korean people can be found in the writings of Buddhism, Confucianism or Christianity, religious thought as a part of basic personality and as a direct part of cultural pattern can be best approached directly by the analysis of ritual services performed at home. During the last two or three decades, there have occurred tremendous changes in Korean society. As the apartments in suburban areas of larger cities illustrate, industrialization and urbanization have seriously influenced social change, especially in family living patterns. The changes that have occurred in the religious life of the family in urban areas reflect these changes in contemporary industrialized Korea.

TYPOLOGY OF THE KOREAN FAMILY

Until recently, especially in rural areas, there had been no major changes in family type. The typical family in Korea is a stem family, including old parents and one couple with their offspring residing together in a single domestic unit. The couple who live together with the parents is usually the eldest son and his wife. The eldest son remains the most important child in the Korean family. He is treated as the most important figure at home, being the direct lineal descendant. He is supposed to take care of old parents and perform the ritual services related to the ancestors. He is thus, the basis of the psychological security of the parents in their old age as well as being the symbol of family continuity. The eldest son of a direct lineal descendant bears the particularly heavy responsibility of maintaining the continuity of the main family.

The distribution of family property in Korea is characterized by an unequal division, with the bulk going to the eldest son. If there are 12 acres of land and 3 sons, the eldest son can receive 6 acres, the second son 3 and the third 3. Naturally there are many variations from this norm according to local custom and the economic condition of the family. But, without exception, the eldest son receives more than the other sons. This unequal division and the superior treatment of the eldest son is justified by his responsibility to care for the parents and to perform the rituals of ancestor worship.

The first son lives permanently with his parents, but the other sons must leave the family of orientation either on marriage or after spending several years after marriage with the parents. Their time of departure is determined by local custom and the economic condition of the family during the period of the sons' marriage. In the past, younger sons stayed longer with their parents, sometimes more than 10 years, but recently the period has become shorter. Today the younger sons leave immediately after marriage. The new families established by them are known as branch families while the family composed of the parents and the eldest son is called the main family.

The main family is a stem type of family whereas the branch family is a conjugal family. Because of this process of extension of families and of the proportion of sons in general, when a census of family type is conducted in a particular locality about 30 per cent or less of the families are found to be of the stem type, and 70 per cent or more are the conjugal type.

The conjugal family established by younger sons becomes a stem family after the marriage of its own eldest son, that is, the conjugal family has the potential of becoming a stem family, so that the stem family is the "typical" family in Korea.

In terms of family type, the Korean family like the Japanese stem family differs from the Chinese, which is characterized as an extended family type. The Korean type stem family is characterized by consanguineous lineality, whereas the Japanese family is characterized by fictive kinship ties.

Religious life can be explained as based on the stem family. Before proceeding it is useful to describe the spacial arrangement of a typical house. (A typical house from the central part of the Korean peninsula is depicted in Figure 1.)

A Korean house usually has two separate buildings; an "inside" and an "outside" building. There are two rooms in the inside building; an "inner" room and an "other side" room. The inner room has an under-the-floor heating system (*on-dol*) and is used for sleeping. Between the inner and the other side room there is a large, wooden-floored platform on the same level as the two rooms, open toward the inside garden, and usually facing south. The kitchen is always located next to the inner room.

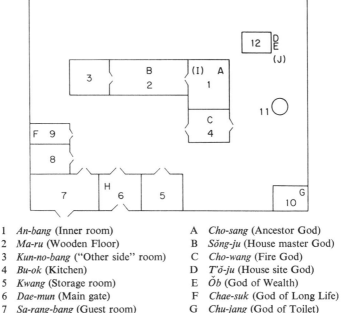

1	*An-bang* (Inner room)	A	*Cho-sang* (Ancestor God)
2	*Ma-ru* (Wooden Floor)	B	*Sŏng-ju* (House master God)
3	*Kun-no-bang* ("Other side" room)	C	*Cho-wang* (Fire God)
4	*Bu-ok* (Kitchen)	D	*T'ŏ-ju* (House site God)
5	*Kwang* (Storage room)	E	*Ŏb* (God of Wealth)
6	*Dae-mun* (Main gate)	F	*Chae-suk* (God of Long Life)
7	*Sa-rang-bang* (Guest room)	G	*Chu-jang* (God of Toilet)
8	*Cha-kun-bang* (Small room)	H	*Su-mun-jang* (God of Gate)
9	*Kwang* (Storage room)	I	*Sam-sin* (Goddess of Child)
10	*Byon-so* (Toilet)	J	*Yŏng-dong* (Goddess of Wind)
11	*Umul* (Well)		
12	*Chang-dok* (Jar platform)		

Fig. 1. Plan of a Typical House in Central Korea.

The outside building can be more varied in the number of spaces contained than is the inside building. The important spaces of the outside building are the guest room, the storage room, and the main gate. The storage room is a small room that can be converted into a stable or a cellar. If the family is rich and has many members, the house includes more rooms or more spaces in the outside building.

One of the characteristic features of a Korean house is the jar platform on which are deposited many jars of various sizes for containing soy sauce, bean paste, red pepper paste and *kim-ch'i*.

The guest room in the outside building is occupied by the family head, the father, since he represents the family to the outside. He attends community meetings as the spokesman of the family and he participates in the ritual ceremonies of the lineage. His occupation of the guest room clearly symbolizes a father's rights and duties as the family head. He receives guests from outside in his guest room, where he spends much time and where he sleeps. The family head also has the right to manage the family property and to control the family members.

The inner room in the inside building is occupied by the wife, the mother. She is in charge of household management, such as housekeeping, controlling storage, and supervising daily life of the family members including food, clothing and sleeping. But her rights as a housewife are subordinate to the rights of the family head. For example, the right of a housewife to control the storage is subordinated to the husband's right of management of family property.

Even though ideally the right of a housewife is subordinate to the right of family head, the role and status of the housewife in a Korean family is of great importance. Her role and status are symbolized by occupation of the inner room, which contains the important gods, as will be discussed below.

Above all, the inner room is the living room of all family members except the head, who stays in this room only when he falls sick. The family members come together for meals in this room. During the hot summer the wooden floor area is used as a dining room. But especially during the winter time, family members are accustomed to sit together in the warm part of the inner room for chatting, in addition to taking their meals there.

The "other side" room in the inside building is occupied by a married son, generally the eldest son of the family head, and his wife. The youngest offspring of this man sleeps together with the parents in this room. When this young child has a younger sibling, he moves into the inner room and sleeps with his grandmother. When a child more than 7 years old has another younger sibling, the child moves into the guest room and sleeps with his grandfather.

When the family has more space, the young boys sleep together in one room, and the girls share another. In traditional society it is not customary for a girl to have her own room before marriage.

This sharing of rooms reflects the sexual and age role differences among the family members. The inside building is the domain of the housewife, while the outside building belongs to the family head. Division of domain by sex is more clearly reflected in the upper class. Some bigger houses of the nobility or *Yang-ban* have walls and gates as well in the inside garden which separate the lady's domain from that of the man.

As the two buildings that comprise a house site indicate the separation of space and harmony or working place, so the right of the family head and that of the housewife reflect the division of labor by sex and the cooperative roles of the family life. The two polarities function as two different centers of security for the family. Patriarchal power is based on social status and therefore family members receive their social security from the family head. Matrifocal power has no overt symbolic manifestation; rather, it is conceptualized as "emotional" security by family members. Centers of social security and emotional security are the two focal points of Korean family structure.

This polarity in structure characteristic of the Korean family is also reflected in religious practice.

THE HOUSEHOLD GODS

There are several gods which are worshipped by the housewife. The letters in Figure 1 indicate their location. One of the important gods in a house is *cho-sang*, (lit. "ancestor"). But *cho-sang* is to be distinguished from the ancestral spirit which is worshipped by the family head using a Confucian form of ritual service. This household god is widely distributed throughout the country and thus many different names are used according to region, but *cho-sang* and *cho-sang-dan-ji* are the most widely used. The latter means the "jar of the ancestor".

Generally the ancestor god is located in one corner of the inner room, on a high shelf. It is symbolized by a small jar containing rice, the mouth of which is covered with white paper. In some districts people put white paper in a small box which is placed on a high shelf, calling it "the ancestor box". This ancestor box is another form of the ancestor jar but in some districts the box is placed beside the jar.

Even though the god is referred to as "ancestor", it has no direct function like a true ancestor spirit. This god is referred to as "grandmother" and linked with the fertility of agriculture and with the ability of the housewife to produce offspring.

The most important god of the house is *sŏng-ju*, the House Master God, which is usually located in the middle part of the wooden floor or at its corner. In the southern part of the Korean peninsula, a large jar containing rice or barley is placed at one corner of the wooden floor and is called the House Master God. But the most widely distributed form of the god is a small jar containing rice, covered with white paper, placed on a shelf at one corner of the wooden floor. In the central part of the Korean peninsula and in some locations in the southeast, the god occurs in paper form. A white paper is hung over the corner of the wooden floor or on the upper part of a post. In some houses, an old coin is put in the paper or some rice is contained in it.

This house master god is enshrined during house-building. In the earlier stage of building a large ritual service for this god is held when posts, girders and beams are erected. From its enshrinement this god is considered to protect the building itself. He is also believed to afford special protection for the family head.

In addition to the general ritual service for all household gods, the sincere housewife will dedicate a separate table to this god on seasonal holidays or on the birthdays of family members. Whenever special foods are received from neighbors, they are placed in front of the house master god before being touched by the housewife or by a family member.

A most important god for the housewife is *cho-wang*, the Fire God, which is located in the kitchen. A small white cup containing fresh water is placed on the stove. This is the symbol of the fire god. This god is well known throughout all Korea, but it is considered to be the most important household god in the southwestern part of the peninsula. An especially devoted woman changes the water in the cup early every morning. But most wives change the water once a month, on the first day of the month.

Without exception, the fire god is called "grandmother". She supervises the fire, cooking and other activities in the kitchen. But above all she protects the housewife. She has no function of reporting the family affairs to the heavenly god, as is stated to occur in Chinese ethnography. If the housewife has a special wish, she prepares a special place at home to dedicate herself to this god. In this case, the god is represented by a bowl of fresh water.

The House Site God, *t'ŏ-ju*, is located in the backyard, near the jar platform. It is symbolized by a sheaf of straw stood on end and bound at the top. Inside the straw is a jar containing rice. The rice in the jar is replaced after the harvest, like other house gods in jars. This god of the house site is especially honored as the most important god in the central part of the Korean peninsula, but it serves no special function other than the general protection of family members. Side-by-side with the house site god, there is always the God of Wealth, *ŏb*. It is symbolized by a flattened straw heap. The inside of the straw heap is empty, but it is believed that a snake resides there. If the snake is seen to come out from beneath the straw heap, it is believed that the family will decline.

In the storage area is the god called *chae-suk*. It is also symbolized by a small jar with rice or a piece of white paper. Because of the location of the god, it is believed that the god supervises food, thus all stored materials. But he is widely considered to be a god who protects the life of the family members and ensures longevity.

An interesting god among the household gods is the God of Toilet, *chu-jang*. Generally this god is given no symbolic form but it is believed that she resides in the toilet. Without exception this god is considered to be a young woman of perverse character. If a man enters the toilet without caution, he may die suddenly because he has angered this goddess.

The God of the Gate, *su-mun-jang*, is considered to be a general purpose household god; the most humble among the deities he is given no form.

All the household gods of a Korean family have their own particular functions as their locations within the house and their names indicate. They generally overlap in promoting of the health and wealth of the family and strengthening family prosperity by eliminating misfortune and guarding against illness.

The household gods have no functional connections with one another. There is no hierarchical relationship among them, even though there is an order of ritual services in which the same foods are dedicated. It has been explained that the house master god is the highest god and that he controls the god of the gate, and that the god of toilet is controlled by the god of house site [IMAMURA 1938: 256]. But it is generally believed that each of the household gods in the Korean family has an equal status and that each maintains a strongly individualistic character.

One interesting aspect of the worship of household gods is that the ritual performer is almost invariably the housewife. Men do not concern themselves with the household gods. An exception to this has been found in the central part of Eastern Province, where the sexual segregation and division of labor extends even to ritual performances for these gods.

Generally, the housewife purifies her soul and body with a cold bath and by being prudent in word and deed for several days prior to a ritual. Sincere women clean the house and put straw rope on the gate to prohibit the entrance of strangers. The housewife selects one day for the ritual service in October or November by the lunar calendar either by herself or by consulting a fortune teller.

Special preparation of foods for the gods is another aspect of purification. The foods must be prepared personally by the housewife. Steamed rice cakes are the most important food. One dried pollack, a piece of white paper, and a bowl of fresh water must be placed on the ritual table. Some women add jujube, chestnut and persimmon, and some offer rice wine instead of fresh water.

Wearing clean clothing, the housewife performs an evening ritual. The family members leave the room where the ceremony is held. The housewife brings the ritual table in front of the god, rubs her hands together, bows her head repeatedly, and murmurs for several minutes, praying for the good luck of the family under the protection of the god. The housewife then takes the same offering table to subsequent gods and repeats the ceremony. The ritual service begins from the inner room. First, the ancestor god receives the table, then the house master god, fire god, the god of toilet, and the god of gate, in that order. If the housewife is ardently religious and the family has the economic means, she may sponsor a ritual service by a shaman. During shamanistic rituals at home the house master god, the fire god, and the house site god may receive special attention.

There are two other goddesses that may make their appearance in a household, the Goddess of Child, and the Goddess of Wind. The goddess of child comes to the house when a child is born. She stays until the child becomes ten years old and then disappears. The wind goddess comes every year on the first of February, according to the lunar calender. She stays only two weeks and returns to heaven. The goddess of child is worshipped by wives throughout the whole of Korea. But the wind goddess is believed in only in the southern part of the peninsula.

The goddess of child is believed to attend a woman at the beginning of delivery of a child. At one corner of the dining room she is served with a small table on which is rice, dry seaweed and a bowl of fresh water. During a difficult delivery the midwife or an old woman rubs her hands together praying for the protection of the goddess and asking for her help. When the child is born the old woman brings out the small table and cooks rice and seaweed, which are dedicated to the goddess, and then brings cooked rice and soup to the mother.

The dedicated woman prepares a small table with rice, soup and vegetables every day in the corner reserved for the goddess of child. And normally she brings the offering table on the seventh day after the birthday and again on the fourteenth day. On the twenty-first a large celebration is held for the new child after the dedication of the largest table to the goddess.

Even though it is believed that the goddess of child stays at a home until the child becomes 10 years old, there is no dedication of foods or ritual services except when the child falls sick. When the child is sick it is believed that the goddess gets angry, forsakes her protective duties and leaves the house.   She comes back home when the housewife apologizes for her carelessness.

Generally there is no form given to the goddess of child.   In some areas she is symbolized by a piece of white paper attached to the upper part of one corner in the inner room.

The wind goddess descends from heaven on the first of February.   The housewife prepares a large table with various foods on the jar platform.   She rubs her hands together to welcome the goddess.   From the next day the woman brings only a bowl of fresh water to the jar platform, but some dedicated women prepare a small table with food.   On the fifteenth of February the housewife brings a large table once again foi the farewell ceremony, which is also performed on the jar platform.

These two goddesses, the goddess of child and the goddess of wind, have no direct connection with the household gods.   They share only the common functional characteristic of eliminating misfortune and the furtherance of family prosperity.

The main task of all household gods and their functions are a projection of the desires or values of ordinary people, and may be summarized in two words: peace and prosperity.   Peace means the health of the family members, and prosperity of the family means many offspring and good harvests.

ANCESTOR WORSHIP BY THE FAMILY HEAD

While worship of the household gods is the domain of the housewife, ancestor worship devolves upon the family head.   From early childhood a first-born male learns that he is responsible for taking care of his parents while they are alive and later, for performing ritual services for them after they die.   These acts serve as repayment for parental love and affection.   In this manner, ancestors and offspring are considered mutually dependent.   Confucianism from the Yi dynasty on put particular emphasis on ancestor worship as the highest form of moral response.

If a family head is a second or younger son he has no ancestor at home.   As mentioned already, the eldest son lives with his parents and performs ritual service for them after their death.   He performs the rituals not only for his parents but also for the ancestors who were taken care of by his father.   If the ritual officiant is the direct lineal descendant of the main family, he performs the ritual services for his parents, grandparents, great-grandparents, and great-great-grandparents.

Ritual service for ancestors begins in the mourning period. It is believed that there are three souls (*hon*) and seven spirits (*back*) in a human body. When a man dies, the three souls leave the body but the seven spirits remain in the body in the grave. The seven spirits are composed of two eyes, two ears, two nostrils and one mouth.

After death one soul leaves the body and with three messengers as guides goes to the heavenly god who controls the life of the living.   Another soul moves from the body to the small box called *hon-back*, which contains either a mass of strings or paper. The third soul returns to stay with the body in the grave after the funeral.

The *hon-back* is made during the process of putting the body into the coffin.

It is preserved on a small table side-by-side with a photograph of the deceased person during the mourning period. It is then kept on the altar for two years and finally buried in the grave. In the central part of Korea the altar of the deceased is established in a back corner of the open-faced platform. In the southern part of the peninsula, it is located in the outside building containing an altar.

A prominent family will make an ancestor tablet to place beside the *hon-back*. It is made of chestnut wood and takes a fixed form. On the front of the tablet is the name and the title of the deceased. This is written at the grave side during the burial. If there is an ancestor shrine at home, the ancestor tablet is moved from the home altar to the shrine after three months. Each time a ritual service is performed, the ancestor tablet is moved to the ritual table from the shrine. Until the 4th generation of the ritual performer the tablet is kept in the ancestor shrine. Thereafter it is buried in the grave.

Nowadays most people have no ancestor tablet nor ancestor shrine at home. Many were destroyed during the Korean War. In such a case they make a paper tablet for each ritual service and burn it after the ceremony.

The first ritual service for an ancestor is the "returning ceremony," performed when the ancestor tablet or *hon-back* is brought home from the gravesite. There are other ceremonies after the returning ritual. After three months the ceremony for ending the tears is performed. On the next day there is a ceremony for attaching the tablet to the ancestor shrine, if there is a shrine at home. A man performs the ritual service on the first anniversary and the major ritual on the second anniversary. Then, after another two months, the ritual ceremony for normal food is performed. From that time the mourner can eat meat. Prior to this ceremony, all the rituals are called *Hyung-je*, or "bad ceremony". On the following day the ritual *kil-je*, good ceremony, is performed. From that time the mourner can wear normal clothing, which symbolizes a return to a normal life.

The ritual services for ancestors are classified into three: *Ki-je*, a ritual service at home on commemoration day; *ch'a-rae*, a ritual service at home on a holiday; and *si-je*, a ritual service at the grave.

The ritual service on commemoration day is the most important ceremony. It is performed at midnight on the commemoration day in the wooden floor area or in the inner room by the direct lineal descendant. Theoretically, only one ancestor receives the ritual service, but a dead couple tend to be served side-by-side.

During the preceding several days the worshipper and his wife exert themselves to the utmost spiritually. There are two kinds of exertion or meditation: inside and outside exertion. One should concentrate his soul and mind, thinking only of the good behavior of the ancestor. This is "inside" meditation. At the same time, one should not leave the home and should not drink wine or sleep with one's wife. This is "outside" meditation.

The food for the ritual is carefully prepared by the housewife. The special table and vessels for the ritual service are preserved separately from those used daily, even in a normal house.

It is said that "different families have different rites" because the performance of a ritual service is a special family practice.   But there are some standardized arrangements of the ritual table and process of ritual performance.   For the ritual table, for example, everyone knows the words such as "red on the east and white on the west", meaning that red-colored fruits are placed on the east side of the ritual table and the white on the west.   Similar expressions say, "fish on the east and meat on the west", and, "dry meat on the left and sweet drinking on the right".   Viewed from the performer's side, the first row of dishes is for fruits, the next for vegetables, the next for different thick soups, then that for different kinds of meat and fishes, and the last for bowls of rice and soup. Spoons and chopsticks are placed to the left of the rice bowl because a dead spirit is considered to be left-handed. There are rules governing the height of fruit and meat offerings, and the number of thick soups are in keeping with the official rank of the ancestor and the status of the family.

In front of the large ceremonial table is a small table on which incense is burned.   On the floor is placed a small cup containing a small bundle of straw or pine needles put on sand or rice.

The direct lineal descendant, the master of ritual service, sits in front of the small table and burns the incense, which indicates the beginning of the service. He then stands up behind the table, bowing deeply twice, and then sits down again. He takes a glass of wine and pours the wine three times into the small bowl of sand or rice, which symbolizes the meeting of heaven and earth or descent of the ancestor spirit to the table.   Everybody bows twice to the ancestor.   The ritual master dedicates the first wine glass, after rotating it three times in the smoke of the incense.   The dedication of the first wine glass is the most important duty of the direct lineal descendant. A helper removes the cover of the rice bowl and puts the spoon and chopsticks in an empty bowl.   All participants bow deeply twice.   Next, a sentence is read in a loud voice paying respectful and affectionate tribute to the memory of the deceased ancestor.

The second glass of wine is dedicated by the wife of the ritual master or by the second son of the ancestor.   The action of the second is just the same as the first. After the dedication of the third glass by a relative of the third category, a spoon is placed in the rice bowl. Then follows the ancestor's mealtime. A folding screen can be set between the table and ritual performers, or they leave the room for a short while.   Thereafter, the folding screen is removed or the participants return to the room.   The wife brings a bowl of water which is put on the table in place of the soup. All the participants bow deeply twice and then the ritual master announces the end of the service.   The participants take a little of the food from the table or a glass of wine, to share the meal with the deceased ancestor.

There are some noteworthy aspects to this ritual service.   A peach cannot be used as a fruit on the ritual table; the spirit is considered left-handed; and the ancestor is served with wine whether he or she drank or not during life.   The most important aspect of the ritual service is the sharing of food with the ancestor.

Other ritual services which are performed at home are semiannual festivals.

In general, nowadays, they are held on New Year's Day and in mid-August, by the lunar calendar. Some families add one other day, "cold food day", in spring. If one more day, "beginning of winter", is added four such festivals can be held annually.

In general, the services of annual feasts are the same as for the commemoration service, but they differ slightly in the kinds of foods utilized. Seasonal special cooking instead of rice and soup is dedicated. Further the annual feast is held in the morning whereas the commemoration is performed at midnight.

The ritual service on commemoration day and the annual festivals are performed for all ancestors whose tablets are kept at home. There are different numbers of ancestors at home according to the status of the family head. There is no ritual service for ancestors in a newly established branch family. But in the house of a direct lineal descendant there are generally ancestors of four generations. If he honors 4 couples of ancestors and holds 2 ritual services on annual festivals, there is a total of 10 ritual services per year at the house of a direct lineal descendant.

When the direct lineal descendant reaches the fifth generation, the ancestor tablet should be given to a branch lineal descendant who is, theoretically, still in the fourth generation. But most ancestor tablets are kept by the direct lineal descendant and buried in the grave of the ancestor. This is called "*mae-hwan*" (lit. "returning by interment"). Thereafter the ritual service is held once in a year in the graveyard. This is the reason for the formation of the lineage organization (*mun-jung*).

In the ritual services of ancestor worship there are two kinds of ancestors: the ancestors who receive commemoration day service at home, and those who receive the ritual service at the grave. If the ritual service of ancestor worship is not performed the ancestor spirit becomes a wandering ghost, but has no power to punish the descendants directly. However, it is nevertheless believed that the ritual service for ancestors protects the offspring from the evil effects of malevolent ghosts and helps to ensure the material prosperity and health of the living family members.

Among the ancestors there is hierarchical order according to the generation principle during the ritual service. For example, during the performance of ritual service on a holiday the first glass of wine is dedicated to the great-grandfather among the four generations of ancestors. But a more recent ancestor is more intimately regarded than is a remoter one.

Ancestor worship reflects the concept of future life, as Janelli [1973] showed. He observed that a retired man is served three meals a day by his offspring; during the mourning period he receives one meal a day; for four generations he is served four times a year; and after that he receives food once a year. In this context death is considered only a stage in a continuity of life. That is why ancestor worship is developed so fully in Korean society. The ancestor spirits live with their offspring in this world after death, but slowly fade away with the passage of time.

CHANGES IN THE MODERN FAMILY

During the past three decades Korean society has undergone a rapidity of change never before experienced. After the Second World War several million people returned to Korea, which then had its productive facilities destroyed by the Korean War (1950–1953). A continuing high birthrate outstripped agricultural production. The rapid industrialization of the 1960s became one facet of a revitalization movement which brought about a large geographical shift in population. Korea went from fifty-eight percent of the population living in rural areas in 1960, to less than 45 percent in 1970. The population concentrated increasingly in larger cities. For example, the population of Seoul was 2,600,000 in 1960 but became 7,363,000 by 1970. It is estimated that more than 8 million people now live in Seoul.

Two factors have greatly influenced the modernization of the Korean family: urbanization and family planning to limit the family to 2 children. Thus the modern family is now characterized as a "conjugal" type. There is an increasing number of old couple conjugal families, a new phenomenon in both urban and rural areas.

The first son received the largest portion of the family property and lived with his parents to form a stem family in traditional Korean society. In recent times, however, the first son receives a higher level of education than the younger sons. When he finishes his education he usually goes to an urban area for a job. Most never return to their parental home, unless they somehow fail. When the first son settles down in an urban area, the second and later sons follow their elder brother to find a job in the urban area. The old couple who remain in the rural home may then be invited to join their sons, especially the first son, who remains responsible for taking care of them in their old age. But because of the difficulty of adjustment to urban life, old couples frequently return home, giving up the better quarters, food and clothing supplied them in the urban area. The old parents tend never to feel lonely because they are busy in the countryside; they work hard to produce now more expensive farm products such as vegetables and red peppers for their offspring in the city. The house is not empty since it is visited by the grandchildren during vacation times.

The restricted space of city living quarters has influenced the lifestyle and division of roles among the family members and workers. Notable phenomena occurring in urban areas are the increasing number of white-collar workers and changes in the role of the housewife. Young male white-collar workers spend time and energy mainly in an office, thus giving rise to what has been termed a "fatherless" complex among the younger generation. Even though a young man works hard, his salary is not enough to support his small family. If his wife's household management is poor, it is hard for the family to keep up with the high cost of urban living.

The popularization of electric kitchen appliances has decreased the amount of labor for the Korean housewife, but her psychological responsibilities as wife and mother have been increased. Not only must she be the wife and colleague of her husband but also the benevolent mother and strict teacher of her children. The boundary of her activities is extended to the public office, post office, and bank.

The traditional social order and division of labor by family members has been disrupted.

The change of the family in outside form and inside order is also reflected in modern religious life. The household gods are disappearing in newer households, especially in those with an educated wife. Many educated young women have been converted to Christianity, Buddhism or to one of several eclectic new religions. Besides conversion to other religions, the number of adherents to shamanism is also increasing in urban areas. The sponsors of shamanistic rituals in urban areas are often people with higher incomes such as an owner of a taxi company, a large textile company owner or the owner of a large restaurant. Among more humble women it is said that they still dedicate themselves to the household gods when they have some special wish such as the safety of their son during his military service or good luck in the university entrance examination.

Ancestor worship is performed by people in rural as well as urban areas, even though practices have become simplified or changed from more elaborate traditional forms. Especially in urban areas, the ritual service on the commemoration day is held in the early evening, after dinner, because the participants from other houses must return home before the midnight curfew.

Younger men no longer know the form of writing required by ancestor tablets and now they tend to use pictures instead of tablets. The order of dishes on the ceremonial table has been disrupted. Sometimes a dish of bananas or pineapple is used, and recently whisky has been substituted for rice wine because whisky is more expensive and the deceased father usually drank it. Ancestor worship is especially popular among urban people. On the day of the ritual service for an ancestor, brothers and cousins who live in different areas, even in the same city, come together to perform the ceremony and exchange information.

CONCLUSION

The traditional family in Korea has been characterized by the dominant position of family over individual. The highest value of this "familism" was to ensure the peace and prosperity of the family. One felt sorrow for death of an outside person, but a far more sorrowful thing was the death of a family member. Once established a family must be continued forever, and thus an individual should do his best to ensure the continuation and prosperity of his or her family.

Not only the living family members but also those who have passed away must sacrifice themselves for the family. Producing and bearing offspring was the most important duty to an ancestor for the prosperity of the family. Filial piety and ancestor worship were also the most important duties of offspring. The household gods reflected this familism in their characters and roles. In a word, religion in Korea has been characterized as a family religion.

The division of labor among the family members, especially between husband and wife, has reflected their mutual dependence in conformity with a harmonious family life. Sharing of family religion between housewife and family head also has reflected the division as well as the unity and conformity of family life. The house-wife still takes care of ritual services for household gods and the family head remains responsible for ancestor worship. Division of labor and conformity to role eases conflict and maintains harmony within social groups.

Disturbances in the value system of modern Korean society may imply the disappearance of this balance of conflict and harmony in group or in society. But despite change there seems to remain structural continuity, especially in family and religion.

On the surface the modern family has become an isolated unit of small size. But in the subjective experience of the people, the family is never isolated, it has just been extended geographically. For example, the conjugal family of an old couple in a rural area is connected economically and psychologically with that of their offspring in an urban area. The structural principle of family and functional cooperation of the families maintains continuity even in a fast-changing society.

The same phenomenon can be seen in the sphere of religion. The household gods have disappeared in the modern home. But the conversion to other religions can be considered as an extension of the worship of household gods. Yu explains that Korean religion is characterized by supplication for family prosperity rather than by the character formation of individuals, whether it be shamanism, Buddhism, Confucianism or even Christianity [YU 1978: 107]. In this sense, the modernization of the Korean family and religion may be witness to what is only an extension of traditional familism.

BIBLIOGRAPHY

IMAMURA, Domoe
    1938   *The Collection of Korean Folklore.* Tokyo: Kitakang.
JANELLI, Roger L.
    1973   Anthropology, Folklore and Korean Ancestor Worship. *Korean Cultural Anthropology* 6: 175–190.
KIM, Doo-Hyŏn
    1969   *The Study of Korean Institute.* Seoul: Press of Seoul National University.
LEE, Kwang-Kyu
    1975a *Structural Analysis of the Korean Family.* Seoul: Il-chi-sa.
    1975b *Kinship System in Korea.* 2 vols. HRAFlex Books. New Haven: Human Relation Area Files.
    1977   *Historical Study of the Korean Family.* Seoul: Il-chi-sa.
    1981   *Psychological Study of the Korean Family.* Seoul: Il-chi-sa.
YU, Dong-Shik
    1978   *Folk Religion and Korean Culture.* Seoul: Hyondae-Sasangsa.

Chapter 13

Ancestor Worship in Contemporary Japan: Continuity and Change

KIYOMI MORIOKA

INTRODUCTION

Accompanying the change of *ie* after the Second World War, ancestor worship among the Japanese has also changed considerably. The concept of ancestor has largely shifted from a unilineal descent to a bilateral orientation. This change has been accelerated by a widespread acceptance of the nuclear family form. As to the function of ancestor worship, jural or political functions such as those that legitimize one's social status have weakened, whereas personal or informal functions as a memorialization of one's dead ancestors or an emotional consoling of their spirits have been strengthened. The *butsudan* or Buddhist altar, the central object of ancestral rites inside the private house, is still kept in many Japanese households. Variations exist, however. There can be temporary delays in setting up a *butsudan*, establishing a shelf in a corner of a room to serve as a *butsudan* substitute, as well as direct disuse of the custom. Even among those who own a *butsudan* the rate of the ritual performance is not high, and the forms of practice vary. These tendencies are all related to an increasing significance of personal over formal functions of the worship.

In this chapter the form of practice based on the *ie* or household is referred to as "classical ancestor worship". That which has appeared in the process of the transition of the *ie* is called "modified ancestor worship". In present-day Japan, classical ancestor worship is still found in agricultural and mountain villages, and the modified form tends to occur in urban areas. Further, even "modified ancestor worship" is rare among some nuclear family households.

"Ancestor worship" refers to the totality of the belief in the superhuman power of the dead who are recognized as ancestors, and the rituals based on this belief. The dead are not always ancestors. Ancestors must have real or adopted descendants who are admitted as legitimate in the context of ancestor worship. Legitimate descendants are those who succeed to the social status of the ancestors and who consequently assume the right to worship ancestors. Ancestor worship is, therefore, indivisibly connected with the patriarchal family and the patrilineal descent group.

Ancestor worship is neither simply a mental representation of ancestors nor an action of love and respect extended to them as if they were alive. The performance of a set of rituals is a requisite of ancestor worship, with a belief that dead ancestors have a superhuman power. In this sense, ancestor worship is a central problem in discussing the relationship between a patriarchal family and religion, and was in fact the core of the relationship between the Japanese *ie* (traditional family household of Japan) and religion. In contemporary Japan, however, the nature of ancestor worship has been changing, responding to, and forming one aspect of, the change in the *ie*. This chapter attempts to analyze the continuity and change in ancestor worship of the Japanese in this process of recent change.

ANCESTOR WORSHIP AND ITS FUNCTIONS

The *ie* or household is a social institution which has continued in Japan over generations unilineally through the male line. According to research findings, ancestors in an *ie* comprise all the household heads together with their wives since its founding. When a founder established a new *ie* as a branch household, ancestors from the main household were sometimes transferred over. In addition, the founder of a main family was sometimes connected genealogically to the Imperial Household or to other powerful families in previous periods. Ancestors under the *ie* system were shown systematically on a lineal genealogy that included not only actual ancestors but not infrequently, imaginary ones.

The generational depth of ancestors differed greatly depending on social class. Not a few politically powerful families claimed an imaginary descent from the gods recorded in the Japanese sacred scriptures, the *Kojiki* or *Nihongi*. But for most commoners, it was difficult to trace their actual ancestors back beyond a few generations.

Japanese folklorists maintain that an ancestor retains his individual characteristics for a period of time but gradually frees himself from the impurity of death and loses his individuality, finally merging into the general ancestral soul of the *ie*. This is true only for commoners, however. Among politically powerful families or those with religious authority, each ancestor retained his individuality and was separately worshipped. Even among commoners, the spirit of a founder or of a special restorer of an *ie*, or that of an ancestor who died an unhappy death was not fused into the general ancestral soul.

Among the principal functions of ancestor worship are:

1. *Status Legitimization*

Ceremonial attention to the ancestors serves to prove that the present head of a household has legitimately succeeded to the social status of his ancestors. This is especially important for households holding political power or religious authority. In such households, there is more tendency for each ancestor to retain individuality in order to demonstrate that power and authority have been properly handed down.

2. *Stabilization of Inter-generational Relations*

Demonstrating symbolically the ethics of filial piety to the dead helps an heir resolve his ambivalent feelings toward his living parent. This supports the well-known proposition of M. Fortes (1961, 1965). In Japan, the practice of shifting the headship of the household to the heir while the former head is still alive is widespread. The functional resolution of ambivalence is not as important as in a society where the domestic power of the head can be handed down to the heir only after his death. Nevertheless, such resolution was especially meaningful for the socially privileged.

3. *Unification of Kin*

N. Hozumi pointed out this function while discussing Japanese law in terms of ancestor worship [HOZUMI 1912: 21–25]. This can be applied generally to unilineal descent groups or *dozoku* in Japan. It is, of course, pertinent to an *ie* that may be under stress.

4. *Strengthening Motivation for Household Continuation*

Periodic ceremonies strengthen motivation for household continuation by deepening one's appreciation of ancestral benevolence and teaching one to pray for their help. Appreciation and prayers were urged by the "Ancestor Religion" espoused at the turn of the century, and, more significantly, by the doctrine of ancestor veneration taught to schoolchildren with the aid of official textbooks.

In parallel with ancestor worship, offerings were made to *muenbotoke*, dead who had no legitimate offspring to worship them as ancestors. These offerings were intended to prevent unhappy incidents which might be brought about by troubled souls. Hence, it can be said that the rites for them had the function of easing the psychological tension of people.

In modern Japan, lower class urban workers lacked the physical means necessary for guaranteeing the maintenance of their households and had to work hard to provide the necessities of everyday life. Under such circumstances, it was not easy for them to perceive any benefit as being bestowed on them by their ancestors, and thus it was not easy to recognize ancestors as those to whom one owed gratitude. Instead, their poverty-stricken situation was often explained as due to the presence of ancestors who could not successfully achieve a state of bliss. While misfortune could be attributed to *muenbotoke* in the propertied classes, the misery of the disinherited could be explained as being caused by ancestors who were not properly worshipped by their offspring. Therefore, a central function of ancestor worship for lower class people was to relieve themselves of tension concerning their present plight as well as to avert further disaster and misfortune.

CHANGES IN THE IE AFTER THE SECOND WORLD WAR

Concomitant with changes in other social institutions and economic development, the *ie* was gradually changing over the past century following the Meiji Restoration. Changes in the *ie* following the Second World War, however, have been notable especially. As the *ie* changes, ancestor worship supported by *ie* is also transformed. It is important therefore to delineate how the *ie* has been legally and socially transformed since 1945.

Formerly, the *ie* was physically based on a continuity of property. The corporate family tended to be self-employed in its own occupational specialization. As such it was an independent enterprise based on its own property and capital. However, a meta-economic concept of property as handed down from the ancestors to the present generation has lost influence. Instead, now more salient are newer notions of property as a means of production, or as a commodity for negotiation as in the case of farms now part of suburbs and metropolitan areas. In addition, changes in the industrial structure of Japan have led to marked reduction in the number of self-employed workers. Households of salaried employees are now in a majority. Even in the remaining self-employed households, not all members are engaged in the family business. Some are gainfully employed outside as is true for part-time farming households. Thus, the diminution of property and occupation as the material bases of the *ie* has made a steady advance [MATSUMOTO 1981: 110–111].

Primogeniture is not only legally abrogated but has also lost popular favor. Attitude surveys reveal that the rate of those in support of an equal division of parental property among children had reached nearly 50% by the 1960's. Even among those remaining in favor of primogeniture, a predominant majority connected the right of exclusive inheritance with the full responsibility to take care of aging parents. Only a small minority continued to think that all property should be handed down to the heir along with the headship of the *ie*. Although 70% or more remain in favor of the combined residence of parents and a married son or daughter, the assumed reason is the convenience which this arrangement may provide in caring for the aged rather than as a means of continuing an *ie* form of living. Those who think it unnecessary to adopt a child in order to continue an *ie* line when there is no real offspring now number about half the population, while those who stress the necessity to adopt for household succession has fallen to about one-third of those contacted [MORIOKA 1980]. Thus, the notion that the *ie* should be handed down generationally has become less and less popular.

As to family composition, along with urbanization, the increase of nuclear family households has become marked in postwar Japan. However, because of the drastic decrease in the number of children per woman it is estimated that the percentage of nuclear families will remain constant or decline, and the stem family household in which parents and their married child live together will become more common. Yet the so-called contemporary stem family household is more like a generational combination of two nuclear families of parents and their married child rather than the single unified household in existence under the *ie* system of former days. In the *ie*, the axis of family life lay in the parent-child dyadic ties. Thus two nuclear families were bound together firmly by a filial relationship. On the other hand, the focus of the present-day family, especially those formed recently, is placed on the husband-wife relationship. Therefore, even when there is a three generation family, it is merely a residential alliance of two nuclear families. The notion of a continuation of *ie* over generations has almost totally evaporated.

Because of vulnerability to weather conditions or to the economic fluctuations, the households with an independent small-scale business worshipped guardian deities often associated with the ancestors who laid the foundation of the business. Now, since workers' households depend on large enterprises that employ their bread-winners, it is unlikely for them to practice such ancestor worship. In a family centering around the parent-child relationship, the extension of filial piety to their dead ancestors lead immediately to ancestor worship. In a conjugal family, however, this sort of attitude does not tend to occur.

As noted above, the drastic change in the *ie* system, which may well be called a collapse of the traditional family, naturally should have devitalized ancestor worship. However, the "Japanese National Character Study" reveals that the ratios of re-spondents who affirmed their paying reverence to ancestors were 77% for 1953 and 72% for 1978, the decreasing trend being less conspicuous than anticipated [TōKEI SūRI KENKYŪJO 1979: 42]. This suggests that the meaning of "ancestor" changed between 1953 and 1978. Presumably, the concept of "ancestor" in 1953 was close to that defined at the beginning of this chapter, but by 1978 had changed considerably far from its original meaning. A change in the view of ancestor is assumed to have taken place. With the decline of the concept of ancestor based on the *ie* system, a new concept devoid of the *ie* premise may have emerged. Along with such change, the pattern of worship may also have become modified.

CHANGE IN THE CONCEPT OF ANCESTOR

I will review the actual status of the concept of ancestor by making use of re-search findings completed since 1960. Since the data were obtained only from community studies, they are fragmentary but nevertheless they are mutually support-ing. According to a survey of 87 households conducted in 1974–75 in a farming community in Okayama Prefecture, "ancestors" meant, for more than 70% of those interviewed, the founder of household, the household heads since the foundation, ancestors of the main household, or the household heads of all generations including those of the main household. That is, a majority held the traditional concept as defined above. However, for the remaining 30% or less, ancestors were either all those who died in their households or all the dead enshrined at their *butsudan*, or their deceased parents, etc. In other words, all deceased family members were in-cluded in their concept of ancestor. For them, closeness of blood relationship was more important than lineality [YONEMURA 1981: 153]. A 1972 study of 142 house-holds in a hotspring town in Yamagata Prefecture revealed that two thirds of the respondents considered the founder of an *ie* or all the deceased heads and their wives as ancestors, while for 20% or more ancestors were the dead close kin on both husband's and wife's sides. S. Yonemura, who made the Okayama study, interpreted his findings as an extension of the concept to ordinary family members beyond household heads and their wives. Yet it is questionable whether this is a change that occurred after the war; it is possible that the system of ancestors held by commoners was so extensive as to include some ordinary household members. At any rate, the regarding of deceased bilateral kin as ancestors, which was entertained only by a minority of the respondents in the Yamagata study, is different in quality from the traditional concept of ancestor.

Behind one family of procreation exist two families of orientation on the husband's side and on the wife's side. On this basis a bilateral concept of ancestor may emerge. It has been kept latent, however, under the *ie* system. Again, we should not hastily summarize this as a new postwar phenomenon, though we admit that it certainly accords with the decline of the *ie* in postwar Japan.

This contention is based on replies to the question asking whom the respondents regarded as ancestors. Other than this, the tablets installed in a *butsudan* permit an estimation of the extension of "ancestor". In 1963 R. J. Smith employed this method in studying 429 urban households in Tokyo, Kyoto and Osaka and 166 rural households in Iwate, Mie and Kagawa Prefectures [SMITH 1974: 152–186]. According to his findings, 93% of the tablets were of the dead on the descent line of the *ie*, whereas those for nonlineal kin including relatives on the wife's side averaged only 6% of the total. Because the percentage of nonlineal tablets was higher in cities than in rural areas, Smith concluded that the presence of nonlineal tablets is a newer trend and serves as the opening wedge of family-centered ancestor worship as opposed to household-centered ancestor worship [SMITH 1974: 174]. Also, in Yonemura's research conducted in Okayama Prefecture, a few instances of tablets for the nonlineal deceased such as kin on the wife's side were reported. In addition, there were tablets for siblings who died unmarried, divorced or childless even when married. In other words, a unilineal concept of ancestor remained dominant, yet an emergence of a bilateral concept was indicated by the data [YONEMURA 1981: 154]. The coincidence that both Smith and Yonemura confirmed an emerging bilateral concept of ancestor suggests that a shift is taking place from a concept of household-centered ancestor to family-centered ancestor.

This shift can be summarized as a change from a unilineal view which includes distant ancestors beyond even indirect experiences, to say nothing of direct personal contact, to a concept which limits ancestors to close kin within the range of direct experience, but extends bilaterally; and as such a change from an obligatory concept which should include all the dead on one's descent line regardless of personal preference, to an optional one which limits ancestors to the deceased close kin whose memories are cherished by offspring. This should indicate a trend toward the collapse of the concept of ancestor as defined in the opening paragraph of this chapter.

The change of concept should accompany a change of function in ancestor worship. The original four functions are social, whereas the newer functions are much more personal; that is, they release psychological tensions through affectionate reminiscence of the dead and consolation of their spirits [SMITH 1974: 183; TAKAHASHI 1975]. The former functions contribute to the stability of household and society, whereas the latter seek to bring solace and peace to one's heart. Although the percentages of those who affirmed the reverence they paid to their ancestors do not indicate any marked drop, a shift from an obligatory ancestor of an *ie* to an optional ancestor of an individual, and "privatization" of the function of ancestor worship may be in progress behind the scenes.

CHANGES IN CEREMONY

Under the *ie* system ancestor worship was commonly practiced at a household altar such as a *butsudan* where tablets or objects symbolizing ancestral spirits were installed. Therefore, any change in ancestor worship may be manifest in the possible increase in the number of households keeping no *butsudan*.

According to the comparative study of three areas we conducted in 1965–66, the percentages of *butsudan*-keeping households were 92% in an agricultural community in Yamanashi Prefecture (92 households), 69% in a business area in Tokyo (103 households), and 45% in a white-collar workers' residential area in Tokyo (106 households). The variation among areas was in the same direction as anticipated. We classified the households into two types; nuclear family households (without old people) and extended family households (with old people). Almost 100% of the extended family households kept a *butsudan* regardless of rural-urban or occupational differences, as the following figures show: 98% in the Yamanashi farming village, 93% in the Tokyo business area, and 100% in the Tokyo residential area. In contrast, among nuclear family households, the percentages varied considerably: 83% in the farming village, 51% in the business area, and 31% in the residential area. In addition, the percentages of nuclear family households were 38% in the farming village, 58% in the business area and 80% in the residential area, all contributing to the regional variation mentioned above [MORIOKA 1975: 97–98].

In my 1967 research on a suburb of Tokyo, I observed the *butsudan* ownership rate by dividing the sample into the local residents (54 households) and the newcomers (65 households), and then subdividing them into extended family households and nuclear family households. Although the difference was small among the extended family households (97% for local families and 100% for newcomers), the rates varied widely among nuclear family households (73% for local families and 38% for newcomers). The result obtained was similar to the findings from the comparative study of three areas [MORIOKA 1975: 99–100].

From these studies, it has become clear that the *butsudan* ownership rate was lowest among nuclear family households of full-time workers. Since the number of such households is assumed to have increased in postwar Japan, it is estimated that the *butsudan* ownership rate has generally decreased.

According to a study of the middle-aged or the aged conducted in 1973 in Kakegawa City, the *butsudan* ownership rate for nuclear families was as high as that for extended families where two couples of successive generations were alive. In both household types the *butsudan* ownership rate was significantly higher for the households of the aged (65–74 years old) than for the households of the middle-aged (55–64 years old). This suggests that the incentives to set up a *butsudan* accumulate as time passes even in nuclear families, especially with the death of the senior generation. Among extended families the *butsudan* ownership rate was significantly higher for households with widows (91 %)than for those with two couples intact (68 %). The reason for this difference would be that the death of husbands of the senior generation provided a decisive incentive to set up a *butsudan* earlier for the households with widows [TAKAHASHI 1975].

The above mentioned Kakegawa study made it clear that the low *butsudan* ownership rate for nuclear family households reflected a moratorium phenomena in *butsudan* ownership. Along with the increase in the number of nuclear family households, however, it cannot be denied that those who never set up a *butsudan* during their lifetime are also growing in number. The Kakegawa research also revealed that some of those lacking a formal *butsudan* had a simplified altar resembling it [TAKAHASHI 1975: 43]. *Butsudan* like equipment may indicate a stage prior to setting up a formal *butsudan* or may be a relatively permanent altar for ancestor worship. In short, formerly it used to be normal as well as commonplace to set up an ancestor altar such as a *butsudan*; nowadays, the norm has waned especially in large cities. This is partly responsible for the great increase of non-*butsudan* households among nuclear families. Among them, some have an altar resembling a *butsudan* or dispense with it for the time being, whereas others, it is estimated, do not set up a *butsudan* throughout their lifetime. A public opinion poll conducted by the Asahi Newspaper in 1981 revealed that the *butsudan* ownership rate reached 63 %. This suggests that a majority of the Japanese have a *butsudan* even today. I would like to call attention to the fact that, however, a few patterns of non-ownership have emerged.

Our next question is about the ways of worship. According to Smith's tablet study in 1963, 457 households had ancestral tablets in their *butsudan*. Of them, 63 % worshipped ancestors on the day of *Bon* (Buddhist All Souls' Day); 62% practiced a daily morning rite; 60% observed periodic anniversaries of death; 56% practiced a monthly deathday rite. Only 21 % observed all four rituals. Judging from the above figures, ancestral tablets may have been almost neglected in about 30 % of the total households.

In our 1964–65 comparative study of three areas, senior students of elementary schools were asked whether they were told to worship ancestors at the *butsudan* by their elder family members. The results were as follows: among nuclear family households, the *butsudan* ownership rate was as low as 48 %, out of which a worship-demanding rate was 55 % (26 % of the total). In contrast, among extended family households, the *butsudan* ownership rate amounted to 97 % and the worship-demanding rate was 66 % of the *butsudan* owners (64 % of the total). In the farming village, the *butsudan* ownership rate was 92 %, among which the worship-demanding rate was 65 % (60 % of the total); in the business area, the *butsudan* ownership rate was 69 % out of which the worship demanding rate was 51 % (35 % of the total); and in the residential area, the *butsudan* ownership rate was 45% among which the worship-demanding rate reached 71% (32% of the total). The ranking order of *butsudan* ownership rates was: first, the farming village; second, the business area; and third, the residential area with a large difference. Worship-demanding rates were highest in the residential area, then the farming village and finally the business area, with small discrepancies. For the residential area, the *butsudan* ownership rate was the lowest, whereas the worship-demanding rate was the highest. This is presumably because wives of white collar workers in that area were mostly full-time housekeepers, and tended to be attentive to their children. On the contrary, in the farming and the business households, for which the *butsudan* ownership rate was high, farming or business is assumed to have occupied too much time and energy of elders for them to be attentive to the little ones [MORIOKA 1972]. This reasoning suggests that the worship-demanding rate may not exactly indicate the practice rate and that the practice rates for farming and business households must be more or less greater than their worship-demanding rates. Anyhow, it is estimated from these rates that about 30% of *butsudan* owning households perform no ancestral rites, thus almost neglecting their *butsudan*.

We should not hastily conclude a decline of ancestor worship from the above observations. There are two reasons at least. First, comparative data for the prewar period and for the period right after the war are lacking. Second, it is possible that the practice rate remains almost the same as before though a change has occurred in the meaning of practice. For example, remember the extremely high *butsudan* ownership rate for the extended family households with widows which the Kakegawa study brought to our attention. For these households, the practice rate must be also high. The meaning of the practice is assumed to lie in the function of consolation of worshippers themselves by means of warm remembrance of the dead, comforting of their spirits, and spiritual contact of the living with the dead which was kept latent in ancestor worship under the *ie* system.

The following remark by Smith [1974: 113] summarizes such a change in the practice of ancestor worship:

> ...With the weakening influence of institutionalized Buddhism, households no longer need to be so concerned as they once were with the formally prescribed occasions of worship. The household may now worship its ancestors in the way it deems fitting and most efficacious. This may well represent the ultimate effect of the privatization of worship, for it is significant that no household reporting the most common patterns of worship apparently feels constrained to observe the seasonal, semipublic rites to the exclusion of all others...

The privatization of worship is nothing other than the increasing dominance of personal functions in ancestor worship. It has broken down the preeminent and orthodox pattern of worship, diversified the way of keeping a *butsudan* and helped to create forms of worship which are free from the constraints of sectarian and local customs.

RELIGIOUS GROUP MEMBERSHIP AND ANCESTOR WORSHIP

Ancestor worship of the Japanese was combined with Buddhism for many centuries. This was a characteristic of both Buddhism and ancestor worship in Japan [TAKEDA 1981: 19]. In prewar Japan, every family belonged to a religious group, mainly to a local Buddhist church, and a funeral ceremony and ancestral rites were performed in the manner prescribed by the religious group and local customs. Postwar economic growth, however, promoted regional migration and change of occupation; as a result, a population with no religious affiliation has increased in urban centers.

In the above mentioned 1967 Tokyo suburban study, we asked both local residents and newcomers whether their households had experienced a funeral as the chief mourner, and, if not, whether they could think of any religious man to whom they might apply for a service when a death occurred. The funeral experience rate was 89% for local extended families, 54% for local nuclear families, 43% for newcomer extended families and 9% for newcomer nuclear families. Among non-experience households, the rate of respondents who had no idea about any religious man to whom they might apply for a service was 0% for local extended families, 12% for local nuclear families, 43% for newcomer extended families and 50% for newcomer nuclear families. Among the local households, the funeral experience rates were high, and for the non-experienced local households an affiliation with a religious group was generally definite, whereas among newcomer households, as represented by nuclear families, the funeral experience rates were strikingly low, and further, half of the non-experienced newcomer households did not know which religious group to ask for a service. They might be called a "religiously floating population".

The religious affiliation of the newcomers viewed from the kinds of the religious bodies to which they would apply for a funeral service were: (1) established religions (about 40%); (2) new religions (about 10%); and (3) undecided (about 50%). All the households of the third category kept no *butsudan*. About 80% of the first and the second category had a *butsudan*. Among the *butsudan*-owning households, only one third practiced the "Bon" rite. The practice rate for the newcomer households in a Tokyo suburb was far lower than that in Smith's study. On the other hand, among local households, about 90% were affiliated with established religions (1), and the remaining 10% were new religion adherents (2) or had no definite affiliation (3). All of the first category households, except those with living founders, kept a *butsudan*, and 85% of them observed the Bon festival.

In short, those households as represented by local extended families are affiliated with established religions, mostly own a *butsudan* and practice the Bon rite. On the contrary, those as represented by newcomer nuclear families have neither religious affiliation nor a *butsudan*. In between these two poles, there are households affiliated with an established religion, keeping a *butsudan*, but lacking the Bon practice, and also those with established religion orientation but without *butsudan* ownership, and so forth. These instances are found more frequently among newcomer households than among local resident households.

Established religions, centering around the services for ancestor worship of the household, meet the needs of an individual family to perform rituals. Despite the declining popularity of established religions, people remain firmly connected with them in practicing ancestral rites. The ways to practice ancestor worship are largely prescribed by the established religion to which people belong. On the other hand, for those whose affiliation with an established religion has become tenuous because of residential shifts or other reasons, a variety of forms tend to emerge in the way of keeping a *butsudan* or of practicing ancestral rites.

Some of those who drifted away from the established religion to which they once belonged have come to be affiliated with a new religion. Among those religions, such sects as *Sōka Gakkai* and *Tenshō Kōtai Jingūkyō* do not make much of ancestor worship; yet, a majority including *Reiyūkai* set ancestor worship at the center of their rituals. *Reiyūkai* and offshoot sects from it conceive of ancestors bilaterally, totally different from the traditional concept of ancestor which was based on unilineal descent. They expound that the anguish and agony one suffers at present are caused by dead ancestors unable to arrive at a blissful state and hence in distress; in this respect, too, their concept of ancestor contrasts with that of *ie*, which emphasizes the benefit and the protection afforded by ancestors [KŌMOTO 1978].

For about ten years in the wake of the last war, when the Japanese were suffering from serious economic shortages, the teaching that ancestor worship would relieve people from distress was persuasive; however, after rapid economic development took place and the living conditions of the people improved markedly, the notion of suffering ancestors lost its appeal. Yet the concept of bilateral ancestors has become much more acceptable for the Japanese with the increasing popularity of nuclear family households.

The Japanese view of ancestor has been fundamentally conditioned by the way of household life and its change, but also influenced by the doctrine of the religious group to which the family belongs. Established Buddhism, once having been assured its influence by the feudal powers, had controlled the pattern of ancestor worship and, being supported by local customs, it continued to regulate ancestor worship even after the Meiji Restoration. However, it has now lost such influence because local customs which buttressed ancestor worship have collapsed under the impact of rapid social change. Thus, a variety of forms have appeared including a total absence of ancestor worship and partial or fragmented performance of the ritual. The weakened influence of established religions has led to the increased tendency of people to accept a new religion, and as a result, the concept of ancestor and the ways of worship expounded by new religions have also expanded their influence.

CONCLUSION

Along with the change of *ie* after the Second World War a striking change has occurred in ancestor worship which had been supported by the *ie*. In the concept of ancestor, a shift has been observed from a unilineal descent to a bilateral orientation.

This has been reinforced by the concept of ancestor expounded by some new religions and has been accelerated by the general acceptance of a nuclear family form. As to the function of ancestor worship, jural functions such as to legitimize one's social status have weakened, and personal functions such as to recall one's dead parents warmly and to console their spirits have been strengthened. The *butsudan*, the central object for the practice, is still kept by a majority of Japanese households, although various alternatives such as a temporary delay in setting up a *butsudan*, no ownership through one's life, or the equipping of a shelf resembling a *batsudan*, have emerged. Even among those keeping a *butsudan*, the worship practice rates are not always high and variations are also found in the ways of practice. This tendency is connected with the increasing significance of the personal function.

If ancestor worship of the Japanese has changed in this way, it must be said that the emerging forms are not ancestor worship as defined at the beginning of this chapter. If we call the traditional one "classical ancestor worship", the emerging one which is bilateral kin centered and personal function oriented, free from the pre-scribed patterns of established religions, may be called "modified ancestor worship". Both the view of ancestor and rites of worship have been modified. In present-day Japan, classical ancestor worship is kept not only in farming villages but also among local households in cities, whereas the modified form has been accepted by newcomer households in cities or in suburbs. We may add that even modified ancestor worship hardly occurs among some newcomer nuclear family households. The above tendencies coincide with the variety found in continuity, change and breakdown of the traditional household in present-day Japan.

Although I emphasized a shift in ancestor worship among the Japanese, I do not deny that the modified ancestor worship existed in former days side by side with the classical one. The latter was the norm claiming to be legitimate and proper, whereas the former was regarded as deviant and hence kept latent. Since the war classical ancestor worship has virtually ceased to be the norm. It may remain only a norm, but no longer the sole norm. The modified one also has gained an informal legitimacy. If we can look at the shift from this perspective, we are in a position to treat both continuity and change impartially.

BIBLIOGRAPHY

FORTES, Meyer
    1961   Pietas in Ancestor Worship: The Henry Meyers Lecture, 1960. *Journal of the Royal Anthropological Institute* 91: 166–191.
    1965   Some Reflections on Ancestor Worship in Africa. In M. Fortes and G. Dieterlen (eds.), *African Systems of Thought: Studies Presented and Discussed at the Third International African Seminar in Salisbury, December 1960,* Oxford: Oxford University Press, pp. 122–141.
HOZUMI, Nobushige (Rev. ed.)
    1912   *Ancestor Worship and Japanese Law.* Tokyo: Maruzen.

Kōmoto, Mitsugi
1978 Minshū no nakano senzo-kan no ichi-sokumen (1): Reiyūkaikei kyōdan no baai. In T. Sakurai (ed.), *Nihon Shūkyō no Fukugōteki Kōzō*, Tokyo: Kōbundō, pp. 357–381. (One Aspect of Ancestor Cult among the Common People (1): A Case of the Reiyūkai Sect. *Complex Structure of Japanese Religions.*)

Matsumoto, Michiharu
1981 Ie no hendō nōto. In Dōshisha Daigaku Jimbun Kagaku Kenkyūjo (ed.), *Kyōdō Kenkyū Nihon no Ie*, Tokyo: Kokusho Kankōkai, pp. 83–114. (Some Notes on the Change of *Ie* System. *Joint Study on the Japanese* Ie *System.*)

Morioka, Kiyomi
1972 Kazoku patān to dentō-teki shūkyō kōdō no kunren, tokuni shōgakkō jōkyū jidō ni tsuite. *Shakai Kagaku Jānaru* (ICU) 11: 71–97. (Relationship between Patterns of the Family and Training in Traditional Religious Practices, with Special Attention to Primary School Senior Children.)

1975 *Gendai Shakai no Minshū to Shūkyō.* Tokyo: Hyōronsha. (*People and Religions in the Contemporary Society.*)

1980 Sengo no kazoku kōsei no henka to ie ishiki no hōkai. *Rekishi Kōron* 50: 122–127. (Change of the Family Structure and Vanishing *Ie* Consciousness after the War.)

Smith, Robert J.
1974 *Ancestor Worship in Contemporary Japan.* Stanford: Stanford University Press.

Takahashi, Hiroko
1975 Kazoku keitai to senzo saishi. *Kazoku Kenkyū Nempō*, 1: 37–52. (Family Structure and Religious Services for Ancestors.)

Takeda, Chōshū
1981 Nihon no ie to sono shinkō. In Dōshisha Daigaku Jimbun Kagaku Kenkyūjo (ed.), *Kyōdō Kenkyū Nihon no Ie*, Tokyo: Kokusho Kankōkai, pp. 5–29. (Japanese *Ie* and Its Belief System. *Joint Study on the Japanese* Ie *System.*)

Tōkei Sūri Kenkyūjo (Institute of Statistical Mathematics)
1979 *Kokumin-sei no Kenkyū Dai 6 kai Zenkoku Chōsa*, 1978 nen.: *Sūken Kenkyū Report No. 46.* (*A Study of the Japanese National Character Based on the Sixth Nation-wide Survey Conducted in* 1978: *Sūken Research Report No. 46.*)

Yonemura, Shōji
1981 Gendai nihonjin no senzokan to senzosaishi. *Gendaijin to Shūkyō* [Jurist *Sōgō Tokushū* No. 21], Tokyo: Yūhikaku, pp. 151–156. (Contemporary Japanese View of Ancestors and Their Religious Services for Ancestors. *Contemporary Men and Religion.*)

Part V

Woman's Role and Status in the Family

Chapter 14

Family and Interpersonal Relationships in Early Japan

Takao Sofue

INTRODUCTION

The most fundamental group during the 8th century was one of bilateral kindred based on the mixture of both patrilineal and matrilineal principles. It may also be added that lower the class, the more dominant was bilaterality, whereas patrilineality was much stronger in the upper class. Both duo-virilocal and uxori-virilocal residence rules were common and polygyny was practiced among the upper class.

The most frequent theme among the myths in the *Kojiki* compiled in A.D. 712 by the government is "brother-brother relationship", while there was no myth illustrating the mother's sentiment toward her children. This is very important when compared with contemporary Japanese movies and TV dramas in which the mother's strong affection for her son and the tendency toward mutual dependency between them are both emphasized. This could be a reflection of the real mother-son relationship in early Japan. Each family member should have been much more independent and should have expressed sentiments much more freely.

With the beginning of the Heian Period, however, women's status became gradually lower and they were supposed to suppress their emotions. It was probably around this time that the mother-son relationship came to be characterized by mutual dependency and *amae* became one of the fundamental traits of Japanese psychology.

At the same time, there should have been a noticeable continuity, and "receptivity" must have existed as characterizing the Japanese interpersonal relationships since the earliest part of the history, while sensitivity to vertical relationships developed with the change of society after the Heian Period.

The family and kinship structure of the early Japanese have been widely studied by historians, anthropologists and sociologists. [ARIGA 1952a, 1952b, 1957; KOYAMA 1952; ŌMACHI 1958; OKA 1958; YOSHIDA 1980]. The oldest known Japanese census was taken in A.D. 702, shortly before the beginning of the Nara Period (710–794). Some of the largest households recorded in this registration numbered more than 100 members. Based on this data, some historians maintain that large extended families existed in ancient Japan. However, this idea has been refuted since it is evident that the members of each household unit recorded in the 702 census did not always dwell under one roof, but were divided into several residences. The average number of residents per household has been estimated at 6–10 suggesting that the fundamental living unit was usually a nuclear family consisting of a married couple

217

with children. However, this unit was not considered to be entirely independent, but rather existed as part of a larger social group.

The core of this larger social group of which the nuclear family formed a part was probably composed of bilateral kindred. While various data indicate that among the upper classes patrilineal ties based on ancestor worship were very strong and that the patrilineal kinship group (*uji*) was the most important unit there was no rule of exogamy excluding marriage within the group.

According to various 8th century documents, there were four kinds of incest taboo: incest with one's mother; incest with a daughter; incest with a wife's daughter from a previous marriage; and incest with one's wife's mother. These four taboos were strictly enforced. But on the other hand, marriage with one's own siblings born of different mothers was not uncommon. It should be noted that siblings born of one's own mother were denoted by the prefix *iro* to distinguish them from those born of different mothers. These facts suggest that matrilineality was also considered important.

In sum, the most fundamental social group during the 8th century was one of bilateral kindred based on the mixture of both patrilineal and matrilineal principles, although there was neither a bilineal nor a double-descent system. It may also be added that probably the lower the social status, the more dominant was bilaterality, whereas patrilineality was much stronger in the upper class. Upper class men exercised considerable power as war leaders as well as chief supervisors of intensive agriculture and various kinds of construction. These leaders added non-kin peasants and servants to their own domestic units. Frequently these units were politically powerful organizations with a very strong sense of solidarity.

Regarding marriage residence rules in those times, scholars agree that both uxori-virilocal marriage and duo-virilocal marriage were the most common types. In uxori-virilocal marriage the couple initially took up residence where the wife lived. After a few years, or after the birth of the first child they moved to the husband's residence prior to formalized "marriage". In duo-virilocal residence the husband and wife lived separately for a few years after the marriage or until their first child was born. The husband made "night visits" to his wife, returning home in the morning. Later they took up residence where the husband lived. In addition to these two types, neolocal marriage also existed. It should be emphasized also that polygyny was common among the upper class and that duolocal residence was also practiced. The husband made night visits to his wives who lived separately. This type of residence became very common among the aristocrats during the Heian Period (794–1185) and is illustrated in the famous *Tale of Genji* written around 1000 A.D.

During the Kamakura Period (1192–1333), however, warriors (*samurai* or *bushi*) gradually assumed political power. With the increasing emphasis on masculinity and the husband's dominance during this period, traditional residence rules (both uxori-virilocal and duo-virilocal) were gradually replaced by virilocal residence, and from the outset married couples lived in the husband's residence.

Probably this new residence rule became the dominant practice among warrior classes during the Muromachi Period (1338–1573). Gradually this form of residence was adopted by the upper status commoners. Only by the beginning of the 18th century, in the middle of the Edo or Tokugawa Period (1603–1868) did virilocal residence finally become widespread among the lesser commoners of castle towns. It was not until the latter half of the Meiji Period (1868–1912) or during the beginning of Taisho Period (1912–1926) that virilocal residence became a standard type of marriage in smaller towns and rural villages [NOGUCHI 1969: 97].

Finally it should be noted that the early written records referred to above are from Nara, Kyoto and other centers in which the ancient culture developed. Inevitably, therefore, academic discussion based on these data is valid for these regions only. Even at that time, considerable regional variation was probably to be found in specific localities. Among some mountain hamlets of the Shirakawa region of Central Japan, for example, it was customary up until the late 19th century for only the eldest son to live virilocally with his wife after marriage. Younger married sons had to stay alone at their natal houses. Every night after supper they visited their wives, but during the day they had to work to help their parents and eldest brother. Their children were raised by their wives. Since most households had several daughters and each daughter was responsible for her children (ranging up to about 10 in number), the total number of family living under one roof at the middle of the Meiji Period must have been on the order of 30–50. Land was extremely scarce in this mountainous area, thus cooperative work by brothers remained indispensable for their system of slash-and-burn agriculture. With the development of heavy industries, roads and railroads toward the end of the 19th century, younger sons began to leave their village to work in the urban centers. Consequently, this formal traditional large family soon disappeared [BEFU 1968; KOYAMA 1954].

Similar cases are reported from other isolated areas. According to the records of a mountain village in Kochi Prefecture, Shikoku, written in 1853, duolocal marriage was generally observed [ŌMACHI 1958: 182]. It is quite probable that these and other local variations in marriage customs existed since the earliest times in Japanese history despite inducements to conform to the centrally controlled census regulations.

INTERPERSONAL RELATIONSHIPS AS SEEN THROUGH JAPANESE MYTHS

Japanese myths can be analyzed from the perspective of interpersonal relationships to throw some light upon intrafamilial tensions existing among the early Japanese. A book entitled *Kojiki* (*Record of Ancient Matters*) compiled in A.D. 712 by the central government and known as the oldest history book in Japan is a collection of the most important myths inherited orally from ancient times. It is clear that the major purpose of the *Kojiki* was to show that the Emperors are legitimate rulers descended from the proper Ancestor God. However, I think that interpersonal relationships illustrated in these myths should reflect the social reality of the time, although, of course, there should be anticipated exaggeration. It is from this view-point that I have taken up the myths as important data. Many historians and anthropologists have studied the *Kojiki* but it seems that none have taken a psycho-social approach.

Among the 91 myths included in the *Kojiki* 34 are stories of some kind of intra-family relationship as follows:

Brother-brother relationship	15
Husband-wife relationship	10
Father-son relationship	3
Father-daughter relationship	2
Brother-sister relationship	2 (including one case of incest)
Mother-son relationship	1
Sister-sister relationship	1

Thus, in the ancient records, the most frequently described family stories involve a brother-brother relationship. (Both "brothers from the same mother" and "brothers from different mothers" are included here.) Among the fifteen myths, only three describe friendly relations; the remainder depict competition and aggression among brothers. In eight of these twelve stories, brothers are killed (in six cases elder brothers are killed by younger ones). This seems to be a frequent theme in the *Kojiki*. To take one example, the Emperor Yūryaku killed two of his elder brothers because they were not brave enough to cooperate with him in avenging their eldest brother's murder. Prince Yamato Takeru killed his elder brother by tearing off his arms and legs, simply because he did not join a repast. Umihiko, a god of the sea, attacks his younger brother, Yamahiko who rules the mountains. But finally Umihiko surrenders. In all three examples, the brothers are of the same mother. There are also stories about fights among brothers of different mothers. One such story is about Ōkuninushi-no-Mikoto, who was attacked and killed by his eighty half-brothers. He subsequently revived.

The second largest group of stories is about husband-wife relationships, in which heterosexual love is most openly emphasized. In three stories the main theme is the very strong jealousy of the first wife toward other wives.

As illustrated above, one of the most remarkable characteristics of these myths is that the sentiments and emotions existing among brothers and married couples are most openly and vividly expressed. But on the other hand, those between parents and children are not so well described. The father-son relationship appears in three myths, but in none does the patriarchal and strong image of father exist. Rather the father seems to be gentle and amicable toward the son. The mother-son relationship appears only once in the myths. A young, brave and violent prince, Susanoono-Mikoto, cried ceaselessly after his mother's (Izanagi-no-Mikoto) death. He cried so loudly and continuously that most of the trees in the mountains perished. His father became so angry at this that he banished his son from the country. Even in this story there is no interaction between mother and son, and there is no myth whatsoever in which the mother's sentiment toward her children is illustrated. Neither does the mother-son relationship appear in any of the myths included in the *Nihon Shoki* (lit. *Chronicle of Japan*) compiled by the government in A.D. 720, shortly after the compilation of the *Kojiki*. The *Manyōshū*, the oldest anthology said to have been compiled at the beginning of the 9th century, contains more than four thousand poems, the majority of which express very openly the heterosexual love between lovers or spouses——again the mother-son relationship received no representation.

The above facts seem to be most important when compared with the situation in present-day Japan. From the end of World War II, until about the beginning of the 1960's the favorite recreation for the Japanese general public was watching movies, especially Japanese movies. The most popular movies were "haha-mono" (lit. "mother films") stories dealing with mother-son relationships. Frequently a mother and her illegitimate son exist under sad circumstances but the mother's very strong affection toward her son is emphasized repeatedly [MINAMI 1957: 575–576]. More recently, movies have been replaced by television viewing as the major form of recreation. In 1964, for example, the most popular TV program was a drama entitled "Okāsan" (Mother). During this period, more than 300 serialized stories were aired, each of which was a different story about a mother and her son. The most frequent basic theme has been that of the mother's strong affection for her son and their continuing mutual dependency [YAMAMURA 1970].

The psychiatrist Takeo Doi has compared Japanese and Americans, including psychopathic patients, and presented the concept of *amae* as the key to understanding Japanese psychology [DOI 1962, 1963, 1971]. *Amae* is a popular word in Japan frequently used by the general public to express interpersonal relationships. It is defined by Doi as "to depend and presume upon the other's benevolence". He points out that a child forms *amae* relationship with its mother early in life, and this ultimately leads to a so-called "mother-complex". This relationship is maintained into adulthood and emerges as a very strong continuing dependency need. My own research indicates that *amae* also exists among Japanese high school students [SOFUE 1979: 15–16]. It should not be surprising, therefore, that *amae* between mother and son is the most frequent theme of Japanese movies and TV dramas. That such a theme never appears in any ancient writings similarly should be considered a reflection of the prevailing mother-son relationships of the time.

Following the Nara Period, discussed in the preceding section, came the Heian Period (794–1185), and in A.D. 905 around the middle of this period, a new anthology, entitled *Kokin Wakashū* (lit. *Collection of Old and New Poems*), was compiled. Comparing the approximately one thousand poems included in this anthology with those in the *Manyōshū*, compiled about one hundred years earlier, scholars agree that there are apparently considerable differences between the two groups of poems. *Manyōshū* poems are characterized by open expressions of very strong interpersonal sentiments, most noticeably in heterosexual relationships. Both men and women do not suppress their sentiments of love, and express them openly in poems. Among the *Kokin Wakashū* poems such sentiments are suppressed. This suppression is especially true for women [MARUYAMA 1981: 3–5]. The causes of these differences have been discussed by scholars but the principal causal factor was probably that the Fujiwara family gradually became the most powerful of aristocrats in the central government, and polygyny became increasingly common among them. In addition, the number of court ladies increased rapidly. As a consequence, a type of femininity was greatly stressed in which ladies were supposed to suppress their emotions [ŌNO 1961: 110–111].

A related fact is the existence of a large vocabulary of words used exclusively by women, which may have become a unique characteristic of the Japanese language from the beginning of the Heian Period. Court ladies should appear to be graceful and as part of their comportment use only "feminine" words. A special ladies' vocabulary was further developed during the Muromachi Period; later, there was a gradual increase in such usage among common women [ŌNO 1961: 65–66]. It should be recalled that virilocal residence became popular at the beginning of this period.

Another related fact to be stressed here is the changing role played by women in the field of literature. During the Nara Period women could express their emotions openly in poems, whereas during the Heian Period they had to suppress their feelings. However, they could still express themselves by writing poems, essays and even novels. The famous *Tale of Genji* and a collection of essays entitled *Makura no Sōshi* are typical examples; both were written by intellectual court ladies. After the end of this period, however, women writers disappeared completely from the scene [ŌNO 1961: 112–113]. Transitions in social background should be closely related.

The position of women as well as intrafamily relationships thus changed considerably after the Heian Period. The question arises as to when *amae* relationships came into prominence. As already discussed, this relationship never appears in *Kojiki* or in *Nihon Shoki*. Thus it may be concluded tentatively that mother and son at that period were more independent of each other and the tendency of mutual dependency did not exist or at least was much weaker. The earliest description of the very close relationship between mother and son appears in a novel entitled *Sagoromo Monogatari* (lit. *Tale of Sagoromo*), which is said to have been written around A.D. 1050 by a court lady who obviously tried to imitate the famous novel *Tale of Genji*, written around A.D. 1000.

The hero of this tale is an aristocrat called Sagoromo, who is very handsome and good at music and poetry. This novel is actually a story of how his parents raised him with great care. The following describes what happened when he was eighteen years old:

"His parents tried to protect him not only from the rain but even from the sunshine and moonlight. However, Sagoromo himself gradually came to feel ill at ease about his parents' excessive care. When Sagoromo went out pleasure-seeking at night, both parents never went to bed but kept waiting for him until early morning.

When he came back, the parents never scolded him but just smiled with great joy about his safe return.   They just looked ridiculous.   Even when Sagoromo did something very dishonorable, his parents hesitated to stop him and could not say anything to him about it".

It should be noted here that the earliest record in which the word *amae* appears is the *Tale of Genji* [ŌNO *et al.* 1974: 53], and I suspect it was around this time that *amae* became one of the fundamental traits of Japanese interpersonal relationships, and especially of the mother-son relationship.

CONTINUITY AND CHANGE

So far I have discussed the historical changes in intrafamily relations since the Nara Period.   At the same time, however, I should point out also that there is a noticeable continuity in some fundamental psychological traits of the Japanese.   Such characteristics as group-orientedness and other-directedness are most frequently mentioned traits of the Japanese [CONNOR 1977: 9–10; SOFUE 1963, 1980], but "receptivity" may be worth considering here as an example of a long continuous existent trait.

"The Japanese are willing to copy anything from abroad."   This has been pointed out very frequently as one of the most remarkable traditional characteristics of the Japanese.   But it is only recently that this trait became a subject for analysis among social scientists.   Among them, an anthropologist, Masuda [1967: 6–29], carefully examines Japanese prehistory and history and shows that from about the 1st century B.C. through the beginning of the 16th century A.D. the Japanese admired the Chinese civilization, which they accepted with such enthusiasm.   During the 16th century the Japanese became attracted by Portuguese culture.   Some of the upper class tried to copy the Portuguese costumes and other usages.   Then, after the Meiji Restoration, in 1868, the Japanese eagerly absorbed traits borrowed from the German, British, French and other western cultures with which they made contact.   Masuda emphasizes, however, that such "receptivity" may have existed since the Stone Age.

In Japan, settled agriculture began around 300 B.C. (at the beginning of the Yayoi Period) and the Japanese State was established in the earliest years of the 4th century (at the beginning of the Kofun Period).   The interval between these two fundamentally important events is only about 600 years.   On the other hand, intervals between the beginning of settled agriculture and the establishment of the historic state took 3,500 years in Mesopotamia, 3,000 years in Egypt, Mexico and Peru.   The same can be said of Indian and Mediterranean cultures.   Clearly then, culture change in Japan was much faster even during prehistoric times, and it should be noted that the beginning of sedentary agriculture in Japan was obviously a result of the ready acceptance of a new culture involving wet rice field cultivation, which probably came in from southern China.   At the same time, the establishment of the state is today generally interpreted as a result of influences from Central Asian nomads, who periodically probably entered Japan via Korea.

Therefore, it is obvious that the ready acceptance of alien cultures was occurring rapidly in Japan as early as the Yayoi Period. However, Masuda points out also that the earliest evidence of such receptivity may date back even to the Jōmon Period which preceded the Yayoi Period. One suspects various alien cultures, probably from Southeast Asia and Oceania, as influential, especially during the Middle Jōmon Period (around 2,000 B.C.).

If such receptivity has existed since the Stone Age, as suggested by Masuda, then the interpersonal relationships of the early Japanese were already characterized by this trait, although early Japanese may have been more independent or more individualistic than those of later periods.

Finally I would also like to refer to the prevalent Japanese sensitivity to "vertical relationships." This trait has been pointed to by many scholars (e.g., NAKANE 1967, 1970). Historians maintain that this trait originated and was developed by the very strong feudal system that characterized the Edo Period. Then the question is, did this hierarchical sensitivity exist before the Edo Period, and to what extent? One of the clues to answering this question may lie in the history of honorific terms (*keigo*) which characterize the Japanese language.

According to linguistic studies, honorific terms appeared in the oldest written records in Japan of the 6th century [KASUGA 1971: 35–36], as well as in the *Kojiki* and *Nihon Shoki*. But the terms of the time were mostly those addressed to the Emperor and to the gods. These terms are thought to be the origin of all honorifics [TSUJIMURA 1968: 82–3, 1971: 119]. People probably had a strong feeling of awe and respect toward the Emperor and gods who were believed to have strong magical powers. Animistic beliefs were very strong among the early Japanese and probably the feeling of awe toward natural objects was extended to the Emperor and gods [ŌNO 1961: 46–49, 74–75]. However, fathers and elder brothers lacked autocratic powers over sons and younger brothers; and women and wives were not submissive to men and husbands. Vertical relationships must have developed with the change of society in the Kamakura Period. Honorific terms became more elaborate and complicated, paralleling the changes occurring in interpersonal relationships.

BIBLIOGRAPHY

ARIGA, K.
   1952a Kazoku. In Japanese Society of Ethnology (ed.), *Nihon Shakai Minzoku Jiten* vol. **1**, Tokyo: Seibundō Shinkōsha, pp. 166–172. (Family. *Dictionary of Japanese Society and Folk-customs.*)
   1952b Kon'in. In Japanese Society of Ethnology (ed.), *Nihon Shakai Minzoku Jiten* vol. **1**, Tokyo: Seibundō Shinkōsha, pp. 449–452. (Marriage. *Dictionary of Japanese Society and Folk-customs.*)
   1957 Bokeisei. In Japanese Society of Ethnology (ed.), *Nihon Shakai Minzoku Jiten* vol. **3**, Tokyo: Seibundō Shinkōsha, pp. 1328–1329. (Matrilineal System. *Dictionary of Japanese Society and Folk-customs.*)

BEFU, H.
1968   Origin of Large Households and Duolocal Residence in Central Japan. *American Anthropologist* 70: 309–319.

CONNOR, J. W.
1977   *Tradition and Change in Three Generations of Japanese Americans.* Chicago: Nelson Hall.

DOI, T.
1962   Amae: A Key Concept for Understanding Japanese Personality Structure. In R. J. Smith and R. K. Beardsley (eds.), *Japanese Culture*, Chicago: Aldine, pp. 132–139.
1963   Some Thoughts on Helplessness and the Desire to Be Loved. *Psychchiatry* 26: 266–272.
1971   *Amae no Kōzō.* Tokyo: Kōbundō. (*The Structure of the State of Amae.*)

KASUGA, K.
1971   Kodai no keigo: I. In T. Tsujimura (ed.), *Keigoshi*, Tokyo: Taishūkan, pp. 35–95. (Honorifics in Early Japan: Part 1. *History of Honorifics in Japan.*)

KOYAMA, T.
1952   Kazoku seido. In Japanese Society of Ethnology (ed.), *Nihon Shakai Minzoku Jiten vol. 1*, Tokyo: Seibundō Shinkōsha, pp. 172–174. (Family System. *Dictionary of Japanese Society and Folk-customs.*)
1954   Daikazokusei. In Japanese Society of Ethnology (ed.), *Nihon Shakai Minzoku Jiten vol. 2*, Tokyo: Seibundō Shinkōsha, pp. 862–863. (Large Household. *Dictionary of Japanese Society and Folk-customs.*)

MARUYAMA, Y.
1981   *Manyōshū Yōkai.* Tokyo: Yūseidō. (*Notes on Selected Poems from Manyōshū.*)

MASUDA, Y.
1967   *Junsui Bunka no Jōken.* Tokyo: Chūō Kōronsha. (*Japanese Culture under the Impact of Alien Cultures.*)

MINAMI, H.
1957   *Taikei Shakai Shinrigaku.* Tokyo: Kōbunsha. (*Outline of Social Psychology.*)

NAKANE, C.
1967   *Tate Shakai no Ningen Kankei.* Tokyo: Kōdansha. (*Human Relations in Vertical Society.*)
1970   *Japanese Society.* Berkeley and Los Angeles: University of California Press.

NOGUCHI, T.
1969   Mukoirikon, yomeirikon: Nihon no kon'in seido o bunsekisuru. *Kagaku Asahi*, April, pp. 95–100. (Uxorilocal Marriage and Virilocal Marriage: Japanese Marriage System.)

OKA, M.
1958   Nihonbunka no kisokōzō. In M. Oka *et al.* (eds.), *Nihon Minzokugaku Taikei vol. 2*, Tokyo: Heibonsha, pp. 5–21. (The Structure of Japanese Culture. *Outline of Japanese Volkskunde.*)

ŌMACHI, T.
1958   Kon'in. In M. Oka *et al.* (eds.), *Nihon Minzokugaku Taikei vol. 3*, Tokyo: Heibonsha, pp. 175–202. (Marriage. *Outline of Japanese Volkskunde.*)

ŌNO, S.
1961   *Nihongo no Nenrin.* Tokyo: Yūki Shobō. (*Annual Rings of Japanese Language.*)

ŌNO, S. *et al.* (eds.)
    1974   *Iwanami Kogo Jiten.* Tokyo: Iwanami Shoten. (*Iwanami's Dictionary of Japanese Archaic Words.*)
SOFUE, T.
    1963   Nihonjin no kokuminsei ni okeru renzokusei to henka. In T. Sofue (ed.), *Nihonjin wa Dō Kawattaka?*, Tokyo: Shibundō, pp. 5–32. (Continuity and Change in the Japanese National Character. *How Have the Japanese Changed?*)
    1979   Aspects of the Personality of Japanese, Americans, Italians and Eskimos: Comparison Using the Sentence Completion Test. *Journal of Psychological Anthropology* 2: 11–52.
    1980   Continuity and Change in the Japanese Personality. [paper presented at the International Symposium on "Asian Peoples and Their Cultures: Continuity and Change", December 8–10, 1980 at Seoul, Korea.]
TSUJIMURA, T.
    1968   *Keigo no Shiteki Kenkyū.* Tokyo: Tokyodō. (*Historical Study of Japanese Honorific Terms.*)
    1971   Keigoshi no hōhō to mondaiten. In T. Tsujimura (ed.), *Keigoshi.* Tokyo: Taishūkan, pp. 5–32. (Methods and Problems of the History of Honorifics. *History of Honorifics in Japan.*)
YAMAMURA, K.
    1970   Terebi ni miru hahano kyozō to jitsuzō. In T. Takuma and H. Matsubara (eds.), *Oya to Ko*, Tokyo: Shibundō, pp. 156–172. (Ghost Images and Real Images of the Mother in Japanese TV Dramas. *Parents and Children.*)
YOSHIDA, Takashi
    1980   Narajidai no shakai-soshiki. In M. Inouye (ed.), *Nihon Kodaishi*, Tokyo: National Center for Broadcast Education, pp. 101–108. (Social Organization during the Nara Period. *Ancient History of Japan.*)

Chapter 15

Maternal Authority in the Japanese Family

MASAKO TANAKA

INTRODUCTION

Casual observers of Japanese society may form the impression that Japanese women are passive and obedient to men, and that they are relatively content to play secondary roles in a male-dominated society. At the same time I have frequently encountered just the opposite characterization, according to which Japanese women are said to be quite strong despite their surface meekness. So strong are they in fact that they not only manage their households with little or no help (or interference) from the men, but are said to "move the world from behind the scenes", for men are heavily dependent emotionally on their women, specifically on their wives and/or mothers. Men are thus considered to be firmly controlled by women. This second view seems to be willingly shared by some Japanese males, who fondly insist that whether a man succeeds or not in his enterprise depends on his woman, saying that because *uchi no kaachan* ("my wife" [lit. "the mother of my house"]) is strong he cannot do a thing without her permission. Where lies the truth?

This paper examines the Japanese woman's status and roles in the family through a study of the pattern of her normative behavior vis-à-vis other members of the household, particularly the husband and son. These interpersonal relationships seem to be supported by, or closely correlated with, certain kinship ideology, the characteristic features of which are described here and compared with those of the American system prevalent among the middle-class White Anglo-Saxon Protestant families.

Put simply, the Japanese woman's expected roles at home can be summarized as those of the family care-giver, even in her capacity as daughter or sister, if the family lacks a mother or wife. That this, particularly for the mother-wife, should be so might appear as a worn and redundant truism, but what is peculiar about the Japanese woman's case is that be she a wife, mother, sister, or daughter, she could, unless too young, assume the role of the *sole* care-giver vis-à-vis all other members of the household, including not only her children and husband but also aged parents (or parents-in-law) and ritually the ancestors. She is the *shufu*, or "the woman" of the household (the word *shufu* consists of two characters meaning "main" and "adult woman". The *shufu* is ideally and most often the wife of the household head, but could be any other adult woman of the house). The important point is that in this capacity her relationship to her husband, or to her adult son, as well as to the aged parents (-in-law) and ancestors is not essentially different from her relationship to her

227

young children. Everyone in the family is totally dependent on her for his/her comfortable daily existence at home.

The prototypical relationship between the care-giving woman and the care-receiving members of the household is undoubtedly that of the mother and her infant child. That, of course, seems to be a universal characteristic of the mother-child relationship anywhere while the child is young and dependent. What is unique in the Japanese case, though, is that such a dependency relationship is often maintained even after the child becomes an adult, especially when the child is male, and that when he marries, the mother's role is taken up by his wife, whom he symbolically begins to address and refer to as "mother" as soon as a child is born. Because of this overlap of mother and wife roles, there often develops an emotional conflict between the two women vying for the position of the sole care-giver, a situation which can become critical in a traditional stem-type household where a young couple lives with the husband's parents. Hence the notorious "mother-in-law problems" (conflict between a man's mother and his wife) which are themes of so much Japanese fiction and essays in the family column of newspapers.

Mother or wife, the mature Japanese woman's authority appears to be derived from her role as the sole care-giver of the family. As the sole care-giver vis-à-vis all the other family members, living and dead, she is the unifying force in the family. She also epitomizes the continuity of the family by producing and raising children, as well as through caring for aged parents and ancestors. In this sense, she is the custodian of the family's past and future.

JURAL VS. MORAL AUTHORITY

The Japanese woman's position as the sole care-giver of the family is formidable. This, however, does not mean that she has jural and/or legal authority over other members of the household, nor does it imply that she can maintain an independent identity in society at large. Though legally independent under the present Civil Code, an ordinary Japanese woman's jural status is still largely defined in Confucianist terms by the status of her father while she is single, and by that of her husband after marriage. At birth a woman automatically acquires the family name of her father, and she assumes her husband's name upon marriage, unless her husband is an adopted son-in-law (*mukoyōshi*). She is always a daughter, wife, or mother of somebody. Her status in society is largely defined and determined by the status and career of her father, husband, or son. Even today only few Japanese women succeed in establishing their own social identity. Thus, it may be said that jurally the Japanese kinship system continues to exhibit a marked "patrilineal" bias. Outside the family context the Japanese woman's status is even lower, despite Article 14 of the Constitution, which stipulates that no one shall be discriminated against on the basis of, *inter alia*, race, creed, or sex. Japanese society remains a staunchly male-dominated world, where women are expected to be either "pretty flowers" or handy but inconspicuous and polite assistants to men who alone manage the world. Clearly such a male-female relationship results from the general pattern of sexual division of labor in the society, as shown below.

However, it is important to emphasize that the jurally dependent status in and outside the household does not necessarily mean that the Japanese woman has only low moral or spiritual authority (Chapter 4). In a sense the situation is just the opposite. Since family members are totally dependent on her for a comfortable existence, and males cannot replace her in this capacity owing to the general division of labor, the woman is truly indispensable. It is perhaps not accidental that the mother should be regarded as the very incarnation of the family (*ie*) and the "*furusato*", or one's birthplace. The *furusato* ("old village"), however, is more than just a birthplace for most Japanese, since it is also where their parents and ancestors are, and where a person can always return and be accepted without condition. Japanese seem to feel that the person who lacks a *furusato* is rootless. In this sense, the mother may be said to be the very root of one's existence. But before examining the nature of the Japanese woman's moral authority, a glance at the general pattern of sexual division of labor in society is necessary.

SEXUAL DIVISION OF LABOR

In traditional Confucianist Japanese ideology man and woman are thought to have distinct, heaven-sent, complementary and sex-determined roles. Man works to earn the living while the woman takes care of the family, including children, aged parents and deceased ancestors. A competent woman is expected to keep the household in perfect order both physically and emotionally without the help of her husband. In fact, she should not even bother him by mentioning family problems. On the other hand, a truly manly husband is supposed to concentrate on his work, completely free of domestic cares. Neither man nor woman is supposed to interfere with the other's business. Thus the typical Japanese man will not "meddle" in the kitchen, nor will he say much about the children's socialization. And many a Japanese wife is quite ignorant about her husband's job.

Such a strict division of labor may have been worked out first among the salaried *samurai* class during the Edo Period, and adopted later by other classes when urban growth and industrialization after the Meiji Restoration transformed farmers and peasants into wage-earners and housewives. Whatever the origin, the tradition persists. Higher education for women (as well as for men) and the women's liberation movement have made some inroads in changing the general pattern, but compared with other industrialized societies, change in the status of a Japanese woman has been minimal. So much so that many a working woman today still exerts herself to do a "perfect" job of house-keeping, just like the housewife who stays home, and feels guilty for not being able to do so. In short, the two sexes are supposed to belong to two complementary but distinct domains, where they perform interrelated but separate roles as follows:

Male domain and role	Female domain and role
outside (society)	inside (home)
public	private
job or profession	house-keeping
	child rearing
	care of the aged parents (-in-law)
	care of the ancestors
care-receiver at home	care-giver
(dependent on woman)	(emotionally or morally dominant)
jurally independent and dominant	jurally dependent

HUSBAND-WIFE AND MOTHER-SON RELATIONSHIPS

One of the biggest social changes undergone by Japanese society after World War II is said to be the *kakukazoku-ka*, or break-up of the large extended family (more precisely, "multi-generational stem family") into nuclear families. Indeed, nearly 75 percent of families today are nuclear, or incomplete nuclear type of households. According to the New Family Registar Act (*kosekiho*) introduced after the War, a new family is created when a man and woman marry. The family grows as children are born, and shrinks when children leave upon marriage to establish their own families. It shrinks further when one of the spouses dies, and disappears with the death of the other.

On the surface such a nuclear family is structurally no different from the typical family of any Western society. But is it really so? For example, is the Japanese nuclear family comparable with a typical middle class WASP American family, as described by Schneider [1968] and Parsons [1943, 1954], in terms of the husband-wife or the mother-son relationship?

In American kinship the husband-wife and mother-son relationships are structurally distinct in that among all the so-called kinship relationships only the former can be established by the will of the two concerned individuals and it is based on mutual personal love, "erotic" or "sexual" love as Schneider terms it. Consideration of any other factor in initiating the relationship (such as family background, wealth, religious affiliation, class) is regarded as "calculation", and therefore not "right". The resulting family may be said to be conjugal in the true sense of the word.

Needless to say, this ideology, or the myth of "true love" marriage, does not prevent most Americans from marrying homogamously, but the ideology is there all the same. This conjugal love ("sexual love") contrasts sharply with all other kinds of love, which Schneider calls "cognatic" because they derive from the partners' sharing of something (such as "blood"). According to this distinction, the husband-wife relationship is based on "sexual love" whereas "cognatic love" occurs in the mother-son and any other parent-child relationship. The two love relationships are thus entirely different. In other words, when an American male marries he contracts an entirely new love relationship with a new woman, which should not compete with his "cognatic love" for his mother.

Not so in Japan. Many young people today say that they prefer a "love marriage" (*renai kekkon*) to a traditional arranged marriage (*miai kekkon*). However, I would say that a true "love marriage" comparable to an American love marriage is rare [De Vos 1973: Chapter 5]. Even when partners declare theirs to be a "love marriage", there are always some elements of the arranged marriage. Parental consent is regarded as very important, if not essential. Parents of both sides weigh (Americans might say "calculate") meticulously various extraneous factors, such as social ranking and income of the family, educational background, profession, age and personalities, among other things, of family members as well as the partner him/herself. The wedding will be very much an affair of the two families rather than of two independent individuals. It is normally the groom's family which "takes" (*morau*) the bride from her family. And even though the new couple establishes a new household neolocally, it is usually expected that when the husband's parents grow old, or if one of them dies, the couple should take care of the parent(s) along with the ancestors, sometimes even at the expense of the couple's career. Aged parents and ancestors, ancestral land and a house, if any, are symbols of the continuity of the Japanese family, and few Japanese will feel free to dispose of them. Many people still consider it a *sacred* duty to produce children for the continuation of the family line. All this remains despite the new Civil Code and the new Household Register. In a sense many Japanese nuclear families may be seen as a temporary arrangement, or rather a condition which really should not be, unless parents and the other symbols of continuity are already properly taken care of by one of the husband's siblings.

Compared to those weighty matters, it is not surprising that some Japanese consider personal affection not vital for a good marriage. In fact, love is not regarded as a necessary condition for a marriage to be contracted. Instead, conjugal love is expected to develop "naturally" as the couple grow old together and share many experiences.

In such a husband-wife relationship, sexuality is much downplayed, or even repressed, and a decent couple should not express mutual affection before others, including family members. Unlike an American couple who sleep in a master bedroom undisturbed, the Japanese husband and wife often sleep with their child(ren) between them, largely because it is considered "natural" and "good" to do so. From a very early age an American child is expected to become aware of the special relationship between his parents by the existence of the master bedroom with its double bed, by watching their intimate interaction, and by knowing that after a certain hour in the evening he is sent to his own room so that the adults can spend time together. Japanese children experience nothing of the sort, and mother and her young child are often thought to be inseparable twenty-four hours a day.

The two different sleeping arrangements seem to me to symbolize the difference of the husband-wife and parent-child relationships in America and Japan. In the American family children are, at least in certain contexts, definitely separated from the parents, who can retire to the best and largest private room of the house, the master bedroom. No such sharp division between adults and children exists in the Japanese family. As stated already, in many families parents and children sleep in the same room, with the children between the adults. Even when children become somewhat older and sleep separately, rooms are often separated only by thin paper screens. There is simply no space in a traditional Japanese house which is comparable to the American master bedroom. Any room can be used for any purpose during the day (e.g., for eating, entertaining guests, family relaxation) and at night can serve as a bedroom for any member of the family. In short, sexuality of the married couple is explicitly recognized neither in the room organization nor in the sleeping arrangement in Japan. Of course every adult Japanese recognizes sex as an essential component of a marital relationship, but the Japanese couple is expected to manage it unrecognized. In other words, sexuality between husband and wife is regarded as a strictly private matter and some people even consider it frivolous.

In contrast parenthood is essential for most Japanese. This is quite understandable since parenthood alone assures an indisputable position in the society—particulary for the woman—because the family is regarded as the basic social unit and the continuity of the family line was (and still is by some people) regarded as a sacred duty to the ancestors. Many Japanese also seem to feel that only by becoming a parent can a person be properly cared for after death, an important consideration since, according to a recent opinion poll, 60 percent of the sample believes that souls remain in this world after death [ASAHI SHINBUN May 5, 1981]. Because the soul of a person who dies without issue is believed to become a wandering ghost instead of a contented ancestor, it may be said that only parenthood enables an individual to achieve a sort of immortality in the everlasting chain of human existence. Few Japanese today will admit this openly, but their quite meticulous observance of memorial services for ancestors and their strong desire to produce offspring seem to reveal their unconscious preoccupation with this question.

In American ideology, on the other hand, children can be seen as transient members of a family who leave the parents when they grow up, whereas love as the basis of marital relationship should be "eternal". Maturity and independence from parents are thus synonymous in America. Neither the parents nor the children should, when the latter become adult, be dependent on each other. In the American nuclear family the "dominant dyad", to use Hsu's terminology [HSU 1971], is the husband-wife relationship.

In Japan, it is the parent-child relationship which is dominant. Moreover, of the four possible parent-child dyads (father-son, father-daughter, mother-son, and mother-daughter), it is, as Sofue correctly noted [SOFUE 1971: 285], the mother-son dyad which is morally or emotionally ("implicitly" in Sofue's word) dominant, although the father-son dyad is the jurally ("explicitly") critical one.

The dominance of the mother-son dyad in Japanese kinship may, at least partially, be the result of the general sexual division of labor, by which child rearing is assigned to the mother almost exclusively. It is also related to the marriage system in which daughters are "given away" (yaru) in marriage, whereas sons, particularly the eldest son, remain in the parental household "taking" or "getting" (morau or *toru*) wives from outside.   That few married Japanese women could be economically independent, and the general expectation that aged parents should be taken care of by sons, may also be relevant in this connection.

The Japanese mother-son dyad displays four of the attributes pointed out by Hsu: inclusiveness, dependence, diffuseness, and libidinality [HSU 1971: 11, 15–17].   The American mother-son dyad also shows the same characteristics.   But I consider the mother-son relationships in the two societies are markedly different in terms of dependence and libidinality.

The newborn child everywhere starts life completely dependent on its mother or on her substitute.   In America, however, the child is expected to become less dependent as he grows older, until he is completely freed from his mother's protection (and/or interference) by the time he marries.   Neither son nor mother, for instance, expects to live together in the same house after the son's marriage.   And though the mother-son relationship is by no means terminated by his marriage, everybody knows that his first loyalty and responsibility is to his wife and children, not to his mother.   As discussed above "cognatic" mother-son love and "erotic" husband-wife love are structurally distinct, and therefore should not compete with each other.   Libidinality in the mother-son relationship, if it existed at all, ought to have been healthily dissolved by that time.

The Japanese mother-son relationship does not go through a comparable transformation.   A good mother is believed to care for and worry about her son eternally. It matters not at all that he has become a vigorous middle-aged man with social responsibilities and she a feeble old lady, since the relationship between mother and son as the care-giver and the care-receiver should last as long as they live.   In a sense it may even be said that the relationship continues well after the mother's death, since she continues to watch over him and his family as an ancestress.

Such a dependency relationship is no doubt related, at least partially, to the sexual division of labor   A Japanese male who at home is completely dependent on his mother for satisfying his basic needs is not an autonomous person.   He will never be as long as the current division of labor is maintained.

At the same time, though it may sound paradoxical, the mother is dependent on the son.   For it is only through bearing and raising him that she acquires an unchallengeable status in the household into which she married and that the husband-wife relationship, however intimate, cannot bestow upon her.   Thus, mother and son are mutually dependent.   The son is dependent on the mother for his birth, and for personal care which he himself cannot perform by the division of labor, and the mother is dependent on the son in many ways.   For motherhood alone can legitimatize a woman, who otherwise cannot be an autonomous person; motherhood bestows on her a respectable status both in the household and society at large, it furnishes her with a deeply satisfying though demanding life-work of caring for the child, it guarantees her support in old age, and it enables her to fulfill her duty to the household and the society.   In short, she can become a complete person only by becoming a mother.

The strong bond binding mother and son is often tinged with libidinality or un-resolved sexuality. The way in which a typical Japanese mother tends her adolescent or adult son, helping him change clothes and fastidiously looking after his belongings and person, might shock an American observer by its intimacy and by her almost servile attitude. But the Japanese interprets it as an "natural" and "beautiful" expression of affectionate motherly love.

Here I think Doi's concept of *amae* [DOI 1971] and Okonogi's analysis of the Ajase complex [OKONOGI 1978] are quite relevant. The mutual dependency relation-ship between mother and son is convincingly presented by Okonogi. Contrasting such a dependency relationship between an ancient Indian prince, Ajase, and his queen mother with that of Oedipus and his parents, Okonogi sheds light on the Japanese mother-son relationship as well as on the Japanese personality in general. But what is important in the present context is the implication that this mutually dependent mother-son relationship could be seen as the prototype or model of all male-female relationships in the Japanese society, including the husband-wife re-lationship. In any case, the existence of libidinality and the never-ending dependency relationship in the mother-son dyad, and the repression of sexuality in the husband-wife dyad, make the two male-female relationships structurally quite similar in certain aspects.

What, then, are the basic ingredients of the Japanese mother-son relationship? The following premises seem to be generally present:

1) That the mother is the bearer (=creator) of the son. The feeling that the mother is the life-giver is enhanced by the absence in the Japanese religious system of a creator god on the one hand and by the now generally accepted family planning on the other. The two factors together have made the decision to have or not to have children a personal and controllable choice of the parents, thereby considerably magnifying parental authority;

2) that she assumes the role of a devoted giver of care, the only active role she is permitted to play in traditional Japanese society without inviting reproach; and

3) that the mother's devotion is conceived as the "perfect" act of perpetual selfless sacrifice, which in turn induces in the son a deep feeling of guilt and indebtedness sometimes tinged with resentment [De Vos 1973: Chapter 5].

The "motherly" care is symbolized, among other things, in the act of preparing and serving food. It is therefore understandable that in many parts of Japan the transmission of the housewife's status (from the adult male's point of view, from his mother to his wife) is symbolically acted out by ceremonially handing over a rice scoop (*shakushi, shamoji*, or *hera*). It is also noteworthy that the National Housewives Association (*Shufuren*), which is active in various social causes from better education of children to clean elections, chose a rice scoop as its symbol. The Japanese male's persistent longing for the "mother's taste" or "mother's foods" (*ofukuro no aji*) seems to signify the symbolic nature of this act of feeding. Maybe this is an expression of his unconscious wish to be fed and otherwise taken care of in the complete dependency state of *amae*.

Regardless of who plays the role of the care-giver, a man must always depend on a woman for necessary personal care, owing to the sexual division of labor. In a typical Japanese household he receives it first from his mother, who is then replaced by his wife in this role. But since Japanese society rarely permits a mature woman to play any other respectable role, it is only natural that she should resist or resent, at least unconsciously, the handing over of the status of chief care-giver to her daughter-in-law. In any case, she continues to care about her son emotionally, if not physically, even after he has taken a wife.

The conflict arising from such a situation is explicit in the traditional multi-generational stem family where the household head's mother and wife live under the same roof. But even in a manifestly nuclear type of family, conflict and tension can be observed. This should be expected since the suppression of sexuality in the marital relationship, the continuous maternal interest in her son, and the conceptualization of the wifely care after the model of maternal care, all make the wife-husband relationship and the mother-son relationship dangerously similar. In Japan there is simply no distinction between "cognatic" maternal love and the explicitly "erotic" conjugal love, as it is supposed to exist in America. And if there is to be only one care-giver for a man "mother-in-law problems" are bound to arise. It may even be said that the conflict and tension between a man's mother and wife are structurally inevitable.

SUMMARY AND CONCLUSION

The Japanese woman's status at home seems low at first sight. On closer ex-amination, however, it is found that despite her relatively lower jural status and surface meekness, her moral authority, which she wields as mother and wife, is considerably higher. I have argued that her high moral standing vis-à-vis her son and husband should derive from her being the sole care-giver of the family. Owing to the rather strict sexual division of labor, an adult female's place is said to be in the home, the affairs of which she manages almost single-handedly without interference (or help) from the men. As a result, the Japanese male, whatever he may do outside, is a helpless dependent at home, since he is supposed not to be able to, and normally does not, perform any of the household chores. The Japanese wife-husband relationship is, in this respect, an asymmetrical one between a female care-giver and a passive male care-receiver. As such, the nature of the relationship does not substantially differ from that of a mother and her infant child. The suppression or unrecognition of sexuality in the marital relationship on the one hand and the continuous presence of unresolved libidinality in the mother-son relationship on the other make the two cross sex relationships almost identical in certain aspects. In fact, the mother-son relation-ship may be said to be the model of all female-male relationships in Japanese society. Thus, Japanese women are said to feel a "maternal instinct" towards males of all ages, because all men are helpless in satisfying their basic personal needs. In effect, of course, the dependency relationship is mutual because the existence of a woman would be devoid of meaning if she did not take care of males.

Such a male-female relationship is obviously correlated with the general sexual division of labor and the traditional family and marriage systems. But what keeps this system really working may be the sacred quasi-religious myth of motherhood, according to which the woman is created to perform the sacred role of life-giver and care-giver, without whom no one can live. As a mother she is supposed to be always "perfect", sacrificing all her personal ("egoistic") pleasures for the sake of her children. No wonder that the man should be perpetually bound to her in eternal indebtedness, for who can get even with someone who is "perfect" and "selfless"? Her moral authority is also likely to be related to the structural position she occupies in the household connecting the past and future, by taking care of the aged parents and ancestors and by bearing and raising the children.

BIBLIOGRAPHY

Asahi Shinbun
  1981 Morning edition. May 5.
De Vos, George
  1973 *Socialization for Achievement.* Berkeley and Los Angeles: University of California Press.
Doi, Takeo
  1971 *Amae no Kōzō.* Tokyo: Kōbundō. (*The Structure of the State of Amae.*)
Hsu, Francis L. K.
  1971 A Hypothesis on Kinship and Culture. In F. L. K. Hsu (ed.), *Kinship and Culture*, Chicago: Aldine, pp. 3–29.
Okonogi, Keigo
  1978 Nihon-jin no Ajase complex. In K. Okonogi, *Moratorium-ningen no Jidai,* Tokyo: Chūō-kōronsha, pp. 194–258. (Ajase Complex among the Japanese. *The Age of Moratorium.*)
Parsons, Talcott
  1943 The Kinship System of the Contemporary United States. *American Anthropologist* 45: 22–38.
  1954 The Father Symbol: An Appraisal in the Light of Psychoanalytic and Sociological Theory. In Lyman Bryson, Louis Finkelstein, R. M. MacIver, and Richard McKeon (eds.), *Symbols and Values: An Initial Study, 13th Symposium of the Conference on Science, Philosophy, and Religion,* New York: Harper & Row. [reprinted in Talcott Parsons, *Social Structure and Personality.* 1964. Glencoe: Free Press, pp. 34–56.]
Schneider, David M.
  1968 *American Kinship: A Cultural Account.* Englewood Cliffs: Prentice-Hall.
Sofue, Takao
  1971 Some Questions about the Hsu Hypothesis as Seen through Japanese Data. In F.L.K. Hsu (ed.), *Kinship and Culture,* Chicago: Aldine, pp. 284–287.

Chapter 16

Religion and Socialization of Women in Korea

HESUNG CHUN KOH

INTRODUCTION

Studies on Korean religion to date have examined one of four major religious traditions in Korea—Shamanism, Buddhism, Confucianism, and Christianity or any of the indigenous religious movements, such as Ch'ŏndo Kyo of the 19th century, or one of the many 20th century sects called "new religions." This approach, which isolates one religious tradition from other co-existing and complementary elements, is not suitable for an analysis of how religion affects Korean men and women. All of these "religions" have co-existed for hundreds, even thousands of years, and together they have met the different needs of men and women of various life situations, social strata, and backgrounds.

Another assumption, implicit in many studies of Korean religion, is that the family unit is the core of Korean society. Therefore, the appropriate unit of religious study is the belief system, ritual procedures, and practices of the family rather than those of the individuals. However, there is significant evidence that in Korea, religion to some extent is a matter of personal choice and practice, rather than simply the individual's acceptance of the belief system and practices common to all members of the family.

Statistics of religious affiliations reinforce the above two characteristics of Korean religion. Ch'oe Chae-sŏk's study of four South Korean villages [CH'OE 1975: 190–191] indicated that in 1968, ancestor worship was practiced by 93% of the rural families; 32% attended Buddhist temples, and 9% attended Christian churches. As to Shamanism, according to Youngsook Kim Harvey's calculation [HARVEY 1979], there were 208,424 fortune tellers throughout Korea in 1970. If only half of them were practicing Shamans, one out of every 316 people in South Korea would have been Shaman. She argues that although Shamanism, unlike Confucianism and Buddhism, has never been the official religion of Korea, it has provided the religious foundation for Korean society since the Three Kingdom period.

Off hand, these figures indicate that some families have been counted more than once. In other words, some family members who go to a Christian Church or Buddhist temple, also perform ancestor worship (the ritual of Confucian tradition) and/or participate in Shaman's ritual, *kut*.

Also according to Ch'oe [1975], 8 of the 9% of Christian families have some, but not all members who go to church. Similarly 28 or 32% of the Buddhist families have some, but not all of the members worshipping at temples. These figures seem to indicate that an individual practices and performs rituals of two or more religious traditions and participates in more than one type of religious organization. Thus, an individual's religious practices are often different from those of his family members.

Another general pattern that emerges in all of these studies is that more women than men practice Shamanism, Buddhism, and Christianity. For example, Ch'oe's study shows that in 65% of the families that were identified as Buddhist, only the female members worshipped in the Buddhist temples. This is only one of many more evidences indicating that women are more involved in religious practices than men in Korea where sex segregation is still practiced.

CIRCUMSTANCES OF RELIGIOUS PRACTICE IN KOREAN WOMEN

The aim of this chapter is to examine *how* and under *what circumstances*, which combinations of religion bccame essential to women. This chapter also will explore the way the Korean women approached and relied on or practiced various *combinations* of beliefs, values, rituals, and religious organizations drawing from Shamanism, Confucianism, Buddhism, and Christianity. As to socialization, it is the process, effect, or outcome in relation to women, and not so much who socialized women, that is the concern here. The life stories of five Buddhist nuns and their autobiographic essays will be analyzed first. These in turn will be compared with five life histories of female Shamans [HARVEY 1979: 17–240]. Admittedly, the number of cases is small for the purpose of generalizing about Korean women as a whole. Also, the sample may be biased in favor of the educated population. But this approach is intended to define the type of questions that need to be addressed and establish a beginning for new directions of inquiry which will examine the impact of religion on the individual/ personal level.

Let us now turn to brief summaries of the life stories of five Korean Buddhist nuns. Except for Iryŏp, these nuns are living today. Thus, these are accounts of contemporary Korean women.

Summary of Five Nuns' Stories

Case 1: Chihi

PERSONAL DATA: Chihi was born in Seoul and was the eldest daughter of an upper middle-class family of comfortable means. She graduated from a women's high school and later from the Korean Language and Literature Department of Seoul University.

EVENTS WHICH LED HER TO NUNHOOD: During her college years she was active in a literary circle. In this circle of friends she met Mr. X who was two years older than herself. They saw much of each other on weekends and shared many thoughts. Whenever each rendezvous was over she felt very, very happy. He wrote poetry and, perhaps because of his unfortunate childhood, his poems were usually sad and melancholy. Frequently, he wrote of death.

Ritualistically, every Sunday he went into the mountains. One spring day after graduation, she went mountain climbing with him. By the time they reached the top it was pouring rain and it made their descent very slow and tiring. When they finally reached the outskirts of Seoul it was 11 : 00 p.m. They were wet, cold, and hungry, and they *had* to get a hotel room and food.

During the night, Mr. X requested to have sexual relations with Chihi. She assured him that her "purity" was his and that she would never give herself to anyone else. However, since both parents were anticipating their marriage soon, she begged him to wait until their wedding night. She was sure that a woman's virginity was to be kept for only her "true love" and was to be given in a sacred and beautiful way. She felt that that night was not the "right" time, and she could not bear the thought of giving her "purity" in a cheap and careless way. Mr. X was very offended and didn't seem to understand her viewpoint and beliefs about virginity. He did not call or get in touch with her after that incident.

About a month later, Mr. X's brother called Chihi to tell her that her friend had fallen from a mountainside and was in the hospital. She ran all the way to the hospital and arrived just in time to see the sheet pulled over his body. His brother urged Chihi to forget him and go on with life. He tried to assure her that his brother was depressed and sad most of the time and that she was really better off without him. Chihi thought her tears would never end. She was overwhelmed at the quickness of death, that one could be living one moment and dead the next. She had unbearable emptiness and guilt. She wished then that she had given her "purity" to him that night at the hotel. After months of mourning his death, she decided to seclude herself by becoming a Buddhist nun, living on a "mountain" where he always liked to be. Thereby, she would be keeping her promise to him regarding her "purity."

SEVERE QUESTIONING FROM THOSE AT THE TEMPLE: When Chihi reached the temple, an elderly nun questioned her severely. "Why would a college graduate want to become a nun? Is it out of anger that you wish to shave your head, and live the life of a nun?" the elder nun asked. She was told they could not accept her if her reason was anger. "Do you realize that to live the life of a nun is not something just anyone can do? If you are seeking to become a nun because you were jilted by a man, or because your husband by whom you've had a baby has left you, or because you have been treated disrespectfully by your daughter-in-law we cannot help you!" [YI *et al.*: 1980: 220]. "Do you have your parents' permission?" Chihi did not. It was not easy to convince them that she was indeed serious about her commitment to become a nun and to get them to accept her as a novice.

Case 2: Chin'a

PERSONAL DATA: Chin'a was the oldest and only daughter of Myŏnjang, the head of the village of Ch'ungchŏng namdo in South Korea. She graduated from a local grammar school and the Sookmyŏng girl's High School in Seoul. While attending school in Seoul, she stayed at a paternal aunt's house where she encountered harassment from a number of men, thereby developing a strong dislike for men in general.

In college she met a handsome 25-year-old man and fell in love with him. Later, she found out he had a wife and a child. She struggled to sever the relationship with him and in the midst of that struggle she received a telegram informing her that her mother had died.

FAMILY RESPONSIBILITY: Her father said he would not remarry and that he needed Chin'a to care for the two younger children, ages 13 and 5, who were still at home. She consented to stay home and run the household. However, two years after her mother's death, her father who was 41 years old, married a 32 year old maiden. The main reason for her father's remarriage allegedly was so he could re-place Chin'a in the household and get her married. He could not afford to send her back to college. Chin'a was disappointed because she had been studying at home in preparation for her return to college. While Chin'a's family searched for a suitable groom for her, she was trying hard to forget her lover. The search for a groom was of long duration.

BUDDHIST NUN IRYŎP'S ESSAY AND ITS IMPACT ON CHIN'A: During this frustrating period, she read Iryŏp's essay on Buddhist philosophy. Chin'a was an avid reader, but no other writing had ever moved her to the extent that *Musang* (NIRVANA) did. Chin'a often thought about the mind and its freedom to go beyond the here and now. She had never contemplated becoming a nun before, but under the influence of this book and her life circumstances, she made up her mind overnight to become a Buddhist nun.

FAMILY RESISTANCE: Her father took to his bed from shock after Chin'a's departure for the temple. Her brother wrote to urge her to come home because they were suffering unkind treatment from their step-mother. In spite of all this pressure, six months after entering the temple Chin'a shaved her head and entered nunhood. She wrote clearly and firmly to her brother that she would not be coming home.

CHIN'A'S REASON FOR BECOMING A NUN: In her letter to her family she wrote, "How can I be of help to you when I do not even know my own self or my life?... I will discard all my personal feelings and wish to seek an *endless resting place...* To my late mother, I shall introduce the grace of Buddha which is eternal. There will be no parting in Buddha. Just as I went to school to prepare myself for entering into society, I have come to the temple to become a whole person before I enter society... Only after severe confinement will great freedom come. When a girl becomes a nun, this unfilial act is the very resource with which she will try to fulfill her filial duty to her parents, who will be reborn many more times."

Case 3: Iryŏp

PERSONAL DATA: Iryŏp was born in Pyongyang, North Korea. Her father was a Christian minister. Her father was an only son for five generations, and Iryŏp was his only child. Her parents died early in her life and her maternal grandmother supported and loved her through her college and post graduate work years in Japan.

A pioneer woman who was the first modern woman poet and writer in Korea, she was also the editor of the first women's magazine, called *Shin Yŏja* (New Woman) and published many of her own essays. She became a nun at 32, after suffering the failure of two marriages and having no children.

MOTHER'S SPECIAL LOVE AND EARLY DEATH: Iryŏp had had four younger siblings, but all of them died during early childhood. Since Iryŏp was the sole surviving child, the mother was determined to educate her well and make her "a greater person than any ten sons of others". Her mother influenced her to study hard because she believed education could make even a woman successful. When Iryŏp became ill, her mother cried and prayed out loud to God saying, "If this child dies, I am also a dead person." Her mother died when Iryŏp had just graduated from grade school. [KIM, Iryŏp 1980d: 136–139].

FATHER'S DEVOTION AND HIS DEATH: Her father was a very sincere, gentle and devoted Christian. He loved Iryŏp very much. After Iryŏp's mother died, her father wrote to her at school and came to see her more frequently. She loved the days her father came to visit her at the school dormitory. He often said that Iryŏp was "my only flesh and blood." He died when Iryŏp had just graduated from high school. She was alone and an orphan.

Iryŏp prayed to her father's spirit for guidance as she climbed the many hills in life [KIM, Iryŏp 1980b: 141–145]. She longed for her parents' love desperately. She sought for that kind of love in a man trying to replace through a relationship with a man, the love lost because of the death of her parents and siblings [KIM, Iryŏp 1980a: 29].

UNSUCCESSFUL MARRIAGES: Her first love relationship received much publicity in Japan, and the relationship did not last long. Many of her writings were about her intense love and longing for this man and were directly descriptive of their love relationship.

In 1923, at the age of 27, she went to Sudŏksa Temple where she became deeply engrossed in Buddhist teachings. Subsequently she met and married a Buddhist monk (one of the marrying order), who also had studied Buddhism in Japan. Her writings described three years of this relationship as peaceful and beneficial to her. She said this marriage allowed her to have both the opportunity to deepen her faith in Buddhism and to continue her writing and publishing. However, this marriage did not last either. She believed one had to have the courage to burn oneself in order to live deeply and have an eternal life.

In 1928, Iryŏp entered the Sobongam Temple on Diamond Mountain where she became a nun at the age of 32.

DREAM CHILD: There were never any children around her to grow up with, as she had no brothers, sisters, cousins, nieces or nephews. And she never had any children of her own. She was so unfamiliar with children that she could not comprehend the devotion some of her friends had for their own children. When her friends would wish a child for her, she would quickly comment that she had all she needed!

However, she often dreamed of a child about 3 or 4 years old who was simply adorable. Iryŏp sensed great comfort each time this dream child would appear, so much so that she would lose her sense of self. She wondered about the cause of the dream. She thought perhaps it was due to her few but fond memories of her younger siblings for whom she had cared. But her dreams of this child were 20 years after her siblings' deaths. Perhaps her dreams of this child were the revelation of a subconscious mother love. She thought, "Who was this baby who could have been born from me? and, Why does the baby only appear in my dreams?" Iryŏp wrote an essay on this in 1927, one year before she became a nun.

IRYŎP'S PHILOSOPHY OF LOVE: When Iryŏp was the editor of the first woman's magazine Shin Yŏja she and her advisors and colleagues Pang Chong Hwan, Yu Kwang-yol, (women artists) Ra Hye-Sŏk, Pak Indŏk, Julia Shin and Helen Kim would meet once a week as members of the Ch'ongt'ap hoe (Blue Pagoda Club). It was at these meetings that she would advocate her notion of "new chastity," that is "a person is free from the time of his/her birth. Free love, free marriage, and free divorce are holy things. To hinder these events is a negative thing to do."

Iryŏp not only preached these things but she also lived them. She said that it was Buddha who gave her insight during her many struggles of living alone after her marriages. To know oneself, one must seek love and be loved . . . love shakes the inner spirit of all human beings of the world, and even a strong man is very weak in front of a woman he loves. Iryŏp said, "love is the sum total of the Universe . . . all things are born as a result of love . . . love is everywhere!" She describes her love of two men as being due to her loving personality and her belief in the sacredness of love itself.

Her essays have long been known for her philosophy on love. Her name, Iryŏp, meaning single leaf, truly characterizes her lonely life without parents, siblings, and relatives. The motif here is unmistakenly Buddhistic.

Case 4:   Kyŏngmo

PERSONAL DATA: Kyŏngmo was born in Kwangju, in Chŏlla namdo province in South Korea. She was the daughter of a high school principal and graduated from Kwangju Girls' High School. She later became a nun at the Tŏksan Temple in Kohung, Chŏlla namdo, and is now, a nun at the Kangson Temple of Sunch'anggun, Chŏlla pukto province in South Korea.

CHILDHOOD EPOSURE TO BUDDHIST LEARNING—AN UNCLE WHO WAS A BUDDHIST MONK AS A ROLE MODEL: During her summer vacation when she was eight years old, she was taken to her uncle's temple. At that time, she recalls vividly how she learned Buddhist meditation, memorized the Kyŏng (doctrine), and heard the life-stories of Buddha. She remembers clearly how proud her uncle was of her because she followed very carefully what she was taught, and she took her learning very seriously.

MOTHER'S SOCIALIZATION TO COMPETE—THE PLEASURE OF WINNING: Kyŏngmo's mother was very anxious for her to be socially acceptable. She educated

Kyŏngmo in dance and fine arts and drilled her in writing skills. At the age of 12, Kyŏngmo won a gold medal at a fine arts contest and a literary award in high school. She was the class president in her junior year of grammar school and her teachers and friends expected her to excel in her high school entrance examinations.

ILLNESS DUE TO HIGH EXPECTATIONS TO SUCCEED: Under great pressure to succeed at the entrance examination, she became ill and fainted. As a result she could only enter the school of her second choice. During her high school years she continued to have fainting spells, once during morning assembly. Her illness was diagnosed as serious and her family sought a rare medicine to cure her.

Kyŏngmo's mother, who hated to lose, was determined to find the right treatment to cure her daughter, but with little success. An intestinal illness made it nearly impossible for Kyŏngmo to eat or drink. Out of desperation her mother and grand-mother consulted a shaman. However, they were told that Kyŏngmo would die.

KYŎNGMO GAINS PSYCHIC POWER: Kyŏngmo, near death, lay in her bed and chanted a Buddhist prayer for twenty days. She told her parents that on a particular day she would get up from her bed, and when that day arrived she arose to the amazement of all who knew of her illness. Her grandmother commented, "Perhaps she has received a spirit." Kyŏngmo now believed there was a *hananim* God, and as time permitted, she entered a temple to observe, experience, and study Buddhism. She was determined to learn more, to understand more logically her dream-like ex-perience and validate the origin of that external power. Kyŏngmo wished to become a person with enormous strength. For this reason she entered the Buddhist temple to know the "eternal truth."

DEATH OF HER MOTHER: While studying with a Buddhist nun at a temple, Kyŏngmo received a telegram notifying her that her mother had been killed in a car accident. It was indeed a shock for Kyŏngmo to think of her loving and energetic mother as dead. As she meditated on her mother's life, she came to the conclusion that her mother had lived her whole life sacrificing for others.

RE-EVALUATIONS OF THE PRESCRIBED WOMEN'S ROLE: She thought "Should I also live a life of eating, sleeping, having children and always serving the interests of others; then laugh, weep and die?" The more she thought about her mother's hectic life and how she never had a single moment to search for truth, the more Kyŏngmo thought of living a Buddhist's life. Thereby, she felt she would be really filial to her mother. She heard her mother's voice saying "I didn't really die. There is a new world. Although my body will perish, my life continues. Only because we are in different worlds are we not able to see and recognize each other. All those who are born must die and those who someday meet must someday say farewell. Our time to say farewell came somewhat sooner than expected." And she felt her mother's close embrace. In the midst of this experience Kyŏngmo promised her mother that she would go the way her mother had shown her. Kyŏngmo brought her mother's tablet to the temple where there were already 12 ancestral tablets, including her maternal grandmother's, paternal grandparents', maternal uncle's, and older brother's.

Case 5:   Chinsŏn Piguni Sŭnim

PERSONAL DATA: Chinsŏn was born in Chúngch'ong namdo, the eldest and only daughter, with several younger brothers.   Her father died in the 1951 Korean War as an anti-Communist fighter.   She graduated from a well known Christian girls' school in Seoul.

"WHEEL OF REBIRTH" AND HARD FAMILY LIFE WITHOUT A FATHER: In her junior year of high school, while full of dreams about college and the hopes of a first job, she heard something which touched her heart.   It was a lecture on the Buddhist theory of the "wheel of rebirth".   She often felt that she must have been sinful in her past life if this life was the result of what she had done before.

Chinsŏn was a sentimental girl.   When she would see her friends being happy and living with two parents she would become envious and melancholy.   She wondered what sins her mother and her siblings must have committed in their previous lives to have reaped such hardship.   In the midst of Christian Bible study and prayers, in her high school, she would keep thinking, "How can I live my life now to insure that my next life will be happy?"

TO MARRY OR NOT TO MARRY: After high school graduation she got a job instead of going to college.   Doing so meant she was obligated to get married and have babies.   During her first three years on the job she often pondered the questions, "Should I get married and have babies and be a slave to a man?   How can I live alone without marrying?   Shall I start a business?"

Chinsŏn truly was not interested in marriage.   She feared that her life might be just like her mother's and remembered what a neighbor lady used to say, "Daughters often become like their mothers."   She recalled also her grandmother's saying that women who die without marrying will become a *Tongdeny* spirit.   She felt pressure from her family because she was the eldest child.   Her family was trying to arrange for her to marry the son of an immigrant family in the United States, and that meant Chinsŏn had to choose her life course, soon.   She was undecided as to whether to become a Buddhist nun or a Catholic nun, but she was quite sure she was not going to marry.

LIFE AT A BUDDHIST TEMPLE: During her first few months in the temple, she often thought of a woman's life as it would be in marriage and as it would be single.   She also missed her family very much, especially her grandmother.   Chinsŏn was already influenced by the society's negative image of unmarried women.   For instance, once a senior nun at the temple scolded her, and Chinsŏn commented that the nun reminded her of her mother, but she felt the senior nun lacked the rich understanding that her mother seemed to have because the nun had not been married.

While in the temple, however, Chinsŏn was taught the positive aspect of being a nun, such as the privileged position they held.   Whenever a novice left the temple, the senior nuns would comment, "When there is no Innyŏn (Karma) one cannot become a nun.   One can become a nun only when you are specially blessed."   Also, she remembered her grandmother saying that "Chinsŏn has a precious quality."   This made Chinsŏn think she was 'blessed' to become a nun.

FAMILY'S STRONG NEGATIVE REACTION TOWARD BECOMING A NUN: When her family learned of her decision to become a nun, they opposed her. Her brother came to the temple to take her home. She could persuade him to return home only after a long talk. Then her entire family came to see her the second time and said, "Although you say that you have considered becoming a nun for a long time, have you considered what a harsh punishment it is for your family?   Let's all go home.   We will honor your decision."   Then Chinsŏn shook her head that she was not going home.   As her family was leaving the temple, they said, "From today, our gate will always be open for you.   Come home whenever you change your mind."

Many tears later, she wrote her family a letter telling them once again that she would not be returning home, for it was clear in her mind that she desired to become a nun, and that someday she would visit them with her nun teacher and ask her grandmother to forgive her.

Just prior to her ordination, novice Chinsŏn visited her family as she had said. Her teacher gave them an explanation about Buddhism.   Her grandmother listened very intently.   As novice Chinsŏn was leaving, her grandmother took Chinsŏn's hand and stuffed a handkerchief into it.   On the bus, returning to the temple, Chinsŏn looked into the handkerchief and found a gold ring, a most precious possession to a rural Korean woman.   She clasped the ring hard and vowed to herself once again that she would be a filial granddaughter by becoming a Buddhist nun.

INTERPRETATIONS

Ipsan or Ipsa as a Means of Conflict Resolution

Ipsan, meaning entering a mountain, and *Ipsa*, entering a Buddhist temple, mean to become a Buddhist monk or nun. In the title of a nun's autobiographical essays, "Why I Left the Secular World" *Ipsan* is characterized as "leaving family and the secular world." Implicit in these terms is the seeking of escape from the suffering experienced in secular life.

Before we examine the nature of "suffering" experienced by these women, let us examine some common patterns and attributes of all five women.

First, as to their *personal attributes*, they were all sentimental, expressive, conscientious in self-evaluation, goal oriented, self-centered, and persevering. They were all intelligent and received at least a high school education; one graduated from college, and the other, Iryŏp, even studied abroad in Japan.

Second, as to their *family background* and social status, each of them was the eldest or only daughter of a middle- or upper middle-class family where the father was a member of a respected profession, such as a Christian minister, the head of a village, or a high school principal.   All but one was from South Korea, where there are strongholds of Confucianism, such as Ch'ungch'ŏngdo and Chŏlla namdo.   As the eldest daughters of families in a respected class, it is safe to assume that they were under stronger pressure to conform to Korean role expectations of women as taught by Confucianism, than the daughters of families in lower social classes.

Thirdly, they *all experienced a severe conflict when they were a little over twenty years old* when Korean women were expected to marry. In examining the nature of these conflicts we can delineate clearly the common values shared by all these women.

Types of Conflict

Broadly speaking, these women's conflicts can be classified into two kinds. One, the conflict resulting from the acceptance of womens' roles expected by society and the inability to perform it. This may be called the "end and means discrepancy." The other is the conflict resulting from the rejection of society's expected roles of women due to a conflict in goals—those of the society and those of the individual women.

Accepting Role Prescriptions But Being Unable to Perform Them: Cases 1, 2, and 3 can be classified under this type of conflict.

Chihi (case 1), a college graduate who was active in a literary circle, clearly accepted marriage as her future course of life. She promised her lover marriage, but this promise could not be fulfilled because of his premature death.

Chin'a (case 2) met a man, fell in love, and contemplated eventual marriage. However, it was not possible, for he was already married and had a child. Also, her family's search for a suitable groom was not successful.

Iryŏp (case 3), unlike the above two women, was married. The only daughter of an only son for five generations, Iryŏp was married twice but her marriages did not last. She had no children to carry on her family line, which is the sacred duty of any Korean, especially women.

Thus, all three women initially accepted women's roles as expected by the culture. However, they were unable to fulfill the roles because of life's circumstances.

The question arises, "How common are cases like these?" Although we do not know the answer, a senior nun's comment, when Chihi (case 1) reached the temple to be accepted as a novice, is revealing:

> "If you are seeking to become a nun because you were jilted by a man, or because your husband by whom you've had a baby has left you, or because you have been treated disrespectfully by your daughter-in-law, we cannot accept you!" [Yi *et al.* 1980: 220] "Do you have your parents' permission?"

The cases to which the nun is referring are examples of those who accepted society's role expectations for women but were unable to perform successfully.

Rejection of Role Prescription Due to Goal Difference: Kyŏngmo (case 4) and Chinsŏn (case 5) rejected society's expectations that a woman marry and have children. Both Kyŏngmo and Chinsŏn were very close to their mothers, and each assessed her own mother's life critically. Kyŏngmo's mother sacrificed her entire life for her family and died early in a car accident. Chinsŏn's mother struggled through life as a widow having to support her family alone.

Kyŏngmo characterized the life of a married woman as:

"A life of eating, sleeping, having children, and always serving others' interests; then laugh, weep, and die."

Chinsŏn described the life of a married woman with children as being "a slave to a man."

Along with a negative image toward marriage, these women were also unsure about pursuing the life of a single woman. Chinsŏn pondered whether she should live alone without marrying, and, if so, whether she should enter into a business. Kyŏngmo, due to her ill health, couldn't think of living by herself without some support for her livelihood. Chinsŏn must have had similar feelings as indicated in her comment that she was undecided as to whether to become a Buddhist nun or a Catholic nun, but she was quite sure she was not going to marry. Evidently, she never thought she could live alone, away from her family, unless she had an alternative means of support. The Buddhist temple provided both legitimacy for their choices of celibacy and a much needed spiritual and material security.

Values of Common Concern

The first and most obvious factor was the severe conflict each girl experienced during her adolescence, when females are supposed to begin preparing for future adult roles. However, there was no *freedom of choice* available to them. Even today, the dominant expectation of society is for each female to be "a mother and a wife." All the basic requirements related to the Confucian notion of a "virtuous woman," taught since 1432 A.D., such as *loyalty, filial piety*, and *chastity*, were internalized by the five women as desired norms for all women.[1]

Chastity: Chastity has always been considered one of the essential elements in making a woman "virtuous." A Confucian saying which is familiar even today is "male and female children when they reach seven years of age should not sit together." Thus, the policy of sex segregation was emphasized both in the home and outside the home. According to Confucian ethics, a woman must be chaste not only before and during marriage, but even after the death of her husband. Young and old widows alike are expected to remain chaste.[2]

All of these women in our case studies were concerned with their chastity in various ways. Chihi (case 1) refused to have premarital sex with a man she loved very much and intended to marry. However, she promised him marriage and asked him to wait until their wedding night. She believed that a woman's virginity was sacred and should only be surrendered to her husband in a sacred and beautiful way.

---

1) In 1432 A. D., the government first published *Samgang haengsilto*, (The Principles of Virtuous Conduct) for women. In this book, the three values were emphasized as "virtuous conduct" for women. In subsequent years, a number of other books were issued to give guidance in the moral and practical education of women.

2) In the time period between 1414 and 1894 A.D., a law was passed in Korea excluding children of remarried women and of concubines from taking civil service examinations. This law served as a great deterrent to the remarriage of widows.

It was important not only when to give one's chastity and to whom, but also, in what manner. Her lover died by an accident before their marriage was consummated. She decided to live a celibate life, for she had promised her "purity" to him and it was his. To make sure that she kept her "purity", she chose to live in the Buddhist temple as a nun.

Chin'a (case 2), a daughter of a village head, while attending school in Seoul encountered harassment from a number of men. She fell in love with a handsome 25-year-old man, only to find out that he was married and had a child. No doubt,

Iryŏp (case 3), who came to believe in free love, practiced it herself and advocated a "new chastity." Iryŏp wrote the following concerning her new notion of virginity:

> "It doesn't matter whether a woman's body has touched that of a man. If a woman eliminates from her mind even a shadow of a man, she can be reborn as a virgin" (Iryŏp iran naeryŏk. [Yi 1980: 147]).

She advocated the importance of spiritual relations over physical relations between men and women and the holiness of free love, free marriage, and free divorce. Although her view of chastity was radically different from the norm, she was, nevertheless, preoccupied with the notion of chastity.

Chihi (case 1) in her essay describes six novices who were in the temple when she arrived. One high school graduate from Pusan, named Suk, confessed to Chihi one night how she came to be at the temple. Suk's story was that she was raped by three hoodlums on a beach. When she woke up the next day and realized what had happened to her she decided to commit suicide. Instead, she forged a letter of permission from her father and entered the temple. This story underscores the seriousness with which Korean women value *chastity*.

All of these women expressed intense emotion at the time of *sakbal* (shaving of the head)—a part of the ordination rite to become a nun. They commented how their black hair symbolized their virginity and the cutting away of their hair was like the surrendering of it. No other aspect of the ordination process or life at a Buddhist temple was described with such emotion and seriousness.

Filial Piety: Another strongly held value among all of these women was that of filial piety to their parents. Unusually strong emotion for and adoration of their mothers and especially their grandmothers was described by all of these women. Chin'a (case 2) said:

> "When a girl becomes a nun, this unfilial act is the very resource with which she will try to fulfill her filial duty to her parents, who will be reborn many more times."

Kyŏngmo (case 4), whose mother died having given years of dedication to Kyŏngmo's education as well as devotion to her during her illness, brought 12 ancestral tablets to her temple altar, including her mother's and those of her deceased ancestors on both her father's and mother's sides. Thus, she could fulfill her filial duty to them.

Acts of filial piety expected from women not only require respect, care, and obedience to one's parents and parents-in-law. Filial piety also includes insuring continuity of the family by bearing a son, as well as worshipping the parents through ancestral worship rituals after their deaths. When one compares the practices of inheritance, succession, and adoption in Korea with those of China and Japan, one can see how the pressure for a Korean woman to bear a *son*, (not just children) is heavier than it is for her sisters in Japan and China [KOH 1980].

In all three countries the continuation of the family line is of paramount importance, and this is done through the males. However, in Korea only the first-born son of a legal wife can become an heir. When there is no son, adoption is practiced. However, one can adopt a boy only from parents/people of the same surname and clan (Tongsŏng tongbon). In Japan a total stranger, not even a blood relative, can be adopted as a son-in-law and can become an heir.

The social pressure upon the son-less women in Korea is still very strong. Evidence of this pressure has been well documented in various studies such as, "Boy Preference Reflected in Korean Folklore" [CHA, CHUNG and LEE 1977] and "Psychological Problems Among Korean Women" [RHI 1977]. Boy preference is said to be the major deterrent to birth control and family planning in Korea. [CHUNG *et al.* 1974].

In light of this information, one can better comprehend the circumstances of Iryŏp (case 2). She was an only child, and her father was the only son for five generations. She had four younger siblings, and all of them died during early childhood. One can imagine the weight of responsibility upon her shoulders to bear a son and continue the family. Her mother's devotion and her grandmother's and her father's love cannot be overstated. It is not surprising that Iryŏp often dreamed of a child. This was likely an unconscious desire to have a child to appease her need to fulfill her filial duty. She prayed to her father's spirit for guidance as she climbed the many hills of life. At her father's tomb, Iryŏp regretted that she could not even guarantee ancestral worship for her father, because he had no son and there were no cousins or even nephews to look after her father's ancestral spirit. She believed that she could be filial to her father, who was a Christian minister, by becoming a good Buddhist nun.

One common sorrow for all these women was that they left home without the permission of their parents or families. All of them had families who were strongly opposed to their entering the nunhood—except for Iryŏp, who was an orphan when she entered nunhood. They received letters pleading for their return home or repeated visits from family members to take them home. The sadness of these women was genuine. How could they call their act of leaving home against their parents' wishes filial? There is a tremendous social stigma attached to a family that has a young daughter who becomes a nun.   For example, in the case of Chinsŏn, her family questioned:

"...Have you considered what a harsh punishment it is for your family?"

Although she was not persuaded by the urging of her distressed family members, she did promise that she would be a filial daughter and granddaughter by becoming a good Buddhist nun.   This rationalization of filial piety was based on the Buddhist beliefs of immortality, the "wheel of rebirth", "merits and demerits," and Nirvana.

In light of these Buddhist teachings, Chinsŏn (case 5) often felt that if this life was the result of her past life, she must have been sinful in the past.   As she observed her widowed mother's hardship she wondered what sins her siblings and mother had committed in their previous lives to have reaped such a fate. By living meritoriously in this life as a nun, she tried to make sure that in the next life she and her parents would be happier.

Chihi, Chin'a, Iryŏp, and Kyŏngmo all promised eternal life to those beloved parents and lovers who were dead.

Role Dedication: A common aspect among all these nuns is the degree to which they took seriously their duties to fulfill the roles culturally prescribed for women. If a woman had a need for self-fulfillment, she would usually pursue this through her role as daughter, granddaughter, sister, etc., rather than as an individual.   Thus, we see an emphasis on role fulfillment and performance, rather than on self-cultivation.

INTEGRATION OF BUDDHIST VALUES AND RITUALS WITH CONFUCIANISM, SHAMANISM AND CHRISTIANITY

Even casual examination of these autobiographic essays will indicate how each woman combined different elements of different religious traditions to comprise her own unique belief system.

Iryŏp, the only daughter of a Christian minister and a graduate of a Christian missionary school, seemed deeply affected by the Christian value of love.   This is evidenced in her writings about the importance of love, her parents' love and the loss she felt through their deaths, her unsuccessful love relationships with men, and her advocacy of a "new love relationship between men and women." It seems that Iryŏp transposed Christian love into a Buddhistic context.   She spoke of the love of Buddha as if she was speaking of the love of Christ.   At the same time, the Confucian notion of filial piety was strong in Iryŏp's writings. She expressed sorrow that her father, the only son of five generations, would not receive ancestor worship because she, his only daughter and kin, was a Buddhist nun, and therefore childless.

The blending of Christian, Confucian, and Buddhist values, however, did not seem to be stressful or contradictory.   She strongly embraced elements of all three as needed. Thus, she felt her act of becoming a Buddhist nun would make her father, a Christian minister, "very proud of her." It appears that she considers the two values complementary rather than contradictory. Iryŏp, formerly married but later separated from her husband and childless, would have little value as a person according to Confucian views. But through her synthesis of beliefs she found courage to meet life's challenges and maintain her self-respect, as well as justify her life style.

The commonality in mixing Buddhism and Confucianism is characterized in Chin'a's letter to her family, as already cited under filial piety (See above). She felt her Confucian goal of filial piety was being met through her belief in Buddhist teachings concerning reincarnation, merit and reward (wheel of life), and practicing rituals as a Buddhist nun. She combined a belief in the Buddhist notions of immortality, rebirth and reward of merit with the Confucian teaching of filial piety. The rituals themselves—having ancestral tablets at the Buddhist altar, performing the memorial rite for deceased nuns at the temple, and bowing three times to parents and three times to Buddha at the ordination rites—all resemble Confucian marriage or ancestor worship ceremonies, perhaps due to the fact that Confucianism was the orthodoxy while Buddhism, Christianity, Shamanism, and all others are the heterodoxy.[3]

These are only a few examples of the synthesis of values and rituals from various religious traditions within the lives of each of these nuns.

RELIGION CHOSEN BY AN INDIVIDUAL NOT BY FAMILY

What is apparent in all five cases is that becoming a nun meant overcoming strong opposition from family members. It is plain that each woman chose her own religion, and it was different from that of her family. In the case of Iryŏp, for example, her family was Christian and her father a Christian minister. Considering the deep attachment each woman had to her family members, it is impressive that each was able to be self-reliant in her choice of religious beliefs.

The statistics regarding the religious affiliations of four South Korean villages cited earlier (see pages 237–238 above) seem to support my finding that a woman often chose her own religion.

A COMPARISON WITH MUDANG (SCHAMANIC PRACTITIONERS)

How do these nuns' lives compare with those of female shamans, or mudang? An interesting comparison of key issues can be made by summarizing the lives of six Korean mudang compiled from field research by Youngsook Kim Harvey from 1971 to 1975 [HARVEY 1979: 17–240]. Some selective facts will be drawn from the book to illustrate my analysis further through this comparison.

---

3) These cases were somewhat weak in showing shamanistic belief. However, Kyŏngmo's willingness to believe her grandmother's statement that she (Kyŏngmo) must have received a spirit to have so miraculously recovered can be interpreted as a belief in Shamanism.

First of all, the six mudang were born between 1911 and 1937.   Thus, they are contemporaries of the five Buddhist nuns.   Like the five nuns, all but one mudang was the first born or the eldest daughter.   These shamans were children of lower middle class farmers, merchants and a well-to-do shaman.   All the families declined in wealth by the time the daughters reached their teens.

One common experience of all shamans is *sinbyŏng*.   *Sinbyŏng* is a possession sickness, interpreted as a supernatural message to assume the role of mudang.   All these women reported severe physical and psychological illness which was allegedly curable only when they accepted the "calling" of the mudang role through *sinbyŏng kut*, a shamanic ritual.

Without exception, all these women resisted becoming mudang.   Their husbands and family, including their children, were adamantly against it.   Even the women themselves did not wish to accept this highly stigmatized role—one ran away from home to avoid this fate, and another said she would rather die than become a mudang. But all of them finally succumbed after several progressively worse manifestations of their illness and considerable suffering.

There are two push factors: one is an attempt to cure their illness.   The other is a subtle but real need.   Becoming a shaman was a last resort in meeting financial crises and poverty.   For example, one mudang stated that she became a mudang when there was "nothing to sell."   Another said that she assumed the role of mudang when the adults no longer ate three meals a day.

Before we discuss the circumstances leading to *sinbyŏng*, let us consider five common personal attributes and characteristics of these mudang.

First, all of these women were very intelligent, able, strong-willed, self-reliant and enterprising.   Out of six mudang, only one graduated from college, one from a commercial high school, while three were elementary school drop-outs.   One had never been to school at all and was illiterate.   However, the five who went to school were good to excellent students when they were in school.   In most cases, they were forced to withdraw from school because their families met with economic hardship, and these women had to help support their families financially.

Second, all these women, like those who became Buddhist nuns, experienced severe conflict but at different life stages.   Unlike the nuns who turned to Monastic Buddhism in their early 20's, these shamans surrendered to their role of mudang during their mid-thirties.   They experienced illness in their early teens but resisted the repeated and progressive symptoms of illness (such as hallucinations, palpitations, numbness of limbs, fainting, recurrent seizures, etc.) until their mid-thirties when they couldn't endure any more.   While none of the nuns was married, all six shamans had married and had 4 to 9 children.

Third, these women had in common an unusual amount of successive tragedies and highly charged emotional experiences, such as childbirth, deaths of close family members (father, grandmother, siblings and later their own children), and financial crises. As Harvey's table of the shamans' life histories shows, over a period of eighteen years case C, for example, had twelve pregnancies, three ending in induced abortions, and nine in childbirth. She also experienced the death of her father, the death of two sons, five severe illnesses of her own and one of her daughter, the Korean war and her husband's permanent unemployment. Because her first pregnancy was out of wedlock, living with her in-laws during her husband's absence for his mandatory army service immediately following their marriage was extremely difficult. A considerable amount of conflict between husband and wife or with the husband's family with whom they usually lived, is another common phenomenon.

A fourth recurrent phenomenon was the shamans' frequent moves from place to place seeking better financial opportunity. Some were displaced from North Korea during the Korean War; and some moved within Korea from rural areas to Seoul. Others were immigrants to Manchuria and Japan who later repatriated to Korea. They further moved again within Korea. Just before the end of World War II, many Koreans migrated to Manchuria and Japan to avoid the economic hardship or the conscription of their daughters to Japanese labor camps. Without exception, all husbands had either financial failure, bankruptcy, or unemployment. Several husbands remained jobless following their discharge from the army, and became unable to adjust to life as a refugee.

Values

Three cultural values of Korea are manifested in the nun's life stories. These similar values recur in the life cases of these shamans with somewhat differing emphases. First, as to *filial piety*, all these energetic and strong-willed women were dutiful daughters-in-laws; they calmly accepted their responsibility for supporting and caring for their husband's families despite their own hardships.

Second, the women who became shamans seemed less concerned with the Confucian *value of chastity* than did those who became nuns. In fact, two of the six shamans became pregnant before their marriages. Because of this they suffered considerable scorn and mistreatment from their parents-in-laws and elder daughters-in-law of their husbands' lineage. Thus, although these women themselves were less preoccupied with chastity than their contemporaries who became Buddhist nuns, nevertheless, they were equally affected by the social reaction and the strong cultural expectation that women should be chaste.

A third common value shared equally by both shamans and nuns was that of *role dedication*. All women took seriously the culturally expected role of women to be a wife and mother. In the case of the women who became shamans, they got married and bore children. But when their spouses could no longer fulfill their role of economic provider, these women also resolutely took up financial responsibility, not only for their children, husband and themselves but for the members of their husband's family, despite the fact that they had received no training from family, society or culture to assume such multiple responsibilities. They had no marketable skills. For instance, in three cases, the women had not even been brought up to cook, sew, or manage a household. One, a daughter of a onetime palace shaman who had many servants, had no role model, nor the opportunity to learn domestic skills. The other was born the first child of a family of *samdae tokcha* (only son for three consecutive generations) and the entire extended family pampered and spoiled her to the point where she never did any housework. Still another woman, from an old lineage of Suwŏn who went away to Seoul to attend high school and college, hated housework and never learned domestic skills.

In summary, these women were unable or unequipped to meet all the challenges set before them. Yet even under these circumstances, most of these women did not question their duty to take on the entire responsibilities of their families and those of their in-laws.

Thus, we can characterize the severe conflict of the mudang as the result of imbalance between their heavy sense of responsibility and the scarcity of resources available. Their strong commitment to role fulfillment and the successive human tragedies they encountered made their internal conflicts unusually severe.

As to their religious practice and commitment, all integrated Buddhism and Christianity with Shamanism while adhering to the notion of family loyalty and role dedication emphasized by Confucian ethics. For example, one mudang was baptized into the Protestant church at age 12 and attended both Bible school and a regular school ran by the church. But she later became a mudang. Another was baptized into a Catholic church after the marriage with her husband, but later turned to shamanism. A third mudang who practiced for nearly 10 years became a Christian and was baptized at age 41. She is now an active deacon at a Protestant church. A fourth mudang grew up in her husband's family as *minmyonuri* (a child adopted as a prospective daughter-in-law) where she learned and practiced Buddhist rituals throughout the year. She was also a devoted Buddhist while she was a war refugee. However, she assumed the role of mudang after she became seriously ill and fell into a coma for several days and then miraculously recovered. Now, while being financially successful as a mudang, she resents her life as mudang and plans to retire to a Buddhist nunnery when her youngest son is in the 8th grade and her eldest son can provide for the college education for this youngest son. All these women, as they went through different stages of the life cycle, resorted to four different sets of Korean religious rituals as they needed them. They did not consider moving from one religious form to the other or practicing both at the same time to be improper or undesirable.

CONCLUSIONS

How has religion influenced or affected Korean women and their socialization?

Although Confucianism is not even listed as a religion in the present-day official statistics, the 15th century Confucian principle of virtuous conduct for women still profoundly affects Korean women and society today. Koreans still support the notion that it is of paramount importance to fulfill one's expected role both within the family and in society generally. For women it is expected that their role will be primarily to marry and have at least one son, thus continuing the family line. Being "a wife and mother'' is still the major criterion against which a woman's performance is measured.

Examination of the life stories of five Buddhist nuns and six shamans demonstrates how each of these women had internalized the Confucian values of role dedication, loyalty, and filial piety.   While chastity was more an issue for those who became Buddhist nuns, it was not as strongly upheld by the women who later became mudang.   As an adolescent, being pressured by society and family to make decisions about her adult life, each was preoccupied with the future wife-mother role expected of her.   It was not despite these Confucian values but rather because of them that each had to find an alternative way to fulfill her prescribed roles at particular life stages and to legitimize her deviance from the norm.   It was through the teachings of Buddha and the support of the Buddhist temple or by becoming a shaman that these women found identity, security, and purpose in life.

Under what circumstances does religion become essential?

For the five Buddhist women in our study, religion became essential during adolescence, that time of physical growth and sexual maturing, as their families were pressing them for decisions regarding the roles to be taken in their adult life. They were either unable or unwilling to abide by usual normative expectations and thereupon sought an alternative norm and life style by turning to Buddhist nunhood. For the shamans, reliance upon religious roles occurred during midlife when they were forced to fulfill both conventional and unconventional role expectations.

Religion defines the place of the individual in some total cosmic scheme.   However, within Confucianism and in the family system of Korea there was no room for role choice for females.   There was no place for the unmarried, widowed, separated, divorced, or barren.   Nor was life easy for a mother/wife who also had to assume the role of economic provider as head of the household.   Religion, therefore, took on added significance as a legitimizing force for each of these women when her role preference and/or performance became different from the norm and her self-worth became severely challenged.   Religion vs. belief provided a path for conflict resolution.

Another common factor among the five nuns was the recent *loss* of a mother, father, grandmother, or lover, upon whom they relied for emotional support.   Thus, when one lost a deeply loved and supportive person, one turned to religion as a source of support.   Likewise, shamans often came from displaced families who experienced successive tragedies such as the death and illness of close family members or financial devastation.   Therefore, they too found in religion a source of power and a last resort for survival.

In Korea, religious belief is a matter of personal belief and practice rather than the passive acceptance of the religion of the family.   Even in a society with a strong family orientation due to the influence of Confucianism, these women could develop their own unique belief system by combining various aspects of four major religious traditions—Confucianism, Buddhism, Shamanism, and Christianity.   Since Confucianism and the family prescribed that women choose primarily the wife/mother role, a woman who was unwilling or unable to become a "wife/mother" had to choose some other religious alternative. For some unmarried women, Buddhism provided a doctrine which could legitimize their celibate role choices and provide a family-community to replace their own families; one could even believe that she was fulfilling her filial role by providing for her family's peaceful afterlife.

For six married women with children who had to assume the breadwinner's role in the midst of successive tragedies, becoming a shaman, provided much needed economic relief to meet family needs, to gain psychological and physical well-being, and to find one's self worth.

Thus, through religion, these Korean women could and did satisfy personal quests for identity, security, and life purpose by developing unique combinations of religious beliefs and practices, drawing from the four rich and varied religious traditions available within their culture.

BIBLIOGRAPHY

CHA, Jae-ho, CHUNG Bom-mo and LEE Sung-jin
    1977 Boy Preference Reflected in Korean Folklore. In Sandra Mattielli (ed.), *Virtues in Conflict*, Seoul: Royal Asiatic Society, Korea Branch, pp. 113–128.

CH'OE, Chae-sŏk
    1975 *Hanguk nongch'on sahoe yŏngu*. Seoul: Iljisa. (*Studies of Korean Rural Societies.*)

CHUNG, Bom-mo, CHA Jae-ho and LEE Sung-Jin
    1974 Anthropological Study of Boy Preference in Two Rural Communities. *Boy Preference and Family Planning in Korea.* Seoul: KIRB.

HA, Chi-hi
    1980 Tasi too isesang e t'aeyŏnado. In Yi, Kyŏng-jin, Chinsŏn Kim and Chi-hi Ha, *Na nŭn wae sokse rŭl ttŏnanna*, Seoul: Tong'guk ch'ulp'an sa, pp. 215–297. (Even If I am Reborn. *Why Did I Leave This World?*)

HARVEY, Youngsook Kim
    1979 *Six Korean Women: the Socialization of Shamans*. St. Paul, Minnesota: West Publishing.

KIM, Chin-sŏn
    1980 Yŏllyŏ issottŭn tugae ŭi mun. In Yi, Kyŏng-jin, Chin-sŏn Kim and Chi-hi Ha, *Na nŭn wae sokse rŭl ttŏnanna*, Seoul: Tong'guk ch'ulp'an sa, pp. 161–214. (Two Gates That Were Open. *Why Did I Leave This World?*)

KIM, Ir-yŏp
    1980a Ch'ongch'un ŭl pul sarŭgo. In Kim, Ir-yŏp, *Ch'ŏngch'un ŭl pul sarŭgo*, Seoul: Chungang ch'ulp'an kongsa, pp. 9–109. (I burned my youth. *I Burned Up My Youth.*)
    1980b Ir-yŏp iran naeryŏk. In Il-ig Yi (ed.), *Akkyŏ muŏthari ch'ŏngch'unŭl*, Seoul: Man-hak Ch'angjo sa, pp. 141–147. (Why Named Ir-yŏp? *For What Should I Save My Youth?*)
    1980c Nunmul kwa insaeng kwa haengbok kwa. In Kim, Ir-yŏp, *Ch'ŏngch'un ŭl pul sarŭgo*, Seoul: Chungang ch'ulp'an konsa, pp. 111–127. (Tears, Life and Happiness. In *I Burned Up My Youth.*)

1980d Omŏni ŭi mudŏm. In Kim, Ir-yŏp, *Akkyŏ muŏthari i ch'ŏngch'un' ŭl*, Seoul: Munhak ch'angjo sa, pp. 136–139. (Mother's Tomb. *For What Should I Save My Youth?*)

KOH, Hesung Chun

1980 Korean Studies in a Cross-cultural Perspective. *Papers of the 1st International Conference on Korean Studies*, Seoul: Academy of Korean Studies, pp. 1439–1457.

RHI, Bou-yong

1977 Psychological Problems among Korean Women. In Sandra Mattielli (ed.), *Virtues in Conflict*, Seoul: Royal Asiatic Society, Korea Branch, pp. 129–146.

YI, Il-gi (ed.)

1980 *Akkyŏ muŏthari ch'ŏngch'unŭl*. Seoul: Munhak Ch'angjo sa. (*For What Should I Save My Youth?: Writings of 12 Korean Women Pioneers.*)

YI, Kyŏng-jun

1980 Na nŭn han mari mang'gak ŭi sae. In Yi, Kyŏng-jun, Chin-sŏn Kim and Chi-hi Ha, *Na nŭn wae sokse rŭl ttŏnanna*, Seoul: Tong'guk ch'ulp'an sa, pp. 13–159. (I Am a Forgotten Bird. *Why Did I Leave This World?*)

YI, Kyŏng-jun, Chin-sŏn KIM and Chi-hi HA

1980 *Na nŭn wae sokse rŭl ttŏnanna*. Seoul: Tong'guk ch'ulp'an sa. (*Why Did I Leave This World?*)

List of Contributors

Masahide Bito is Professor of Japanese History at Chiba University. Previously he taught at the University of Tokyo, from which he retired in 1984. His major interest is early modern Japanese history and especially the trend of Confucian thought in Japan in comparison with philosophical trends in China. Among his recent articles are "Society and Social Thought in the Tokugawa Period" (1981) and "Bushi and the Meiji Restoration" (1985), both in English. He is the author of *History of Thought During the Tokugawa Period* (1961) and *Ogyū* (1974), and coauthor of *The Mito School of Thought* (1977).

George De Vos is Professor of Anthropology and Research Associate with the Institute of Personality Assessment and Research and the Centers for Korean and Japanese Studies at the University of California, Berkeley. His principal fieldwork research has been done in urban Japan, starting in 1953. He has studied minority and delinquency problems in Japan, as well as Japanese achievement motivation. He is the author of *Socialization for Achievement* (1973); the coauthor of *Japan's Invisible Race* (1966), *Koreans in Japan* (1981), and *Heritage of Endurance: Family Patterns and Delinquency Formation in Urban Japan* (1984); editor of *Institutions for Change in Japanese Society* (1984) and coeditor of *Ethnic Identity* (1975).

Masao Fujii is Professor and Chairman of the Graduate Course of Religious Studies at Taisho University in Tokyo. His major interest is Japanese Buddhism and its sect rituals. He has made a comparative study of cemeteries in Japan and Europe. Among his numerous articles are "Maintenance and Change in Japanese Traditional Funerals and Death" (1983, in English). He is the editor of the *Dictionary of Buddhist Rituals* (1977), *Problems in the Jōdo Sect* (1979), *Encyclopedia of Modern Japanese Buddhism* (1980), and *Encyclopedia of Cemeteries* (1981). He is the author of *The Belief Structure of the Modern Japanese* (1974), and coauthor of the *Encyclopedia of Buddhist Ceremonies* (1980).

Laura Kendall is Assistant Curator in charge of Asian Ethnographic Collections at the American Museum of Natural History in New York. She is the author of *Shamans, Housewives, and Other Restless Spirits: Women in Korean Ritual Life* (1985), and coeditor of *Korean Women: View from the Inner Room* and *Religion and Ritual in Korean Society*. Her current research includes a study of contemporary Korean marriage customs and an exploration in ethnobiography.

259

Hesung Chun Koh, who earned her doctorate in sociology, is currently directing the Korean History and Cultural Project at the Yale Center for International and Area Studies. She is Director Emerita of East Asian Area Research for the Human Relations Area Files. She has taught at Boston University, the Yale Law School, and Yale University, and has also been a Visiting Professor at the National Museum of Ethnology, Osaka, Japan, where she is now a Collaborative Research Fellow. Her books include *Religion, Social Structure, and Economic Development in Yi Dynasty Korea* (1959), *Social Science Resources on Korea* (1968), *Korean Family and Kinship Studies Guide* (1980), *Korean and Japanese Women: An Analytical Bibliographic Guide* (1982), and *Koreans and Korean-Americans in the United States* (1974). She has also edited and produced a set of educational videotapes, *Korean Culture Through the Arts* (1984).

Lewis R. Lancaster is Professor of Oriental Languages at the University of California, Berkeley. He is a member of the Group in Buddhist Studies, which is in charge of the doctoral program in this field for the university. He also serves as an adjunct Professor of Buddhist Studies for the Graduate Theological Union of Berkeley and the Institute of Buddhist Studies. He is the editor of *Prajnaparamita and Related Systems: Studies in Honor of Edward Conze* (1977), *Early Ch'an in China and Tibet* (1982), and *Buddhist Scripture: A Bibliography* (revised, 1982), and the author of *The Korean Buddhist Canon: A Descriptive Catalogue* (1979) and *The Dirty Mop: Paintings of Unlimited Action of Jung Kwang* (1984).

Kwang Kyu Lee is Professor of Anthropology at Seoul National University. Awarded a doctorate in anthropology from the University of Vienna in 1966, he has done fieldwork throughout the Korean peninsula. His main interests are the family and kinship and culture and personality, with special emphasis on traditional Korean culture and ethnicity. He has also done field research in Japan and China for comparative studies of the three East Asian cultures. He has written three books on the Korean family (1975, 1977, and 1980), as well as *Koreans in Japan* (1983). In addition, he is the author of *Introduction to Cultural Anthropology* (1971) and *Social Structure* (1980), which are the first books in Korean on the discipline of anthropology.

Kiyomi Morioka is Professor of Sociology at Seijo University in Tokyo. He is presently Dean of the Faculty of Literature and Arts and Director of the Institute of Folklore Studies at that university. Until 1978 he was a professor at Tokyo University of Education. His major professional interests are the life cycle of Japanese families and sociological studies of Shinto, Buddhist, Christian, and other religious organizations in Japan. He is the author of *Cycles in Japanese Families* (1973), *Religion in Changing Japanese Society* (in English, 1975), *Family Structure in the Shinshū Sect of Buddhism* (1978), and *Changing Family and Ancestral Festivals in Japan* (1984).

Masaharu Ozaki is Senior Librarian at Ohtani University of Kyoto, where he has specialized in Buddhist culture. His major interest is the history of Chinese religion, especially Taoism. He did research on Taoist scriptures, organizations, and rituals through library studies and fieldwork in both Japan and Taiwan. Among his articles are "A Study on the Taoist Scriptures Established During the Six Dynasties" (1976), and "Some Problems Concerning the Ssŭ-Chi-Ming-K'e" (1977). He is the editor of *Index to Wu-Shang Pi-Yao* (1983).

Kokan Sasaki is Professor of Religious Anthropology at Komazawa University in Tokyo. His major interest is shamanism and its rituals, focusing upon their social and cultural contexts; he has conducted fieldwork in village settings in Oshima, Okinawa, and Amami in the Ryukus, Taiwan, Malaysia, Singapore, India, and Pakistan. He is the coauthor (in Japanese) of *Introduction to Cultural Anthropology* (1979) and *The Science of Religion* (1981), and author of *Man and Religion* (1979), *Shamanism* (1980), *Spirit Possession and Shamanism* (1983), and *The Anthropology of Shamanism* (1984).

Takao Sofue is Professor of Anthropology at the newly instituted Hoso Daigaku (University of the Air) in Chiba near Tokyo, and Professor Emeritus at the National Museum of Ethnology, where he was, until 1984, Professor and Director of the Research Department of East Asian Studies. With a major interest in psychological anthropology, he has conducted fieldwork both in Japanese villages and among the North Alaskan Eskimo. Among his articles is "Aspects of Personality in Japanese, Americans, Italians, and Eskimos" (1979, in English). He is the editor of *The Japanese: Readings in Culture and Personality* (1971), and the author of *Prefectural Characters in Japan* (1971), *Culture and Personality* (1976), and *Introduction to Cultural Anthropology* (1979).

Melford E. Spiro is Presidential Professor of Anthropology at the University of California, San Diego, where he founded the Department of Anthropology in 1968. Spiro has conducted fieldwork in Ifaluk, Israel, and Burma. A Fellow of the National Academy of Sciences and the American Academy of Arts and Sciences, he is the editor of *Context and Meaning in Cultural Anthropology* (1965), the coauthor of *An Atoll Culture* (1953), and the author of *Kibbutz: Venture in Utopia* (1956), *Children of the Kibbutz* (1958), *Gender and Culture: Kibbutz Women Revisited* (1979), *Burmese Supernaturalism* (1967), *Buddhism and Society* (1971), *Kinship and Marriage in Burma* (1977), and *Oedipus in the Trobriands* (1982).

Michio Suenari is Professor of Anthropology at the University of the Sacred Heart in Tokyo. His major interest is family, kinship, and religious practices, especially ancestor worship. Focusing upon these subjects, he has conducted fieldwork in Taiwan among the aboriginal Ami and Puyama as well as the Chinese; he has also done field research in Korea and in Japanese villages and is presently writing a comparison of these three areas. Suenari is the coauthor of *Formation of the Peer Group in Japan* (1979) and author of *Social Organization and Its Changes Among the Ami in Taiwan*

(1983). Among his articles are "Kinship Structure Among the Puyuma in Taiwan" (1970) and "The Cult of the Ancestors in Taiwan" (1980).

Masako Tanaka is Associate Professor of Anthropology at Ochanomizu University in Tokyo. Her major interest is kinship and social change; she has conducted fieldwork in Okinawa, New Zealand, and the United States. She is the coauthor of *Ethnic America: Assimilation Within a Pluralistic Country* (1984). Among her articles are "Kinship and Descent in an Okinawan Village" (1974), "Categories of Okinawan 'Ancestors' and the Kinship System" (1977) (both in English). In Japanese she has written "Okinawan System of Kin Classification and Social Categories" (1977) and "Kinship and Descent" (1982).

Tu Wei-ming is Professor of Chinese History and Philosophy in the Department of East Asian Languages and Civilizations at Harvard University. He is also Chairman of the Committee on the Study of Religion at Harvard. Formerly he taught at Princeton University for four years, and in the Department of History at the University of California, Berkeley, for ten. Tu is the author of two recent publications, *Confucian Ethics Today* (1984) and *Confucian Thought: Selfhood as Creative Transformation* (1985).

Index

Italicized numbers refer to a contributor's chapter in this volume.